THE BUREAU

THE BUREAU

Inside the Modern FBI

Diarmuid Jeffreys

HOUGHTON MIFFLIN COMPANY

BOSTON • NEW YORK

1995

For information about permission to reproduce
selections from this book, write to
Permissions, Houghton Mifflin Company,
215 Park Avenue South, New York,
New York 10003.

Library of Congress Cataloging-in-Publication Data
Jeffreys, Diarmuid
The Bureau : inside the modern FBI / Diarmuid Jeffreys.
p.   cm.
Includes bibliographical references (p.   ) and index.
ISBN 0-395-67283-X
1. United States. Federal Bureau of Investigation
I. Title
HV8144.F43J44   1995   94-33524
353.0076 — dc20   CIP

Printed in the United States of America

MP 10 9 8 7 6 5 4 3 2 1

Book design by Robert Overholtzer

For Patsy

CONTENTS

PROLOGUE

A S THE LARGE BLACK HEARSE rolled to a halt at the base of the Capitol, the rain, already a miserable drizzle, deepened to a steady downpour. Two ranks of ceremonially dressed soldiers, flanking the steps up into the building, stood rigidly to attention. There was absolute silence.

Eight of the young servicemen, their eyes fixed straight ahead, marched slowly and in perfect time to the car. They stopped, hoisted the vast coffin to their shoulders, and turned to face the building. To those watching it seemed for a moment as though the burden would be too great. But then, with agonizing slowness, the soldiers began to climb. By the time they reached the last of the thirty-five steps, their faces were wrenched with effort and damp with rain and sweat. It was 11:25 A.M. on Wednesday, May 3, 1972. The body of J. Edgar Hoover, director of the Federal Bureau of Investigation, had come to lie in state.

The pallbearers moved through the massive bronze doors and into the Rotunda. There, in the great room, 96 feet in diameter, 180 feet high, members of the Supreme Court and the Cabinet, senators, representatives, and other dignitaries stood packed in a tight circle behind velvet ropes. Most had been there for some time, arriving in strict order of precedence, first the justices, then the Cabinet members. Last to file in were members of the House, led by Speaker Carl Albert, Democrat of Oklahoma. Governor Ronald Reagan of California joined the back of the procession.

In the center of the circle lay Abraham Lincoln's black catafalque. Until this day, this modest thing of wooden boards had been reserved for presidents, military heroes, and members of Congress. It had been used only twenty-one times, the last nearly nine years earlier — for the body of John Fitzgerald Kennedy. Now for the first time in history the honor was being accorded to a civil servant.

As the bearers gently relinquished their flag-wrapped burden, a presidential honor guard, made up of one member of each of the four services, took up a vigil at each corner. A lone special agent stood at the head of the casket. The deathly hush was shattered briefly as an unattended telephone rang nearby. Then silence returned once more. The Reverend Dr. Edward I. R. Elson, chaplain of the Senate and pastor at Hoover's own National Presbyterian Church, moved forward for the prayer.

"We thank Thee this day for thy servant J. Edgar Hoover, for his lifelong trust in Thee, his steadfast devotion to the nation, his elevated patriotism, his fidelity in a position of high trust, his commitment to justice and peace in the nation."

The minister's clear voice carried to all parts of the high-domed room, to the front row of mourners made up of Hoover's fifteen top FBI assistants, to the fifteen congressmen who had once been special agents, now grouped with their peers in the ranks of politicians and dignitaries, to almost all of official Washington, who, with bowed heads, stood, and marked the end of an era.

All present, Dr. Elson continued, should be "brave as he was brave, loyal as he was loyal, serve as he served, love the nation as he loved it, worship Thee as he worshipped Thee."

Another brief silence fell, and then Chief Justice Warren Burger, draped in black robes like the other members of the Supreme Court, took his place at the podium. Once a Hoover nominee for the post, he owed a great deal to the dead director, and his address was equally reverent.

"John Edgar Hoover, who was known to his intimates as Edgar and to two generations of Americans as J. Edgar Hoover, was a man who epitomized the American dream of patriotism, dedication to duty, and successful attainment. His role in perspective," Burger said, "will be seen as that of a man trained as a lawyer who always tried to strike the difficult and delicate balance of efficiency in enforcement of laws but within the law and within constitutional limitations. I am proud to join in this salute to a great American who served his country so well and earned the admiration of all who believe in ordered liberty."

It was a striking epitaph, one that would be echoed across the United States in the coming days. But as the ceremony came to an end and the gathering slowly dispersed, there were those in the crowd whose appreciation of Hoover's career was not so glittering. Wisely, though, they kept any such thoughts to themselves. While the director's reputation would take a battering in the years to come, Hoover's presence still seemed almost tangible, the disposition and scale of his rumored secret files as yet unknown. Most important, the agency he had led for the last forty-eight years was still operational. Even in the Washington of May 1972 it didn't pay to put one's head above the parapet.

For the rest of that day and night Hoover's body lay in state, the presidential honor guard in constant attendance. They were joined by thousands of Americans who filed slowly, and for the most part in silence, through the east entrances of the Capitol. Some were grief stricken, others merely curious. All of them came to take a last look at a man who had served under eight presidents.

As the long line of people shuffled up the east steps, a few passed the time by flicking through that day's newspapers. The *Washington Post* of May 3, highlighting the alarming success of the advance by North Vietnamese troops into Quang Tri Province, described the sagging state of morale in Saigon: "For the first time since this latest offensive began there is widespread talk of how badly things appear to be going." The *New York Times* focused instead on the results of the primaries in Indiana and Ohio, and on the growing race between Senators Humphrey and McGovern for the Democratic nomination in the upcoming presidential elections. But in common with other American newspapers that day, both reserved most of their attention for the shocking news of Hoover's death. In page after page of obituary they pored over his career, from the successes of the gangster era and World War II to the excesses of more recent times. The *Post*, in a guarded editorial, captured the general mood:

> While we do not count ourselves among Mr. Hoover's great admirers, especially in his later years, we would not minimize those genuine contributions he made to the well being of the country. His early fame was based, and rightly so, on his performance in taking an incompetent and corrupt investigative service and turning it into a fully professional and honorable police force. During the 1930's when heroes were scarce and public distaste of police corruption was widespread, he filled a public need by projecting the image of the perfect cop. That image lives on —

tarnished somewhat by events of later years — in the awe and respect that most Americans have for the words Federal Bureau of Investigation.

The Hoover mourners were not the only people on Capitol Hill that day. Huddled in a rain-swept corner of the west steps, a small but vociferous group of antiwar protesters were trying to make themselves heard. One by one, throughout the day, they took turns reading out the long list of American servicemen killed in Vietnam. As *Washington Post* staff writer Paul Valentine put it later, "Thousands of Americans were at the Capitol mourning the death of one man, while a handful of others were mourning the deaths of 48,000."

The protest was part of a continuing thirty-six-hour "emergency moratorium" of antiwar actions that had been planned a week in advance. It was unfortunate for the demonstrators that it had coincided with Hoover's death, but it was a happy coincidence for others — particularly for some in the White House. They had known for some time that the protest was to be the first in a number of demonstrations across the city that week, including a rally at Macpherson Square and a march on Congress to pressure the Nixon administration to cut off funds for the war. They now seized their chance to create a little embarrassment.

Shortly after Hoover's death and his lying in state were announced the previous day, White House counsel Charles Colson had telephoned Jeb Magruder, deputy director of CREEP (the Committee for the Re-Election of the President), and, hinting that the orders came directly from Richard Nixon, asked Magruder to arrange a counterdemonstration. Magruder conferred with his boss, the former attorney general John Mitchell, and together they approached a former FBI agent, then CREEP's intelligence chief, G. Gordon Liddy.

Liddy's first thought was to turn to a fellow "plumber" — White House consultant Howard Hunt. Like Liddy, Hunt was no novice in the murky world of intelligence, except that his experience came from the CIA. Among his more notable exploits was his work on the agency's Cuban invasion plans. Those contacts now came in handy. Hunt called Bernard Barker, an old colleague from the Agency days. One of Barker's other claims to fame was that he had once been an FBI informant inside the Batista regime's secret police. Working feverishly over the phone, these three quickly assembled a small group of Cuban expatriates and old Agency freelancers, ordering them to get to Washington on the first available plane and disrupt the "hippies, traitors, and communists" who were out to "ruin Hoover's big day."

By evening the group of antiwar protesters on the west steps had swelled to more than five hundred. Among those present were a number of nationally known activists such as Pentagon Papers figure Daniel Ellsberg (the White House's current bête noire), Harrisburg Eight conspiracy defendant Sister Elizabeth McAllister, radical lawyer William Kunstler (another hated figure), and movie actor Donald Sutherland.

The demonstration was by now beginning to attract some attention, and a number of passing congressional aides stopped to join in. More help came from four Democratic House members: Bella Abzug, Ed Koch, and John Dow from New York and Don Edwards of California. Together they read a "Liturgy of the Air War" consisting of quotations from Indochinese peasants, U.S. bomber pilots, and others on the dreadful effects of the conflict.

Bernard Barker and his men, with a few local additions provided by Hunt and Liddy, stood farther down the steps. Holding placards that read SUPPORT OUR PRESIDENT and DISBAR KUNSTLER, they struggled to make themselves heard, shouting "Commie" and "traitor" every time someone stood up to take over the reading. When this didn't work, they edged forward and started a few minor scuffles. As the threat of a violent confrontation grew, two of Barker's men, Frank Sturgis and Reinaldo Pico, were hustled off by Capitol police. They were released on a side street moments later after the intercession of an anonymous figure in a gray business suit.

As an attempt to halt the antiwar protest, the Liddy-Hunt counterdemonstration was a failure; as an embarrassment to those protesters it was singularly successful. The next day's newspapers would all refer to it, and to the disparaging comments of some of the Hoover mourners who considered the action "disrespectful of a great man."

After the demonstration Gordon Liddy and Howard Hunt picked up Bernard Barker for a debriefing. Liddy later claimed that while driving through the rain-drenched streets they passed by the Watergate office complex, which he pointed out to Barker. It was, he explained, to be their next job.

By midnight, the Capitol was peaceful once more. The antiwar activists, the counterdemonstrators, the press, tourists, and mourners had mostly gone. The rain had stopped, and the normal Washington humidity had been replaced by a slight breeze. A flag set at half-mast flapped gently in the wind. In the Rotunda, the honor guard of four servicemen and a solitary special agent stood silent vigil, Hoover's casket touched only by the quiet of the night.

The story of Hoover's funeral conjures up an extraordinary period in American history — the early 1970s, when conspiracy and intrigue ran rampant, when institutional and individual hypocrisy made cynics out of the most idealistic of citizens. May 3, 1972, is like a time capsule containing the ingredients of scandals so far-reaching that they would rock the nation's political foundations for years to come. But the story of that day is also worth recalling because it marks the death of the only director the FBI had ever had and the difficult birth of the modern Bureau.

Hoover's death raised an obvious question: How would the Federal Bureau of Investigation — the most powerful investigative agency in the world — survive him? For almost half a century he *was* the FBI. He had built it from nothing to an organization at the apex of the country's legal and political establishment. Hoover's name is now synonymous with scandal, but at the time of his death he wielded more individual power than almost any other American of his age.

Of course the FBI did survive Hoover, and more than two decades later it is still a remarkable institution, still at the top of the tree, still carrying its banner of fidelity, bravery, and integrity. It has survived the many embarrassments and exposés of the years since Hoover's death and has reforged its reputation as the greatest law enforcement body in the world. It is justly famous for its high-tech sophistication, its successful investigations against organized crime, public corruption, fraud, espionage, and terrorism. The Bureau's agents labor diligently on the difficult and complex inquiries they are called upon to pursue. The FBI has its faults, but it is back in favor with the American people. Its public relations machinery works overtime to project an image of efficiency, integrity, and almost frightening competence, but there is another side, a side the public rarely sees, of an agency that is still tied to the sclerotic bureaucratic and procedural obsessions of J. Edgar Hoover. Walk the corridors of FBI headquarters and his ghost will come to meet you.

One agent, with twenty years' service behind him (in narcotics, organized crime, and counterintelligence), explained why: "Nobody here talks much about Hoover anymore, nobody even thinks about him much. But his spirit is still with us. He's still the best director we ever had. Sure he did some dreadful things and he made some big, big mistakes, and I for one will tell you that that makes me ashamed. But there's this other side that is always ignored. He built an organization that couldn't be intimidated by anyone. To this day people think twice before they take on the FBI, and for good reason. Let me tell you, every time I go out there on the streets I give thanks that he did so."

Many inside the Bureau share these sentiments, and all will agree that Hoover's legacy to America was an organization dedicated to protecting the nation from hostile intelligence efforts, subversion, and major league crime. His perception of what constituted a threat may have been radically different from many people's, but the machinery was put in place nonetheless. Since his death the Bureau's agenda has changed a number of times; now special agents spend most of their time on matters of more relevance and concern to the nation. But the institution Hoover built remains largely intact, following many of the principles laid down by its founding father. It is here, in the tension between Hoover's powerful legacy and the Bureau's need to adapt to a rapidly changing world, that the story of the modern FBI can be found.

CHAPTER 1

THE MISSION, THE MYTH,
AND THE MEN

The overall mission of the FBI is to uphold the law through the investigation of violations of Federal criminal statutes, to protect the United States from hostile intelligence efforts, to provide assistance to other Federal state and local law enforcement agencies, and to perform those responsibilities in a manner that is faithful to the Constitution and laws of the United States.

— FBI MISSION STATEMENT

THE J. EDGAR HOOVER BUILDING sits on a block of prime real estate, halfway between the White House and Capitol Hill on Pennsylvania Avenue in Washington, D.C. A vast, cream-colored, multistory bunker, it can easily lay claim to being the city's ugliest building. But the complex is famous for more than its architectural brutality. It is the national headquarters of the Federal Bureau of Investigation, the most powerful law enforcement agency on earth.

Most of what goes on behind its fortresslike walls is hidden from the public's view, but several times a day, every week of the year, parties of curious tourists are allowed a heavily sanitized glimpse of the agency's operations. The FBI tour, which was instituted in the 1930s as a public relations exercise, is now one of the capital's top attractions. Millions of people have followed the immaculate guides on a brief trip around a special exhibition designed to celebrate the FBI's many achievements. As people walk past John Dillinger's death mask, the Bureau's incredible collection of guns, the FBI forensic laboratory, and quirky items of stolen property, they are provided general information about the organization's many investigative programs. The tour ends with a demonstration in a specially designed firing range, where a special agent shoots off a few rounds from some of the weapons the FBI uses in its work.

For the vast majority of tourists, this slick, professional, and utterly bland excursion will accord with their vivid, if ill defined, impressions about the FBI. This is hardly surprising, considering that for almost seventy years the public has been bombarded with movies, TV shows, books, and articles devoted to the Bureau's activities. As a result the FBI has become firmly entrenched in American mythology, as much a national icon as baseball, Marilyn Monroe, and the Statue of Liberty. Its fame is truly global, its celebrated initials as well recognized in London, Paris, and Tokyo as in Dallas, New York, or L.A.

In reality, most first-time visitors to the Bureau's headquarters, like most of the public, know remarkably little about what the FBI actually does. When pressed they will volunteer that it fights crime and hunts spies — and of course that it was once run by J. Edgar Hoover (almost everyone knows something about Hoover). But beyond that, few people have more than a superficial understanding of its operations.

This collective ignorance is one of the more apparent consequences of the Bureau's culture of secrecy. Even though the agency has recently made some efforts toward opening its doors to the outside world, many in the FBI would prefer to keep the public at a distance, content with the rosy portrait that the Bureau's public relations machine works so hard to paint — that of "the most successful investigative agency in the world." But although this image is not completely without foundation, it isn't completely correct either. Worse, it is now so deeply embedded in the national consciousness that an accurate perception of what the Bureau does is difficult to achieve. Even agents are affected by the power of the image. Some, when asked to sum up the Bureau and what it stands for, are either unwilling or incapable of assessing it in anything other than the most simplistic terms. One, pushed into thinking about it little longer than usual, replied, "It's just one big complicated son of a bitch."

Such remarks, while undoubtedly true, do nothing to peel away the layers of mystique in which the Bureau has been wrapped for so long. Anyone hoping to gain a good understanding of the modern

FBI might better begin with a few important facts. The Bureau, which has always had a love affair with jargon, might call it the overview. Here, then, is an overview.

The Federal Bureau of Investigation is the principal investigative arm of the Department of Justice of the United States — in effect, a quasi-autonomous body that acts as the nation's primary law enforcement and domestic intelligence agency. Its authority is drawn principally from Sections 533 and 534 of Title 28 of the United States Code, which authorizes the attorney general to "appoint officials to detect crimes against the United States." Under this authority the Bureau performs most of its work, investigating persons or incidents where there is reason to believe that a crime has been committed or is likely to be committed. Other specific areas of investigative authority come from individual statutes or from executive orders issued by the president. The Bureau is also authorized to investigate noncriminal matters or matters where no prosecution is contemplated — gathering information about activities that jeopardize the security of the state, for instance, or conducting background checks on people about to be appointed to sensitive or executive positions in government service.

Although the FBI draws much of its authority from the attorney general and from the Justice Department, and in legal terms is a division of the department, in most respects it operates independently, with its own budget, procedures, and practices. To carry out its twin missions — of investigating crime and protecting the United States against espionage and terrorism — the agency has approximately twenty-four thousand employees, of whom about 45 percent are special agents. The rest are support staff of one sort or another, mainly technical, clerical, administrative, legal, or scientific.

In organizational terms the FBI has a pyramidic structure. At its apex sits the director. Appointed by the president, usually from within the ranks of the law enforcement community, the director is responsible to the president, the attorney general, and Congress for the investigations and operations of the Bureau. Although J. Edgar Hoover, by a combination of political skill, organizational genius, and blackmail, managed to hang on to the director's job for forty-eight years, appointments are now made for a maximum ten-year term — although the president can if he wishes fire a serving director and nominate another in his place. To date, no agents have been appointed directly to the post, although Clarence Kelley, the Kansas City police chief who had the job in the mid-1970s, and the current incumbent, Louis J. Freeh, were both special agents at some point in their careers. No woman has ever even been considered for the position, which is not surprising in an organization known for many years for its Neanderthal attitudes toward women.

The director is ultimately responsible for the day-to-day operations of the FBI and for the tens of thousands of ongoing investigations carried out by its agents. It is he who appears before the various congressional committees that oversee the agency's affairs, he who justifies its colossal multibillion-dollar budget, he who takes the blame if things go wrong. In direct contrast to Hoover, who usually refused to acknowledge mistakes, the last few directors have all had to take their fair share of criticism.

The director's role is significant, but for most practical purposes the modern FBI's operations are overseen by its senior managers, career executives who have spent most, if not all, of their working lives in the Bureau, rising up through the ranks to the top table where decisions are made and where the secrets are the most sensitive. Until recently, the director's immediate subordinates were a deputy director and two associate deputy directors (investigations and administration). Beneath them came ten divisions and four offices. The deputy director, as well as being the director's "executive officer," with comparable overall responsibility, also looked after the inspection and legal divisions, the equal employment office, and the congressional and public affairs office. Shortly after his appointment in 1993, to the private satisfaction of less exalted agents in the field, Louis Freeh shook things up a little by doing away with the two ADD posts and making all the Bureau's senior executives directly accountable to him rather than to his deputy. Further upheavals are anticipated.

The other divisions and offices are roughly arranged into two blocks. The first is "operational": criminal investigations, intelligence, training, laboratory, and liaison and international affairs. The other is "administrative": identification, administrative services, records management, and technical services. Each of the divisions is run by an assistant director, each of the offices by an inspector-in-charge.

These executives — the director and his senior managers — compose what is in effect the FBI's board of directors. Officially they have responsibility for every facet of Bureau operations. Occasionally the senior executives on the investigative side will get drawn into an important case, but generally they spend most of their time on policy. To the agents in the field, the role of these high-ranking bureaucrats often isn't clear. More than one agent, up to his eyes in paperwork and loaded down with unresolved cases, has wondered out loud, "What the hell do all these people do?"

While this attitude reflects the sort of distrust that can be found between employees and management in any organization, it is particularly prevalent in the Bureau. The FBI may be the world's most sophisticated law enforcement and intelligence agency, but it is also one of the world's most hidebound bureaucracies. As one veteran remarked, "To get to the top of the Bureau its senior executives must have one key attribute — they must be skilled bureaucrats. An intelligent and inquiring mind doesn't even come a close second."

All of the senior executives, with one exception, work out of FBI headquarters. They are joined by almost eight thousand people who provide "program support and direction" to the FBI's field operations. Translated, this means that in effect FBI headquarters can do anything from controlling a major hostage or siege operation (such as the one in Waco, Texas, during the spring of 1993) to running fingerprint checks for the Dallas FBI's bank robbery squad. Here can be found, among much else, the fabled and massive FBI laboratory, the Bureau's mainframe computer systems, hundreds of unit chiefs and supervisors with responsibility for the process and administration of categories of cases, the finance departments, and the sophisticated public relations machine.

It is also the place where careers are made and lost, where reputations are built and destroyed, and where committees sit in conclave over the entrails of FBI policy. There is almost as much intrigue along its endless corridors as there is in the rest of Washington put together. With good reason FBI headquarters is known to many agents as the "puzzle palace." Despite this vast administrative apparatus, the Bureau's day-to-day operations are almost exclusively carried out through its fifty-six field offices and its four hundred satellite resident agencies. The field offices are found in almost every large city in the country, the resident agencies (R.A.'s) around them in smaller cities and towns, or in places of particular investigative importance (such as those with numerous defense-related industries or the suburbs of big metropolitan areas). The field offices vary in size; some such as New York and Los Angeles have several hundred agents and support personnel, while others such as El Paso or Anchorage merit only a few dozen. The situation is likewise with the R.A.'s, which at their largest can be as big as the smallest field offices, but in other areas may be staffed by only one agent who acts as chief cook and bottle-washer for the local law enforcement community.

New York, long considered for obvious reasons the largest and busiest field office, provides the exception mentioned earlier. Unlike the other offices, which are all run by a special agent in charge (SAC), New York has its own assistant director, with three SACs under him. Although he works out of the Federal Building in downtown Manhattan, he is accorded the same status as an assistant director at headquarters.

Each field office is a fiefdom, run by its special agent in charge with the help of various assistant SACs, unit chiefs, and supervisors. Currently the SACs are all men — the Bureau's first and only woman SAC was promoted out of the Anchorage field office to an administrative post at headquarters in 1993. To most agents, their SAC is the most powerful figure in their lives. He assigns them to squads and decides what operations are to be carried out in his geographical territory. A good SAC can make a field office an invigorating place to work; a bad one can make it hell. An SAC is a bit like a captain in charge of a ship. He is ultimately responsible to a higher authority but for most practical purposes is God in his domain. The job is regarded as highly desirable within the Bureau, and competition for appointments is intense.

Unlike the CIA, its intelligence-gathering cousin, the FBI has limited overseas resources; it is almost exclusively a domestically oriented organization. It does, however, maintain twenty-one overseas offices, each run by a legal attaché (LEGAT). The LEGAT's responsibility is to liaise with host countries' police, security, and intelligence forces on matters of common interest, from narcotics to international terrorism. Hence Jim Greenleaf, the LEGAT in London, will spend much of his time in contact with MI5, MI6, Scotland Yard, and the various regional police forces around Britain.

His counterpart in Paris will be similarly engaged with the Sûreté, the DGSE, DST, and the gendarmerie. Many of the LEGATs are where one would expect, in major capitals from Bonn to Tokyo; other cities, such as Hong Kong and Montevideo, are regionally important. LEGATs have a special status within the Bureau, and many see such postings as the crowning of a successful career. Greenleaf, for instance, is a former assistant director of the FBI.

On occasion, usually connected with attacks on American property, commercial interests, or individuals, FBI agents are dispatched from the United States to "assist" foreign police and security forces in an investigation. The bombing of a Pan Am jumbo jet over Lockerbie in 1988 sparked a major international manhunt, and special agents worked closely with Scottish police in identifying the two Libyan terrorists allegedly responsible. Under certain circumstances, agents are now allowed to arrest suspects overseas without the approval or knowledge of the countries concerned.

Despite all these management structures and hierarchies, the real work of the Bureau — the investigations carried out under its twin missions of combating crime and protecting the security of the United States — is done by the special agents.

On paper there are few apparent differences between the agents who work at headquarters and those who work in the field. They carry the same gold badge, have sworn the same oath, and have the same legal responsibilities. But as the management professionals rise up the ladder, their immediate contact with cases diminishes and their administrative responsibilities increase. The street agents, by contrast, do all the legwork. They knock on doors, work undercover, hunt fugitives, monitor wiretaps, meet informants, engage in occasional gun battles, man the hostage rescue and SWAT teams, check out the backgrounds of applicants for FBI or other government services, and carry out all the other tasks, big and small, that the agency is mandated to do.

Perhaps inevitably, the field agents tend to have different feelings about their job and the organization they work for. (This is reminiscent of the military, of the way front-line troops relate to the general staff of an army.) Some legitimate generalizations can be made about both the management's and the field operatives' point of view.

People at headquarters think in broad terms — of strategy, policy, and rules. Since they operate in the hothouse atmosphere of intrigue and politics that is part and parcel of Washington, D.C., they are also more cautious, more secretive, and more rigid about procedure. Perversely, this also makes them more romantic about the FBI and its historic role as the guardian of the United States' national security — as though the closer they are to the source of the myth, the more they tend to believe it. As a consequence, although they know they have to put in time at headquarters if their careers are to flourish, many administrators become deeply sentimental about the "good old days" on the street.

Field agents, as a rule, tend to have fewer illusions about the organization. Because they feel its effects every day, they are more cynical about the FBI bureaucracy and the agency's effectiveness. Not that the esprit de corps is any less obvious in the field; on the contrary, it is hard to think of another organization whose employees are as bound together by a common set of principles. But the idealism of the average field agent has more to do with the respect he feels for his immediate colleagues than with abstract historical notions. Field agents prefer to keep their rose-colored glasses for special occasions — and for outsiders, of course. Where strangers are concerned, special agents will always put the FBI first.

Currently there are about ten thousand SAs. As money and priorities dictate, this figure fluctuates by a few hundred, but the number of special agents has stayed about the same for the last five years. The vast bulk are still white, middle-class American men, but slowly things are changing. Roughly 10 percent are women, 5 percent African American, 5 percent Hispanic, 0.5 percent American Indian, and 1 percent Asian American. Virtually all have some kind of college degree, and many are lawyers, accountants, or social science or language experts. Quite a few have served in the military or law enforcement, or both.

These men and women nominally work on about 270 categories of federal violation, although this number varies as legislation changes and priorities are redefined. Some of the categories are effectively obsolete (No. 43H, for example, which has to do with "unauthorized use of the Smokey Bear Symbol" — although the FBI is still legally allowed to open and maintain a case file on any individual caught abusing old Smokey in an unauthorized fashion). These statutory specifications aside, the cases covered fall into six main categories: organized crime, white-collar crime, narcotics, violent crime, counterterrorism (incorporating what used to be known as subversion), and foreign counterintelligence.

In each of these areas the Bureau deploys a complex array of investigative techniques, from the use of undercover agents, informants, and electronic and wiretap surveillance, to the more mundane process of interviewing witnesses and suspects. Every operation is supported by the much vaunted FBI laboratory, which can analyze DNA or a bank robbery note, provide sophisticated listening devices or nighttime optical equipment, advise on how to detect a computer virus, and much more. Lab staff are often agents, and indeed the laboratory is run by agents, but many of the scientists are outsiders hired for their expertise.

Another crucial part of the operation is the FBI Academy at Quantico, Virginia, which provides new agent training courses, in-service training for qualified special agents, a National Academy for senior police officers from around the country, and a variety of quasi-academic support services for the Bureau at large. The most famous of these is the Behavioral Science Unit, which is among other things responsible for tracking down the nation's most infamous serial killers. Quantico is also the home base of the Hostage Rescue Team, an elite force of fifty special agents trained, like the British Special Air Service (SAS), to deal with hijackings, sieges, and the like.

Special agents can also draw on a deep pool of technical skills provided by agents with particular expertise — pilots, engineers, and communications specialists, to name but a few. Whenever an agent joins the Bureau, any specialized knowledge he has is noted and logged into a central computer. More than one new recruit has been startled to find himself shuttled off to the other side of the country to lend his arcane expertise to an ongoing investigation. Further support comes from related agencies like the U.S. Customs, the Drug Enforcement Agency, the Bureau of Alcohol, Tobacco, and Firearms, and local police, who often work with the Bureau in specific task forces.

All this takes money — a lot of money, more than $2 billion a year at current levels. The FBI, as might be expected, makes much of the fact that this is less than the cost of one Stealth bomber and a fraction of the cost of the overall defense budget of the United States. But it is still comparable to the gross domestic product of a number of small Third World nations.

A portion — and not an inconsiderable portion — of the FBI's budget is spent on telling taxpayers that the money is very well spent. The FBI is a remarkable self-propagandist. Hoover learned early on the power of public relations; he used it brilliantly to create a myth of infallibility, and both the myth and Hoover's interest in good P.R. continue. But this myth has little connection to reality and does a disservice to the difficulties faced by special agents on a daily basis. Agents operate in an increasingly chaotic and violent world. No matter how well trained and experienced, they will occasionally make mistakes, sometimes very bad ones.

But if the Bureau is to be understood, if myth is to be divorced from reality, then it must be through the field agents. Each one may have a different background and personality, but each holds a small part of the puzzle. Spend some time with an agent — any agent, in any office — and the Bureau begins to make sense.

John Morris had been called many things in his time, but "a typical FBI agent" was not one of them. For reasons known only to himself he found the suggestion a little amusing. But then, as he liked to explain at great length given the opportunity, there were few laughs to be had out of the Bureau and he had to take his fun where he could find it.

He was working under this principle one afternoon in the spring of 1993 as he prepared to hit the streets of Los Angeles. Morris was engaged in a favorite pastime — teasing the stuffing out of an impressionable younger colleague. His victim was Mark Van Steenburg, whose starched white shirt, polished shoes, and trusting good nature made him a perfect target.

Van Steenburg, it was obvious, was a jealous man. He was green with envy. He hadn't managed to get out of L.A. for months, and he wasn't taking his confinement well. And now Morris had just told him that he had wangled a Bureau-sanctioned trip to Palm Springs — to a golf resort, of all things.

Morris watched the obvious struggle in Van Steenburg's face and, ever so gently, rubbed some more salt in the wound.

"You think that's good. Well, how about this? In three weeks' time I'm off to Australia. It shows a little respect to age and experience, don't you think? Who knows, Mark. Maybe if you behave yourself, they might let you take a ride down South Central."

Van Steenburg loitered wordlessly. He resisted asking for details, knowing that Morris was trying to get a rise out of him. But eventually he gave in.

"You're off to Australia? Well, so what. I hear it's a dump anyway." He paused for a moment. "So how come you get all the breaks?"

Morris stuffed some more papers into his battered briefcase, checked to be sure he had his gun, and walked to the door. His parting shot was thrown casually over his shoulder. "When you've been around a while and you've learned a thing or two, you'll figure out how I manage it."

It was not a brilliant exit line, but it was good enough. The timing was perfect. By the time Van Steenburg had thought of a suitably stinging reply Morris was long gone.

On the way out to the elevators Morris paused by a bulletin board, on which one large black-and-white poster was pinned: WELCOME TO LOS ANGELES — BANK ROBBERY CAPITAL OF THE WORLD. He gazed at it absent-mindedly, rubbed the side of his nose, and then confided a little sheepishly that actually the trip to Australia was for a Rotary convention. "But you know, it doesn't hurt to bring a little joy into these guys' lives once in a while. Once they've been around a little longer they'll figure out when I'm bullshitting."

On the short trip down to the lobby Morris reflected on the day so far. It had been pretty good, all things considered. He had spent most of the morning sitting in on a polygraph examination of a suspect in a major bank larceny investigation. His early expectations were not high, but after four hours she had finally cracked. The case — involving huge unauthorized withdrawals from a string of Wells Fargo cash machines — looked as if it was finally breaking.

Outside, the Los Angeles smog was taking a rare break, and the warm California sun bounced off the concrete plaza in front of the Federal Building. Halfway down the steps Morris was brought up short by Mike Waters, an ex-cop working security for Wells Fargo and an interested party in the case. Morris filled him in on the latest developments.

The case itself presented an old story with a few new twists. One day a Wells Fargo bank teller was made responsible for the security codes of the bank's downtown automatic teller machines. Sue was a big lady, a widow, and a little lonely. When a man named Roland, whom she'd known slightly for the past three years, began to show a romantic interest in her, she was flattered. He wined and dined her, brought her flowers, and after a while they got to know each other very well. Then her new friend started to take an interest in her work. Before long she was talking animatedly about her job, her boss, her responsibilities. Morris had had cases like this before, particularly during his time on espionage investigations in New York. A vulnerable person in a sensitive position would be befriended, blackmailed, and used. It was the oldest trick in the book.

Sue had passed on access codes for a couple of Wells Fargo ATMs to her new friend Roland, and Roland had shared this information with his associates. A short time later the bank was a couple hundred thousand dollars short. Sue immediately realized that Roland had to be responsible, but she was too scared to say anything. And soon Sue realized that she was not the only bank employee he had been wooing; Roland and his associates must have developed quite a few "friendships" among Wells Fargo staff, because the list of robbed ATMs quickly grew to nine. The company was now out several hundred thousand dollars, but still it hesitated before acting. Like most banks that are robbed, Wells Fargo was not eager to advertise the fact, since the news wouldn't do much for customer confidence. But now the thefts were hitting the bottom line and something had to be done. Embarrassment was swallowed, the police were called.

As it turned out, two of the robberies occurred at branches covered by the Federal Deposit Insurance Corporation, and so the FBI got concurrent jurisdiction. Special Agent John Morris of the bank robbery squad asked for the case. He had just come off a major investigation in which he had put the infamous Nasty Boys in prison, and he wanted a change from "takeovers" — straightforward armed robberies that, though often extremely violent, lacked subtlety. Morris liked subtlety; he enjoyed pitting his wits against those of professional criminals, and over the years he had developed a reputation for his tenacity and investigative skills. He got the assignment, and by the time he bumped into Mike Waters on the steps of the Federal Building he had been working it for five weeks.

Morris needed Wells Fargo's help and, for the moment, was unwilling to give Waters the impression that the case was as good as solved: "This thing isn't going to be easy peasy, you know. It's just the beginning." But as he trotted down the steps and strolled toward the parking lot, he whistled to himself — a clear sign that things were going well.

In the first four months of 1993, the Los Angeles FBI investigated over 550 armed bank robberies and dozens of other bank larceny cases. The year before, the office dealt with 2,500 cases in all. The poster on the bulletin board was no joke — L.A. really is the bank robbery capital of the world. Recession or no recession, California still has a massive economy and the City of Angels is its financial heart. There is a lot of money around, and inevitably that means a lot of banks, in an assortment of shapes and sizes. Customers, whether corporate or individual, can deposit their money in, or extract it from, a bewildering variety of institutions. There are investment banks, merchant banks, savings banks, late-night banks, early opening banks, drive-in banks, shopping mall banks, and even Sunday-opening banks — not to mention the hundreds of neighborhood savings and loan branches, which offer much the same services, and the thousands of ATMs in prestige shopping plazas and local grocery stores. Consumers appreciate the convenience and variety of these services and make liberal use of them. Unfortunately, so do the bank robbers. The big banks, like Wells Fargo, American Bank, First Interstate Bank, and Bank of America, have the most outlets and so get most of their attention.

Most of them are covered by the Federal Deposit Insurance Corporation, a system established in the aftermath of the 1929 Wall Street crash to protect investors' money from willful speculation, fraud, and corruption. Deposit insurance was meant to prevent the American banking system from collapsing like a house of cards at the first sign of trouble, but it also means that banks get the protection of the federal judicial system. Title 18, United States Code Section 2113, gives the FBI jurisdiction over bank burglary, larceny, and robbery at any institution covered by the FDIC.

Ken Jacobsen is the supervisor of the Los Angeles bank robbery squad and is John Morris's immediate boss. Jacobsen's difficult task is to stretch his limited resources to meet a massive problem. He supervises sixteen agents in his squad; a further eighteen are spread out in resident agencies across the region. All of them are heavily burdened with work — some are carrying more than 150 cases at any one time, compared with an average of 20 or 30 for other squads.

The problem has become so acute that the squad can no longer respond to every bank robbery. The rules of investigation have had to be altered; now the squad only covers those cases where the amount stolen is more than two thousand dollars, and even then agents will think twice before taking on cases where no violence was involved.

Even so, the L.A. squad has a good clearance rate: more than 85 percent of the cases they cover end in a conviction. This statistic would undoubtedly be a lot worse were it not for the video security systems that most banks now use. The walls outside Jacobsen's office are covered with snapshots of robbers in action. Some of them are using disguises — ski masks, dark glasses, and false beards are the most prevalent. Many, though, are openly recognizable, an indication perhaps of the stupidity of those involved. In the ranking of dull-witted criminal activities, robbing a bank while thousands of dollars' worth of video technology records one's every move must come near the top. Frequently the walls depict a suspect in his own photo montage — a collection of pictures taken by security cameras at each bank he has robbed. Some thieves will hit four or five banks before they get caught; after spending some time in jail, they often emerge a few years later to start all over again. It would almost be funny if it weren't so violent. Virtually every picture shows a robber brandishing a gun. Shootings, even fatalities, are common.

The squad has become adept at processing these cases smoothly, which is not surprising given the amount of practice they get. The FBI normally hears of the robberies through the Los Angeles Police Department radio network, and whichever agent is nearest to the scene will be dispatched to back up the police. Once at the scene, the officers and the agent divide up the chores, the police doing the fingerprinting and taking statements from the public, while the agent talks to the staff and retrieves the surveillance film. Usually, despite occasional attempts by robbers to destroy the cameras, the images have survived. From there it's a quick trip back to the office to print up some copies. The gallery on the office wall is never short of pictures.

Jacobsen knows these investigations sound easy, and indeed they would be straightforward were it not for the sheer scale of the problem his agents have to cope with. There are over 3,500 banks in L.A., and most have been robbed at some time or other. His squad and the agents in the R.A.'s have to cover an area of seven counties with 14 million people. It means a lot of legwork.

Special Agent John Morris had been on the bank robbery squad for years and he had seen pretty much everything. So whenever an unusually challenging case came up he tried to grab it. The alternative — spending the day showing photospreads of suspects to unwilling witnesses and plowing through video surveillance film for useful evidence — had long since lost its appeal. A juicy larceny case like the Wells Fargo ATM scam had a touch of class; it called for some real detection. His only real problem with the case was that it was taking several weeks to resolve and all the while he had other duties that kept getting in the way. That afternoon he was on standby, meaning that at any moment his deliberations could be interrupted by a call to a crime scene.

Morris approached his car, but before getting in he went through a little routine. It never varied. He unlocked the trunk, took out his pump-action shotgun, and put it on the floor beneath the passenger seat. The gun took a rifle slug; Morris didn't like firing buckshot because it was too indiscriminate, whereas a slug would go through a wall or an engine block if necessary. Next, he looked over the 9mm Bureau-issue automatic on his hip; then he checked to see that his bulletproof vest was on the back seat.

Morris's car was an ordinary looking Buick Regal, but it had hidden qualities. It was more an office than a form of transport, and he spent as much time hunched over the wheel as he did at his desk, planning investigations, checking out leads, and responding to crisis calls. From the outside, apart from a small forest of antennas on the trunk, it didn't give much away. Inside was another matter; there were mobile phones, beepers, a radio tuned to the FBI dispatch network, another to the Los Angeles Police Department. From them all came snatches of messages, instructions, and requests, a bewildering background noise to his work.

That afternoon the police network was the busiest, but occasionally traces of radio chatter came through from a big FBI surveillance operation downtown. Agents were tailing a suspect they believed was using extortion to get school kids to hold up banks on his behalf. Many of the special agents involved were working overtime on the case because they felt so strongly about it. Morris, though, was something of a loner and liked to do his sleuthing on his own. Partners got on his nerves after a while. Not that it made that much difference anyway; the Los Angeles FBI had neither the means nor the manpower to put two agents on every job.

He climbed into the car and drove out onto the street toward the banks and expensive apartment buildings of West L.A. Although the agents in the squad didn't have official beats, many took to the streets in the afternoons so that they could finish the day somewhere convenient for getting home. Morris lived with his wife, a former nurse, in Simi Valley, and anywhere in West L.A. or Hollywood was good for him. Other agents would gradually work south or east, keeping close to the freeways so they could beat the city's unbelievable traffic at the end of the working day. As he drove, Morris kept an ear out for the FBI radio network, knowing that at any moment the voice of Linda Webster, the bank squad's dispatcher, might come through with a call in his neighborhood.

Like many people in Los Angeles, Morris loved Hollywood and had a secret longing to be a movie actor. He was a particular fan of Clint Eastwood and had even met him a few times. Morris's sister-in-law had once worked in the small California town of Carmel during the time the movie star was mayor there, and on one occasion Eastwood asked if her family and friends would like to visit him on the set of one of his pictures. It was a great day out and helped feed one of Morris's fondest fantasies: that when he eventually left the Bureau, he would be able to get a character part or a walk-on role in a film. The reality, though, as Morris sadly conceded, was that when that time came, he would probably have to become a private investigator to eke out his small FBI pension. He wasn't looking forward to the prospect very much. The only plus was that he wouldn't have to go near any more banks. Morris was getting a little tired of banks.

Accelerating through a set of lights, he turned off Wilshire Boulevard toward West Hollywood and slowed down again as he pondered the vagaries of being a special agent. Only a couple of years away from retirement, he had spent a lot of time recently looking back on his career and wondering whether he should have done something else with his life. But every time he asked himself that question he got the same answer.

"I've been in the Bureau for twenty or so years," he explained, "and to be honest I still get a kick out of it. That's not to say that everything is perfect; no organization ever is. You know the bureaucracy can really get to you sometimes, and you think, why am I putting up with this bullshit. And it's because every now and then you get a case like this Wells Fargo one which kind of stretches you, know what I mean? It's still fun once in a while. This is something that we don't get a chance to do very often, to do an investigation where you use your skills. It's more than just taking a picture of a guy and running around and doing photospreads to get him for as many robberies as you can. Ninety percent of the time they confess anyway; they're disposed of pretty quickly. Three months and they're in prison. This takes more effort."

Morris joined the Bureau right after his Vietnam service because it seemed to offer a decent career doing something worthwhile. Most of the time the decision had worked out, but it hadn't always been easy, and he reckoned that the job had cost him his first marriage. His early years were spent in New York on foreign counterintelligence and espionage cases; then he worked kidnapping and hostage rescue for a while. Ironically, given his love of Clint Eastwood, during that time he got involved in an operation that could have come straight from the script of *Dirty Harry*. One day a fugitive hijacked a schoolbus, took it to Kennedy Airport in New York, and demanded a plane to make his getaway. Morris was part of the local FBI SWAT team that was sent in to sort things out. The incident ended in a gun battle, and was one of the few times Morris had fired his weapon in anger. The fugitive was injured but eventually gave himself up. The children were released unharmed.

Then, a couple of years later, Morris found himself behind a desk at FBI headquarters in Washington as a supervisor. If he was going to climb the career ladder he had to put in his time there, but it was a dramatic change of pace from the hustle and bustle of the streets. After four years and a messy divorce, he decided it wasn't for him. He applied for a transfer back to the field and he got L.A. All these years later he believed that he had become a good student of human nature, especially when it came to what made an agent effective against "the criminal mind."

Morris's theory was that a good agent knew how to use thieves' own criminal thinking against them, and even how to play psychology with them. He maintained that the best training for becoming an FBI agent was not going to law school or studying accounting, as the recruitment literature claimed, but learning about people, maybe through spending time in the military, working as a schoolteacher or as a sports coach. As he explained it, "The whole thing about being an FBI agent is gaining people's confidence. The first five or ten minutes you're with them, they size you up to determine whether or not you're competent, whether they can trust you or can't trust you, or whatever. If you can't make them think that, you've got a real problem."

Psychology was the whole key to his current case. Morris felt that Sue had confessed that morning partly because of her employment agreement with the bank, which required her to take a company polygraph test and even to allow her bosses to search her home if they thought it necessary. Her dread of her employers was so great that she had agreed to take a more demanding FBI polygraph, even though she was under no legal requirement to do so. The session had started at ten o'clock, but it had been two before she was ready to talk.

"This girl knew she was lying," said Morris, "and she wanted to relieve the burden of guilt. She just wanted a little coaxing. I mean, she figured, as she was suspended, that she was probably going to lose her job anyway. So what else did she have to lose? She knew that we probably wouldn't send her to jail. She is a nice person, basically, and she didn't get any money out of it, so we'll probably get her immunity as a federal witness. Even if she admitted going and doing the larceny herself, because of her past record they'd probably just give her probation. Hell, they don't put people in jail for bank robberies unless they are armed. I mean, the system is up the creek anyway. So it's the first in the lifeboat theory. Whoever gets in that lifeboat with us first doesn't flounder. The rest we throw to the sharks. She's the first in the lifeboat."

After five weeks on the case Morris now had a reasonable idea of who was involved. Sue's statement had just confirmed some of what he already suspected. There were three or four in the gang besides Roland, and they had been running this sophisticated scam for several months, following a standard pattern. Their first step was to work their way into the friendship and confidence of a number of targeted bank employees and then extract individual ATM access codes from them. Once that was done, it was relatively simple to pay an unobtrusive late night visit to the machines to clean them out. Morris also suspected that the money was being used for narcotics deals farther down the coast. The group had some sort of tie-in with the Palm Springs golf resort he had mentioned to Van Steenburg, which meant that he could legitimately practice his golf while conducting some clandestine inquiries in the area.

Unfortunately, suspicion, even certainty, did not always add up to proof. Morris still needed to make a case against the gang. He was hampered by the fact that they had somehow found out the FBI was watching them and were lying low. He was irked because he thought the bank might be to blame. It was obvious to him that someone inside the company had been helping the criminals, but he didn't know who. Because there were too many possibilities, and because the gang was already suspicious, he now planned to put a body recorder on Sue to see if Roland would incriminate himself, provide enough evidence to convict his associates, and reveal the identities of any other bank employees involved.

The car phone beeped. It was Mike Waters, the Wells Fargo security chief, asking for advice on the next move. Should the bank reinstate Sue for a while, so none of the other employees would find out that she had been volunteering information, or was she too much of a risk?

Morris was in a difficult situation. He wanted to protect a possible witness, but he knew that if Wells Fargo wanted to it could just fire her. He had to proceed carefully because he suspected Roland would soon turn up asking awkward questions and he didn't want to put Sue's life at risk or jeopardize his case. He still had not had time to take the case to a U.S. attorney and before a grand jury — legally he had no influence over her at all until he did — and she could easily be scared off.

"Look, Mike," he finally replied, "she's not going to do any more illegal activities, that's for sure. I don't want to alarm her, but by the same token we don't know if these people followed her. I'm sure Roland is going to drop by in a couple of weeks just to find out what's going on, and I want to be prepared for that. I don't want her to initiate conversation with him right now because he'd be too suspicious. I mean these guys are waiting for us to knock on the door."

Eventually they decided that she should be put up in a safehouse at the bank's expense. Morris didn't seem to mind that the bank would have to shell out a little of its own money. Like other agents on the Los Angeles bank robbery squad, he felt little sympathy for companies that spent comparatively little on security, treated their employees with constant suspicion, paid them next to minimum wage, and often failed to report thefts of money to the police or the Bureau because of the bad publicity it would cause. He also resented the way they used the presence of the FBI as excuse to fire employees — regardless of their guilt. He was happy to track down the robbers, but he knew the banks were not totally innocent victims.

Morris stopped the car for a moment to concentrate on an incoming message. An armed robbery was in progress downtown. At first it looked as though he would have to respond, but then it became clear that it was way out of his area and could safely be left to someone else.

He turned down the volume on the radio and returned to his theme: the frustrations agents sometimes faced in assembling sufficient evidence in cases like the Wells Fargo investigation. Juries were becoming increasingly fickle and hard to persuade. They had to be given irrefutable proof before they would convict, and in various cases he had had in the past, they had let an obviously guilty person go free. Even if Morris stopped Roland in his car and found fifty thousand twenty-dollar bills in the trunk, he could do little. The money could perhaps be confiscated for a few days, on the suspicion that it was drug related, but eventually the Bureau would have to hand it back. An unfortunate feature of ATM thefts was that banks were often unable to trace or identify stolen money from cash machines. The rapid and random outflow of money from them meant that there was no point in marking the bills with hidden distinguishing stamps.

Tracing money from more traditional armed robberies was much easier. Banks frequently put "bait money" in with the cash handed over the counter to the robbers. Sometimes the bank employees managed to slip in dye packs among the bundles of banknotes. These would later explode and give off heat, tear gas, and clouds of sticky red smoke. On numerous occasions agents had arrested a suspect only to find unmistakable, and obviously painful, signs that the robber had stuffed wads of cash down the front of his pants while making his getaway.

"There was this case the other day." Morris laughed. "The bank offered a $250 reward to its people if they handed over a dye pack to anyone when there was a robbery. It's kind of risky, you see, because they might be sussed doing it. Anyway, there was this takeover and the tellers stuck nine dye packs into the money. The guy stuck some of it down his crotch, and the dye packs went off a little early. All the bank people could see was this tremendous cloud of red smoke coming out from this guy's pants. I'll tell you, he left the bank like he had a torpedo up his ass."

Of all the cases he had worked in recent years, catching the Nasty Boys was the most satisfying for Morris, who described them as "the worst, the absolute rock bottom." Most of Los Angeles would probably agree with him. Even in a city that has become so used to violence, the Nasty Boys — two black teenagers, Clarence Sanders and Harold Walden II, and their followers — managed to make a big impression. Starting in September 1991, the two led a number of others on a massive robbery spree across southern California. During the months they were at large they attacked twenty-seven banks, terrorized hundreds of customers and employees, and stole hundreds of thousands of dollars. A favorite tactic was to herd everyone into a vault, holding guns to their heads, and threatening to kill them. Sometimes, for fun, the Nasty Boys would fire a few rounds next to someone's head. Other times they would fondle a woman and threaten her with death if she told anyone about it. Some of the victims were so disturbed they quit the next day. Others were still receiving psychiatric help months later. According to John Shepard Wiley, the assistant U.S. attorney who prosecuted them, Sanders and Walden "were everyone's violent nightmares come to life."

Inevitably the FBI led the hunt to find them, although for most of the investigation the agents had no real clues as to whom they were looking for. They weren't even aware the gang members were calling themselves the Nasty Boys. The agency christened them the White Maxima bandits instead, after the kind of getaway car they often used.

Then, on Friday, January 9, 1992, shortly after ten in the morning, Sanders and Walden hit the Great Western Bank in Mission Hills. They followed their standard procedure, firing a few shots at a bank teller before taking $150,000 from the vault. This time they made off in a green Lexus. Three hours later police were called to a wreck on the northbound lane of the freeway, near Ventura. The car involved was a green Lexus. When they arrived, the police had no way of knowing that the dazed young man in the car was one of the Nasty Boys, but when they checked his license through the computer, they found that he was one Clarence Sanders, a convicted felon. The name meant nothing to them, but since he had a loaded gun in the car they were able to hold him while they checked the Lexus for narcotics. They thought they might have hit on a drug dealer. During the search they found banded money with a code for the Great Western Bank still on it. That's where Morris came in.

"So I went up to interview him at the county jail," he said. "I didn't know then — none of us did — that this was one of the Nasty Boys. I thought he'd done just the one bank. But then I was going through his property and I saw that he'd once bought a Jeep Cherokee by trading in a white Maxima. So I began to put two and two together. He wouldn't tell us a thing, so I got his picture and started doing photospreads. The next day there was another hit and they took $100,000 or so from a bank over here in Rancho Park — four guys firing shots. The same M.O."

"Now these guys obviously had no idea what had happened to Clarence. I had his beeper and I kept it on. They were trying to call it all the time. Then they just disappeared for a few weeks. At the end of February I got a call from the FBI in Kansas City who said the local police had arrested two guys with banded money on a train to Detroit. They'd been trying to flush it down the toilet, but they'd forgotten the bands, which said WELLS FARGO BANK, RANCHO PARK. The cops held on to the money, but they had to let the guys go because they couldn't hold them on anything firm. At least they'd managed to get the name Harold Walden. So I got this photo out and sent it off, and eventually we caught up with them in Detroit. I still had nothing much on them, you understand. But I brought them back here and started doing an investigation. And we found out that Walden had been in Jamaica, where they'd been laundering the money for major drug deals into Miami. So we were able to trace it all back and bring it to court. Sanders and Walden got about 150 years between them on federal sentences, and because there's no parole, that means life, right?"

Unfortunately, the Nasty Boys were more the rule than the exception in L.A. Although violent crime is on the increase across the United States, Los Angeles has often seemed on the verge of chaos in recent years, most recently during the riots of April 1992. Even though the FBI responded aggressively to the disturbances, quickly forming a task force hours after the violence began, and eventually tracking down and arresting three men for a savage attack on a truck driver which was broadcast live across the country, it is continually confronted by the underlying racial tensions that have dogged the city for so many years. Racial tension is L.A.'s Achilles' heel, and the riots can be partly attributed to the obvious economic discrepancies between different sections of the community and to black Americans' legitimate complaints about discrimination. For the Bureau, though, there were no doubts about who was behind most of the violence and who was out to manipulate the protests for their own ends: the black and Hispanic gangs that effectively control large areas of the city. Although their roots go back to the 1930s, these gangs have evolved during the last ten years into significant criminal enterprises, and the Bureau has had to mount a response.

There are an estimated 150,000 gang members in the Los Angeles metropolitan area. While the Hispanic groups are often the most violent, running the narcotics traffic in the San Fernando Valley with a breathtaking ruthlessness, the black gangs have achieved the most notoriety and are a criminal force to be reckoned with. Drive-by shootings, armed robberies, bank takeovers, auto theft, narcotics distribution, extortion, contract murder, prostitution — you name it, they do it.

The problem has become so serious that the FBI, which would otherwise have left these crimes to the police, has formed squads to tackle gangs in much the same way that it has tackled traditional organized crime. Laws passed by the federal government for use against the widespread criminal conspiracies of the Mafia are now being used on the streets of Los Angeles.

In concert with the LAPD and other local police forces, the Bureau deploys its full range of investigative techniques against the gangs: electronic surveillance, wiretapping, informants. Of course, sending in undercover agents, one of its favorite techniques, is something of a problem. Close-knit communities, where everyone knows everyone else, are hard to penetrate, and the agency's stock of suitable black and Hispanic agents cannot meet every case.

And of course, although gangs and violent crime are good head-line-grabbers for the Los Angeles FBI office, it does, like every other office in the country, have many other demands on its time and resources. There are squads for narcotics, organized crime, counter-intelligence, white-collar crime, and much else besides. The office is a busy place.

The man ultimately responsible for all this effort, at least as far as the public and his superiors in Washington are concerned, is Charles J. Parsons, the special agent in charge (SAC). Forty-nine years old, tanned, balding, and well dressed, Parsons is a native of Tennessee, and he brings a certain Southern charm to his job. This is perhaps fitting in a city where the media and the public prefer their officials to have a flashing smile and a firm handshake.

But his colleagues stress the dangers of assuming he is a superficial character in any way. Parsons reached his position by sheer hard work, including many years on the streets working on organized crime in New York and Nevada, a stint at the FBI Academy teaching "gambling technology," two years as SAC in Kansas City, and a period at headquarters running the Bureau's internal inspection unit, a section one of his subordinates darkly described as "the thought police." He is also, by all accounts, a man used to getting what he wants, a lesson he learned perhaps from J. Edgar Hoover, whose autographed picture he put in his office when he first moved in.

Beneath him are assistant special agents in charge (ASACs), squad chiefs, supervisors, task force leaders, supervisory resident agents, and of course hundreds of men and women engaged in tasks like John Morris's case. Most of them are content to be in Los Angeles. Housing costs are high and the commuting is terrible, but the weather in southern California makes up for a lot. Even agents who dislike the laid-back West Coast mentality prefer L.A. to any of the Bureau's gloomier outposts. "Anything is better than New York," they say. But in L.A., as elsewhere, the workload is onerous.

The cases the agents pursue fall under a bewildering range of government statutes. For example, take the white-collar crime section, the largest unit of its kind in the country, with 180 agents headed by two assistant SACs. In ASAC Tom Parker's unit, agents cover public corruption, fraud against the government, bankruptcy fraud, health care fraud, copyright violations, boiler room scams, and much else. In early 1993, SA Mary Jo Marino was investigating allegations of corruption in the L.A. County transportation system, focusing on possible fraud in a Department of Education scheme to help disadvantaged children. SA Bob Kilbane, who was involved in more than one hundred other investigations, had just joined a squad set up to target telemarketing scams. SA David Chainer was running a squad dealing with everything from securities fraud to hazardous waste dumping. SA Dennis Buche had a case involving a local police chief who had been accused of taking bribes to fix cases. It is the same story in every squad in the division — too many cases, too little time, and often too much stress.

Almost all the L.A. agents, like Parsons, have had spells of duty elsewhere. In Hoover's era postings were arbitrary and agents were frequently sent to locations far from home. Nowadays things are easier, and after the first few years agents get the opportunity to pick their postings. But frequent transfers are still a problem.

No one knows this better than Chuck McCormick, a former Vietnam veteran turned agent, one of only two full-time FBI counselors in the country. He runs the Los Angeles FBI's Employee Assistance Program (EAP) out of a small corner room in the field office. He spends his time dealing with agents who have fallen victim to drug and alcohol abuse, relationship problems, and other symptoms of stress.

"Transfers are the number one cause of stress," he said. "We have done more harm to our agents on the inside than the bad guys on the outside have ever done, because this organization has the ability to destroy motivation."

Another common problem is posttraumatic stress disorder, particularly for agents who have been involved in shootings. "Until the mid-eighties, PTSD victims were treated with benign neglect," McCormick explained. "Then the FBI's own psychologists launched a study to discover the long-term effects of shooting incidents on agents. They found out that often more trauma was caused by the subsequent administrative inquiries into the affair than by the event itself." It wasn't for nothing, he added, that the agents in the Office of Professional Responsibility, which carried out such investigations, became known as the goons, because they would put the agent through an inquiry that assumed he was guilty until proved innocent. Now, any Los Angeles agent who is subjected to a traumatic event beyond the range of normal experience is counseled by McCormick for weeks and attends follow-up seminars held twice a year. This helps them get through the inquest period in one piece.

For all the program's good intentions, though, McCormick knows he is fighting against the strong self-image agents are supposed to have, of being normal, well-balanced professionals who can take the stresses and strains of the job without complaint. As he put it, "Coming to see the EAP officer is without doubt one of the scariest things an agent can do. Given the choice, they would all really rather walk into a barricaded building and face an armed man than walk in here and say they have a problem they can't deal with. That is an agent's worst nightmare."

But the EAP is at least one sign that the FBI has changed since the Hoover era, when people with personal problems were seen as candidates for punishment rather than help. Although McCormick concedes that there are plenty of people in the Bureau who still see the program as a "dodge for malingerers," he maintains that attitudes have generally changed. It helps that the program has official support, though it also depends on the approach of the SACs, some of whom began their careers in the late sixties and early seventies and rose through the Bureau by having a Hoover mindset. But fortunately, as McCormick pointed out with a quiet smile, in a few years even they will all be gone.

Back out on the street Morris negotiated his car through the heavy traffic on Sunset Boulevard. Some commuters were trying to beat the rush hour by leaving work early, but already traffic jams had begun to form. Cursing, Morris slid to a halt. To pass the time he called his voice mail to see if there were any messages. Most were relevant only to his ongoing case load: a subpoena had been served here, a meeting had been arranged there. But one stood out. It was from Sue, his witness. Her voice was strained and frightened. She had just left his office and checked her answering service from a pay phone. Roland had left three messages and was urgently trying to contact her. It was clear that he knew she had been talking to the FBI.

"Oh, boy," said Morris softly. "Oh, shit."

He stopped the car and sat frozen for a moment as the implications of Sue's call hit home. In the silence that followed, a fresh outpouring of messages from the LAPD dispatcher seemed strangely surreal: "Vehicle driven by an Hispanic . . . Suspect is believed to be armed with a stolen handgun . . . Witness says he stole it the same time as the black Scottish terrier." Morris paid them no attention. His face was a mask of concentration, and his fingers were tapping nervously on the steering wheel. He knew his next move could be critical. If Sue spoke to Roland, she could blow the whole case and end up dead in the process. If she refused to see him, he would probably guess what was up and the result could be the same.

"They must have been following her or something," he said. "I don't want her going home. I wonder if she's got a car phone. Shit, all I've got to do is get my main witness killed, huh? I should have told her I wanted to videotape her confession. That's what we do to the organized crime guys in case they are not around for the trial, you know what I mean? The problem is it has a kind of chilling effect on some people. Aw, Christ! What can I say. You sleep with the dogs, you get bitten by fleas."

Morris picked up the car phone and tried Sue's number again. She was still not home. "Sue, this is John Morris. Don't talk to Roland. If he's at your house, don't talk to him, okay? Tell him you've got an appointment to go somewhere. Don't let him into your house. Call me or beep me as soon as you get this message. Talk to you later."

"He must have been following her or something," he repeated. "She's just started telling the truth now, and this could really blow it. You can tell by her message that she's scared as hell."

He called Mike Waters, the Wells Fargo security chief, once again. "Mike, I'm up in Hollywood. Roland's been trying to get hold of her. Do they have a police department up in Arcadia? They have a station there? Shit. Okay, can you get hold of her and tell her not to go home? See, I got this message that she's on her way home so I told her to avoid him if he's there. I don't know if it's going to be a problem."

He paused while Waters told him why it was not going to be easy. Morris had a disconcerting habit when he was thinking of puffing up his cheeks. It made him look as if he were having a seizure. A middle-aged woman, out exercising her dog, walked past the car and did a double take. Then, very carefully, she crossed the road. You can never be too sure in Los Angeles. He ignored her.

"Yeah, well, I don't really want to send a black-and-white out to her at this stage. It could end up blowing the whole thing. Why don't you head down there and see if he's around. If it looks like he's staking it out or something, screw it. I want to record their conversation because I don't have any positive proof at this stage. It's his word against hers, you know. If you see her coming, try and head her off. You could legitimately be with her, you see. Tell him it's Wells Fargo business or something, and tell him to take off. Then get her the hell out of it, okay? . . . Right, so where are you going to take her, the Holiday Inn or something? . . . Let me know. I'll be in the car."

At moments like this it was important to play it by the book. Sue might be a great witness, but Morris was not certain he could make the case stand up. He called his supervisor, Ken Jacobsen, for advice.

Jacobsen pressed him about the state of the evidence. Despite Sue's polygraph examination that morning it still wasn't clear whether she had admitted giving Roland the codes for the two banks covered by federal insurance. Jacobsen was worried that if she had not, the FBI might not have jurisdiction over the case, and if it did not have jurisdiction, he was unwilling to commit Bureau resources to protecting her. Might it not be better to hand the case over to the LAPD?

Morris resisted. He told Jacobsen of his plan to fit Sue with a body recorder before her next meeting with Roland. Once he had enough evidence to go before a grand jury, Sue would become a federal witness, entitled to round-the-clock protection.

Finally Jacobsen came to a decision. In the morning, Morris would have to go to the U.S. attorney's office and file a "475" — a request for the use of a recorder. As soon as he had it, Morris could see whether Roland would incriminate himself while speaking to Sue. Until then, Sue was on her own. The bank and the LAPD could help protect her, but there was little else Morris could do for now.

Frustrated, Morris made yet another phone call and told Mike Waters that Sue's safety would have to be the bank's responsibility for the next few hours. Waters should get to her house as fast as he could. If Roland was already there, he should try and intercept Sue and stop Roland from seeing her. If Roland gave him any trouble, then Waters should make a citizen's arrest and call the police for help.

Morris slammed the receiver back in its cradle and swerved past a bag lady pushing a shopping cart packed with cardboard down the center of the road. Abstractedly he pulled out the list of jobs in this case. There were nine of them — several hundred thousand dollars had been stolen so far. Two jobs alone had netted $300,000 between them.

"Jesus, who can you trust," he complained. "There's a snitch in this office — I can feel it. It's gotta be someone next to this security guard. He's the only one I trust; he was hired after all these jobs started. But look at all that money. It's big, it's worth killing people over. Hell, what do I care. This is Wells Fargo's problem. We're hanging out liability here. Most of the cases aren't federal cases, except for these last two, and if she had admitted to giving him the codes for those two, then I'd be okay, but she hasn't yet.

"The problem is, these banks use us as their security to hammer their employees. They say the FBI did an investigation and then they fire everybody, but nobody ever goes to jail. It's like the old theft and interstate shipment cases we used to work — someone steals a truck full of jeans and we go over and interview everybody and take fingerprints and the thefts stop for six months. You might never catch anybody, but it was a deterrent. Plus the agents get good jobs with all these companies, when they retire. It's the same with Wells Fargo, they even offered me a job. The problem is, the higher-ups are only concerned with the bottom line. These thefts are really hitting their bottom line, so now they're screaming.

"These people doing the jobs, they could go and get some little people and pay them a few bucks and get them to hit nine or ten locations in a few hours, and they could get a million dollars a day. The only reason they haven't is because they know we are on to them. Now they're trying to cover it up. Which is good, because even if I don't make it on the case, I got them for obstruction of justice, threatening a witness, and lying to the FBI. They ain't gonna walk away, that's for sure. I've got to take my fun where I can."

The phone beeped. It was Sue once more. Roland had called her again and she was worried. Morris was reassuring. Mike Waters was on his way and everything was going to be okay. "Let me hear the message," he said. "Look, none of this matters, it's just calls, right? Sounds like he's drunk. Hey, what are you crying for? Listen, tomorrow we are going to make some phone calls to Roland. We have to get him to discuss the jobs. Don't erase that message; we might need it."

Twenty minutes later Mike Waters called; he had finally caught up with Sue, and she would be safe for the moment. The bank would pay for her accommodation until she was under federal protection.

Morris sighed with relief and looked at the dashboard clock. He was officially off duty, and he knew he should be heading home to Simi Valley, but maybe he would have a beer first. After all, it had been a stressful day. "What the hell, there's not much I can do until the morning anyway," he said.

The Yamashiro bar and restaurant was set back on the hillside off Sycamore Avenue in Hollywood. Its imitation Japanese architecture would have been out of place anywhere else, but here among the trees it somehow looked natural. Even in the fading light the view was one of the best in the city, stretching away for miles toward the Pacific. A few blocks away the red taillights of homeward-bound commuters flickered and glowed on the freeway heading south. Beneath the veranda the green Buick Regal, complete with its forest of antennas and its deadly arsenal, sat under the nervous but watchful eye of a Filipino attendant. He knew a cop vehicle when he saw one, and he was worried that someone would try to steal it on his watch. Every now and then he flicked his eyes up at Morris, who sat nursing an ice-cold Sapporo on the balcony above. But Morris had forgotten about him and the car. He was back on the subject of the Bureau.

"All this violence and stuff — it seems to be a lot worse these days. We all have a lot more to contend with than we used to, especially in this city, with the riots and everything. People have lost some of their respect for law and order. I don't mean to sound all righteous about it, because I'm not a hang-'em-high kind of guy, but things have definitely changed.

"It's the same with the Bureau. When I joined it, Hoover was still in charge and things were different. There was a lot more respect and camaraderie among street agents. A lot of us were Vietnam vets who'd lived through some heavy stuff and we used to hang around together — go out for a few beers, hang out with each other's families, look out for each other's backs, you know the kind of thing. I felt I knew these guys and I could trust them. Now I'm not so sure. The Bureau is getting to be like any other government organization. These young guys see it just as another job." He sipped his beer for a while, lost in thought, and stared out through the gathering dusk toward downtown L.A.

"I suppose what I'm trying to say is that things have changed and not all for the better. Hoover died in, what, 1972, right? Jeez, that seems such a long time ago now. I met him once, after Quantico. I couldn't get over how small he was. I mean, we all knew he was a shortass, but there was this image of him as a big man. It was a very powerful image, you see, a hangover from the G-man thing. It drove the whole FBI. Everything centered on him and this image he generated. Today there's nothing quite like it. . . . Hey, what the hell, maybe I'm just a tired old agent at the end of his career."

Morris finished up his beer, paid his bill, and lumbered out to collect his car from the nervous attendant. He wanted to get home to spend a little time with his wife. In the morning he would be back on the Wells Fargo job. He was fatalistic about his chances of success. Maybe he would crack it soon, maybe he wouldn't. He knew that cases were often shaped by events beyond his control. Changes or no changes, twenty years in the Bureau had taught him never to take anything for granted.

CHAPTER 2

LEARNING TO LOVE THE FBI

THE FBI ACADEMY at Quantico lies deep in the heart of Virginia on sixty acres of leafy land ceded by the U.S. Marines. To get there you drive forty miles south of Washington on Interstate 95 and turn onto neatly paved roads running through a couple of miles of gently forested countryside. Every half mile or so there are clearings with army trucks and small prefabricated huts. Road signs, covered with the Delphic abbreviations favored by the military the world over, stand at every junction. Finally, just when it seems you've missed it, the FBI Academy comes into view. An impeccably polite armed guard sees you through a checkpoint and makes sure you know the way to reception. Quantico isn't a place to go wandering around unannounced.

At first sight the place is mildly disorienting. The honey-colored buildings have been built in that modern architectural style most often associated with new hospitals, industrial parks, and small Midwestern universities. But the moment you get out of the car, the illusion that you've arrived at a sleepy campus dissolves as the crack of nearby gunfire reaches your ears. Somewhere behind the trees that surround the complex, a group of FBI rookies is being put through its paces. For here at Quantico is where it all starts — where trainee agents take their first faltering steps toward their gold badge.

To get here, they have to meet some of the strictest recruitment criteria for any job in the federal government. In an average year more than ten thousand people apply to become special agents and about four hundred make it through the selection process. Who gets chosen depends, to some degree, on Bureau requirements at the time. Although a hiring freeze has been in effect for a couple of years, in normal times the Bureau may need more accounting graduates, or lawyers, or agents fluent in Italian. Once headquarters decides on the relevant criteria, personnel managers go looking for applicants with the right qualifications. Anyone who wants a job as a special agent has to have either a designated degree, in an area such as law or accounting, or a nondesignated degree and three years' work experience.

Each potential agent is asked to fill out a long form, take intelligence and aptitude tests, and face an interview panel of three serving special agents. The applicant is graded at each stage on his or her potential as Bureau material. After the initial selection has taken place, an extensive background check is carried out. Many a family has been startled to find an FBI agent on their front porch asking pertinent questions about the character, habits, and interests of someone they know. The standard Bureau procedure is to talk to as many people who know the applicant as possible: teachers, former employers, friends, parents of friends, anyone in fact who can give some insight into the character of the man or woman who has applied. If an applicant has a shaky credit history, has run too many red lights, or has exaggerated his educational achievements, he can forget it — the Bureau will find out. It goes without saying that anyone on Christmas card terms with Abu Nidal or Saddam Hussein has more chance of being the subject of an FBI investigation than of conducting one. If, after all this, the Bureau decides there are too many men, or too many white men, among the applicants, the potential agent can still fail to get through, although he might be encouraged to apply again. Finally, a few hundred will be offered a job and will make it to Quantico, in batches of thirty-two at a time. Here the selection process begins in earnest. One of the first things the instructors tell them is that at least 10 percent will fail to get through the course.

Opinions differ on the value of the sixteen-week training program. It is stoutly defended by the Quantico instructors and by the Bureau managers who claim it is one of the most sophisticated training courses in the world. Many agents in the field will tell you that it was lousy at the time but that the lessons they learned there have stayed with them ever since. Others will mutter darkly that its chief value to the Bureau lies in the way it enforces conformity and inculcates the FBI value system.

It can certainly be tough, especially the physical side. Most new agents are not Rambo-like figures, all bulging muscles and no brain. The high premium the Bureau puts on fitness can trip them up if they have come prepared for long days in the classroom or on the firing range. Rookies are expected to spend several hours a week in the gym and jogging through the woods, and if they don't shape up it will be noticed and counted against them. If anyone is foolish enough to complain, he is reminded that being able to run a couple of miles without breaking into a heavy sweat could save his life sometime. But then those people don't tend to stay around too long anyway.

Days start early and stretch into the late evening. Typically rookie agents begin at 7:00 A.M., and over the next twelve hours they could go through the U.S. Marine Corps leadership reaction course, which involves lots of charging across rope bridges and over corrugated iron walls; a period in the classroom learning the details of the 270 or so statutes over which the Bureau has jurisdiction; some practical lessons on how to use sophisticated electronic wiretap equipment; another spell in the gym for unarmed combat; and more classwork on organized crime, the most commonly used narcotics, or computer fraud. If they have had an especially tiring day, they may be given complicated legal problems to solve — on the theory that even an exhausted agent has to be able to think straight.

Of course all this hard-won expertise is useless if it leaves agents unprepared for the real-life crises they encounter in the field, so, every few days, trainees pack their guns, cross Hoover Road, and walk through the trees to the FBI's Practical Applications Training Unit. Here they enter another world, a world where Mafiosi stalk the streets, where prostitutes and drug dealers mingle with crooked cops and corrupt politicians, where banks are robbed, hostages are taken, and terrorists plant bombs with little regard for the innocent bystander. Here they find a town living at the sharp edge of the war against crime, a town where crime pays and armed FBI agents fight a ceaseless battle against the forces of anarchy, a town where nothing is quite what it seems. The town is called Hogan's Alley.

At first sight Hogan's Alley looks as if it should be home to Mr. and Mrs. America. Set back from the sidewalks among the neat brick and wooden buildings are a bank, a drugstore, a used-car lot, a courthouse, a laundromat, and a post office. In the unlikely event that an unsuspecting bus driver managed to slip past security, he could drop off his passengers at the town's Greyhound bus station, check himself into the Dogwood Inn at the reasonable rate of forty-eight dollars a night, pop into the Pastime Bar for a quick beer, and still be faced with the competing attractions of the pool hall and the Biograph cinema. The movie — *Manhattan Melodrama*, with Clark Gable and Myrna Loy — might be a little dated, but then these small, quiet, out-of-the-way places are always a little behind the times. Soon the unsuspecting visitor might ask himself, What's all this shooting about? Where have all those FBI agents come from, and what's going on at that bank over there? What is this place?

This place is one of the world's most sophisticated "reality" training centers. Built in 1986, shortly after two agents were killed and five people wounded in a Miami shootout, the town was designed to give agents as much authentic street training as could be packed into the schedule. Here mistakes can be made on a colossal scale without any blood being shed or any lives being lost. Agents can be put through their paces in a wide variety of "real life" situations and learn enough to get them through any crisis they might face when out in the field. At least, that's the theory.

Days at Hogan's Alley unfold against a background of squealing tires, gunfire, and shouts of *"Freeze — FBI."* At one end of town the Bank of Hogan might be under armed siege, while at the other agents could be conducting covert surveillance on a suspected Libyan terrorist. Somewhere in the middle employees of the post office could be under investigation for a complex wire fraud, and on the sidewalk a prostitute might be deflecting questions about a narcotics-related homicide. The principle is, if it happens in America, it happens in Hogan's Alley.

The "bad guys" are played by both amateur and professional actors and actresses, who are employed by an agency under contract to provide suitable criminals for whatever scenarios the Bureau's carefully choreographed scripts call for. All undergo serious background checks (to prevent the Bureau's investigative techniques from finding their way into the wrong hands), and for between eight and ten dollars a session they are encouraged to be as unhelpful as possible to the rookies who are out to catch them. Experienced agents sometimes play leading parts. Everyone sticks to an agreed script, but beyond that there are few restraints on what the crooks do.

All this play-acting is designed to teach the rookies how to conduct a crime scene investigation, how to react to trouble, and, most important, how to follow Bureau procedures and satisfy all legal requirements. During every course a few trainees make the mistake of assembling their evidence in the wrong way, so that when their cases come up in the Hogan's Alley courthouse, they suffer the indignity of having them thrown out by the presiding judge (retired from the local circuit). They also learn something of the tedium of an agent's life, of the long hours spent on stakeouts for little result, and the best way to question reluctant witnesses.

Here too many of the lessons they have learned on the firing range come into play. Special agents still generally adhere to the principle that armed force is to be used only when lives are at risk. When agents have to fire their guns, they shoot to kill, never merely to wound. As one instructor said, "It isn't like in the movies, when you can just shoot someone in the leg and they'll give themselves up. Real life isn't like that. If someone is pointing a gun at you, then it's you or him. If he takes a shot at you, you can't take the chance that he might miss or shoot wide. As far as you are concerned, he is trying to kill you, and you have to protect yourself or any members of the public that might be around. It would be irresponsible to think that you are a good enough shot to be able to wing the guy. If you try and do that, the chances are that you will miss. Remember that the majority of firefights take place in bad light as well."

Not surprisingly, though, the Bureau is not keen on having its people blast away without any thought of the consequences. Agents are never allowed to forget their firearms training. Throughout their careers they put in regular hours at the range and occasionally come back to Quantico for in-service training. Despite this, some will go through their whole lives without ever hearing a shot fired in anger. For those who do, good decisions are crucial. Every time a gun is fired on an operation, agents have to file a detailed report in triplicate justifying the incident. A wrong move can cost an agent his career.

Nowadays, if rookies get tired of practicing their shooting on the range or at Hogan's Alley, they can always go play with FATS, the Firearms Automated Training System, a new Bureau toy that allows rookies (and experienced agents) to sharpen their shooting skills in simulations of real life. FATS is a little like a video game, only deadlier. The agent stands in front of a screen on which a computer projects kidnappings, hostage situations, multiple shootouts, and the like, all designed to test the agent's ability to react to rapidly changing circumstances. If he or she shoots the wrong person or reacts too slowly, the video freezes and the words POOR JUDGMENT appear.

Dave Martinez, the FATS instructor, explains: "Regular firearms training has its benefits, and it's very difficult to duplicate the actual functioning of the weapon and the recoil of the weapon and the knowledge that every time you pull the trigger there's a live round under the firing pin. But here we can provide a lot of scenarios that can't be duplicated on the range because of safety considerations. Here they are using a weapon that is safe — it's firing a laser beam at a screen — so we're able to do a little bit more than we can just out shooting at targets."

The classroom lectures on deadly force policy, the practical training in Hogan's Alley, and the marksmanship practice on the range are all supposed to come together in the FATS room. Here too the rookie can learn to handle some of the heavier weapons he might have to use in his career, such as the M-16 assault rifle and the Heckler and Koch submachine gun. The FBI loves FATS, not least because it saves large amounts of money. Live ammunition is very expensive.

Both FATS and Hogan's Alley might appear to be places where rookies can get some fun and relief from the intensive classroom and fitness routine, but in fact these constitute some of the most important parts of the course. Instructors watch the rookies' every move and assess the way they cope with the practicalities of the job. If they foul up here, they could be out. Every few weeks they are given tests to monitor their progress, and they have to make the grade in every department. A trainee who is a genius at solving complex legal dilemmas but fails the fitness program may be given another chance, but he or she will have to make it through. Another who shows considerable talent in practical arrest situations but can't get his head around the complexities of the RICO statutes might be quietly told to take his handcuffs to the local police academy. Occasionally a trainee will decide after a few weeks that life as a special agent isn't for him; sometimes the instructors decide it for him.

The instructors believe that for people to get through the course they must be properly motivated. The right attitude is vital. Grumblers and whiners are not tolerated, teamwork is encouraged, bearing is all-important. Here, for instance, rookies are encouraged to wear uniform blue shirts and khaki slacks, whereas out in the field they will always be in ordinary clothes. Apart from the practical and legal aspects, the whole process seems unashamedly designed to inculcate a value system, to reinforce a sense of belonging to a large and powerful organization. Here the rookies are let into the secret society, where the Bureau's esprit de corps is hammered into them. The messages are simple: Don't let your partners down. Don't let the Bureau down. You are the cream of the crop. The taxpayer is spending a lot of dollars getting you trained. The FBI is the finest law enforcement body in the world. You are one of the few. You must never embarrass the Bureau.

The rookies have no shortage of people to look up to and learn from. Almost all the instructors have been active street agents at one time or another in their careers, and dozens of specialists come in from around the country to lecture on aspects of life in the field. If these role models are not enough to sustain the trainees through the sixteen-week course, Quantico has other larger-than-life characters for them to emulate. For instance, down in a bunker in one corner of the Academy is a small unit at the cutting edge of the Bureau's fight against crime, run by a man with a worldwide reputation. Gruesome though the unit's task is, it has become so famous that movies have been based on it, and one of them even featured a rookie.

The Oscar-winning *Silence of the Lambs* must be one of the most commercially successful films about the FBI ever made. Based on a book by Thomas Harris, the story is now famous. A rookie agent called Clarice Starling, played by Jodie Foster, is plucked out of training and sent to interview Hannibal Lecter, a cannibalistic mass murderer incarcerated in a maximum security jail. Hannibal the Cannibal, played with chilling authenticity by Anthony Hopkins, will, it is hoped, help the Bureau track down another serial killer before he strikes again. Starling has to trade her own darkest secrets for Hannibal's advice and in the process comes close to jeopardizing her sanity and safety. Her mentor and father figure throughout this terrifying process is an older agent named Jack Crawford.

Crawford was based on John Douglas, the head of the FBI's Investigative Support Unit. Although the job carries a number of responsibilities, in laymen's terms only one seems to matter — he catches serial killers. Douglas is also something of a Bureau celebrity.

In real life he is much gentler and more humorous than the man played by Scott Glenn in the movie, qualities that perhaps help him cope with astonishing amounts of misery, suffering, and death. Every week, indeed every day, he sees things and hears things that most people would find impossible to deal with: photographs of dismembered and mutilated bodies, video- and audiotapes of screaming, hysterical victims, details of child abuse, rape, and torture. He has been doing this since 1977, and it is remarkable how unaffected he seems. A more well-balanced person would be hard to find anywhere.

His unit's task, in essence, is to provide a service of last resort to the FBI's own investigators and to the nation's twenty-four thousand hard-pressed police agencies. The unit's specialty is building psychological profiles of serial killers, rapists, arsonists, and other violent offenders.

It's a desperately needed service, even taking only homicides into consideration. Twenty years ago there were about fourteen thousand murders a year in the United States. Of those, 92 percent were ultimately solved by police. In 1992 there were twenty-five thousand murders, but the resolution rate had dropped to 62 percent. That left over nine thousand unsolved homicides. Many of them were committed by strangers to the victim, which gave law enforcement officers no ready pool of suspects to follow up. A large proportion, as Douglas knows, were undoubtedly the work of serial killers.

Compiling accurate figures on the true number of serial killers in the United States is obviously very difficult, but Douglas believes a conservative estimate would put one in each of the fifty states. As evidence, he cites the huge nationwide increase in apparently motiveless murders over the last twenty years — incidents in which love, sex, money, or revenge have not obviously played a part. His unit's task is to study some of these crimes, assessing why the killer might have attacked and mutilated the victims in the way he did. From these clues the unit is often able to put together a profile of a likely suspect.

The science of profiling is based on the theory that some kinds of violent crime and serial murder follow a pattern. Most serial killers, for instance, are men; often they kill within their own ethnic group.

Most follow the same procedures each time they murder, such as mutilating the bodies or arranging them in a certain way, in essence leaving behavioral clues behind at the crime scene. They also frequently come from disturbed backgrounds, have been abused as children, or are the product of broken and violent homes.

Douglas and his team know these facts from their own investigative experiences and from talking to serial murderers after they have been caught. Although in real life a rookie like Agent Starling would never be sent on such a job, the basic idea of *Silence of the Lambs* was not too far from the truth. The unit frequently deals with convicted killers; Douglas's telephone often rings with calls from people he has jailed. It can sometimes be a macabre game. One of his current callers, for instance, has not told the authorities about every murder he has committed. Douglas plays him along with a line of friendly conversation in the hope that one day he will admit to more.

"You have to be a chameleon," he said. "You have to get in these guys' shoes, laugh with them and get on their level. We've had agents here who have interviewed a suspect who they know has been killing and sexually abusing children, and they think of their own kids and get angry. You just can't do that. Sometimes you have to show that you are kind of amused by what someone did. You tell him it's interesting. In fact, if you are doing your job right and someone walks by the cell, sometimes they can have a hard time differentiating between the killer and the interviewer, because you're laughing, maybe, at how he killed this girl, at how he took this bitch out of society."

Of course, finding a suspect in the first place is the most difficult task. It isn't made easier by the common assumption that the profiling unit can work miracles. A couple of years ago Douglas did a profile on Joseph Paul Franklin, an assassin and bank robber whose favorite method of murder was to shoot, from a long range, black men out driving with white women. By studying the pattern of Franklin's past activities, Douglas was able to predict that his next crime would be committed in Mobile, Alabama. When the local special agent in charge got a copy of this assessment, he called Douglas and demanded to know which bank the suspect would be hitting.

Other law enforcement agencies have had to learn the value of

profiling the hard way. One of Douglas's favorite stories concerns
the time he was invited to the United Kingdom to help during the
famous Yorkshire Ripper investigation. At the time the local police
believed their best lead was a series of cassette tapes that allegedly
came from the killer, who had murdered several prostitutes in the
north of England. But the leads were going nowhere. In desperation
the police had played the tapes on national television, at press
conferences, even over loudspeakers at soccer games, all to no avail.

Douglas remembers sitting with a colleague in the lounge of a
police building waiting to meet the officer in charge of the investigation. When the man finally arrived, Douglas saw he was not
carrying any investigative reports and that he wore a look of weary
resignation on his face. It was clear he resented having to take time
out from his busy schedule to be nice to the American visitors. The
officer walked over, sat down, and explained that although he was
grateful for their interest, the British police had everything in hand.
Douglas was careful not to bruise the officer's ego any further and
stressed that he was happy to have a quiet drink and then go. But
he did tell the detective one thing: he had heard the tapes of the
Yorkshire Ripper, and, based on what little he had read about the
crime scenes, he was certain that the recorded voice did not belong
to the killer. The detective was skeptical, but predictably, when
Peter Sutcliffe was arrested as the Yorkshire Ripper a couple of years
later, the voice on the tapes was found to be a hoax.

One of Douglas's most famous cases came in 1982 in Atlanta,
Georgia, where at least twenty black boys from poor neighborhoods
had been brutally strangled. Police were at a loss, not knowing
whether the crimes were racially motivated or even if they were the
work of one person. The FBI was called in.

Douglas quickly realized that a white person could not be responsible. Serial murderers driven by racial hatred usually left highly
symbolic clues at the crime scene, but there was no such evidence
in Atlanta. It was also unlikely that a white person would have gone
unnoticed in the all-black neighborhoods from which the victims
came. And when Douglas investigated the backgrounds of the victims, he learned that they were usually bright, inquisitive children,
the kind who would be susceptible to an approach from the right
person. That person, he decided, would be a black homosexual in
his mid-twenties, someone with a friendly manner and clever enough
to gain his victims' trust.

The pattern of the killings showed that each time the police or a medical examiner made a statement to the press, the killer responded with a fresh murder. Taken in sequence, the bodies had been left progressively more open to view, as though the killer was gaining confidence with each crime and was playing a "catch me if you can" game. It was clear too that the killer followed the media's reports of the case with intense interest and was probably very knowledgeable about police procedures.

During one press conference, police told journalists that hairs and fibers had been found on some of the corpses. Based on his analysis of the murders, Douglas predicted that the next body would be found in the river, where the water would wash away any such clues. The police began watching the banks of the Chattahoochee River, and sure enough, Wayne B. Williams, a music promoter and police buff, was apprehended. His hair and fibers from his clothes matched samples from twelve of the victims.

During the subsequent trial, the prosecutor had a hard time portraying the bespectacled, soft-spoken, mild-mannered Williams as a brutal killer. He turned to Douglas for help. The agent advised that he "get into his face and infringe on his body space." He told him to speak in a low voice, and say to Williams, "What was it like, Wayne, what was it like when you put your fingers around that child's throat? Did you like it, Wayne? Did you panic? Did you panic?"

Williams, clearly controlling himself, softly denied this at first. Then he flew into a rage and began pointing his finger and shouting, "I know you've got that FBI profile on me, but you're not going to get me!" He was later sentenced to two consecutive life terms.

The key to the Atlanta case, as to many investigations, is what Douglas's team defines as "victimology" — an analysis of the likely responses of the victim to a killer. Douglas explained: "Say you find out that a rape and murder victim was very passive, that she was an asocial kind of person, and the killer has done all these things to her — tortured her, pressed and squeezed her flesh, pierced her skin. If it was only rape on his mind he could have raped her. She might have gone along with that to save her life. So you look at that, and you try to experience what she would have felt. If she was passive, her response might have been what he was looking for — he wanted to see the tears streaming down her face, he's inflicting this pain and suffering on her so that she's crying, she's sobbing, and he's really getting turned on by it. That's what's really exciting him. He wants to dominate, to control. Sex is secondary. Things like that can give you a picture of the kind of person you are looking for."

Not surprisingly, perhaps, profilers have to be particularly emotionally healthy people in order to do this kind of work. Sometimes empathy with the victims makes the job almost unbearable, and that is one reason why Douglas chooses his staff with great care. In the first few years after the profiling unit was set up, academic qualifications, such as a Ph.D., were the major prerequisite. After a while Douglas realized that the right state of mind was just as important, if not more so. As he pointed out, "No one can ever really shrug it off. None of us can take our families for a walk in the park or the woods without looking around for a body. There you are, walking around, when you get this flashback and think, Gee, this is similar to a case we had one time when we found this body, or, Wouldn't this be an excellent disposal site."

Like many offices in the Bureau, Douglas's unit has an overwhelming workload. Of the thirty-six agents in the unit, only ten work profiling cases. The others work in other investigative analysis programs such as VICAP, the Violent Criminals Apprehension Program, and ABIS, which deals with arson and bombing, or they assist prosecutors who are preparing to cross-examine suspects, prepare interrogation techniques, testify in court as expert witnesses, or advise on hostage situations. Most of his team members are involved in forty or fifty investigations at a time, and Douglas constantly has to turn down work. What's more, the team has to work out of a cramped maze of offices, set sixty feet underground in what used to be a nuclear fallout shelter for the FBI director and his top staff.

"We have people burning out from stress down here," Douglas complained. "There's too much work, too much demand for what we do. We work ridiculous hours, in lousy space. We haven't the resources to take on any more people, and meanwhile the floodgates are open."

In spite of his difficulties, and his outspokenness, which is still unusual in the FBI, Douglas is held in high regard throughout the Bureau. Many of the rookies hold him in awe. Whenever he can snatch enough time to lecture at the Academy, his classes are always particularly well received. Whether he and his somewhat maverick unit would have been tolerated in the more regimented Hoover era is open to question, but that both are flourishing now is a clear sign of the more liberal atmosphere that prevails at Quantico today.

Another sign of that liberalization is the increasing number of women recruits and people from minority groups who pass through the Academy's doors. Throughout the Hoover era the FBI was often accused of sexual and racial prejudice in its hiring policy. Since then the Bureau has been actively recruiting women and nonwhites and has done much to improve their working conditions. However, in spite of these moves, it has continued to be dogged by well-publicized cases of discrimination.

Don Rochon's story is perhaps the most invidious. A black cop with an excellent six-year service record at the Los Angeles Police Department, Rochon was keen to go one step further. So he joined the Bureau, even though the weekend before he was due at Quantico he was warned by an experienced black FBI agent that racism was still a problem. During training he was reassured to find no signs of it, but once he was in the field his problems began.

His first posting was in Omaha, a thousand miles away from the liberal West Coast atmosphere in which he had been brought up and almost as far from the progressive East Coast where he had been trained. The office was run in an old-fashioned way and had attitudes to match. At first it was all petty stuff. He asked the guys on his squad where they worked out and they gave him the name of a gym several miles away; when he went there, he was told by puzzled staff members that all the FBI agents used a gym a few blocks from their office. He was never invited to go for a drink or to meet any other agent's family. All petty stuff, but hurtful just the same. Then it began to get serious.

"It came both subtly and blatantly," said Rochon. "They'd make derogatory remarks about civil rights leaders like Martin Luther King and Jesse Jackson. They'd put a picture of a monkey over the picture of my children that I had on my desk, or there would be invitations to an office party and on my invitation they would write the words 'Don't Come.' There would be photographs in my mail slot of a black man who'd been beaten up — that kind of thing."

When he began to get harassing phone calls at home, Rochon, whose white wife was pregnant, started to complain. At first none of his supervisors would listen, so he had to file an official complaint. He requested and was granted a posting to Chicago. When he reported for work, he was horrified to find that one of the Omaha ringleaders had been sent there as well. The abuse started all over again.

"The very first day I got there," Rochon continued, "someone had put chocolate on my phone receiver so when I put it to my ear I got covered with the stuff. Then there were the phone calls — annoying, harassing, even obscene calls, in fact even some death threats. This went on for months, and I was reporting it to my superiors, but they did absolutely nothing. They refused to record the calls and even told me not to record them."

In 1987 Rochon finally filed a racial harassment suit. At first it was fiercely fought by the Bureau, but after the appointment of a new director, William Sessions, in 1987, the agency capitulated and settled out of court. Now Rochon has left the FBI, on full salary with increments for the rest of his life. But he is still bitter about what happened, as he explains: "The FBI has had problems for years with black Americans — you know, the Martin Luther King business, the spying, the blackmailing. It's all part of the legacy that's been left by J. Edgar Hoover. But you know, just because I was born black and I was standing up for my rights doesn't make me some kind of provocateur."

Some agents who knew Rochon at the time insist that his allegations were unwarranted and that he was a difficult man who couldn't take the ribbing that is sometimes handed out to new employees. But there have been other examples of discrimination. Not long after Rochon's case was settled, five hundred Hispanic agents filed a class action suit alleging that they were routinely assigned the more tedious cases and that they found it impossible to get off the "taco circuit" — the border states and Puerto Rico.

As a result of the press attention such cases received, Director Sessions implemented changes in the Bureau's recruitment and employment policies, and there have been other changes for the better. But many in the FBI still deeply resent the way race has come to dominate hiring procedures.

Women too have complained of discrimination. Take the case of former special agent Kathryn Ann Askin, for example. In 1990 she told a congressional committee that when she was transferred to an office in Michigan, she was told by a supervisor that he "had no use for girls in the FBI," that it would take "more than blonde hair and a pretty smile to impress him," and that he "did not feel females were capable of handling certain types of work." Subsequently, she claimed, she was assigned low-level casework and was eventually fired for allegedly not accepting an immediate transfer to New York. The real reason, she told Congress, was that she had filed a complaint with her local equal opportunity counselor which the Bureau had been unwilling to investigate. The agency had shown, she said, "that it is not capable of stopping or properly reacting to unlawful discrimination within its ranks. The vestiges of the Hoover mentality still present in the FBI cannot be allowed to remain."

It is hard to judge how isolated such cases are. Certainly the FBI says it is making much greater efforts to attract more female recruits. Nowadays as many as 10 percent of new agents are women, although Tom Picard, the Bureau's chief of personnel, says he wishes there were more. He insists that the FBI has liberalized its entry requirements so that women can work part-time when their children are young and that there is nothing to prevent women agents from progressing in their careers in the same way as men. He would be happy, he adds, to see women make up half of all FBI agents but says that the Bureau is still hampered by a traditional public view that sees the job of FBI agent as a man's. Obviously, however, as American society becomes more heterogeneous, racial and sexual prejudice will have to follow Hoover into history. By the year 2000, whites will be just another minority in the United States, and the FBI, like all other branches of the federal government, will be unable to allow any illegal discrimination practices, even if it wants to.

There is also another, more practical reason behind the changes in recruitment policies. Increasingly, the modern FBI relies on covert techniques to meet its responsibilities. Informants are as important as ever, but the Bureau now uses undercover agents and clandestine surveillance methods much more widely than before. For obvious reasons, the stereotypical clean-shaven, white agent in a suit would not be very productive using these techniques. Agents these days have to blend into the communities they work in. That means employing more women, blacks, Asians, Arabs, Hispanics, and American Indians. For instance, the Bureau has even tried to recruit more Japanese Americans and Vietnamese in order to penetrate the new organized crime gangs that have sprung up in these communities in the last few years.

Few agents ever report such discrimination at Quantico, however, and it seems that there at least the rookies are treated equally, regardless of sex or ethnic origin. By the end of the sixteen-week program, the ones who have survived know where their first field assignments will be and are ready to go through the graduation ceremony to become fully fledged agents. The ceremony hasn't changed much over the years. Every few months family and friends proudly gather to watch and applaud as the new special agents go up on-stage to meet the director and receive their diplomas. As they do so, they are reminded that they are joining an elite organization, carrying on a tradition that can be traced back to the 1920s and 1930s — back to simpler times when the young J. Edgar Hoover was carving out a unique place in American history.

According to Bureau folklore, when Hoover took over the agency in 1924 it was corrupt, politicized, and incompetent. The organization that was destined to become the acme of American law enforcement was in those days a tiny affair, staffed by an assortment of sleepy vigilantes, failed cops, and political bullyboys. In the sixteen short years since it had been set up during the Progressive Era, the Bureau of Investigation (as it was then called) had become involved in a number of major imbroglios, such as the controversial Palmer raids on radicals and aliens in 1919, and had been used as a mercenary antilabor force by Chief William Burns, a colorful but crooked former detective who ran the Bureau for his own personal gain.

The Bureau of Investigation as originally conceived was meant to provide the federal government and the Department of Justice with some response to the growing number of interstate violations that were outside the responsibility of local organizations. These included bank fraud, land fraud, antitrust matters, and, most infamously, offenses against the Mann Act, which made it a crime to transport women over state lines for immoral purposes. The agency had not been terribly effective at dealing with any of these crimes, but clearly federal offenses were only going to increase with time and something had to be done to get the Bureau into a state capable of responding. Since many of its problems resulted from slack management, the agency needed a competent administrator as much as a high-profile legal eagle. Hoover, although only twenty-nine, seemed to have all the relevant skills. On May 10, 1924, Attorney General Harlan Fiske Stone appointed him acting director.

Various FBI historians have seen this as an astonishing, even inspired appointment, but at the time director of the Bureau of Investigation was not the most sought-after post in Washington. A Senate inquiry had exposed the deep corruption in the Bureau, and it had a poor reputation, even among state and local police forces, which were often no paragons of virtue themselves. But Hoover threw himself into the task with great enthusiasm, and within a decade he managed to create the basis of the FBI as we know it today.

At first sight, there was nothing remarkable about J. Edgar Hoover. He came from a long line of minor Washington bureaucrats who had served the government in one capacity or another since the nineteenth century. His father, and his father before him, worked for the U.S. Coast and Geodetic Survey; his brother Dickerson was an official of the U.S. Steamboat Inspection Service. His roots were English, German, and Swiss, his outlook strictly white, Southern, and conservative.

He was patriotic, an orthodox Presbyterian, and to a great extent a product of the middle-class beliefs of the day: in self-reliance and self-improvement. Critically, perhaps, he may also have been shaped by growing up in a city where racial segregation was still enshrined in law. In other regards, his childhood, spent in the modest Washington suburbs of clerks and low-ranking officials, was straightforward and traditional. He seems to have been a diligent if not outstanding student who applied himself with equal enthusiasm to his studies and to his church. He was also a keen member of the High School Cadets, becoming a company commander. From there he went to law school and found his way without any problems into a minor job in the Department of Justice.

At Justice he seems to have found his role in life. From very early on he began to hone his interest and expertise in the machinery of bureaucracy. Combined with his appetite for hard work and his natural conservatism, this helped him to make his mark. He worked in the Aliens Registration Department and developed a knowledge of political radicalism that would prove very useful in the future. One of his more notable positions was as one of the coordinators of the Palmer raids, where he developed a reputation as a tenacious redbaiter. Hoover's many biographers have all speculated about the effects of his childhood and early career on his later life, and it does seem true that his preoccupation with Communism, political radicalism, and race, which were such a feature of the Hoover FBI, had their roots in that period.

Whether Harlan Fiske Stone had a premonition that his choice of Hoover as director would not turn out quite as he expected is not known. But when he announced the appointment, he made a portentous statement to the press:

> There is always the possibility that a secret police may become a menace to free governments and free institutions because it carries with it the possibility of abuses of power which are not always quickly apprehended or understood. The enormous expansion of federal legislation, both civil and criminal, in recent years, however has made a Bureau of Investigation a necessary instrument of law enforcement.
>
>   But it is important that its activities be strictly limited to the performance of those functions for which it was created and that its agents themselves be not above the law or beyond its reach. The Bureau of Investigation is not concerned with political or other opinion of individuals. It is concerned only with their conduct and then only with such conduct as is forbidden by the laws of the United States. When a police system passes beyond these limits, it is dangerous to the proper administration of justice and to human liberty.

With this ringing statement of principles echoing in his ears, Hoover set out to examine his inheritance. As bequests go it didn't add up to much. In sheer physical terms the Bureau was ill equipped and underresourced. It had a budget of just over $2 million, 441 agents, 53 small field offices (quickly cut back to 25), and few friends in Congress, the White House, or even the Department of Justice.

In view of these facts Hoover's achievements were remarkable. When he died forty-eight years later, the FBI had a budget of $334 million, 19,000 employees (of whom 8,526 were agents), 59 field offices, a forensic division that was the envy of police forces across the world, an expanding program for keeping computerized crime and fingerprint records for the nation's police forces, jurisdiction over hundreds of federal statutes, and an ongoing $125 million construction program for a new headquarters in downtown D.C. Between the Prohibition era and the Vietnam War the Bureau slowly but surely consolidated its position as the mightiest federal agency in the United States of America. The director himself went from being an unknown and little-regarded bureaucrat to arguably the single most powerful man in the country.

Perhaps Hoover's most extraordinary achievement, though, was the creation of the myth of the G-man, a composite figure based on Hoover himself and personifying many of his traditional middle-class values. The G-man provided the Bureau with a brilliant public relations tool, and if the myth made real agents vulnerable to criticism and the FBI to corruption, it also opened the door to power.

From the very beginning Hoover decided that the FBI and its agents should be the mirror image of himself: neat, disciplined, serious, and conservative. As originally cast, the "perfect special agent" was well educated, with clean-cut good looks, a smart but orthodox taste in clothes, and a quiet, polite manner. Probably married, he might be religious in a modest, nonflamboyant way, and he would spend his off-duty weekends coaching his son's baseball team or building his daughter a doll-sized replica of their modest suburban home. But he wasn't a wimp, and no one who ever thought so made the mistake twice. He kept himself in shape, eschewed alcohol and other strong stimulants, and was a crack shot with his Bureau-issue revolver. At work he was tireless and conscientious, both a leader of men and a team player. His loyalty to the FBI, his director, and his colleagues was matched only by his belief in the Constitution and America. He was fiercely patriotic. He despised Communists, radicals, criminals, and corrupt politicians. Though he would never say it publicly, he probably felt a sneaking contempt for liberals and other bleeding hearts who might take a velvet glove approach to the nation's problems.

Above all he was a meticulous and unswerving investigator. He followed orders to the letter, but he also had the rare insight and cunning with which only the best detective minds are blessed. Incorruptible, unshakable, brave, determined, and clever, he was Sherlock Holmes, Davy Crockett, Babe Ruth, and Charles Lindbergh in one neat package. The G-man was the best, and everyone had better believe it.

Many people did believe it, but of course it was difficult for real special agents to live up to a social norm that only really existed inside the director's own head. Any deviation from the ideal, be it for marital indiscretion, homosexuality, support of a left-wing party, refusal to work overtime, or even baldness or mild obesity could cost an agent his job. Discipline was harsh, the demands great. It was hard to get into the Bureau, and once an agent was in, there was never any question where his loyalties should lie: to Hoover, to the FBI, and to his country, in that order. Meeting the demands made on that loyalty could be dangerous, exhausting, and often tedious. A special agent's life was bound by strict codes of behavior and appearance. Transgression of the rules, wittingly or unwittingly, could bring transfer, suspension, extra duties, and reprimands from superiors.

It seems surprising, given all this, that so many wanted the job. But the Bureau never had a problem attracting applicants, because of the power of the image. Even though the idealized figure of the G-man ultimately came to dog the weary agents — slogging through cases, filling in forms, interviewing suspects, and trying their best, albeit unconsciously, to live up to this comic book champion of Middle America — that never mattered. From the moment the G-man forced his way into the American consciousness, special agents were burdened not only with the reality of Hoover's strict codes of conformity, but also with the expectations of a society that fell in love with the idea of an organization dedicated to defending the American way. Without the G-man myth, the FBI might have been a saner, more reasonable institution, less tied to the ideals and prejudices of one man and more open to other influences and ideas. With it the Bureau was condemned to years of slavish adherence to a fantasy that served only to boost the reputation of the man at the top.

The term itself was first heard on the lips of George "Machine Gun" Kelly in 1933. Cornered by special agents, the gangster pleaded, "Don't shoot G-men, don't shoot." He later explained that he was using street slang for "government men." The press picked up the term, and before long it was in common use.

Hoover loved it. Throughout the late twenties and early thirties the bad guys had been getting all the good publicity. The Depression was eating into the nation's prosperity, and the dissatisfaction that many people felt with the inadequacies of government and big business found a symbol in gangsters, who opposed the established order. A series of successful films such as *Little Caesar* and *Public Enemy* made folk heroes of comparatively small-time crooks like

Al Capone. Every week movie theaters showed newsreels recounting the exploits of John Dillinger, Ma Barker, Pretty Boy Floyd, Baby Face Nelson, and others. The longer they escaped arrest, the greater the attention they received. Before long many of them attained the status of latter-day Robin Hoods, taking from the rich to give to the poor. Most of these celebrity criminals were also vicious killers who kept their ill-gotten gains for themselves, but it didn't seem to matter.

The infamous deeds lost some of their appeal, though, when they began to come closer to home, and the gloss really began to rub off after the kidnapping of the Lindbergh baby in March 1932. That the infant son of a famous American could be snatched from his home in the middle of the night caused national outrage. Coming at the height of a minor kidnapping wave, this case gave the Bureau one of its earliest public relations victories. The bumbling inefficiency of the state and local police, and new legislation that made kidnapping a federal crime, allowed the FBI to muscle in on the investigation — and on the publicity. Although the child's body was eventually discovered in a shallow grave a few miles from the Lindbergh home and an arrest was not made until 1934, the Bureau came out of the experience quite well, gaining some positive newspaper coverage. Above all, the case helped to turn the public relations battle back in favor of the "guys in the white hats."

By early 1934 public attitudes toward the gangsters had changed, creating a growing anticrime movement. The New Dealers in the Roosevelt administration, particularly Attorney General Homer Cummings, were firm believers in the concentration of authority in federal hands. With the nation faced by a crime wave, gathering such power was vital to maintaining law and order. And so, cheered on by Hoover, Cummings whipped up general public alarm about the growing problem of Mob violence. In speech after speech he asserted that "organized crime is a menace to our society." The nation was at the mercy of an "armed underworld"; drastic action was needed. Ironically, the aggrandizement of even ordinary criminals into major public enemies became an important part of Hoover's ability to gain and maintain power, in the 1930s and beyond. Though gangsters were becoming less popular, it was vital that they should continue to be perceived as a serious threat to American society. As the FBI became the nation's leading law enforcement agency, it had to make clear that its "enemies" were the mightiest, the most dangerous to the public at large.

The ploy worked beautifully. In May 1934 the first of nine major crime bills passed unopposed through Congress. For the first time the federal government had a comprehensive criminal code and a "national police agency" to enforce it. Special agents of the Bureau of Investigation were given the right to make arrests, execute warrants, and carry firearms. From now on they were no longer just investigators, they had enforcement muscle as well.

But Hoover had a peculiar genius for recognizing the potential for public glory in any situation, and this made the myth of the G-man really take off. Until 1934 the agency had been a comparatively small organization with only a few hundred agents and limited jurisdiction. But after this point its resources increased dramatically, and in less than three years congressional appropriations more than doubled. At the same time, Hollywood adopted a censorship code and even banned some gangster films. New heroes were needed, and Hoover's G-men fit the bill perfectly.

As head of the nation's top crime-fighting agency, the FBI director became the "public's favorite cop." He milked it for all it was worth. For example, in a scene at the end of a newsreel in the mid-1930s, an avuncular J. Edgar Hoover is shown talking to an admiring group of small boys. The great man smiles his most masculine smile, and the adoring audience hangs on his every word. Finally, one shiny-faced youth, his voice cracking just a little, pipes up, "Gee, Mr. Hoover, your G-men sure are good. I'd like to be one when I grow up." Hoover, his bulldog face glowering benignly, barks back, "Well, if you work hard and play hard and live clean, you'll certainly be one." The youth, his career now assured, mumbles a quick "Thank you," and the scene fades to the accompaniment of rousing music.

From the mid-thirties onward, the special agent grew more and more important in popular culture. Countless Bureau-approved articles appeared in the pages of national magazines. The press, particularly the newspapers of the Hearst empire, glorified Bureau exploits. The FBI tour, including exhibits from some of the agency's most famous cases, became one of Washington's favorite tourist attractions. A host of new movies, such as *G Men*, the 1935 Jimmy Cagney hit, "educated" the public about the heroes of the FBI and the evils of crime. Junior G-men clubs sprang up across the United

States. There were even popular songs: one favorite had the immortal chorus "I wanna be a G-man and go Bang, Bang, Bang, Bang." Hoover himself wrote (or at least had others write for him) numerous articles, speeches, and books extolling the glory of the FBI's crusade against criminals.

As Hoover's tough face and gruff voice became familiar to moviegoers and radio listeners across the United States, the image became increasingly important to him. He allowed nothing to tarnish it. When it emerged during the 1934 appropriation hearings that the nation's "number-one cop" had not ever actually arrested anyone, an embarrassed Hoover issued instructions that if "Public Enemy Number One" Alvin Karpis, a noted bank robber of the time, were apprehended, the agents should notify him so he could participate in the arrest. Headlines such as KARPIS CAPTURED IN NEW ORLEANS BY HOOVER HIMSELF, as the *New York Times* put it, were everything he could have wished for.

It was vital, of course, that the myth of the omnipotent G-man never be personified in anyone except the director. Any public credit that was due should go to him and him alone. He could be vicious in ensuring that no agent ever became more famous than the Bureau itself. Time and again throughout Hoover's tenure, the role of individuals was played down. Any agent who was tempted to walk under the spotlight of publicity was quietly reminded by colleagues of what had happened to Chicago SAC Melvin Purvis, "the man who got John Dillinger."

In the early 1930s Dillinger was America's most famous outlaw, its first "Public Enemy Number One." From an inauspicious beginning as a grocery store thief, he had gone on to become a leader in a band of moderately successful Midwestern bank robbers. Like many of his peers, he had a reputation boosted out of all proportion by the screaming headlines of an overenthusiastic press. If he had any particular talent at all, it was his capacity for getting out of difficult situations, often in circumstances highly embarrassing for the forces of justice.

One night in July 1934, after getting a tip from a brothel madam, Melvin Purvis tracked Dillinger to the Biograph cinema in downtown Chicago and, with a few colleagues, waited for the gangster to emerge. Dillinger was killed in the resulting shootout.

But if Purvis thought he would be thanked by Hoover for this, he was mistaken. The press latched on to him as the hero of the hour and reported his triumph in glowing terms. The director held it against him. When Purvis's actions against other noted gangsters of the time received equally enthusiastic coverage, Hoover hit back, sidelining him by sending him on a series of meaningless errands to out-of-the-way field offices. Eventually Purvis resigned. His attempts to capitalize on his nationwide fame by opening a detective agency fell apart when FBI headquarters put out the word that he was to receive no help from law enforcement. Official Bureau accounts of the Dillinger case were doctored to minimize his role. In 1960, after contracting cancer and by then a broken man, Purvis took his own life. He used a gun that agents had given him when he left the FBI.

Purvis was one of the earliest victims of the rigid disciplinary system that was such a feature of Hoover's Bureau. At the same time that the public was being fed an idea of an elite organization of dedicated professionals all pulling together under the inspired leadership of their director, Hoover was ruthlessly enforcing a conduct code of unredeemed austerity.

Consequently, the Bureau's efficiency became hampered by an obsession with regulations and procedures, which stifled initiative and distorted objectives. The G-man image served to get the public on the Bureau's side, and Hoover was determined to keep things that way. The greater his reputation, the more authority he had over his agents, a happy side effect being that his status and power in Washington rose accordingly.

Purvis's story was not unique. Each successive generation of special agents had plenty of other examples to take heed of. Everyone knew that to cross Hoover was to put one's career on the line. At the top of the list of sins came anything that might be seen as an embarrassment to the Bureau or to the director — a sin whose seriousness didn't diminish with the passing years, as Special Agent Jack Shaw found out to his cost.

In 1970 Shaw, who had seven years of commendable service behind him, was allowed to attend graduate school at the John Jay College of Criminal Justice in New York. He was something of a high flier, a language specialist and intelligence expert who was being groomed for greater things. His intention was to get a master's degree in preparation for a new teaching post at Quantico.

While in New York, Shaw attended classes given by Dr. Abraham

S. Blumberg and was dismayed to hear what he thought were unjustified criticisms of the FBI. He decided to write privately to the
professor to set the record straight. Unfortunately he made the
mistake of being honest. Though mostly complimentary, his letter
contained some mild criticisms that Shaw thought *could* justifiably
be leveled at the Bureau. The agency, he admitted, was hindered by
the cult of personality that operated around the director. Discipline
was often arbitrary and harsh, and personal initiative was dampened
as a consequence. The Bureau's relations with other law enforcement and intelligence bodies were weakened by professional jeal-
ousies and the whole organization was too rooted in tradition. "And
it all revolves around one key figure," Shaw concluded. "The life
and exploits of J. Edgar Hoover."

The document was never intended for public consumption and
would have remained confidential had Shaw not asked a Bureau
stenographer to type it up neatly. Another agent picked a rough copy
out of her wastebasket, and within hours Hoover had a copy on his
desk.

His response was as quick as it was vicious. In a telegram he
accused Shaw of "atrocious judgment" and ordered him to present
himself immediately to the FBI field office at Butte, Montana, the
Bureau equivalent of exile to Siberia. Shaw, whose wife was seriously
ill, refused to go and submitted his resignation. Hoover responded
with another telegram saying, "Your resignation is accepted with
prejudice." This made it impossible, as Shaw soon found, to get
another job in law enforcement. It took a lengthy court action to
get the "with prejudice" designation dropped from his record. Finally, after much negotiation, he received fifteen thousand dollars
in compensation, but he was finished in the FBI. Today he is back
in government service, working for the investigative division of the
Department of Immigration, but he remains extremely bitter about
the way he was treated. He still points to the distorting effect the
director's personality had on the FBI and its employees.

"For agents there were always two career tracks," he explained,
"one for those seeking administrative advancement, the other for
the professional criminal investigator. The latter were the ordinary
street agents, the ones who did the work. The others were 'terrorists' who bordered on the brink of stupidity. They wore nice suits
and penetrated the Bureau hierarchy and curried favor for advance-

ment. Many of them lied for a living anyway, so they survived —
they simply came up with enough crime statistics for their supervisors. Hoover was responsible for this. He was the head of a secret
police organization for forty-eight years. If you did a lot of historical
research, it would be difficult to distinguish the workings of the
KGB and the FBI, politically, organizationally, and philosophically,
over those years."

If the G-man myth had been allowed to follow the gangster era
into history, things might have been different. But it was maintained
in various guises for years. Hoover continued to draw power from
his carefully fostered reputation as a man who stood above the
political establishment, a faithful servant of the American people.
The cleaner-than-clean fantasy was too important to let go, and it
was part of a special agent's duties to keep it that way.

As William Sullivan, who rose to the number-three spot in the
Bureau, later claimed, maintaining the image meant that some agents
spent more time on public relations than on investigations. "Flack-
ing for the Bureau" was a major activity. At headquarters, thousands
of man-hours were spent on answering letters from schoolchildren
and other interested members of the public. Expensively trained
agents slaved over such important questions as "Which tailor does
the director use?" and "What does he eat for breakfast?" Sullivan
recounted a story about an agent who replied to a letter asking for
the director's favorite popover recipe. He made the mistake of not
checking with Helen Gandy, Hoover's secretary, and got the recipe
wrong. A letter of censure went into his file, and that was the end
of his hopes for promotion.

As time went on, the image became so powerful and pervasive
that many agents came to believe in it as profoundly as the most
impressionable small boy. It blinded them to the agency's and the
director's failings and encouraged them to believe in the utter infallibility of the organization. It was bound to distort their perspective.
As the threat of the criminal "public enemies" receded and the
Bureau increasingly turned its attention to Communists and subversives, the black-and-white, them and us, view of the world proved
disastrous to civil liberties and to democracy. As Hoover got older
and more determined to hold on to power, whatever the cost, the
image encouraged others in the Bureau to follow him down a more
sinister path. Behind the bright and shining G-man of popular myth

there eventually stood a cynical and sneering agent of political repression.

Three years after Hoover's death the FBI's carefully nurtured image had unraveled almost completely. In the wake of Watergate, the greatest political and criminal conspiracy in American history, the agency was finally subjected to the scrutiny of the press and the public. Had he been around to see it, J. Edgar Hoover would have been horrified. Even today, more than twenty years after his death, the true story of FBI abuses during his period in office has not fully emerged. The Bureau relinquishes its secrets slowly and then only under great pressure.

Nonetheless, it is now clear that during the Hoover era the agency spied on its fellow citizens, interfered with their legitimate and constitutionally guaranteed rights to freedom of speech and political expression, illegally recorded and monitored private conversations, carried out thousands of black-bag jobs (illegal break-ins), spread misinformation to disrupt due political process, manipulated the Supreme Court, compiled dossiers on the murky secrets of the nation's most prominent citizens, and blackmailed hundreds, if not thousands, of people, including congressmen, senators, and presidents. All these activities are thoroughly documented in the hundreds of thousands of papers that have been released under the Freedom of Information Act since Hoover's death. The scale of the abuses is simply astonishing.

An example, by no means the most egregious, is COINTELPRO (an acronym for counterintelligence program), the code name the FBI gave to operations aimed at political and social protest groups it deemed subversive. There were five main targets — the Communist Party U.S.A., the Socialist Workers Party, black nationalist groups, the New Left movement groups, and the Ku Klux Klan — although COINTELPRO techniques were also used against the American Indian Movement and Puerto Rican nationalists, among others. The ostensible aim of the programs was to disrupt each of these groups to such an extent that they would be effectively neutered as any kind of political force. Drawing on authority granted to it by President Roosevelt in 1940 to gather intelligence on domestic subversives (an act that at the time was kept secret from the legislative and judicial branches of the government), the FBI spent the years between 1956 and 1971 violating the civil and constitutional rights of millions of people.

The first target of the program was the American Communist Party. In March 1956, with the full knowledge that the nation's Communists presented only a tiny fraction of the threat that he had claimed they did, Hoover sought secret White House approval for a campaign to disrupt their activities. This request was almost certainly an after-the-fact formality, as many of the techniques Hoover was seeking authorization for had been in use since the 1940s. He told a select gathering of National Security Council members, including President Eisenhower, the chairman of the Joint Chiefs of Staff, the director of the CIA, and others, that he wanted his agents to be able to use every available means open to them. Among the techniques he had in mind, he said, were engaging in surreptitious break-ins, intercepting mail, doing telephone surveillance, planting hidden microphones, inspecting garbage, falsely labeling targets as government informants, encouraging feuds between members of a group, instigating disruptive tax investigations by the IRS, tipping off employers that they had Communists working for them (which would lead to dismissal), mailing anonymous letters alleging marital infidelity to spouses of target persons, mailing copies of controversial newspaper articles to groups to cause disruption, using informants to raise controversial issues within a group, safecracking, forging Party documents to generate controversy, and so on and so forth. No one in the room raised any objections. From then on the FBI was effectively at war with America's political dissidents.

Of course, from then on Hoover's agents also felt free to use these techniques against anyone else they believed presented a threat to the established order. Successive generations of radicals, civil libertarians, antiwar protestors, and politically active Americans fell victim to these techniques, which took up tens of thousands of agent man-hours and tens of millions of dollars. As Tom Hayden, a student leader targeted in this way during the sixties and for many years a respected senator in the California legislature, put it, "This is a case of the abuse of power in extremis, in one of the most, if not the most, democratic societies in the world. Hoover is the evidence of some profound flaw in American democracy. I can't account for it. I don't know what people were doing. I don't know what our past presidents were thinking."

The COINTELPRO operations officially came to an end following a midnight raid on an FBI office in Media, Pennsylvania, in 1970. The burglars, calling themselves the Citizens Committee to Investigate the FBI, stole several hundred documents associated with the program. Over the next few weeks they leaked them to the press, creating a public furor over the agency's domestic intelligence operations. Hoover, ever sensitive to embarrassing publicity, panicked and ordered that the program be dismantled immediately. But the techniques that the agents had been using were not so easily forgotten or readily relinquished. Facets of the campaign continued for years, and even the post-Watergate reforms failed to quash completely the Bureau's ability to conduct such operations.

There are of course numerous other scandals associated with the Hoover era. The Bureau failed to tackle organized crime in any effective way and may even have indirectly aided and abetted mob figures, through the relationships Hoover formed with them, in their corruption of the American system. The agency took credit for successful investigations that rightfully belonged to others. It manipulated statistics to mislead Congress and the Senate about its effectiveness. This list doesn't include Hoover's own moral hypocrisy — his petty corruption, his public expressions of outrage at the peccadilloes of others (gambling and homosexuality, to name but two) while apparently concealing his own private practice of those same activities — or the double standard that had his agents laboring under a harsh disciplinary code while he was able to conceal his own many shortcomings and vices.

It is hard to understand how Hoover was able to get away with all this for so long. The average man in the street remained in the dark because he had no real access to any reliable information. But it is harder to accept that members of the political establishment and opinion makers in the press remained unaware of what the FBI was up to during the many years Hoover ran it. Many may have sincerely believed in the Hoover myth as enthusiastically as other members of the public, or shared the director's politics and beliefs, but plenty of others didn't. Aside from some notable exceptions — Eleanor Roosevelt, the ACLU, and the columnist Jack Anderson, to name a few of the most prominent — the ranks of FBI critics were woefully short of any real establishment figures over those years. If there is any cogent explanation for this, it can perhaps be found in the power Hoover wielded through his files. The director's habit of collecting information about the private embarrassments of his friends and enemies went a long way toward ensuring his own safety from exposure and criticism.

Throughout the latter years of Hoover's life his secret files were the subject of considerable speculation in Washington circles. It was rumored that the director had detailed information about the sexual, political, and financial indiscretions of some of the country's most powerful and famous people and that he had used this information to blackmail his way to power and influence. According to the anecdotes, if you were in any way a well-known public figure, J. Edgar Hoover had something on you. You didn't have to be a radical or even a critic of the FBI or the director; he was just as capable of compiling information on his friends as on his enemies.

The stories that leaked out mostly came from people who had fallen afoul of Hoover or the FBI. Whether you were a political critic who was openly skeptical of some of the Bureau's more dire warnings about Communists in government, a Hollywood star who lent support to a radical cause, or a journalist who wrote an embarrassing article on a questionable FBI operation, you could very easily incur the director's wrath. If you were such a person, you didn't have to be a genius to figure out who was behind the anonymous letter that found its way to your spouse, or the all-too-accurate allegations of Mob connections your opponent made at election time. For every way in which you could anger the director there were dozens of ways in which he and his agency could get back at you. Hoover was a master at collecting and using information. Whispers, rumors, and gossip were his stock-in-trade. And even if your own particular skeleton was well buried at the back of the closet, it often took little more than a very public visit by the local FBI man to make your life difficult.

One of Hoover's favorite tactics was to warn a prominent person that some dreadful story had been circulating about him. This was accompanied by a reassurance that the FBI would do its best to squash the rumor. The unhappy person was then left in no doubt that the Bureau knew all about the potential scandal. It wasn't even necessary to make any threats; the target's "help and cooperation" were usually assured. At the same time, it often didn't matter that the FBI had nothing on the target at all; the thought that it might have something was enough to keep most people in line.

No one thought for a moment that the secret files might not exist, and of course Hoover did nothing to dispel the rumors about them. Why should he? The not-so-veiled threat of their existence was one of the most potent reasons for his continuing hold on power. Some even believed that he had material explosive enough to blackmail each of the eight presidents he had served under. Some of these leaders were prepared to believe it themselves. Often eager recipients of the juicy information he had passed on about others, some presidents were open to hints that he might have the goods on them too. Every politician has something to hide, and none, least of all a president, is immune to fears that those secrets might one day be exposed. Hoover's files attained the status of legend, and that legend was powerful enough to ensure that the director was always treated with some sensitivity by the occupants of the Oval Office.

Officially, the FBI has always claimed that there were no secret files as such, although it has conceded since Hoover's death (in the face of direct evidence) that it did compile material of a gossipy, even salacious, nature on many Americans. The real dispute comes over how that material was used.

The Bureau has always maintained files, of course. It almost has an obsession with them. Even in these computerized times the agency still lives on a diet of paperwork that records operations, investigations, administrative matters, correspondence, and so on. All this material has to be held somehow, and though now the vast bulk of it eventually finds its way onto computers, in Hoover's era it was still all hard copy that had to be stored somewhere. There were criminal files that recorded FBI investigations of murderers, arsonists, rapists, perpetrators of fraud, con artists, and blackmailers. There were also files on spies and the agents of foreign powers. The Bureau could argue that these files were held legitimately under the terms of its constitutionally granted rights of inquiry. Less legitimate were its political files on the thousands of Americans who had committed no crime other than to take stands that were contrary to the attitudes Hoover imposed on the Bureau.

But Hoover's secret files were something else again. They were the mother lode, the gold seam, the carefully cataloged embarrassments of the nation's most powerful and influential people. The word *file* conjures up an image of a cardboard binder packed with separate pieces of paper, but in Bureau jargon it had a broader meaning. A file could be a single sheet of paper referring to one person, or, as in the case of Hoover's most confidential material, it could be thousands of separate documents stored under one generic heading. It was these files that occupied the thoughts of so many people during the weeks after Hoover's death in May 1972. Uppermost in those thoughts were two questions: where were they, and what was in them? It was the start of a mystery that haunts the Bureau to this day.

Being the archbureaucrat that he was, Hoover always believed passionately in the orderly collection of information, and he devised various systems to ensure that it could easily be retrieved when needed. But almost from the beginning he decided to keep separate from the general files the kind of information that should not fall into the hands of people (file clerks and the like) who had no security clearance. This material — presidential correspondence, memos, letters, photographs, case summaries, microphone and wiretap logs, and records of special investigations — was kept in two confidential files in his secretary's office.

The first was called the Personal File and was designated by the letters *PF*. Many now believe that these documents, held in thirty-five file drawers, contained the most damaging and explosive material. Access to them could be obtained only with the director's personal authorization. The second was called the Official and Confidential File and was designated by the letters *O/C*. Although it also contained much damaging material, it was apparently less sensitive than the PF file. Exactly what happened to both of these files after Hoover's death has been the subject of considerable speculation over the years. There are, however, several straightforward clues.

Six months before he died, Hoover, perhaps with his own mortality in mind, began sorting some of the material in his Personal File. He spent only two weeks on the task before abandoning it, but that was enough time for him to extract some eight dossiers that he thought could be safely transferred to the less sensitive O/C file. Perhaps he gave up in the face of the vast amount of material. In the time he spent on the job, he was able to get up only to the letter *C*.

But those eight dossiers, which have survived, prove that, despite later claims to the contrary, Hoover indeed kept material of a highly confidential nature in the Personal File. None of these documents could even remotely be considered personal correspondence; their titles were: "Agreement between the FBI and Secret Service Concerning Presidential Protection," "Bentley, Elizabeth, testimony," "Black Bag Jobs," "Black, Fred B., Jr," "Black, Fred (#2)," "Bombing at the U.S. Capitol," "Bureau Recording Instruments," and "Butts, E. R."

Yet when Hoover's secretary, Helen Gandy, came to testify at a congressional inquiry in 1975, she insisted that all the material contained in the PF file was of a personal nature and had no relevance to any FBI matters. She said she had gone through all the remaining material in the file after the director's death and that, although Hoover hadn't sifted beyond the letter *C*, all the other documents were innocent personal notes and memorabilia. When investigators pointed out that this was a bit hard to swallow, she still would not be moved from her story.

Helen Gandy had been with Hoover since before he joined the Bureau, and she stayed resolutely loyal to him even after his death, although she resigned from the FBI shortly afterward. She was always much feared by special agents, who rightly realized that she had constant access to Hoover and his secrets. Few dared to cross her, and those who did often had great cause to regret it. Almost immediately after Hoover passed away, she assumed responsibility for sorting his private papers.

Some days after Hoover died, Gandy gave twelve cardboard boxes to Mark Felt, one of Hoover's most trusted senior assistants and a deputy associate director of the FBI. The boxes contained 164 separate folders — all that remained of the Official and Confidential File. This material, though highly sensitive, Hoover had wished the Bureau to keep. The folders varied in size and content, but there were 17,700 pages in all, concerning individuals and events going all the way back to the 1920s.

Although Hoover thought the O/C file was safe enough to keep (as opposed to his Personal File, which wasn't), it still contained a mass of damaging material. Included in these innocuous cardboard folders were surveillance reports on and allegations about the extramarital relationships of Eleanor Roosevelt; a detailed and potentially embarrassing set of papers outlining the close relationship between Senator Joe McCarthy's anti-Communist campaign and the FBI; reports of investigations into the alleged homosexuality of Senator

Henry Cabot Lodge, who later became the U.S. ambassador to the United Nations (though the allegations were known to be completely unfounded, these reports were maintained for more than twenty years); details of the secret information provided by Ronald Reagan on the political activities of his Hollywood associates; a list of FBI informants in the White House over forty-eight years; reams of unpleasant gossip about assorted people in show business; copies of anonymous letters (drafted by the FBI) sent to Martin Luther King, Jr., with tape-recorded evidence of his sexual indiscretions; allegations about the supposed homosexuality of Adlai Stevenson, a one-time Democratic presidential candidate; and page after page of information on the scope, nature, and content of the FBI's illicit wiretap and bugging programs.

Some years later, William Sullivan maintained that the O/C file did not contain "the gold," the "sensitive and explosive files containing political information and derogatory information on key figures in the country." One shudders to think what the gold was. But all the available evidence now shows that this material was in the director's Personal File. Despite what Gandy told her congressional inquisitors, various memoranda in the O/C file indirectly refer to the Personal File as a repository for even more sensitive information. According to academic and author Athan Theoharis, who was among the first to gain access to the O/C file under the Freedom of Information Act, the nature of the eight folders that Hoover transferred from the Personal File to the O/C file indicates that the main criterion for including material in Hoover's most secret records was the value of specific information to his continued tenure as director. When that material had served its purpose, had lost some of its sensitivity, or was no longer relevant, it could be downgraded to the less threatening O/C file.

Helen Gandy gave Mark Felt enough files to fill twelve cardboard boxes, but a mass of other material had to be dealt with. Over the course of the next week, some of it was destroyed in Hoover's office and some of it formed part of a shipment of about thirty-five boxes and filing cabinets that were taken by FBI trucks to the director's house, at 4936 Thirtieth Place. Hoover had bequeathed the house to the Bureau's associate director, Clyde Tolson, who had been with him since the twenties and had risen rapidly through the ranks. Tolson's role was to be Hoover's lifelong friend, chief aide, hatchet

man, and even, if some stories are to be believed, homosexual partner. Like Gandy, he had resigned almost as soon as was decently
possible after Hoover's death. He was also desperately sick. Nonetheless, he was the executor of Hoover's will and had the nominal
responsibility for organizing his affairs.

For the next two and a half months, Gandy worked in the basement of the house, sometimes with Tolson or John Mohr, a Hoover
loyalist who was an assistant to the director. As appraisers moved
about the house above them, taking inventory of the furniture and
mementos, Gandy worked steadily through what was left of Hoover's
Personal File, sifting through box after box of paper.

Gandy could never be shaken from her stand that nothing of an
official nature was taken from headquarters to Hoover's home. She
said that she had personally gone through the material page by page
to make sure. Since she did not find a single memo or document
relating to Bureau matters, she said, she tore up the papers and sent
them off to the Washington field office for shredding. She insisted
that they were all purely private documents and that Hoover had
wanted them destroyed. But if this was so, it seemed strange that
at the time a great many other people in Washington were trying to
get their hands on the files — the occupant of the White House
among them.

President Richard Nixon had been one of Hoover's intimates and
protégés off and on since the forties, when as a young congressman
he had received inside information to help with his high-profile
anti-Communist campaigns. This information enabled him to make
a name for himself as a member of the House Un-American Activities Committee and as the man responsible for assembling a case
against Alger Hiss, the State Department official accused of being a
Communist infiltrator. Nixon had also had unofficial help in his
various election campaigns over the years, and on several occasions
he had had cause to be thankful for the juicy tidbits Hoover passed
to him about his opponents.

But nothing is free in Washington, and Nixon must have realized
that he was under some obligation to return the favor. Like many
others, he probably found that one easy way to pay the debt was to
give the Bureau any scraps of information he was able to gather from
among his political and social contacts. It was standard practice.

Nixon wasn't by any means the only one. When Gerald Ford was serving on the Warren Commission, which investigated the John Kennedy assassination, he allegedly passed inside information to the Bureau, and President Lyndon Johnson once told Nixon that he owed his job to J. Edgar Hoover.

The worry for Nixon must have been that the further he went in his political career, the greater a return on his investment Hoover would want. Believing, as he told his aide John Dean, that Hoover had "files on everyone, godammit," he would find it hard to refuse. However, President Nixon was a different figure from the callow young lawyer who went to Congress in 1946, and he thought he could keep Hoover at arm's length.

For a while he managed it. Bob Haldeman and John Ehrlichman, his palace guard, had strict instructions to keep Hoover off his back. This the director both realized and resented. As a consequence, relations, though publicly excellent, became increasingly strained — particularly when the administration sought help against the political radicals of the Vietnam War protest movement. On one notable occasion the White House tried to push through a covert domestic intelligence program called the Huston Plan which would have had the FBI and other intelligence organizations carrying out wiretapping, surreptitious break-ins, and other "black operations" aimed at destabilizing antiwar groups. Most of the proposed participants were already involved in such activities, but Hoover, who hated the thought of sharing his operational secrets or his power base with anyone, obstructed the plan at every turn, and it failed to get off the ground. If he had been more willing to cooperate, or if Nixon had been powerful enough to insist, then the president might not have had to turn elsewhere. Hoover's intransigence, it seems, led to the formation of the infamous White House "plumbers," the administration's covert, and more pliable, intelligence force.

Ultimately the president and his men lost patience with Hoover, whom they saw as little more than an aging bureaucrat determined to hang on to his job. But even though they were desperate to get rid of him, they knew how well Hoover could dig in his heels when he wanted to. Every time Nixon met him and tried to broach the subject of his retirement, he went off on one of his infamous monologues about the good old days of the gangster era. This was one of the director's favorite tactics, and over the years he had become so skilled at controlling any conversation that he was almost impossible to interrupt, even by presidents. At the third such meeting, over a private breakfast in the White House, Nixon was supposed to follow a predetermined script for getting the subject of Hoover's retirement into the open. The plan failed. After an hour or so, the two emerged, wreathed in smiles and with Hoover still in charge of the FBI.

It seems likely that Nixon did push Hoover to the brink, and that Hoover then dropped a few hints about the information in Nixon's FBI file. Perhaps he mentioned — not that he would ever dream of making such things public, of course — that there were those in Washington who knew that the president had established a friendship with a Chinese girl during two trips to Hong Kong in the 1960s, and that Nixon may subsequently have helped her emigrate to his hometown; perhaps he mentioned other, darker secrets. No one except Richard Nixon knew. Although the president was in the habit of taping his Oval Office conversations, he never allowed the recordings of this meeting to be released. If, following Nixon's death, these tapes are released, they will surely resolve the matter once and for all.

But such a conversation could explain why the White House went to great lengths to try to retrieve Hoover's files. Shortly after the director's death, the new acting director, L. Patrick Gray, was given firm instructions by Attorney General Richard Kleindienst to discover their whereabouts. Gray, a Nixon loyalist whom many thought was lucky to get the job, had been deputy attorney general for a couple of years. Unfortunately for the administration, he had had little experience of dealing with Bureau semantics and procedures, which were (and are) impenetrable to outsiders. His attempts to find out from his new colleagues — chiefly John Mohr — what had happened to the records were met with blank faces and protestations of ignorance about any secret files. The fact that the director's Personal File was being stripped from Helen Gandy's office right under his nose didn't bother Gray. He was satisfied with Gandy's explanation that she was getting rid of Hoover's private letters, memorabilia, and personal financial records because the director had been worried that they might fall into the hands of autograph hunters.

Even worse, Gray somehow failed to take seriously an anonymous letter he received a few days later, which told him that the files had been moved to Hoover's house and that "things are being systematically hidden from you." He asked Mohr for an explanation and accepted Mohr's assurances that there was no truth to the allegation. A week later Gray received another letter, this time signed by a former special agent, who told him that he had been misinformed about what was happening to the files. Again Gray took no action. This startling lack of perception might explain why some months later he found himself embroiled in the Watergate scandal — which cost him his career.

Others were also on the track of the files. The undertakers who went to 4936 Thirtieth Place to remove Hoover's body on the morning of Tuesday, May 2, 1972, came across a team of between ten and fifteen men in suits who were systematically and rapidly searching the house. Although they didn't stop to chat, the undertakers assumed these were government agents (the men have never been identified). In the days after Hoover's death his neighbors saw various people at various times loading boxes into the trunks of cars. One was identified as John Mohr, who later claimed he had been taking away cases of spoiled wine (he never explained why he would have bothered with something so useless). Another bore an uncanny resemblance to James Jesus Angleton, the CIA's counterintelligence chief. There were stories that some of the files had found their way to the Blue Ridge Club near Harpers Ferry, West Virginia, a favorite haunt of some senior Bureau executives, including John Mohr. Senate investigators who later tried to follow up this clue arranged a visit; the day before they arrived the club burned down.

Whether the Personal Files were all finally destroyed or whether some survived will probably never be known. If someone spirited some of them away to protect the Bureau in the difficult years to come, it is hard to see how they could have been that effective. During Hoover's lifetime, the threat of the files was as great as, if not greater than, the sum of their contents. With his death they lost some of their potency. Certainly nothing saved the FBI from the beating it took in the investigations that followed the Watergate debacle.

Try as it might, today's FBI can't escape completely from the darker side of Hoover's legacy. For one thing, although many of its current operational rules and procedures grew out of the reassessment of the Bureau's activities which took place in the 1970s, a question mark still hangs over its attitude toward political investigations. There are enough recent contemporary examples to prove that the Bureau has never really lost its appetite for spying on Americans because of their political beliefs.

Hoover was so much a part of the Bureau's DNA, his influence was so pervasive, that twenty-two years after his death, vestiges of his era remain. Many of the organizational structures he established are still in place, and the FBI bureaucracy still functions essentially as it did in his time. His picture still hangs on many walls in Bureau offices around the country; the agency's headquarters still bears his name.

To outsiders, the Bureau sometimes appears unwilling to pay more than lip service to rectifying the mistakes of the past. Certainly many of its employees do not believe they have anything to learn from history. Today the myth of the Bureau's infallibility, though not as powerful as it once was, still forms the thinking of special agents. During training at Quantico, new agents are repeatedly told that they are joining an elite organization that has a special responsibility for the nation's security, but they are not taught anything significant about how that responsibility was abused. Hoover is barely mentioned, and certainly not in any negative sense. Rookies who wish to find out about his tenure as director have to do so on their own time. Many of today's agents confess that they have gained their knowledge of Hoover through discussions with veteran agents, which is perhaps why so many of them have a rosy opinion of him. Even the official FBI tour, still attracting hundreds of thousands of tourists every year, makes no mention of the abuses of the Hoover era.

Despite all this, one point is worth making with some force. The abuses of Hoover's tenure were so dreadful that they have tended to overshadow the Bureau's many significant and effective investigations of real criminals. For all his many faults, Hoover did leave behind an effective and much admired law enforcement organization. Not all agents, not even a majority of them, spent their time undermining the civil liberties of their fellow Americans. Most of them worked in areas of legitimate concern. When Hoover died, his successors began the process of redirecting the Bureau's energies and attentions toward such investigations. Today the fruits of that process are readily apparent, especially in areas like organized crime, which in the last decade and a half has finally been given the attention it deserves.

CHAPTER 3

RICO AND THE WISEGUYS

SPECIAL AGENT JOHN MARLEY was cold and tired, and he suspected he was beginning to smell of fish. He was not particularly fond of New York at the best of times, and whenever he went there he thanked his lucky stars that he had been transferred to New Jersey. But something about the Fulton Fish Market brought back poignant memories. He sniffed the air, smiled, and said, "God, that really is something, isn't it?"

It was four in the morning, and Marley, accompanied by an anonymous Bureau bodyguard, had returned for another look at the scene of one of the Bureau's minor triumphs — or, more precisely, a triumph for RICO, the Racketeer Influenced and Corrupt Organizations statutes, which are the FBI's chief weapon against organized crime. In this small part of Manhattan, the Cosa Nostra had recently taken a beating, and if the price of that was to walk around in a fishy haze, then Marley was willing to pay.

Around him the Fulton Fish Market was operating at full tilt. A curiosity in these days of mechanization, an anachronism even, it occupies five blocks of the Lower East Side, just south of the Brooklyn Bridge, and a few blocks north of Wall Street and some of the most expensive real estate in the world. Here, in crumbling narrow streets that could have sprung from the pages of Dickens, lies the center of New York's multimillion-dollar seafood industry.

Marley stood on the corner of South Street and gazed at a scene of extraordinary chaos. On one side of the street, under the shadow of the freeway, men were pulling a steady stream of pallets, laden with stacked boxes of frozen fish, from the bowels of dozens of freezer trucks. Forklifts scurried here and there, racing up to a truck, claiming a load, and scuttling away again like small orange beetles swarming on a rotten tree stump. In a row of very rundown stores, dozens of workmen cleaned, filleted, and gutted fish with the speed born of long practice. Mullet, shark, salmon, brill, squid, swordfish — as each fresh case arrived, a cleaned load was hustled out onto the sidewalk and piled high on wooden pallets. In the bright neon light, both fish and men looked pale and past their best.

The market had been building up to this pace for hours. Sunday was the busiest night of the week. Trucks had been arriving since ten that evening with loads from elsewhere on the East Coast or from John F. Kennedy Airport, where they picked up crates from as far away as Chile and Scotland. Fish is a perishable commodity, and speed is all-important. From the moment the crates are opened and the fish go on display, the dealers are racing against time. The retailers and restaurateurs who regularly come here to buy will not touch so much as a scale if the fish is off. This is the largest fish market in the United States, and the competition that night, as every night, was intense.

In a quiet voice that contrasted oddly with the hectic activity around him, Marley began his tale. It sounded a little like an old-fashioned recipe for a simple dish with few ingredients. First you took a labor-intensive industry with a perishable product, then you added a corrupt trade union and threw in a pinch of extortion. Finally, as a finishing touch, you covered it with a thick layer of protection and served it cold, very cold. It was called Genovese fish pie, an old Sicilian favorite.

"According to our investigations, the Genovese crime family has controlled this place since at least the 1930s," said Marley. "Back then, Socks Alanza, a Genovese capo, was the president of Local 359, which is the seafood workers' union, and it's stayed with the family ever since, right up to Carmine and Vinnie Romano in the eighties. The family exerted its control here in a number of ways. One was through the unloading crews, the seven or eight groups of individuals who go and unload the commercial haulers. They have to do it quickly or the fish will go bad. We believed that the heads of the unloading crews were designated by the Genovese, who allowed them to demand payments in return for their services. Anyone who didn't pay did not get unloaded. If the fish had already come out but they hadn't paid, their vehicles were damaged.

"At the other end of the chain were the retailers. At about four in the morning they make their purchases, and they have to move the fish from the wholesalers to their vehicles. Now, when they come to the market, they have to find a place to park. The Genovese had decided who would run the parking concessions, which are basically just places on the street. If the retailers didn't pay those guys a fee, their seafood would not be loaded and their cars would be smashed up. And then there were the thefts. A retailer would get home and discover that the fifty-pound box of seafood he'd just bought was filled with ice."

Marley paused for a moment as a truck trundled slowly past, its horn blaring. By now everyone in the market had figured out who he and his colleague were, and hostile stares were coming their way. It didn't seem to bother Marley much, but the eyes of the other special agent flitted anxiously from face to face.

"The Mob enforced all this through violence," Marley continued. "In the eighties, for instance, two individuals were shot — one killed, the other seriously wounded. The first was killed because he was committing thefts without the sanction of the Genovese family. They warned him to stay out of the market, but he didn't, so they killed him. The other was shot because they believed he was a witness in a pending prosecution. There were others — truckers who had a beef with a wholesaler and weren't complying with the system were beaten, retailers were beaten. Interestingly, none of those people were willing to become witnesses."

All this had been going on for decades, Marley explained, and until the mid-eighties there was little that the FBI or the New York Police Department could do about it. They had been eating Genovese fish pie for years and getting nothing but indigestion. Every now and then they would manage to convict a small-time gangster on some minor charge, but such victories were few and far between, and they did nothing to stop the rackets.

But in 1984 a joint organized crime task force of the FBI and the NYPD began a new investigation, which they dubbed Sea Probe. Its aim was to gather enough evidence for the government to be able to proceed with a civil RICO action that would take the Genovese family out of the market. By that time Carmine and Peter Romano, who had been the Mob representatives at Fulton, were in prison on federal racketeering charges, and another brother, Vincent, had stepped into the breach. It seemed clear that if the FBI continued to investigate individual Mob figures one by one, the process would go on for years. Until then the Bureau had been lopping off branches. Now they were going for the whole tree.

"So we had to go back to basics," said Marley. "First, we had to establish that organized crime did in fact control the market. To do that we started up physical surveillances and contacted possible witnesses and informants — that sort of thing. That gave us enough to get authorization for electronic surveillances in the market itself. One of the places we targeted was right here, Carmine's Bar and Grill. The union worked out of the second floor, and we knew that Vincent Romano was holding meetings here. He'd also meet guys on the corner outside — anyone with a complaint or a payment would come to see him there. So we targeted both places for cameras and bugs."

Marley pointed toward the restaurant. It was beginning to get light, and a few commuters had begun to make their way over the Brooklyn Bridge, high above his right shoulder. The frenetic activity in the market was slowing down a little as retailers made their way around the thousands of boxes of fish. The smell by now was almost overwhelming.

The Bureau was lucky, because Carmine's was overlooked by a couple of twenty-story towers on the edge of the financial district, a couple of blocks away. They provided an almost completely secure vantage point for closed-circuit video cameras pointing down into the market. A lamppost with a sealed junction box stood on the corner outside the restaurant — another perfect place for a bug.

Over three years the Sea Probe agents compiled a mass of pictures and recordings to prove that the Genovese family controlled the fish market by force: hundreds of people were being intimidated into making regular illegal payments to the Cosa Nostra. Over $125 million of trade a year went through Fulton every year, but agents discovered that at least 25 percent of the profits from that trade was ending up in the pockets of the Mob.

The FBI used some of this evidence to support a range of criminal racketeering indictments it had been preparing against the Genovese family. But the agents knew that these charges would not be enough to remove completely the Cosa Nostra's stranglehold on Fulton. They took their tapes, transcripts, and photographs to the U.S. attorney's office for New York's Southern District, run at the time

by Rudolph Giuliani, then a noted prosecutor of Mafiosi. He assigned the case to Ed Ferguson and Randy Mastro, two assistant U.S.
attorneys. The prosecutors decided to use a civil clause of the RICO
statutes, and pressed for court supervision of the activities of the
entire Fulton Fish Market. Twenty-nine people, including Vincent
Romano, were named in the action, as was the Genovese organized
crime family itself. The government also asserted claims against
Local 359 and asked for the dismissal of the executive administrator
and trustees. All were ultimately banned from the market — for life.
The Genovese family had been cleared out.

That was the theory. Although the case was counted as another
major success in the Bureau's fight against organized crime, Marley
admitted that it is impossible to eliminate La Cosa Nostra from any
situation where there is a possibility for corruption and large pay-
offs. "I don't know if we can ever really remove the LCN influence
from the market," he said. "We've made an impact and we've loos-
ened their grip, and some people here feel free to conduct business
legitimately without fear of reprisal. But you'll never remove all
criminal activity from a place like this."

Prophetic words. While Marley was talking, a couple of shadowy
figures gathered a few feet away and smirked openly at what he was
saying; the bartender in the all-night joint across the street had
confessed earlier that he was still paying "heavy protection to the
Mob" to keep his business open. But Marley's key point wasn't just
that the operation itself had been a success, but that RICO had been
used in a new and effective way. The Sea Probe case had set a
precedent that agents could draw on again and again.

"Without RICO we would have been nowhere," Marley concluded.
"In the past we would have prosecuted just an individual and when
he got out of prison he'd go back to doing the same thing, or
someone else would do it. With RICO we've been able, or at least
partly able, to ban a whole criminal enterprise from one place. We've
been able to target the upper echelons for once, instead of the
underlings."

He yawned. By now the sun had risen over the East River. It had
been a long, cold, and grubby night, and the watery sunlight fell on
hundreds of discarded cardboard boxes and piles of rotting fish. An
attractive young office worker picked her way through the garbage,
trying to keep her shiny white running shoes out of the garbage and

melting ice. Half the market turned to watch and someone whistled. She blushed and passed on, head down. Marley and his silent body-guard slouched off in the other direction. No one watched them go.

Gambino, Lucchese, Colombo, Genovese, Bonanno — these names have become synonymous with Cosa Nostra activity in New York, where the five families have dominated organized crime for as long as most people can remember. Until comparatively recently the status quo had been maintained. Law enforcement had its successes and failures, the Cosa Nostra had its. It was almost like a war of attrition, with two sides vying to see who had the most stamina. Occasionally one would seem to gain the upper hand, but eventually the balance would be restored. The RICO statutes changed all that.

In numerical terms, the five families don't seem to add up to much. According to recent FBI estimates, the Gambino family outfit, the largest, has about 210 initiated members, called "made guys" or "wiseguys" and just over a thousand associates. The smallest, the Bonanno family, has approximately 75 wiseguys and 375 associates. All told, there seem to be about 675 fully initiated "made guys" and about 3,500 associates. But of course the families have traditionally had much more power and influence than these figures suggest. Their rackets in extortion, loan sharking, prostitution, gambling, narcotics (it was always a naive myth that the Cosa Nostra operates in some kind of drug-free zone), trade unions, politics, and industry are legion. Nor is their influence limited to New York. Every state in the union, every major city and many smaller ones, has some kind of organized crime activity run by its own distinct family.

The Bureau isn't the only agency on these criminals' heels. Like the police in other cities, the New York Police Department has a large and efficient organized crime section (which predates the FBI's by a good many years), and other government agencies, such as the Drug Enforcement Administration (DEA), the Bureau of Alcohol, Tobacco, and Firearms (ATF), and the U.S. Customs Service, also take a keen interest. But the FBI, as the country's leading law en-forcement agency, sets the pace. In New York, organized crime is its main priority. There are currently nine LCN (La Cosa Nostra) squads, each having between ten and fourteen agents, and each covering one family or a geographical area.

Although the FBI has been operating these squads for some years, its interest in organized crime is still a comparatively modern phenomenon. Theories about the reasons for this abound, from the believable to the downright implausible, but all revolve around J. Edgar Hoover, who rarely showed any enthusiasm for chasing the Mob and was fond of saying publicly that no such organization existed. The latest theory, based on shaky evidence, is that Hoover was being blackmailed by the Mob over his homosexuality. It is certainly clear that he had some questionable connections with major Mob figures such as Frank Costello and Meyer Lansky. Whether they had some hold over him or whether he was unwilling to pursue investigations for fear of revealing his relationship with them will probably never be known, but there is no doubt that the Bureau failed in its duty toward the Cosa Nostra while he was in charge.

Neil Welch, a former special agent in charge and once tipped to replace Hoover when he died, certainly believes this to be the case. "It's a mystery to me and I suspect it's a mystery to most agents," he said. "I can't account for it. In hindsight it seems like a terrible dereliction of his responsibilities. I'm not sure that it was all that well recognized in the forties, but by the fifties the Mafia problem was there for all to see. Certainly all the agents saw it because they came up against it in their ordinary investigations, but they weren't allowed to acknowledge its existence. Of course Hoover wasn't alone in this; Congress was equally at fault and his nominal superiors should have brought him to account, but you can't excuse his own failure. It was a very serious omission."

Some agents, past and present, are just as vehement that Hoover's hands were tied by the lack of legislative tools to use against the Mafia. They say that this wasn't remedied until 1957, when the Commission (the national council of the Cosa Nostra) was unmasked by police, who stumbled across a meeting at a farmhouse in Apalachin, New York. Others say the key dates are later and that it took the shocking testimony of wiseguy Joe Valachi before Congress, and the subsequent attempts by Attorney General Robert Kennedy to launch a crackdown on the LCN, to provoke the Bureau's interest in organized crime.

Welch dismisses as totally bogus all the arguments that the Bureau had no legal jurisdiction over Cosa Nostra cases. "They are just excuses and I don't give them any credibility whatsoever," he said. "The first federal anti-racketeering statute was on the books as early as 1934, and there were other criminal statutes which would have given him all the authority that he needed."

Whatever the truth of the matter, it is now clear that it was not until the mid-seventies that the FBI made a concerted effort to deal with organized crime, and not until the end of that decade that it began to achieve the kind of high-level successes that have become commonplace in recent years. Many individual investigations had been undertaken before then, but they had all left the Cosa Nostra structure intact. Mob figures, even top bosses, were willing to endure a few years in jail if the organization they left behind continued to prosper. It would always be there when they came out, or so they thought. But in the last fifteen years or so the FBI has shown that it can and will take on the mobs.

That new determination is in part a result of the tools agents were given to fight with: increasing use of undercover operations, electronic surveillance, informants, wiretaps, and, chief among these, the RICO statutes, described by more than one frustrated investigator as "manna from heaven." The statutes are a collection of interrelated federal laws that allow investigators to prosecute the organizations and conspirators that influence and benefit from crimes, rather than just the individuals who commit those crimes. These laws are now so much a part of the Bureau's arsenal against organized crime that it is easy to forget that they were ignored for quite a while. Although introduced in 1970 (as part of the Organized Crime and Control Act), they languished on the books for almost five years before anyone thought about using them, and then they were applied only to minor labor racketeering cases; for instance, they were once used against a minor Mafiosi caught on a drunk-driving charge. Neither agents nor attorneys seemed to appreciate their true significance.

In 1978, though, Neil Welch, then the SAC in Philadelphia, was transferred to New York, and he took Michael Ryman of his organized crime squad with him. Welch wanted to explore some new ways of making cases, and so he gathered together a small, elite group of staff program managers, each an expert in his field. Ryman was part of the team.

"At that time," said Ryman, "the Bureau had gotten into a situation where agents were producing cases, not justice. We called it 'goal distortion.' The number of cases being investigated had nothing to do with the crimes being committed — they had more to do with what was expected from agents. Every office kept its caseload artificially high in order to persuade headquarters and in turn Capitol Hill that it was doing a great job but needed more men and more money."

The group formed an unofficial think tank to see if it could tackle these problems in New York. One day in August 1979, when kicking around some ideas, its members decided to attend some lectures given by Professor Robert Blakey at Cornell University Law School. Blakey had devised the RICO statutes, and, frustrated that no one was using them, he embarked on a series of organized crime seminars for law enforcement professionals. The agents, Joe Kossler, Jules Bonavalonta, Michael Ryman, Jim Kallstrom, Marty Crow, and Dennis Kavanagh, thought the two-week series of lectures might give them some fresh ideas on how to approach the Cosa Nostra problem.

"We had a plan and we had some objectives, but we lacked a strategy," says Ryman. "We knew that we didn't want to do it in the old way, by working on individual cases. If we'd done it that way, we'd have been looking at a Hundred Years' War. We were locking people up, but it wasn't getting us anywhere. We wanted to strike a blow with all the legal tools available. So we attended a seminar on labor racketeering, which is a kind of offshoot of traditional organized crime, and it started to become clear that Blakey's theories might hold the answers, might give us the tactical and strategic means to strike a crippling or killing blow against organized crime."

The theory was simple enough. Blakey proposed that agents could use "probable cause" to justify making a related series of investigations, thereby amassing enough material evidence to go right to the core of organized crime. In practice, this meant not arresting the first criminals they came across but waiting until they could get interlinking groups of Mafiosi in a criminal conspiracy. They could then bring down the whole structure in a preemptive strike.

This idea came to the members of Welch's group as more than just a revelation: it was a Damascene conversion. They went back to the New York field office full of wild enthusiasm about how the RICO statutes were going to change everything. But they soon realized that they would encounter plenty of resistance, not least because the new approach would turn the culture of the FBI on its head. As Ryman explained, "Traditional investigative behavior — the Hoover legacy, if you will — involved the individual agent working on a lot of individual cases. We had come to understand that to be effective against organized crime, using the RICO statutes, we would have to develop a teamwork approach. That meant changing the approach so we were sharing information. Many people, primarily supervisors and senior managers, resisted this change simply because it attacked the establishment. When we bounced the idea off one of them, he advised me that this would get us into trouble with the politicians, the business establishment, the Justice Department, and with our own FBI headquarters."

For a while Ryman and his colleagues felt they were banging their heads against a brick wall. Finally they decided to get Blakey into the New York field office to convince the doubters. Ryman took a flight out from New Jersey to pick up Blakey, rushed him back to the office in a surveillance convoy, and smuggled him into a room with a few senior supervisors. The professor spoke to them for three or four hours and won them over.

Once the agents had their immediate superiors on their side, they began planning how to conduct their investigations. By placing a wiretap on one Mob group, they could identify another, related group, which in turn would lead them to a third, and so on. At each stage, using visual surveillance and informants as well, they would gather evidence to prepare a conspiracy charge against the leaders of the organization. It would be like doing a jigsaw puzzle: the complete picture wouldn't be clear until the last piece was in place.

The process was risky because the more extenuated the investigations were, the greater the chance that the Cosa Nostra would find out what they were up to. It was also politically sensitive. A few years earlier, during the many anguished congressional investigations in the wake of Watergate, Congress had frowned on intelligence gathering of any kind, and intelligence operations had become dirty words, even inside the FBI. But for RICO to work, detailed intelligence was everything. There was also a danger that the Bureau mandarins would shut down operations that appeared to be delivering no immediate results. In the short term, at least, crime resolution statistics might suffer.

With the support of Neil Welch, though, the unit decided that the risks were worth taking. Slowly they began to reap the rewards. "The more we dug, the more of the LCN structure we uncovered," explained Brian Taylor, a supervisor on the squad. "And the more we realized just how complicated and subtle the Mob's influence was in the unions, in commerce, and in legitimate business ventures. We came to understand that the heart of the Mob's activities was the unions. Without a union card you can't work in New York, and so anyone who controls the unions controls much of the city's industry."

First the New York FBI targeted street crews; then, as it began to get convictions, it moved on to the higher echelons. Eventually the whole business took off, and the Cosa Nostra began to take some big hits. One by one the major New York organizations — first the Genovese family, then the Colombo family — were turned inside out. RICO began to prove its worth, and the whole FBI took note. By 1987 the Bureau had carried out more than one hundred major prosecutions across the country. The boss of almost every Mafia family was under indictment, in jail, or dead, and the agency was pursuing the successors.

But the first case to come close to completely dismantling an entire Cosa Nostra family originated not in New York but in New England. One of the most extraordinary organized crime investigations in recent times, it changed the way the Mob is viewed and uncovered secrets so profound that men have been killed for them.

WETHERSFIELD — The body of William P. Grasso of New Haven, the reputed No. 2 man in New England organized crime, was found Friday washed up on the shore of the Connecticut River with a bullet in the back of his head. Grasso's death and the wounding of another reputed organized crime figure who was shot Friday in Massachusetts may signal a potential takeover of the Providence-based Patriarca mob, said state and federal law enforcement sources.

To most of the people who glanced through the *New Haven Register* on Saturday, June 17, 1989, this story was little more than a curiosity. A few might have paused to wonder what organized crime figures were doing in their quiet corner of Connecticut, but they wouldn't have paused long. Violent death, even in New Haven, the home of Yale University, is an unfortunate part of modern American life, and there was little point in worrying about the murder of some hoodlum who probably got what was coming to him.

But to others, the news was not only of interest, it was of critical importance, another piece in the complex jigsaw puzzle of the Cosa Nostra's struggle for control of New England. Throughout the weekend and for days afterward, shadowy figures pored over the article for clues, referred to it in hushed and coded telephone conversations, and mulled it over in dozens of bars and restaurants. What did it mean? What were the implications? Who was going to be affected by it? Some knew, of course, or thought they knew. But they were keeping their opinions to themselves — for the time being.

To agents in the FBI's New Haven organized crime squad, the story was a day old and singularly lacking in useful detail, but they read it through very carefully anyway — particularly Special Agent Don Brutnell. Although no great fan of Grasso, Brutnell had mixed feelings about his untimely departure from this world. He had been on Grasso's trail for years, trying to pin him down, but he hadn't had much luck. Grasso was careful and avoided all the snares the FBI set in his way. He never held meetings in the same place twice, and he was careful to avoid leaving a trail that could be used to build a case against him. He also made sure, by the enthusiastic and savage application of discipline and example, that his subordinates stayed away from the feds.

Billy Grasso, age sixty-two when he died, had been known to law enforcement agents for years. As early as 1968 his tendency to violence had marked him out. He was convicted of using strong-arm tactics to win control of the garbage-hauling business in southern Connecticut and was sentenced to ten years in a federal penitentiary in Atlanta. There he met and became friends with Raymond Patriarca, who was serving a prison term for fraud and racketeering.

An old-fashioned Depression-era godfather, Patriarca had carved out a small but lucrative crime empire in and around New England. Among his peers he was thought to combine ferocity with wisdom, and as a consequence he was treated with a respect disproportionate to the scale of his enterprise. The Commission, the Cosa Nostra's ruling council, frequently asked him to mediate in disputes between other families, especially among the five major organizations in New York. This made him an important man in Mob circles, and his friendship had great value. When he and Grasso were released, Patriarca asked the younger man to work for him. For someone who was still only a small-time hood this was an honor, and Grasso went to great lengths to make sure he lived up to his boss's confidence. By the start of the eighties he had risen to become a capo, with responsibility for the whole New Haven area.

Some of Grasso's success can be attributed to his uncanny ability to frustrate the efforts of those who tried to trap him. Although he was the target of grand jury probes and various federal and state investigations into illegal gambling, he kept a low profile and steered clear of any major trouble with the law. As other Mafiosi were indicted, convicted, and sent to jail, Grasso prospered. But it wasn't just his ability to stay out of the headlines that endeared him to Ray Patriarca. He also had a talent for making money for the family — large amounts of money, from gambling, extortion, racketeering, and loan sharking, and by infiltrating trade unions.

Grasso was an ambitious man. He quickly realized that one's power within the Mob is proportionate to the amount of territory one controls. New Haven was a profitable piece of turf, but it was too small; he wanted more. Before long, by applying muscle, he had extended his operation to Middletown, Hartford, and Springfield. At the same time, he built a fearsome reputation for violence. A Teamsters union official who made the mistake of telling jokes about Grasso over a few drinks in a Hartford bar later received a visit from Grasso's subordinates, who broke his arms and legs with a baseball bat; Grasso sent a cheery get-well note to the hospital. On another occasion, he thought two prostitutes might be informing on him; they were slashed with razors. Once, in a fury, he kicked a pregnant woman in the stomach. And then there were the killings. One night a former boxer named Eric Miller, who didn't quite know whom he was dealing with, got into a barroom fight with Grasso and beat him unconscious; a few days later Miller was found shot to death in a car in Hartford. Grasso's nickname, "the Wild Guy," was becoming well known throughout the New England underworld, and he was feared. Few were willing to stand in his way.

Until the early eighties Connecticut was a kind of frontier zone for organized crime, a place where no one family had control. The Scibelli faction of the Genovese family and the Gambino family both had New England interests, and until Grasso came along they had a kind of gentleman's agreement not to trespass on each other's turf. But the Wild Guy, egged on by Patriarca, managed to force a realignment of the territory to the Patriarca family's advantage, and by the time the boss died in 1984, Grasso had become underboss of the whole family. In line with tradition, Raymond Patriarca, Jr., took up the reins, but Grasso was far more powerful.

As Don Brutnell explained, "Young Raymond was the boss because his dad had nominated him before he died. But Ray was a wimpy kind of guy, a little guy who was a bit afraid of his own shadow, and he just wanted to stay in his big house in Rhode Island and rake in all the cash, so Grasso ran the organized crime thing for him. And young Ray trusted Grasso, like his old man had. Grasso was a loyal, careful, keep-your-mouth-shut kind of guy — both of them knew that, and both of them knew that if someone had to be killed, Grasso would take care of it."

For Brutnell and his partner, Bill Hutton, Grasso's increasing dominance of organized crime in their area was frustrating, particularly as he seemed so well attuned to their techniques. He always drove alone, so that he couldn't possibly be having conversations of a criminal nature and the FBI couldn't cite those conversations as a probable cause with which to apply for a federal bugging warrant on his car. He usually parked his car facing outward, so that passing police patrols couldn't see his license plate and wouldn't stop to see what he was up to. He never held meetings in his home, preferring to see his soldiers and associates at unpredictable hours in different bars, shopping malls, and drugstores. When using the phone, he displayed all the skills of a master spy. He never called from home; if he wanted to talk to someone in Hartford, he would drive there and make a local call from a pay phone, knowing that it was impossible to tap every phone booth in the city and that local calls costing only a dime would leave no record. He would also speak in a prearranged code that was unintelligible to anyone who didn't have the key.

"He was unbelievably good," said Brutnell. "Just to give you an example, he'd be talking to one of his associates — say, someone like Rico Petrillo — and he'd want Rico to get a message to someone else, like Jackie Johns. So he'd say 'nine sleep place Jackie.' And when Jackie got the message, he knew that at ten o'clock — because he knew to add an hour — he should meet Grasso at the Holiday Inn or the Ramada, depending on which one they had agreed on before."

Such caution made it even harder for the FBI to get to Grasso. It had informants, of course; agents always try to develop contacts within a family, people who feel dissatisfied with their share of the loot or who are vulnerable because the Bureau has something on them. Unfortunately, they were never able to get more than the broadest picture, and none of it could be used in court.

Finally, in 1987, the New Haven organized crime squad got a tip that eventually enabled it to get a much better picture of the Patriarca family's activities. The information came not from a Cosa Nostra contact but from casino regulators 150 miles away.

Almost every week a solid, well-dressed man with graying hair and a heavy, lined face would turn up at the casinos along the boardwalk in Atlantic City, New Jersey, with a great deal of money, which he then deposited in casino accounts. In under three months he left over $1 million. To the casino regulators, who were sensitive to such things, it seemed a clear case of money laundering. They did a little digging and eventually made a call to the Connecticut State Police. Had they any record of a man named John Francis Castagna?

They had. "Sonny" Castagna had been on their target list for years and had only recently emerged from a long prison term for manslaughter. How Sonny, who had no visible source of income and was not thought to be the brightest guy in Hartford, had managed to get hold of so much money was of great interest to everyone, including the New Haven FBI agents. They put out feelers to their informants and discovered that Sonny was moving the money for Billy Grasso. Sonny, the informants said, was seen by Grasso as a reliable subordinate who would keep his mouth shut about such an operation.

The Bureau's informants also told them that in between trips to Atlantic City, Sonny ran an illegal high-stakes dice game called barbute out of a dilapidated old store in Hartford known as the South End Social Club. This gave them sufficient probable cause for a warrant. In spring 1988 the agents persuaded a federal judge to give them a sixty-day permit to tap Sonny Castagna's phone. (Contrary to popular belief, electronic surveillance and wiretap warrants are not granted indefinitely but have to be renewed or abandoned every thirty or sixty days. Although most judges cooperate, the Bureau has to go to great lengths to demonstrate that the information to be gleaned is vital to its investigations of a crime or a criminal conspiracy.)

The tap was not immediately successful. The South End crew used an intricate code of confusing jargon and veiled references. It quickly became apparent that Castagna and his colleagues had been warned by their bosses about the dangers of talking on an open phone line. They knew that the FBI might install wiretaps and that agents might be listening. Close physical surveillance was even more difficult, since a lookout usually sat outside the club and took a keen interest in anyone who came too near. This made it very hard for the agents to get any clear idea of what was going on. But Brutnell and Hutton painstakingly pieced the picture together later from the snippets of conversation that they were able to record.

The South End Social Club, they learned, lay at the center of an underworld network that controlled Hartford's "Little Italy," which ran along Franklin Avenue. Grasso's hand was everywhere. Not only was he the secret owner of Franco's, an Italian American restaurant on the corner of Franklin and Brown, he also had ties to the South End Seaport, a fast-food outlet farther down the street. But the Social Club was where most of the action took place. Besides running the barbute games and an illegal sports betting operation, Grasso's crew also oversaw a numbers racket, protection rackets, and a variety of loan shark scams.

The Franklin Avenue hierarchy also fell into place. Sonny Castagna and his associates took their orders directly from two Grasso soldiers, Rico Petrillo and Billy Grant, a man fond of boasting he was Grasso's underboss in Connecticut. Both men were thorns in Sonny's side, pressuring him to pass on gambling, loan, and racket profits every week. It was also clear that each of them suspected the other of stealing. Grasso, at the top of the tree, was the most sensitive of all, and anyone who failed to pass on the correct amount of the loot had to be very sure that Grasso wouldn't find out.

One day in May 1988 Billy Grant disappeared, and the phone lines buzzed with whispered speculation as to whether the Wild Guy had found him cheating on the take. Brutnell and his colleagues went back to the federal court for another wiretap authorization. The new permits allowed them to bug Castagna's apartment and to tap his home telephone. Tapping the phone was easy — it just meant getting the phone company to divert his line — but installing the microphone was another matter. On June 2, with Sonny under surveillance elsewhere, two agents broke into his apartment and placed the bug, triggering a burglar alarm in the process. Although they quickly turned it off, when they began listening into the bug later that day they were dismayed to hear Sonny Castagna say to an associate,

"I'm afraid they came into my house and bugged it. I'm nervous 'cause you know who comes over here. I had company last night." Company, in Mobspeak, meant an important visitor. Sonny was terrified at the idea that Billy Grasso might be picked up by a hidden microphone.

The skill in any microphone surveillance operation is to determine the one place where the target is most likely to hold conversations — the kitchen, the lounge area, the bathroom. But even if the agents get it right, the slightest background noise can blank out what audible conversation there is. And of course the bug has to be well concealed. Either Brutnell and Hutton got lucky or they found the perfect hiding place for the microphone. They won't say in case they want to use the technique again, but they were able to pick up most of Sonny's ongoing conversations, which began after he searched for a bug but failed to find one. For several weeks they monitored yet more talk about crime.

The most frequent topics continued to be the disappearance of Billy Grant, which most people agreed had been a Mob hit, and how his share of the Patriarca operations would be divided up. Grant, it transpired, had run the family's Hartford area rackets, from loan sharking and extortion to gambling. Now that he was gone, Sonny and his associates were under a lot of pressure to collect on the debts from these activities, but as Sonny complained to a friend, "Nobody is paying. The heat is on but nobody is paying. I saw Grasso yesterday, and he says everybody has got to pay."

Brutnell and Hutton were determined to spread the conspiracy net as widely as possible, so the Bureau's surreptitious monitoring went on for the next twelve months. By the spring of 1989 two other voices were being heard regularly on the their wiretaps. One belonged to Louis Failla, a longtime Patriarca hood who had just come out of jail and was now back serving under Grasso. The other voice belonged to Jack Farrell, the family's "mechanic," who ran casino-type gambling events. He had once been freelance, but after one beating too many from customers who had been cheated, he had sat down with Grasso, who offered him security in return for a piece of the action. Farrell was famous in Mob circles for his skills with loaded dice and a stacked deck. He was making a fortune for Grasso and the two got along well. Louis Failla, though, was from the old school, and he was less than enthusiastic about the Wild Guy.

Failla wasn't the only one. As the agents continued to gather information, they began to realize that almost everyone in the Patriarca family was getting very tired of Grasso. He had been in effective control of the family since 1984, and he was getting more powerful every year. His appetite for money and authority was insatiable, and everyone was feeling the pinch. Many were terrified of his mercurial temper, and everyone knew that soon he would want to start expanding his territory again.

Every Cosa Nostra family experiences times when internal discipline breaks down. Grudges are harbored and insults are traded, and unless there is a strong boss to impose order from above, things can get out of hand. Ray Patriarca, Jr., was far from a decisive character, and everyone knew he was under Grasso's thumb. But Grasso wasn't yet the godfather, and his orders to those outside his immediate territory were often deeply resented. Factions of the family in Boston and in Providence, Rhode Island, were particularly wary of Grasso's growing power.

There had been bad blood between the Boston faction and the other New England branches for some time. Grasso's immediate circle believed that the Boston crew had been infiltrated by the FBI and that it was on the point of being brought down on racketeering charges. For their part, the Boston crew members were convinced that Grasso and the Providence faction wanted to move in on their rackets. Three Boston capos — Vincent Ferrara, Joseph Russo, and Bobby Carrozza — were especially eager to see Grasso cut down to size; none of them felt any real loyalty to the young Patriarca, and Vinnie Ferrara even believed that Patriarca and Grasso were plotting his assassination. The three also hated and feared Frank Salemme, Grasso's man in Boston, who had been told to keep an eye on them. Money, territory, and influence were at stake, and no one felt any inclination to give these up to the Wild Guy.

Furthermore, the bug on Sonny's house and phone revealed that the Hartford Mob was planning something ambitious. It seemed that some of these people were setting up a crooked gambling parlor in Manhattan, with help from the New York families and a casino chief from Atlantic City. This was being done behind Grasso's back. For some as yet unknown reason, the Wild Guy was being cut out of the action.

By now the Patriarca family, and in particular its Hartford–New Haven branch, had been under close surveillance for almost eighteen months, but the Bureau still had insufficient evidence to prove a case under RICO. Brutnell and Hutton were now part of a wider team that included FBI agents in Boston and Rhode Island, Connecticut state troopers, and Hartford cops. The case was absorbing resources, and the pressure to get results was growing. But in spite of the vast amount of material that had been passed on to New Haven, the Bureau's office of origin for the case, a clear pattern had not yet emerged. Brutnell, Hutton, and their supervisor, Dave Cotton, knew that the facts invited as many questions as they answered. For instance, why was one Gaetano Milano, an ambitious young Mafioso, a known Grasso soldier, meeting secretly with the Boston faction of the family? More interesting still, why was he being accompanied to those meetings by Frankie Pugliano, a known soldier in the Genovese family? Something was up, but the details were elusive. Then two fishermen stumbled across the mortal remains of William P. Grasso floating face down in the Connecticut River at Wethersfield.

Dave Cotton, the supervisor in charge of the FBI's New Haven organized crime squad, could not contain a small smile of satisfaction about the break his team got that day. As he described it, "We were told about it fairly quickly by the state police because they knew it was important, right? So we got into a car and went looking — it was an impromptu thing. We went up to Hartford and started going around to all the locations we were familiar with — you know, just driving around from place to place, talking it over. For hours. And there, outside this restaurant called Chef Antone's, were these guys — Gaetano Milano, Louis Pugliano, Louis Failla, Sonny Castagna, and some others. So what? Well, we knew right then that they must have something to do with Grasso's death because they were all showing deference to Gaetano — they were kissing him. It was just too big a coincidence."

Grasso's death changed things dramatically. There was now a leadership vacuum, and it was clear someone would try to fill it. The FBI agents' instincts told them that the most likely local candidate was Louis Failla, so they decided to bug his car. Failla, they had already observed, was a great one for giving rides to his colleagues. He was the proud owner of a blue Cadillac sedan, a car on which he seemed to lavish time and energy. Unfortunately he locked it into a secure garage at night, and it rarely left his sight during the day. Hiding a microphone in it wasn't a job that could be done in minutes. The agents had to figure out a way to separate the car from Failla.

After days of following him, they finally hit on an idea. One afternoon Failla was flagged down by a Connecticut state trooper for a "random" auto check. Two hours later, after a frustrating wait at the local police station, Failla was allowed to go on his way, complaining loudly about the heavy-handedness of the police and their attitude toward respectable citizens. Little did he know that from then on, almost every conversation he would have in the car would be monitored by teams of agents on his tail.

Again, the bug must have been well hidden. Mafiosi frequently take their cars apart to make sure they aren't being overheard, and simple bug detectors can be bought at electronics stores throughout the country. It is never enough to take off the dashboard and conceal the bug in among the gauges and dials behind the steering wheel. The usual practice is to disguise it as a piece of standard auto equipment or seal it into a sill or headrest where it can never be found. This time it worked like a dream.

For the next few months, everywhere Failla went, his shadow went with him. Teams of agents and cops from the organized crime task force followed him and his Cadillac to and from meetings with Cosa Nostra figures across New England. Unfortunately for Failla, he liked the sound of his own voice, and when he got back to Hartford or New Haven he frequently discussed these meetings with his associates in the car. On one occasion he told Sonny Castagna of the growing concern felt by some elements of the Providence Mob that the Genovese family might try to muscle into the Patriarca rackets. On another he speculated that he might be appointed the new man in charge of the New Haven area operations. Some days later he warned his son Mark to stay away from cocaine: "In my business I can't have my kid using junk. They become suspicious of me."

Another major topic of conversation was Failla's ongoing and very lucrative interest in the illegal Manhattan casino that he and his associates had set up behind Grasso's back. It had been built, with the help of the Genovese family, in a large room on the floor above Lino's Restaurant on West Thirty-sixth Street, and much of its

continuing success depended on the gang's ability to lure rich marks
to its tables. To help with this they had recruited William Vuotto,
from Caesar's World in Atlantic City, whose promotional job with
the legitimate casino gave him ample opportunity to spot gamblers
with money to burn and invite them to Lino's, ostensibly to discuss
a trip to Caesar's World. The gang had also hired a hooker called
Karen Devine, who helped lure the gamblers from the restaurant to
the illegal gaming room. Then it was up to Jack Farrell, the mechanic with the weighted dice, and Patricia Auletta, a former Las
Vegas blackjack dealer and an expert with a "crooked shoe," to part
them from their cash. Others were brought in as shills to lend the
place an atmosphere of authenticity, but virtually everyone except
the victims was in on the scam.

Failla and the others had made a lot of money from this operation,
but they knew their good fortune couldn't go on forever. They all
thought it would be better to shut the place down while the going
was good and then consider how to reopen it later in another location. They were also getting fed up with paying a large percentage
of the take to the Genovese family for the rights to operate on its
turf. They wanted to go it alone. So they decided to arrange one last
gala night for July 12, 1989, with some high rollers specially brought
in for the occasion. It was to be the biggest sting any of them had
been involved in and would generate enough cash to keep them in
silk ties for years — or so they believed.

A few days before the big night Jack Farrell made sure that William Vuotto was aware of their plans and had lined up the right
victims. Farrell had put a lot of effort into keeping Vuotto happy,
even going so far as to give him a two-thousand-dollar Rolex. Vuotto
couldn't take his eyes off it. "It's gorgeous," agents monitoring the
conversation heard him say. But for Jack it was more than a flashy
timepiece. "See, that's like a Mercedes, am I right? That's a very
status quo item . . . I've got an old one, you know. I've been in crap
games where I tell the guy, I'm laying you two thousand dollars. The
guy looks at me, but they already saw the Rolex. In other words,
they know I can afford this two G's. You follow what I am saying?
In other words it eliminates bragging about yourself." Such things
were important to Jack.

That night the bogus casino looked better than ever. The shills
played their role as innocent gamblers to perfection, and Patricia

Auletta gave a wonderful performance as a straight blackjack dealer. Karen Devine had been persuaded once again to use her charms on potential gamblers. A large banner proclaiming GOOD LUCK SONNY (one of the marks shared a first name with Sonny Castagna) hung at the end of the room. It was like a scene from *The Sting*, where everyone except the poor suckers with the money was in on the act. But this was for real. The Mob had laid their plans carefully.

At the dice tables players were given "misspots" and "bricks," dice that were either shaved to ensure they always turned up a certain way or were printed with a low number of spots on each side. In both cases winning combinations were almost impossible to throw. The trick was to have a mechanic standing by who was good enough to introduce the dice into the craps secretly and remove them before detection. When a skilled mechanic like Jack was working, even someone who was in the know could stand and watch and still never see the phony dice being thrown in.

At the blackjack table things were just as well arranged. Patricia Auletta was using a "hold-out" dealing shoe. Although it looked just like the shoe in the casinos in Las Vegas or Atlantic City, it was designed to let her draw the second card from the top rather than the first. She literally held all the aces.

Having attended to the details, the Patriarca gangsters and their New York associates settled in for a good night. They were all there: Louis Failla, Sonny Castagna, his son Jackie Johns, Louis Pugliano and his brother Frankie, Salvatore "Butch" D'Aquilla, who had picked up many of Billy Grant's rackets, and Nicholas Auletta, a close associate of the Genovese family boss, Fat Tony Salerno, who was there to make sure that the take was shared. As the only "made guys" present, Frankie Pugliano and Louis Failla went to the restaurant downstairs when play was in progress. As Louis had explained to his son while out driving in his bugged car a few days before, "Me and Frankie got to stand downstairs in the restaurant while the party is going on. If they raid the joint, me and Frankie have got nothing to do with it. Everybody gets twenty years just being with us, organized crime. You just got to stay out of the club while they are making the money."

Of course the one thing the gang was not prepared for was a visit from the FBI. Well before July 12, agents from Boston, Springfield, New Haven, and Hartford and their police colleagues in the organized crime task forces had gathered the intelligence material that told them where the casino was, who would be attending, and when it was to close down. But they faced a dilemma. By breaking up the casino, they might net some of the Patriarca family's big fish, but there were plenty of others who were not involved. Furthermore, they might not get enough evidence to convict those they did pull in of anything more than minor illegal gambling charges. The suspected murder of Billy Grant and the murder of Billy Grasso were still unsolved, as were numerous other crimes, and there was a strong argument for maintaining the surveillance to bring still more people into the investigation.

After days of discussion and deliberation in the Bureau, various police departments, and U.S. attorney's offices in Hartford, Boston, and New York, it was decided that they would raid the casino and disrupt the scam against the "innocent" marks. No one would be arrested immediately, however, although all would be told that they would be prosecuted later. The raid would appear to be a hastily planned, ad hoc operation, so the gang would not suspect that the police or FBI had learned of it from wiretaps and bugs.

Thirty minutes after the casino opened for business, the New York Police, the FBI, and the Connecticut State Police burst in. As they were coming in through the door, Louis Failla and Frankie Pugliano were seen making a hasty departure from Lino's Restaurant downstairs. Almost everyone else was caught card in hand: thirty-five people in all, some futilely trying to beat the odds at the crap table and at blackjack, the shills pretending to be winning when they weren't. Only $45,000 had been taken so far — a tiny proportion of the $500,000 the organizers had hoped to divide among them.

After breaking up the party and confiscating all the equipment, the agents and police officers cautioned everyone that they would be facing prosecution at a later date. Then, as suddenly as they arrived, they left, going back to their wiretaps and bugs as the family tried to sort out what had gone wrong.

The next morning, as agents recorded the conversation via the wiretap at the South End Social Club, Farrell and Auletta were back on the phone, discussing the charges they expected to face. Everyone had to get their stories straight — particularly the shills. They might have to be the fall guys.

"The give-up will be the shills," said Farrell. "You hear me? If we can get together and tell them all, if there is any court fees we'll handle them."

"That's what I had in mind," Auletta said.

"I'm 100 percent for it," said Farrell. "Even if I got to come out of my own pocket."

Meanwhile, the shadow of Billy Grasso's assassination still hung over the Mob. The Patriarca family was on the verge of disintegrating into competing factions, and Raymond Junior knew that unless he did something soon the organization he had inherited from his father would fall apart. In late July he arranged a rare familywide meeting at a private address in East Boston to settle all differences. Although he couldn't attend himself — he considered the risks too great — he gave strict instructions to his lieutenants.

He decreed that one of them, Nicholas Bianco, an experienced Providence capo, should be underboss in Grasso's place. The Boston faction was to be represented by Joseph Russo, who was appointed consigliere, the third most powerful position. The family was to cease this infighting and get back to making money. There had been some lack of discipline and some breaches of security, and they would have to stop. Patriarca would decide who would become capo in Connecticut at a later date.

As the FBI agents learned from the bug in his car, Louis Failla thought he was in line for the job. As he described it to Jack Farrell, he had been singled out at the meeting by Nick Bianco, who told everyone what good friends they were. "He gave it to me in front of everybody special," Failla said. "About our relationship, how many years we go back. My fucking chest popped out. 'Louie and I go back many years,' he said, so I kissed him and I said, 'It's an honor to be under your command.'" But Failla was worried that he might have a rival in Gaetano Milano, who many in the family believed had murdered Grasso.

If Failla had had access to the information the FBI was getting from its informants at about the same time, he might have been less worried. Apparently Patriarca was also convinced that Milano was directly responsible for Grasso's death, and he was not about to reward Milano for the execution of his old underboss. He had become very irritated when Russo, the new consigliere, began pushing Milano for the job.

Patriarca's initial decision was to send an envoy, Matthew Guglielmetti, down to Connecticut to take soundings. Over the course of several meetings at the Ramada Inn in Mystic, the envoy heard arguments in favor of one person and another before going back to report to the boss. When the ruling came, it was a blow to Milano's hopes, but to Failla's too. There would be no Connecticut capo. All money made by the Mob there would be sent to Providence, where Patriarca would decide how much would be returned to them. They were also to stay away from the Boston faction of the family. Any disputes were to be taken directly to Nick Bianco.

The Connecticut Mob accepted these decisions, but behind the smiles and the new agreements to behave, the jockeying for position and authority went on. Ray Patriarca wasn't strong enough to enforce his authority, and Nick Bianco was still finding his feet as underboss. In this atmosphere, the slightest rumor could set the Mafiosi against each other. Failla and Milano, who shared both anger and fear at being cut out of the power structure, agreed to cover each other's backs, but only weeks later Failla was incensed to learn that Milano was asking discreet questions about his rackets. And when he heard that Rico Petrillo was concerned that he was going over to the Boston faction and wanted Failla to keep out of his patch, Failla told Farrell, "What do I give a fuck about Rico? He's on the same level I am." The truce was holding, but only just.

The scams also continued. When members of the Connecticut Mob had bled one racket dry, they dreamed up another one. But the constant search for new ways to make money inevitably led them toward Boston, in spite of Patriarca's warnings. On August 27, one of the Boston capos, Vinnie Ferrara, threw a big birthday party for his father. Louis Failla, Jackie Farrell, Sonny Castagna, and Gaetano Milano all attended. On the way back, FBI agents, listening in yet again to the hidden microphone in Failla's Cadillac, heard Failla describe to Farrell how he had persuaded Ferrara to let him run a gambling operation in Boston. Vinnie Ferrara's friend Gaetano Milano was going to get some of the profits. And henceforth, Failla told Farrell, he would be reporting to Boston, not Providence.

To the listening agents the message was clear: the loyalty Patriarca had once commanded from his subordinates was ebbing away. An informant confirmed it. Joseph Russo had become so dissatisfied with Patriarca's leadership that he was demanding that Patriarca resign as boss. If Patriarca ignored the order, the informant told the Bureau, the Boston faction would make a move on the Providence faction with the support of John Gotti, boss of the Gambino family and the most feared Mafiosi in the country.

By the start of October, Patriarca desperately needed to pull something out of his hat. He lacked the strength to impose discipline on the renegade Boston capos by force, so he tried the only trick he had left — bribery. He would open the family up to new members and make them directly accountable to Russo and Ferrara. If, as everyone suspected, the Boston faction would soon be rounded up by the FBI, the new soldiers would help keep their rackets going while they were in jail. This would enhance the status of Russo and Ferrara within the family, and would reassure them that their interests would be looked after while they served out their sentences. If the FBI didn't make its move, Patriarca hoped the Boston faction would be sufficiently satisfied with its new power to leave him in place as boss. He also hoped that the move would quell unrest in the Connecticut faction, which, considering the dominance of Boston, would have to accept that there was no further point in conspiring against his leadership.

The initiation ceremony would take place in a small suburban house at 34 Guild Street, in Medford near Boston. Patriarca and sixteen of his senior lieutenants would attend as the four new recruits were sworn in.

Unbeknown to them, the FBI would also be there — in a way. For weeks agents had heard rumors that an initiation ceremony was about to take place. But they needed to find out when and where. Their informants and the gossip they picked up from the bug in Failla's Cadillac told them that Russo and Ferrara would be among those present, and this was enough for them to get authorization to install microphones anywhere the two might be found. Then by a stroke of luck they learned that a Boston hood named Vincent Federico had applied for furlough from a state prison on Sunday, October 29. On his petition for day-release he listed the nondescript Medford home of his sister and brother-in-law as the place he would be visiting. Armed with the warrants to bug Russo and Ferrara, the FBI took a chance and wired that house. Only hours before the ceremony was to begin, agents took up their surveillance posts. It was a unique moment. For the first time in history, the agency had stumbled across a Cosa Nostra baptism. They were about to listen in on the Mob's most secret ceremony.

The Medford neighborhood was usually quiet on Sunday mornings, but on October 29 the peace was disturbed by a procession of cars that rolled down Guild Street and came to a halt outside number 34. One by one, men in expensive suits and heavy topcoats got out and made their way to the front door of the modest suburban house. An FBI agent, concealed behind curtains at the second-story window of a house down the street, set the motor drive on his camera and took dozens of pictures. In the house directly across from number 34, other agents placed headphones over their ears and pressed the start buttons on the two tape recorders they had placed on a table. With a mounting sense of excitement, they waited to hear if their bug would reveal how a wiseguy was made.

Being "made" is of extraordinary significance to a Mafioso. It is his coming of age, a formal recognition from his boss and his family that he can be trusted as a member of the Cosa Nostra. To become a "made guy" or "wiseguy," he must have Italian ancestry that can be traced back for generations and he must be recommended by another made guy from within the organization. Being made has many advantages: a wiseguy gets respect from his peers, he sees the wider picture of the family's criminal operations, he runs his own crew of associates, and he is allowed to hold on to a larger share of the proceeds of their activities. He is also a figure of great influence, accorded the protection of his own family and of other families throughout the country. A made guy's special status is underlined by the fact that he is one of a few. A Cosa Nostra family may have hundreds of associates working its rackets, but they will be con-trolled by a handful of initiated members; in all of the United States there are only a few thousand made guys.

But being made also has its pitfalls. It makes it harder for a Mafioso to cream off a little of the take before he passes it up to his superiors. The status and responsibility might be enjoyable, but a wiseguy is considered personally liable for any of the failings of his crew. If they make a mistake, fail to pay their share of the proceeds from the rackets, or bring trouble into the family, the made guy is called to account. The whole system is underpinned by the Cosa Nostra's code of silence, enforced by death, known as *omertà*. A made guy swears to abide by this code. If he talks about his family secrets to an outsider, he risks the ultimate punishment.

The FBI and the police had known about all this for many years, through informants and former Mafiosi who testified in criminal trials, but they had never been able to get direct evidence of an induction. Getting the initiation ceremony on tape would allow the Bureau to refute, once and for all, the arguments of defense lawyers who claimed there was no such thing as organized crime.

Raymond Patriarca, Jr., in time-honored fashion, opened the ceremony with a few well-chosen words. He wanted everyone present to be aware of the importance of what was happening.

"We're all here to bring some new members into our family, and, more than that, to start maybe a new beginning. Put all that's got started behind us. 'Cause they come into our family to start a new thing with us. Hopefully, they'll leave here with what we've had years past. And bygones are bygones and a good future for all of us."

Biagio DiGiacomo, Providence capo and master of ceremonies for the day, wanted to get things moving, so after declaring, *"Il onore della famiglia la famiglia e' aperta"* ("In honor of the family, the family is open"), he administered the first oath to the first inductee, Vincent Federico: "I, Vincent, want to enter into this organization, to protect my family and to protect all of my friends. I swear to not divulge this secret and to obey with love and *omertà.*"

As the FBI agents across the street listened intently, Joseph Russo asked Federico which was his trigger finger. Federico held it up and Russo pricked it to draw blood, which he then smeared on a holy card of the family saint.

Then Charles Quintana, a seventy-five-year-old capo from Revere, took the "count" to choose a *cumpare,* or buddy, for Federico. As the FBI later learned, the sixteen wiseguys were sitting in a circle around the inductee. Now each of them raised a random number of fingers above his head. Quintana added them up. He stopped when he reached forty-two and began counting the seated Mafiosi themselves. In line with tradition, the tenth person from the right was chosen. Federico's *cumpare* was to be Gaetano Milano.

Russo then placed the holy card in Federico's outstretched palm and lit it. Again the inductee repeated a litany. "This is the holy image of our family. As it burns, so will burn my soul. I swear to enter alive into this organization and get out dead."

There was a long, dramatic pause. Then Biagio DiGiacomo asked if Federico understood what had been said. He could never say anything about the family to anyone who was not a member. He could never get out of it alive; there was no such thing as resigning.

"Right," said Federico.

Carmen Tortora was the next to be baptized, and Russo asked him, "If I told you your brother was wrong, he was a rat, he's gonna do one of us harm, you'd have to kill him, would you do that for me, Carmen?"

"Yes," said Tortora.

"So you know the severity of this thing of ours?"

"Yes," said Tortora.

"Do you want it badly and desperately? Your mother is dying in bed and you have to leave her because we called you, it's an emergency. You have to leave. Would you do that, Carmen?"

"Yes," Tortora replied.

Russo said, "All right. This is what you want. We're the best people. I'm gonna make you part of this thing . . . Carmen, oh Carmen, we're gonna baptize you again. You were baptized when you were a baby — your parents did it. But now, this time, we're gonna baptize you."

After Tortora had been through the ritual, Biagio DiGiacomo reinforced its message: "We get in alive in this organization, and the only way we are gonna get out is dead. No matter what. It's no hope. No Jesus, no Madonna. Nobody can help us if we ever give up this secret to anybody, this thing that cannot be exposed."

After the other two inductees, Robert DeLuca and Richie Floramo, went through the ritual, the new wiseguys were given lengthy instructions on how to govern their conduct, from the way they should treat women to the way they should greet each other.

"We're very protective of our women," said Russo. "A woman is sacred. It's different if your intentions are honorable. A man has a sister. You like his sister. Your intentions are honorable. You want to get married and have a family and do the right thing. Nothing wrong with that. We encourage that — intermarriage, we encourage that. But it had better be honorable."

The new soldiers were told that two made members must be introduced by a third who knows both; one cannot introduce himself to another. When introducing them, the go-between says, "Amica nostra" ("He's a friend of ours"). They were told to shake hands, not to kiss. "Years ago we used to kiss each other," DiGiacomo said. But Charles Quintana added, "We try to stop kissing in public. We stand out."

Patriarca explained that made guys were prohibited from trafficking in counterfeit money, drugs, and counterfeit bonds. Discipline is vital. He assigned each of the inductees to a capo and said they had to obey the capo without question: "No matter what transpires, he needs to be told if you go anywhere, any place. He needs to know at all times what you're doing, who you're with.

"All business deals," Patriarca added, "legal or illegal, should be brought to the table. If you know that anybody at this table can aid you in a business, legitimate or illegitimate, your obligation is to come to us first."

DiGiacomo gave them a history lesson. "Everybody fights this thing. They call it Cosa Nostra, they call it 'my organization,' and this and that and the Mafia. It is Mafia. There was a Mafia founded in Sicily. They all got together because there was a lot of abuse to the family, to the wife, to the children. Until some people, nice people, they got together and they said, 'Let's make an organization over here. Who makes a mistake he's gotta pay.'"

Patriarca then pointed out that all the families across the country were related and that in an emergency they were bound to help each other, no matter what. "We respect our families for generations to come. Seven generations," he said. "So in another words, if someone's kid out here is a little faulty, but yet his great-grandfather was one of us, as a third generation we must show him respect and help him if we can."

Once the rites, rituals, and instructions came to an end, the Mafiosi drifted away in ones and twos, out to the cars parked down the street. Joseph Russo and Vinnie Ferrara moved around the house, emptying ashtrays and rearranging the furniture.

"I don't think any of the windows were open," said Ferrara.

"Should I shut it?" Russo asked.

"It's better maybe to leave them open, maybe," said Ferrara.

"The smoke. The smoke ain't out, huh?" Russo asked.

"The smoke and the wine," said Ferrara.

"You smell the wine too?"

"Yeah," said Ferrara. "They left, right? That means we gotta lock the door."

"Better lock up," Russo echoed.

Ferrara pulled the door closed. "Only the fuckin' ghost knows what really took place over here today, by God," he said.

In the quiet house across the street, the bank of FBI tape recorders whirred relentlessly on.

"You just wouldn't believe how important all this stuff was to the case," Don Brutnell said. "We had them — no arguments, no messing, all on tape. It was a wonderful thing. And photographs too. All these made guys driving up and driving away, one by one."

There was more to come. Five months later, after lengthy planning sessions involving the Bureau and the U.S. attorneys across New England, the arrests began, coordinated by the FBI's Washington headquarters. Patriarca family members and associates were hauled out of bed in dawn raids and dragged out of restaurants and social clubs throughout the region. Some of the Mafiosi blustered and protested their innocence; some tried to talk their way out of it. When faced with the evidence, some shrugged and stayed silent, confident that their expensive lawyers would get them off the hook. But then cracks began to appear.

One day, a few weeks after the arrests began, Don Brutnell was having a drink with two friends in a Hartford bar when he got a call from the office. Sonny Castagna, who was in custody, wanted to talk.

Castagna was a worried man. Even though at this stage he had no real idea of the strength of the case against the Patriarca Mob, he knew enough to realize that he was going down on racketeering charges for a long time. But Sonny wasn't worried for himself so much; he was more concerned about his son, Jackie Johns. Sonny was no stranger to prison, but he wanted, if possible, to keep Jackie out of jail. The problem was, Jackie was in deep trouble. He was being held on the same racketeering charges as his father, but Sonny knew that as the FBI investigation continued, agents would inevitably uncover much more serious crimes. To keep Jackie out of jail, Sonny realized that he would have to tell the agents about those crimes while the information was still worth having. He knew he had to cut a deal.

"But Sonny was terrified about his attorney," said Brutnell. "You see, they all know each other, these guys, and he thought that if even a hint of his squealing got out, then his attorney might say something in the wrong place and he'd be dead. The problem was, he had to be represented by an attorney. So we had to figure out a way to get him out of the joint and into the U.S. marshal's office without anyone knowing. We managed it somehow."

A few days later, Brutnell and Castagna sat down in a small room in the U.S. marshal's office in Hartford and began to trade. At first Castagna avoided giving the FBI any information, but then he began to proffer a little, just enough to show that he had some. Then, when he had whetted Brutnell's appetite, Sonny insisted that any further testimony would be conditional on a deal that kept him and Jackie out of prison. Brutnell told him that any deal would depend on the quality of the information. After a pause while he considered the implications of what he was doing, Sonny made up his mind. He and Jackie, he told the agent, could reveal who had killed Billy Grasso.

A deal was struck. Sonny Castagna and Jackie Johns would both be treated leniently if they testified against their colleagues. They would probably have to serve short sentences but afterward they would be put into the Federal Witness Protection Program and given new identities. For the moment the deal would be kept secret and no one except their attorneys would be allowed near them. The danger that they might both be murdered to prevent their ever appearing in court was very real. They would have round-the-clock security. "So we got talking," said Brutnell, "and the first thing that Jackie tells us is that both he and his dad had been present at Grasso's murder."

It was a gory tale, but Jackie told it without any sense of regret. He and Sonny had loathed the Wild Guy as much as anyone else and shed few tears over his murder. There was almost a hint of satisfaction that they had managed to take him.

The plan to kill Grasso had evolved out of a series of social encounters Sonny Castagna and Jackie Johns had had with Gaetano Milano and Frankie Pugliano in May 1989. They all agreed that the Wild Guy was becoming a liability and that life would be much more pleasant without him. There were risks in getting rid of him, but, as Milano explained, they were worth taking. He talked to the Boston faction and learned that the hit would fit in well with their plans to take over the family. The three senior capos — Joseph Russo, Vinnie Ferrara, and Bobby Carrozza — backed the idea, and if they pulled this thing off, they would all share in the proceeds. Milano would become a capo in Connecticut, and he promised that Sonny and Jackie would get made. Their problem was that Grasso's antennae were sensitive to treachery. He was always careful never to put himself into a dangerous or compromising situation. So how would they get to him?

The first attempt, to snatch Grasso from the parking lot of the Monte Carlo Restaurant in West Springfield, Massachusetts, had to be abandoned. The plan was for Milano to meet him for a meal and afterward bring him outside, where the others would be hidden in a minivan. But Grasso turned up with an old friend and left early.

The next opportunity came a few days later, on June 13. That night there was to be a Mob meeting in Worcester. Louis Pugliano and Milano were due to pick Grasso up outside the Ramada Inn in Wethersfield and drive him to Worcester. Milano would sit in the back seat, and once they were on the highway, he would blast the Wild Guy from behind. Jackie Johns would hide in the back of the van with a .22 caliber pistol. If by some chance Grasso was accompanied by Rico Petrillo, Johns was to make sure that Petrillo didn't interfere. Sonny Castagna would drive a backup car in case they needed to get away.

At first, everything seemed to be going wrong. Johns, Milano, and Louis Pugliano waited for Grasso behind the Ramada, but Grasso, who had a compulsion about punctuality, expected to be met in front at 1:00 A.M. It wasn't until 1:30 A.M. that he found the others, and he was furious. But in the van Milano handed him a newspaper article about a gambling raid, and Grasso stopped shouting as he bent forward to read it. Johns, peering out from behind a partition, saw what happened next. As they approached an exit on I-91 northbound, he saw Milano put a gun to the back of Grasso's head. There was a single shot.

"All this explained a lot to us, of course," said Bill Hutton. "It tied up all sorts of loose ends and made sense of some of the more convoluted wiretap material that we had. Up until then we knew that Milano had been involved in some way, but now we had direct testimony that he had pulled the trigger. All the hard work was beginning to pay off."

As the weeks went by, Castagna and Johns proved a mine of information. For instance, Johns told astonished agents and government attorneys how, during Grasso's reign, he and some of the crew had delivered corpses from Mob murders to a hole in the floor of a garage at the back of a house in Hamden, Connecticut. There the bodies would be covered with lime and buried. By the time agents found the grave, someone had removed almost all the remains, but small fragments of bone were identified during forensic tests of the soil.

Between them, father and son implicated dozens of Patriarca gangsters on a huge array of charges. Eventually the news that they were helping the government could no longer be kept secret. Castagna was moved to a jail for federal informants, but Johns needed special protection, and for weeks Bill Hutton, Don Brutnell, and others from the New Haven FBI took turns guarding him at secret safe houses. Knowing the Mob was looking for him, they had to move every few days until they could hand him over to the U.S. marshal's service.

In the meantime, Ray Patriarca's attempts to hold the family together under his leadership had failed. Shortly after the Medford initiation ceremony, his lieutenants forced him to abdicate. The new boss was Nick Bianco, Grasso's successor as number two in the organization. Cautious and conservative, Bianco had been comparatively lucky, slipping free from a charge of sanctioning the murder of Anthony Mirabella in 1984 and narrowly avoiding a charge of conspiring to murder Richard Callei in 1985. Like Grasso before him, he had proved almost impossible to bug, and in all the hundreds of FBI tapes the case had generated, Bianco's voice was never heard. At one stage he had worked out of a lawyer's office, which was almost impossible to tap for privacy reasons. But he wouldn't enjoy his position of authority for long. Louis Failla had bragged openly in his bugged car to his associates about how he took money from Mob activities to Rhode Island and gave some of it to Bianco. It was enough for the Bureau to begin building a case against him.

The complex list of indictments stemming from the Patriarca case involved dozens of prosecutors from local, state, and federal courts. Charges ranged from comparatively minor ones such as contempt of court for refusing to testify, to broader and more serious indictments on various RICO counts, murder, and conspiracy to murder. In all, more than a dozen of the Patriarca family's top members and several other associates were charged. The first big set piece trial took place in the U.S. district court in Hartford during the spring and summer of 1991. There, in a four-month drama, the Patriarca crime family, the dominant criminal organization in New England for over half a century, met its nemesis.

Under the watchful eye of Judge Alan H. Nevas, the eleven men and seven women from among whom the final jury would be selected reviewed thousands of hours of evidence, saw hundreds of witnesses, and heard complex and often heated legal arguments from both sides. In the dock, Nick Bianco, Frank Colantoni, Salvatore D'Aquilla, Louis Failla, Gaetano Milano, Frank Pugliano, Louis Pugliano, and Rico Petrillo sat and awaited their fate. Sixteen others, including Raymond Patriarca, Jr., Joseph Russo, Vinnie Ferrara, Carmen Tortora, and Robert Carrozza, would be tried later that year. Others, such as Matthew Guglielmetti and Biagio DiGiacomo, had already pleaded guilty to racketeering charges.

The testimony given by Sonny Castagna and Jackie Johns was devastating, as were the excerpts of the Mafia induction ceremony, played for the first time in public. At one point Gaetano Milano made a dramatic admission that he was a Patriarca made guy and confessed that he had shot Billy Grasso. Against all tradition, he broke his oath and renounced his membership in the Mob. The prosecution had a field day. At the end of it all, Judge Nevas explained some pertinent points of law to the jury, used a lottery to narrow the panel down to twelve, and gave each member a copy of his 150-page instructions. On July 19, at 11:20 A.M., the jury members retired to their room. On August 8, they delivered their verdicts.

"It was one of the most satisfying moments of my career," said Don Brutnell. "We got everything we had worked for." The eight men had faced a total of thirteen separate counts, ranging from RICO conspiracy to violent crimes in aid of racketeering for the murder of William Grasso, and from collection of extension of credit by extortionate means to wire fraud. The guilty verdicts were spread across the board.

Cases like this, along with other notable successes, such as the conviction of Gambino boss John Gotti, have decimated the Cosa Nostra and show how effective long-running RICO-style investigations can be. But two things are clear. First, the Mob is stubbornly resisting the invitation to roll over and die. Every time a crew gets put away, even when the top men in the family are convicted and imprisoned, new wiseguys are made, the structure is reorganized, and the family somehow carries on. Second, while law enforcement agencies are trying to cripple Italian organized crime, other criminal organizations are flourishing: Chinese triads and tongs, Jamaican yardies, Japanese yakuza, the Chechen and Armenian mafias from the former Soviet Union, the Colombian and Mexican cocaine cartels, the Hell's Angels, black gangs, Puerto Rican gangs. Even the Sicilian Mafia, which until recently shied away from independent operations in the American territory of its cousins, is now involved in the United States. If an organized crime vacuum develops as a consequence of the Bureau's attacks on the Cosa Nostra, all these groups are well placed to step into it.

Given the successes the Bureau has had with the Cosa Nostra, the obvious question is, why are these organizations prepared to take the risk? The answer for most of them is simple: money, particularly the money from narcotics. The sums are too huge and the potential for corruption is too great for those who run the narcotics trade to be overly deterred by anything American law enforcement can throw at them. The annual world traffic in narcotics is now estimated to involve half a trillion dollars — more than the total value of all U.S. currency now in circulation. To put it another way, the criminals are making several times what the United States spent on the Vietnam War or on helping to rebuild Europe after World War II.

In contrast, the FBI's annual budget for fighting organized crime is tiny, about $270 million at current levels, and most of that is taken up by salaries and other overhead. This money will now have to be stretched to meet the threat from those groups that, like the Colombian and Mexican cocaine cartels, have the resources and the motive to plug any gaps left by the LCN.

Laws like the RICO statutes will continue to help, but there are holes in any legal net, and the new mafias are capable of devising ways to get around them. If the Bureau has learned a lesson from its wars on La Cosa Nostra, so has everyone else.

Ultimately, the FBI knows that in cases like these there is no substitute for hard work. Agents have to do surveillance, monitor wiretaps, and painstakingly build a picture of criminal activity. The Bureau is constantly devising ingenious new investigative procedures, but it will always rely on the people who put them into effect. More and more these days, this burden falls on a group of specialists who use a technique that was outlawed by J. Edgar Hoover because he thought it would tarnish the agency's straitlaced image: they work undercover.

CHAPTER 4

WALKING IN THE SHADOWS

THE MOMENT the steel door clanged shut behind him, Bill Butchka realized that this one wasn't going to be easy. He'd seen the inside of plenty of jails in his career but never as an inmate. Nothing could have prepared him for this — being locked up as a murderer, loan shark, and all-around professional criminal.

It had been a difficult day. That morning two U.S. marshals had delivered him shackled and handcuffed to the Federal Medical Center in Springfield, Missouri, part of a high-security penitentiary that housed some of the country's most dangerous criminals. His handover to corrections officers and the strip search that followed were routine — they happen to every hoodlum being processed through the system, every con at the start of his time. But for Butchka it was anything but normal. He was a special agent.

He looked around the tiny cell, with its sparse furnishings and its minimal décor. From now on, he would be locked up for eighteen hours a day, with little to do but stare at the walls and make friends with the colony of ants that scuttled around the floor. He sat down on the bed and took stock. This was definitely going to take some getting used to.

"There is no way you can get ready for something like that, no way you can be prepared for the locks going on that door," he later explained. "There's a feeling of total isolation. Even though I was there to do a job, it was hard to get away from the idea that I was being locked up for good. It was scary."

Butchka was undercover, deep undercover. Only a handful of people knew his real identity, and they had been sworn to secrecy. As far as most inmates and staff knew, he was inside for psychological evaluation before being returned to court for sentencing. But Butchka was in jail on a mission: to gather evidence that would help bring a cop killer to justice. By holding on to that fact, he would somehow get through the weeks to come.

In an identical cell next door was Roy Lee Clark, the target of the FBI investigation. "This guy was the worst," said Butchka. "He was involved in everything — stolen cars, drugs, you name it. He ran this crime syndicate in Tennessee and was connected to people in Florida, Vegas, Atlantic City, all over. He thought he was untouchable and that he was being real clever by not saying too much in prison. But he didn't realize how even the simplest thing could set a trail for us." Like Butchka, Clark had a secret. One of Tennessee's most notorious dealers in stolen cars, he was under suspicion for the murder of Michael Rector, a state motor vehicle enforcement officer, who had been his brother-in-law. For two years prior to his murder, Rector had been helping the FBI in a major auto theft investigation involving Clark's operations. On a number of occasions he had worn a body wire to record conversations with Clark, and he had helped the Bureau amass evidence to get an indictment against him. The first Roy Lee Clark had known about it was when agents got a warrant to search the offices of Westwood Enterprises, the company he used as a front for his operations. Six weeks after the raid, on the evening of May 31, 1990, Michael Rector was shot several times with a 9mm handgun as he got out of his car.

To the homicide detectives who investigated the killing and to Rector's FBI colleagues, there was not much doubt about who was responsible. But suspicion wasn't proof. There were no witnesses, there was little forensic evidence, and Clark's fervent protestations of innocence were difficult to dispute. He was charged with a variety of auto offenses based on Rector's evidence, but it looked as if he would evade the murder charge. Then one day in September 1991, Don Provonsha, an agent in the Knoxville FBI office, received a tip that Clark, who was now in prison, had dropped a hint to other inmates that he knew who had killed Rector and even implied that he had pulled the trigger. It wasn't a clear-cut statement, but it was enough to confirm the Bureau's suspicions. Unfortunately it still wasn't enough to get a conviction.

The agency decided to send two undercover agents into the federal prison to get more evidence. To send them both at the same time would be too obvious, but if they could be introduced into the system one at a time, as though they were ordinary inmates, they might be able to gain Clark's confidence and extract a confession from him. The operation required detailed planning and took several weeks to set up. Inmates in cells on either side of Clark were moved to another part of the institution, and the rooms were bugged. A few weeks later Bill Butchka, selected from a file of potential undercover operatives, was briefed. He learned his "history," rehearsed his lines, and became Clark's new neighbor.

Butchka, a short, muscular man with sandy hair and a piercing gaze, has made undercover work a specialty. Nominally based in Connecticut, he rarely works in that state in case he is recognized. In his twenty-year career he has posed as an arms salesman, an art expert, and a Mafioso. His longest time undercover was spent as an upmarket fence, buying jewelry and paintings stolen from glitzy Manhattan apartments. One of his most successful cases involved his playing a crooked arms dealer in a major 1980s FBI sting against gun-running by the Irish Republican Army. Not all his work has been so exciting, of course; on another occasion he was sent to the Bank of Boston to work in a division that counted quarters taken from the city's parking meters. He uncovered a ring of people who, over a two-year period, had embezzled over $500,000 in small coins.

But although Butchka had posed as a mob figure before, he had never had to play the role of an incarcerated killer, and he was more than a little nervous about it. "I had to be convincing," he said, "because it would have gotten around very fast if anyone had guessed who I was. So I was treated just like an ordinary inmate. That's why only two or three people were allowed to know why I was there. They even arranged for this girl, a Bureau employee, to write me love letters in jail and send me some pictures of herself so I could act like she was my girlfriend. They open your mail in federal prison, you see, and it helped to make me appear legitimate."

The only time Butchka could meet Clark was during the periods of free association. But he had to take things slowly. An obvious approach would make Clark suspicious, and the Bureau knew that he had reverted to his normal close-mouthed behavior. A new inmate who asked too many questions would stick out like a sore thumb.

So, in the first few days after he was put inside, Butchka kept away from his target and bided his time. Then after lunch one day he joined a game of cards in which Clark was also participating and struck up a conversation. It was the start of a friendship of sorts. Butchka played his target like a fish, reeling him in a little and then allowing him to pull away, sometimes chatting about crime, sometimes about sports or women. Occasionally he would go out of his way to avoid talking to Clark, all the time aware that he could blow the whole operation by being too pushy. Eventually the two men became so close that they were sharing one another's letters and talking in general terms about the crimes they had committed. Butchka realized Clark was impressed by his fake record as a convicted killer with mob connections, and he made sure his exploits sounded convincing.

After three weeks, the second agent, Steve Salmieri, appeared on the scene. He too tried the subtle approach, joining the two new friends over lunch one day, staying away the next. But there was something about him that Clark distrusted. He began to think Salmieri was an informant, and one day took Butchka to one side and warned him against the new guy. But Butchka had his story ready. Salmieri, he said, was well known to him, by reputation at least, as a big-time narcotics trafficker and hit man. He had underworld connections and could be trusted. Reassured, Clark accepted Salmieri's bona fides, and the three began to spend all their free time together.

For the agents, those weeks were tough. They constantly had to be on their guard to avoid giving the inmates or the staff any reason to think they weren't who they said they were. There was obviously no suggestion of special treatment. Butchka even had to endure several sessions with the prison psychiatrist who was supposed to be writing a psychological evaluation of him.

But after a while Clark began to talk about the Rector murder and how it was connected to his auto theft case. At first he only skirted the subject, but when he saw that his two fellow inmates had at least a passing interest in the matter, he kept returning to it. One day, sitting in Butchka's cell, he began to share some of the details of the killing, telling the agents facts that had never been publicly released and could have been known only to the murderer. He pantomimed pulling a trigger and told them how he would have shot Rector "if I had had a chance." Not surprisingly, his description exactly matched the manner in which Rector *had* been killed. Butchka and Salmieri knew they had their man.

Two weeks later, the agents had enough incriminating recorded testimony to get a conviction, although Clark had never come right out and admitted the killing. To their considerable relief, Butchka and Salmieri were allowed to return to the real world. Another Bureau undercover operation had been successfully concluded.

Although undercover operations, or UCOs, are now a common investigative tool, they have not always been so popular with the Bureau. J. Edgar Hoover, ever mindful of the possibility of embarrassing publicity, disliked them because of the danger that his agents could be compromised in some way. He hated the idea that FBI agents might have to dress like hoods or even socialize with them, and he was always wary of exposing them to possible corruption. Given what is now known about Hoover's personal relationships with a number of suspected criminals, this seems odd, but his own power and that of his agency rested in part on public confidence and trust. He felt that that confidence should not be jeopardized by having agents appear as anything other than well-groomed men with an impeccable reputation for integrity.

But from the sixties on, it became increasingly obvious to some field agents that undercover operations were going to be vital to their investigations. Two New York agents, Paul Brana and Guy Berado, were among the first to experiment with the technique, although they had real problems getting permission because of disapproval at headquarters. As Berado explained, "Our bosses didn't understand. The traditional investigation work, the shoe leather and the interviews, were fine law enforcement techniques, but this was different. Here we were taking the man and putting him in a situation where he wasn't interviewing or writing out a statement but he was actually joining in the action. They didn't really know how to view it."

The early undercover operations took agents into unexplored territory and brought them face to face with new problems. For instance, how should undercover agents react when asked to participate in a crime? Should they prove their "authenticity" to their criminal associates by sampling drugs or prostitutes? How much should they tell their wives and families? What should they do if they were recognized? Eventually the Bureau developed sophisticated guidelines that, even though they didn't cover every possibility, at least gave agents a framework within which to work. But in the late 1960s and early 1970s agents often had to think on their feet.

"Part of undercover work is being a good actor," said Berado. "Once Paul and I were waiting for a bond seller to show in a hotel room, and when he opened the door a guy stepped in with him. I had arrested this guy three or four years before. He looked at me and said, 'You're FBI, your name is Barrago.' He almost had it down perfect. So I jumped up and grabbed him by the throat and started to tell him that I figured he was a stool, that he was the cop and was setting us up. That turned the tables on him, and it seemed like they wanted to deal. We found out later that for a week the bond seller was outside the FBI office every morning and every night to see if we were going in and out of the place. Apparently he was convinced, because he made the sale and we put the arm on him. And he says, 'I knew you guys were who I thought you were.'"

After Hoover died, the FBI's attitude toward undercover operations began to change. The new directors — L. Patrick Gray, Clarence Kelley, and especially William Webster — sought to find ways in which the Bureau could cover investigative areas that had been neglected, and UCOs seemed appropriate. Even so, the first officially sanctioned undercover operations were used against old targets, particularly "subversives." For instance, in the early 1970s agents assumed the role of political radicals and infiltrated groups associated with the Weather Underground in an attempt to locate a number of fugitives. Other early operations were aimed at disrupting fencing scams by having agents pose as buyers of stolen goods. Many of these operations were only moderately successful, but they gave the Bureau an idea of how to approach the increasingly problematic areas of narcotics trafficking, organized crime, white-collar crime, and public corruption.

As undercover operations became more common, they inevitably became more complicated. Agents realized that they could use their imaginations to good effect. At its simplest, an undercover investigation can be little more than an agent masquerading as a crook to involve himself in an existing criminal enterprise in order to uncover evidence that a crime has taken or is taking place. Such operations, like the one that took Bill Butchka to the Federal Medical Center in Springfield, have become an accepted FBI investigative procedure and these days are a matter of routine. But beginning in the late seventies, the FBI also began to develop complex proactive cases in which the criminal activity itself was bogus. In these operations the agents themselves established a criminal enterprise that offered illegal opportunities to those predisposed to take them up.

It wasn't long before it dawned on some people that such "stings" carried with them the potential for serious damage to the nation's democratic institutions and to civil liberties. As the list of successful FBI undercover operations grew, so did the list of people who suffered disgrace, humiliation, and ruin merely because they were under investigation in such probes. Often these people were never charged with, indicted for, or tried for any criminal offense. In other words, some citizens were targeted for investigation when there was only the barest suspicion that they might be involved in criminal activity, and even though in many cases they were found to be completely innocent of any crime, the implication of criminal activity remained. This was a particular problem in cases involving public officials, whose ability to do their job was directly affected by any damage to their public reputation.

Perhaps the most famous early sting was Abscam, an operation in which FBI agents posed as an Arab sheik and his aides and tried to buy political influence in Congress. On February 3, 1980, the media reported that the Bureau had used this elaborate undercover operation to bribe or attempt to bribe a number of well-known national politicians. Of the twenty-seven public officials targeted for bribe offers and the twenty who went to videotaped meetings, twelve were later convicted.

At the time Abscam was trumpeted as a major Bureau success, a sign of the "new FBI," and in some respects it was. Certainly in the old Bureau things would have been handled differently. Rather than investigating and publicly disclosing political misconduct of this sort, Hoover would probably have kept anything so incriminating in his personal files for his own purposes. But the operation also left a number of senior politicians under a cloud, even though there was never any evidence that they had been abusing their offices. Furthermore, the way Abscam had been conducted left much to be desired. During subsequent inquiries, Congress applauded the motives for investigation (it could hardly do otherwise under the circumstances) but identified a number of significant deficiencies: the operation had relied on corrupt middlemen, informants had not been supervised, and initial approval for the operation had been virtually unlimited in scope.

An even more questionable early sting operation involving public officials left the Bureau open to charges that it was manipulating the political process. From 1980 to 1982 the FBI mounted Operation Colcor, a major investigation into corruption and narcotics trafficking in Columbus County, North Carolina. On the face of it the operation was extremely productive: thirty-eight people were convicted, and millions of dollars' worth of drugs, stolen vehicles, and other property were recovered. The two key undercover agents involved, Robert Drdak and Bradley Hoferkamp, took the investigation into areas as disparate as auto theft, narcotics smuggling, and insurance fraud. In the process they had to learn the ways of the tobacco farming community, to gain the confidence of powerful politicians, and to work their way into the inner circles of drug smugglers who bragged openly about how death awaited informers. Drdak and Hoferkamp were undeniably brave men who took a significant personal risk to end a major public corruption problem. As Robert Pence, the SAC for the operation said later, Colcor "was probably one of the most successful cases we've been associated with."

But Colcor also had a dark side. Part of the investigation was meant to establish that state and local politicians were willing to buy votes, so the agency decided to use its undercover operatives to propose and influence the outcome of a referendum in Bolton, a town of some four hundred voters. At issue was whether liquor could be sold by the drink, a local bone of contention. By promising to open a fancy new restaurant in this relatively poor rural community and by offering to pay the local party fixer, the agents managed to get the issue on the political agenda.

Although the issue itself was a minor one, a fundamental principle was at stake. As the congressional Subcommittee on Civil and Constitutional Rights said in a later report, "The point is that the FBI, with the blessing of its attorneys and the Department of Justice, created a local political issue, initiated a petition, and obtained a referendum on that issue and then influenced the outcome." Even more damning criticism came from the North Carolina State Elections Board, which invalidated the referendum and said sternly, "Neither the laws of North Carolina nor the First Amendment to the United States Constitution permit that elections may be initiated or election workers paid with funds supplied by secret government undercover agents."

If Abscam and Colcor had been isolated incidents, one could say that the Bureau had simply been finding its feet in the use of a new technique. But the late 1970s and early 1980s saw a number of major undercover operations that appeared to get out of control. Of these, none was more indicative of the threat posed both to individual citizens and to the country's democratic institutions than Operation Corkscrew.

Like many major FBI investigations, Operation Corkscrew began with a tip. In October 1977 a woman reported to the Cleveland, Ohio, FBI office that a local police officer had offered to arrange for her husband's vehicular homicide charge to be reduced. When the FBI investigated, it found that a Cleveland Municipal Court bailiff and another police officer were also involved. These men were arrested, charged, and convicted of bribery.

That could have been the end of it, but in the meantime the Bureau received another tip that people known as "corridors" were regularly taking bribes to act as middlemen in a wider case-fixing racket at the municipal court. Believing that it had identified a major pattern of corruption, the FBI decided to launch a RICO investigation.

Initially the evidence seemed to suggest that whatever was going on was small-time stuff, but one of the FBI's informants identified entries on court records that he thought might indicate case fixing by judges. The Bureau moved to get more evidence. In early February 1978 agents drew up a search warrant to seize all the judges' docket books, the bailiffs' docket books, and three years' worth of other documents. The district court judge who first signed the warrant withdrew his authorization after a day or two's consideration on the grounds that the seizure would "impugn the whole court." The following week the warrant was signed by a more pliant judge from a state court.

On February 14 — Valentine's Day — fifty agents and a large team of officers from the Cleveland Police Department descended on the Cuyahoga County Justice Center and seized 131 volumes of court records, comprising hundreds of thousands of pages and containing over 300,000 entries. At a packed press conference, spokesmen said the investigation showed that there were at least thirteen recorded instances of case fixing, that court employees were involved, and that at least one judge was under suspicion.

However, when the Bureau's agents finally got around to reviewing all the documents, they could not find any of the files pertaining to the thirteen allegedly fixed cases. After reading two thousand files and interviewing all the defendants, witnesses, police officers, and others involved in the cases, agents reduced the number of suspicious cases to 150, and most of those were suspicious only because of irregularities in the records.

After looking at the evidence again, the U.S. attorney decided that there was not enough evidence for a federal prosecution. But the Bureau refused to give up. Indeed, it decided to intensify its investigation and began plans for an undercover operation. By now agents had persuaded a "corridor" to work for them. Albert Hodson was a janitor at the municipal court, and he had openly bragged that he had access to records through a stolen master key. He had told FBI informants that he had been dealing with two judges through their bailiffs and had paid off various court employees, including security guards, who kept watch while he pilfered documents. The FBI set Hodson up, and when he was confronted, he agreed to reveal his contacts. These turned out to be two bailiffs, Marvin Harris and Marvin Bray.

For about a year Hodson recorded several conversations with these bailiffs and arranged to have several cases "disposed of," paying up to $1,500 per case. But the operation still wasn't delivering hard evidence of judicial corruption, so the FBI decided to move on to another phase. The Cleveland office sought and obtained agreement from FBI headquarters for an operation in which Hodson would introduce an undercover FBI agent to bailiffs and other "corridors" in order to bribe judges to fix cases. The cases would be real ones involving minor nonviolent crimes, and at the end of the investigation they would be put back into the system for proper disposition.

Special Agent Robert Irvin from the Cincinnati field office was chosen to pose as "Bob Graham," a car thief working on behalf of a Cleveland crime network. Soon Hodson introduced Irvin to Marvin Bray, and Irvin began taping their meetings with a recorder concealed in a plaster cast on his arm. One of his first acts was to pay Bray three hundred dollars to fix three cases by pulling a warrant from the clerk's office.

Once he had gained Bray's confidence, Special Agent Irvin began to look for evidence of judicial involvement in the case-fixing racket. To do this he needed to meet the judge face to face. He told Bray, who worked for a number of judges when their usual bailiffs were sick, that he would have to speak to a judge so that he, Irvin, could pass a lie detector test administered by the criminals he worked for and prove that the judge had confirmed the fix. At first Bray was unwilling, but when Irvin increased the bribes to between five and ten thousand dollars and stressed that all he needed was the vaguest of assurances that a case had been dealt with, Bray agreed.

Over the next few months Irvin met with judges a number of times, although these were less meetings than chance encounters. Each of the meetings was recorded on Irvin's concealed arm cast recorder. Strangely, however, despite Bray's repeated statements that he had set up the meetings so Irvin could discuss recent cases that had been fixed, the judges never seemed to acknowledge Irvin's veiled allusions to them. The Cleveland FBI and the U.S. attorney's office had labored long and hard to devise a seemingly natural conversation in which Irvin could elicit four crucial pieces of evidence implicating the judge and Bray: the name of the defendant; a statement by the judge that the case had been "handled, disposed of, taken care of"; a statement by Irvin that he would "settle up with Bray and then Bray would settle up with the judge"; and an agreement by the judge to this arrangement. But none of the twelve conversations that took place included all of these elements. In some of them the name of the defendant was not mentioned; in others there was no indication that the name mentioned referred to a defendant; and in at least six of the encounters the judge made it plain that he didn't recall the case or that he did not know what Irvin was talking about, or he put an innocent interpretation on an otherwise incriminating statement.

After a while, since none of the meetings seemed to be producing definitive evidence, Bray introduced Irvin to two more judges, Clarence Gaines and Lillian Burke. Although the conversations were still vague, the two targets apparently volunteered that the cases in question had been taken care of, and they repeatedly alluded to Bray's role. The FBI thought it had struck pay dirt. But there was a minor problem: these judges were imposters. In reality they were Marvin Harris (the other bailiff named by Hodson as a case fixer, whom the FBI apparently did not recognize), and Betty Smith, a fifty-three-year-old former bus driver with absolutely no knowledge of the law. The only resemblance between Betty Smith and the real

Judge Burke was that they were both black women. Marvin Harris and Judge Gaines were also both black, but Gaines was sixty-six at the time, Harris barely thirty. Astonishingly, Irvin never peeked inside the courtrooms where the real Judge Gaines and Judge Burke were at work every day.

Another thing the FBI seemed to overlook was a dramatic change in Bray's lifestyle. Over the past few months he had begun to wear expensive shirts and flashy jewelry, and he took frequent trips out of state, often as far away as Canada. Although the FBI agents believed their bribe money was finding its way into the pockets of judges, in fact, Bray, who had a string of convictions for larceny, check forgery, and breaking and entering, was taking it all for himself. The FBI was being scammed but didn't know it.

In the meantime, the effects of the ongoing investigation were being felt throughout the Cuyahoga County Justice Center. Although no one was aware that an undercover operation was in effect, everyone in Cleveland knew that a veil of suspicion hung over the municipal court system. Every few weeks one of the city's newspapers or television stations would carry some sort of story. A few were based on the growing conflict over the Valentine's Day raid, which had been heavily criticized by the local bar association; some told of the anxious meetings among various authorities in the Cleveland justice network. A few were almost certainly engineered by the FBI, which gave some juicy leaks to friendly reporters to keep its suspects off balance. But their effect was to undermine the faith of the people of Cleveland in their judicial system and to destroy many patient years of encouraging people to turn to the law in their civil and criminal disputes.

Judge Burke began to feel the breath of suspicion toward the end of 1980 when she decided to run for the position of administrative judge, a post that involved day-to-day handling of the court's affairs. When she courteously informed the incumbent that she would be running for the office, he told her that the FBI had presented its findings to a grand jury and that some judges would soon be indicted. At the time his remarks had no special significance to her, but later she perceived a warning in his words. When, several months later, she failed to get endorsements from the local bar associations, she realized that she was being damaged by rumors.

Finally, on April 20, 1981, Lillian Burke bowed to pressure from the media and agreed to go on prime-time television. That evening she gave an unequivocal interview and strongly denied any involvement in any kind of case fixing. Someone from the FBI was watching and realized the appalling truth: that the woman they knew as Judge Burke was an imposter — Betty Smith, the former bus driver.

Incredibly, Operation Corkscrew didn't end then and there. Agents continued to rely on Bray, who had disappeared from the court some five weeks earlier. When they finally caught up with him, he admitted that Betty Smith was an imposter but claimed that the real Judge Burke had agreed to use her as a stand-in. Astonishingly, they believed him. For some reason they made no effort to find out whether Judge Clarence Gaines had also been impersonated. When the FBI got around to giving Bray a polygraph test three months later, agents ignored their own examiners, who said his answers were "indicative of deception."

An even more astonishing decision was made when the FBI put a body recorder on Bray to trap the real Judge Burke. He faked her voice on the tape, a ruse too transparent to ignore. When agents asked him why he had done it, he told them blithely that he was not comfortable dealing with Burke and would rather deal with another case-fixing judge. The FBI handed over another $2,500 of the taxpayers' money so that he could bribe this judge and wired him up once more. Bray, who probably couldn't believe his luck, came back with a blank tape and told them the recorder hadn't worked. Nonetheless, he said, the bribe had been taken. Yet again the FBI believed him.

This extraordinary comedy of errors went on and on. Ignoring the most obvious signals that something was wrong, the agency continued to prepare indictments against a number of judges, including Burke and Gaines. In August 1981, it asked the Internal Revenue Service to track the money supposedly paid to the targets. Not surprisingly, the IRS found no trace of this money in any of the judges' accounts, but they did find that Bray had tens of thousands of dollars in his. Only then did Bray tell the FBI that Gaines had been played by an imposter as well.

Ultimately, the FBI's only evidence of a case-fixing scam was Bray's claim that he had bribed judges and some not very incriminating tape recordings of meetings between Irvin and several municipal court targets. But the agents packed it all up and presented it to U.S. Attorney James Williams with a recommendation that indictments be sought.

In early 1982 Williams issued his opinion: "In light of the manifest credibility problems caused by Bailiff Bray's actions and the lack of any other direct evidence to prove that money was paid to any judge of the Cleveland Municipal Court, it is impossible for this office to conclude that acts of judicial bribery have taken place in the twenty-six meetings with Bailiff Bray and Special Agent Irvin." He recommended that Bray be charged with tax evasion relating to the bribe income he had received as a middleman. Bray was prosecuted in Michigan, well out of reach of any embarrassing press coverage, and was sentenced to two concurrent sentences of three years each for tax evasion and embezzlement. He was also fined $2,500. He was never asked to return any of the other money he had been given in the previous two years. Just prior to his conviction, the Cleveland FBI office issued a statement, saying that "the prosecution of Bailiff Marvin Bray concludes the investigation of case fixing in the Cleveland Municipal Court which began on February 14, 1978. No further prosecutions are contemplated based on information presently available."

In the summer of 1982 the FBI conducted an internal review of Operation Corkscrew, and as a result "administrative action" was taken against the special agent in charge, the case agent, and Robert Irvin, the hapless undercover agent. In other words, they received the Bureau equivalent of a slap on the wrist. No one at FBI headquarters, which had kept a tight rein on the operation, was ever disciplined.

The damage and stress Operation Corkscrew caused to the judges and employees of the Cuyahoga County Justice Center can only be imagined. Even today, both Judge Gaines and Judge Burke are still feeling the effects. As Gaines said, "I prided myself on my honesty, and it was very important to me, throughout my career, never to take a dime. If you are honest, you know who you are. Yet after this, I felt dirty. And when I sat on the bench I would think, These people think I'm a crook. From the day I learned that the FBI thought I was fixing cases for money, I stopped feeling good about myself." Lillian Burke spends her days as she always has, working for the black community. She has set up a scholarship fund that sends deserving children to music school, and her small apartment is decorated with photographs of her accepting various awards and honors. That this remarkable woman, who was once offered a senior post by the White House, could ever have been thought to be corrupt is extraordinary.

The year after Corkscrew fell apart, Judge Burke appeared before a congressional committee looking into FBI undercover operations. At that gathering she raised the question of whether the investigation was racially motivated. She also said, "I believe the FBI owes not only the judges of the Cleveland Municipal Court but the citizens of Cleveland a public apology, or at the very least a statement that none of the judges of the court did anything improper." But to this day the FBI has never apologized for Operation Corkscrew.

By the early 1980s, many inside the Bureau privately thought that major operational blunders like Operation Corkscrew had to stop. However, the Bureau's most consistent shortcoming is its inability to admit publicly that it has been wrong. After all, the "best law enforcement agency in the world" is not supposed to make mistakes. As a consequence, its response to congressional and other criticisms has been at best a grudging acknowledgment that things might have been done better, and at worst a stony silence.

But in fairness, the agency and its parent, the Department of Justice, had already made a major attempt to tighten up the rules for undercover operations by the time Congress began its investigation in 1982. In January 1981 the internal Bureau regulations that governed such operations were amended and incorporated into a formal set of guidelines issued by Attorney General Benjamin Civiletti. With a few minor adjustments, these rules have held sway ever since. They provide a framework for authorizing, costing, and reviewing UCOs, which are divided into two main groups: those that have to be directly approved by headquarters, by the director or one of his assistants, and by the FBI's Undercover Operations Review Committee (designated Group I); and those that can be directly authorized by a special agent in charge (Group II).

In general, a special agent in charge can launch UCOs without any interference from headquarters, provided that they last less than six months and don't fall into any of twelve predetermined "sensitive" categories. If a proposed operation fails to meet any of these criteria, it becomes a Group I matter and has to be passed to headquarters for approval. The sensitive areas include any investigation that involves a foreign government, a religious or political organization, any public official, or the news media; any investigation in which an agent will pose as an attorney, doctor, member of the clergy, or journalist; any operation in which the agent might break the law (except by buying and selling stolen property and concealing his or her identity); any investigation in which an undercover agent might attend a meeting between the target and his or her lawyer; any domestic security investigation; and any operation in which there is a significant risk of injury or financial loss to a person.

If an operation is referred to headquarters on any of these grounds, the Undercover Operations Review Committee (and ultimately the director or his designated assistants) is supposed to make a judgment about whether to go ahead. It is supposed to consider whether anyone is going to lose money, be injured or be killed; whether anyone will suffer damage to his or her reputation or an invasion of privacy; and whether the individual agents and their case officers are suitable for the operation. Ultimately, of course, the committee must establish whether the operation is going to deliver the promised result. If it appears likely to do so, some or all of the jeopardizing factors can be set aside. In other words, the committee applies a cost-benefit analysis, deciding whether the convictions the operation would deliver are worth the risks.

The UCO guidelines also include a whole raft of provisions for consultation among all the various parties and U.S. attorneys or the Department of Justice. Underlying the guidelines is the idea that decisions have to be based on both the law and common sense. Unfortunately, there is no way for anyone outside the Bureau or the Department of Justice to know in advance whether the rules have been properly interpreted. By their very nature, undercover operations are secret, and there is no forum other than the courts for questioning how decisions have been made.

Of course, rules and regulations do not necessarily forestall calamity. Rules are obviously only as good as the people who put them into effect, and sadly, the Bureau, like any other large organization, has its fair share of the foolish, the overeager, and the incompetent. Consequently, a number of operations still seem to run counter to the spirit, if not the letter, of the guidelines. For the most part, these failures — for that is what they are — seem to have occurred because a few people in the FBI disagree with the rest of society about what might damage civil liberties or the rule of law.

One difficulty is that FBI agents are expected to be perfect in all circumstances, never making mistakes or being guilty of errors of judgment. But as agents will frequently protest, the Bureau does not operate in a perfect world. Crime and criminals are not necessarily straightforward, and often agents deal with cases so marginal that they have to distinguish not between black and white but among different shades of gray. In instances like this, they say, they have to rely on their own gut feelings, common sense, and a clear understanding of what will stand up in court. However, they also have to know when to draw back from the brink — when they have pushed an investigation to its limits and have to retreat. Sometimes, despite their best efforts, they get it wrong.

One recent illustration of the difficulties of working in the gray areas involved a special agent named Gary Danzer, who was asked to impersonate a hit man in order to get evidence against a convicted thief who was making threats against a former colleague. In the trials that eventually grew out of Danzer's undercover operation, serious questions arose about whether the UCO was justified in the first place, whether the agents involved made mistakes in pursuing it, and, most important, about whether the limits were overstepped in the pursuit of evidence.

On June 30, 1990, Gary Danzer was busy chasing leads on a number of ongoing investigations at a small Bureau resident agency in northern Kentucky, when he took a call from an FBI agent in Little Rock, Arkansas. The Arkansas office needed his help on an operation; could he come? He was on his way within hours. Danzer was used to these occasional jobs and welcomed the break from the routine. He had been specially selected for this task. The Bureau keeps a computerized list of agents who can be called on to fill undercover roles at short notice, and Danzer was known to be good at the heavy roles. A big man with an intimidating presence, he looked and could act tough. He was perfectly cast as "Chuck Ross," murderer for hire — his role for the next few weeks.

On his arrival, Danzer was briefed by local FBI agents and learned that the target of his UCO was a prison inmate named David Pardue, who was serving a five-year sentence for robbery at the Varner Correctional Unit, in Cummins, Arkansas. In April 1987 Pardue and a partner, Bob Harrington, had been shoplifting at a Wal-Mart store when they were caught by a guard. They sprayed Mace in her face and fled. In December, Pardue was arrested and convicted. During the trial, Pardue lied to the court, and later Harrington went to the police and agreed to testify that Pardue had perjured himself. Pardue was indicted on the new charge.

When Pardue heard about his former partner's treachery, he began talking vengeance in the prison to anyone who would listen. Few did; almost everyone there had some sort of grudge against someone outside, and dire threats against witnesses and cops were common. Even when Pardue talked about getting someone to kill Harrington and his wife, no one took much notice.

But one day Pardue's quest for revenge came to the attention of Gary Garrett, an inmate who was unhappy that his parole was taking so long to come through. He had expected to serve only a third of his sentence, but there were no signs that he was about to be released. When he heard that Pardue was looking for a hit man, Garrett saw an opportunity to improve his own situation. He wrote to the district attorney's office in Bentonville, Arkansas, offering to inform on Pardue in exchange for a deal on his sentence. Meanwhile, he told Pardue that he had a cousin who might be able to help and offered to arrange a meeting. He and his cousin would split the fee.

After writing several more letters to the skeptical local authorities (who had heard such stories a dozen times before), Garrett got his wish. The D.A.'s office sent someone down to talk to him. The contact believed his story and passed the information on to the FBI. Believing that Harrington's life was at risk, the agency decided to use Garrett as an informant and intervene.

The FBI made its first move in late June 1990. Agents sent Garrett a letter purportedly from "Chuck Ross," Garrett's cousin, indicating that Ross would help Pardue with "that problem of his." His fee would be ten thousand dollars (later reduced to five thousand). When Pardue read the letter, as Garrett made sure he did, he asked to meet Ross on the upcoming weekend, when his son would be visiting. That didn't give the Bureau much time, but they found their suitable "Chuck Ross" in just a few days.

On Sunday, July 1, Special Agent Danzer drove his pickup truck to the Varner Unit. An FBI surveillance van followed and parked a short distance away. Danzer signed himself into the visitors' log as Chuck Ross and made his way to the crowded reception room.

There he met Gary Garrett, who recognized him from a picture he had been sent a few days before.

While Danzer was talking to Garrett, Pardue was talking to his twenty-year-old son, Michel, a student at the University of Arkansas. David Pardue might have taken a wrong path in life, but he wanted his boy to achieve something. For his part, Michel had seen the cost of his father's life of crime and wanted none of it. But his father had brought him up and the relationship had bred a deep bond of loyalty between them. Michel's weekly visits were his way of showing that loyalty, and he rarely missed a date.

As Michel Pardue later explained, his meeting with his father that day began as usual with some chat about family affairs. But as they talked, Michel realized his father was more agitated than normal. He had lost weight, and he looked as though he hadn't been sleeping well. His depression about being in jail had been getting worse recently, and Michel knew that his perjury trial, scheduled for July 8, was weighing heavily on his mind.

"Garrett is supposed to get a visit today," David Pardue told his son at one point. As Michel had no idea who Garrett was, he let the remark pass. But after a few minutes something about his father's manner told him that it was important and he asked what he meant.

"I'm going to have Bob Harrington taken care of," David Pardue blurted out, as though pleased to get something off his chest.

Michel Pardue was dismayed. He'd heard his father make threats against Harrington before, but this sounded serious. They talked about it, and Michel pointed out that it wasn't a very clever idea and would only make matters worse. But his father was adamant. He told Michel repeatedly that he felt his attorneys had let him down and that Michel was the only one who could help. There was no one else he could rely on.

Eventually Danzer, who had been sitting unobtrusively in a corner with Garrett, came up and sat beside them. There is no official record of this meeting because the body mike that Danzer wore failed to work. At the subsequent trial, Michel Pardue insisted that Danzer said that he had heard David Pardue had a problem that needed taking care of and that he didn't want to talk about it inside the jail. Michel recalled that Danzer said, "Send your boy out to the parking lot."

Agent Danzer claimed that although David Pardue mentioned no names, he indicated clearly that he wanted a man and a woman killed. Pardue said he wanted the woman's body dumped in Oklahoma, at or near a truck stop, and the man's body disposed of where it would never be found. Danzer believed it was clear that Pardue wanted him to make it look as though Harrington had killed his wife and gone into hiding. Pardue told him he would pay five thousand dollars, in installments, for the job.

Whatever the truth of the matter, Danzer soon left and Michel Pardue stayed on for another fifteen minutes with his father. Michel said later, "He asked me if I'd go out in the parking lot and do this for him, and then he asked me how much money I had. I went to the rest room, counted to see how much money I had with me, and came back and told him I had $250. He wanted me to give it to Chuck Ross as a down payment. I just thought this guy was scamming my dad for the money. I really didn't think that it was a murder-for-hire scheme. I was trying to remain loyal to my dad, and if I went out and gave Ross the money, then I would have upheld my end of things. No one would be hurt because this guy would just take off with the cash."

Out in the parking lot, Danzer waited in his truck and discovered that his tape recorder had jammed. He said later that he had no time to get a replacement, even though the FBI surveillance van was parked just a few feet away. When Michel Pardue appeared, Danzer had no way of recording the conversation, and again his and Michel's recollections differ. During later interviews, Michel said that Danzer told him that he understood the murders would have to take place before David Pardue's perjury trial on July 8. Michel replied that this was the first he knew about the murder scheme and that he could pay only $250 of the first installment.

Michel said Danzer then asked him for information about the Harringtons: their address, what kind of car they drove, and what the license number was. He told the agent that he didn't know the answers to most of the questions and hadn't brought any information with him, since he had been unaware that it would be needed. Michel insists that he only gave the agent what little information he had, because he thought Chuck Ross was a con man who was not serious about actually killing anyone. Michel hoped that if he gave Ross some money, then perhaps he would leave him and his father alone.

In contrast, Danzer later maintained that Michel promised him an additional $250 if he followed him right then, so he could show Danzer where the Harringtons lived, and said that his grandfather, Jack Pardue, would pay him the balance of $4,500 when the murders had been committed.

These apparently minor conflicts in the stories are important, because it was later vital to the government's case that Michel, not Agent Danzer, had forced the pace in their meetings. Unfortunately, because of the broken tape recorder, there is no evidence to make clear who was telling the truth.

At 2:30 the following afternoon, Michel Pardue sat in a car outside a convenience store in Gentry, Arkansas, and waited for Danzer to appear. During the previous evening, Danzer had called him several times (each time recording the conversation), and had arranged that together they would make a reconnaissance of the area around the Harringtons' house. Danzer had been aggressive. He wanted the rest of his fee and he wanted a picture of the Harringtons. His intention, he told Michel, was to get the job done as quickly and efficiently as possible. He was so convincing that Michel Pardue began to think that maybe Danzer was a professional killer after all, and this made Michel very nervous. When Danzer arrived and got into Michel's car, the conversation, again recorded via a hidden mike under Danzer's shirt, was abrupt. On the tapes, Danzer sounded hostile and demanding, Michel more hesitant.

"Who's going to be in this house, besides the two of them — anybody staying with them? No kids? No nothing?" asked Danzer.

"Uh, I don't know," Michel replied. "My grandpa said something this morning about having a kid, but I don't know if they got a kid or —"

Danzer interrupted: "What am I supposed to do with that kid?"

Michel was silent for a while, and then replied, "I don't know; that's the first thing I knew anything about it, about the kid. I didn't know nothing about that deal."

"Well, find out what they want done with that kid. Because I'm not particular — [indistinct] don't particularly cotton to having anyone testifying against me. If there's someone in the house, I need to know about it. If I can find them sitting there, I just want to get this thing done, for quick, tonight probably."

For the next fifteen minutes Danzer and Michel drove around the streets of Gentry, passing the Harrington residence several times.

Danzer fired some more questions at Michel: Was there a police department in Gentry? How well did he and his family know the targets? Michel gave noncommittal answers and seemed to retreat into himself in the face of the forceful interrogation.

Some hours later, Danzer again called Michel at home. By then, or so he claimed later, Michel and his grandfather had agreed to try to stall Danzer in the hope he would give up and go away. But, judging by the tapes, and by the verbatim transcripts later made by the court, Michel found it hard to get Danzer to listen.

> MICHEL: That's my grandpa, and uh, I don't know, he's pretty . . .
> DANZER: I understand a little. Let me — let me do — let's do this, Mike, I don't wanna . . .
> MICHEL: He — let me tell you what he's saying.
> DANZER: All right.
> MICHEL: He's saying it is happening too fast for him, and it's a little bit fast for me too.

Later in the tape, Michel Pardue again apparently tried to tell the agent that he did not want to participate in the murder, but again Danzer interrupted him.

> DANZER: Yeah, like I said, I just want — all I wanna do is just make sure the cash is there and everything's ready to go. If there's any details that need handling, we'll handle 'em.
> MICHEL: Okay.
> DANZER: Now, if it needs to be put off I guess it needs to be put off, but, you know, [*indistinct*].
> MICHEL: Well, if it gets — if it had to be put off, uh, you know, we might just, I don't know, 'cause the trial most likely isn't gonna go through anyway because my dad's gonna get rid of his lawyers —
> DANZER: Uh-hum.
> MICHEL: — up there so, uh, —
> DANZER: You said your dad's gonna get rid of the lawyers?
> MICHEL: Huh?
> DANZER: How does he figure that's gonna help him?
> MICHEL: He's gonna, he's gonna fire them when he gets up there 'cause they won't subpoena the witnesses —
> DANZER: All right —
> MICHEL: — that he wants subpoenaed.
> DANZER: Okay. Well, he's still, uh — well, I don't know anything about it, I don't wanna know, I don't need to know anything about it.
> MICHEL: Yeah, right. Well let me call my grandpa and I'll call you back at that number —
> DANZER: Well, like I said, I'll get down there and I'm, I'm on the road anyway, and like I say, all I wanna do is look at the money. I don't even

wanna talk any business. I don't need to talk anything at all. All I wanna do is make sure there's green available and then that's fine, and we'll work out the details for how we make contact later and what you're gonna do with your alibi. There's ways to handle that, but we gotta know.

MICHEL: Right. See I, I think we need to talk about that because —

DANZER: You don't necessarily even have to be there. There could be a drop somewhere, you know.

MICHEL: Yeah.

DANZER: You know, we can make that clean where you can get an alibi, but I need, you know — if I get somebody up here to help me, then they're gonna wanna kill me about the time if I don't be able to come across with the money. Do you understand what I am saying? I got expenses and responsibilities.

Throughout this call Danzer tried several times to spread the net to include Jack Pardue, Michel's grandfather, and got Michel to agree that Jack would meet Danzer to show him the rest of the money he was owed. Eventually, after speaking to his grandfather on another line, Michel arranged with Danzer to meet again that evening in Fayetteville.

Shortly after 9:30 on the evening of July 2, Michel Pardue and his grandfather drove into the parking lot of Shoney's restaurant. While Jack Pardue stayed outside, Michel went in and joined Danzer at a corner table. Michel told Danzer that his grandfather wanted to meet him, but said that he was nervous. He added that both he and his grandfather wanted to have an alibi when the murders occurred. When Danzer replied that he was ready to do the job that night, Michel said that neither he nor his grandfather liked the idea of "going tonight, Chuck, because it's happening so fast."

"In other words, you still want them whacked, you just don't want 'em whacked tonight?" asked Danzer.

Michel, after a pause, agreed, but told Danzer that he would understand if Danzer wanted to leave the area: "We don't mean to put you out, Chuck, you know what I'm saying." They parted company, and Danzer told Michel that he would be in touch in six days' time. As promised, on July 8, Danzer called again and asked Michel if he and his grandfather had their alibis straight. But Michel's reluctance was by now becoming increasingly obvious, and Danzer was having trouble keeping the plan moving. The call ended inconclusively with Danzer again telling Michel that he would contact him.

It is not known how much pressure Danzer was under from his FBI case agents at this point, but he was in frequent contact with the FBI office in Little Rock and agents there would have been keen to know how the case was progressing. As an experienced under-cover agent, well versed in the law, Danzer would have been aware that the case could collapse if defense lawyers were later able to prove he had pushed Michel Pardue into committing a crime that he otherwise wouldn't have committed on his own. His problem was that Michel Pardue was being very noncommittal about the murder scheme. Danzer was entering the gray area that is a feature of many sting operations: where legitimate investigation can all too easily become obvious entrapment.

Meanwhile, back at the Varner Correctional Unit in Cummins, David Pardue was having a change of heart. He had decided to plead guilty to the perjury charge and hoped to get a reduced sentence. His son, Michel, and his father, Jack, had told him that they were frightened of Chuck Ross, and David Pardue was regretting his earlier threats against the Harringtons. He told his fellow inmate Gary Garrett that Ross should stop bothering his family.

For Garrett, this was bad news. His hopes for early parole were fading, and he believed that if the Pardue case fell apart he would remain in prison for some time to come. He was therefore pleased when, on July 31, he received another letter from "Chuck Ross," written, of course, by Special Agent Danzer. After a few opening pleasantries to make the letter seem legitimate, Danzer said, "Tell Pardue I was ready to do the job that night. I made two trips up there. I'm not the one who delayed it. I'm ready to go. But I want to be sure that I get paid. Mike said he didn't have the money and his granddad wouldn't meet with me, or show me any money, or tell me he would pay. I know Pardue can't pay me from the pen. Tell Pardue to write to me."

Danzer gave as a return address a post office box in Poteau, Oklahoma. In a few days, the FBI agents received a letter addressed to Chuck Ross, signed by Garrett and David Pardue (although Par-due later denied that the signature was his). In the letter, Ross was told that the delay was not David's fault, and that Ross had not seen the money "because my boy was leery of bringing the money before the job was done, because that was not in the agreement." The letter concluded that the remainder of the money would be mailed to a box number when David Pardue had proof that the Harringtons had been killed.

For the next six weeks, the Pardues heard nothing more from

Chuck Ross. Nor did Gary Garrett, who wrote several letters to the prosecutors urging action. In one of the letters he claimed that David Pardue "told me the other day if I get out on some act he wants me to finish the job for him and then contact his son after the job is done and pick up the rest of the money."

At the FBI office in Little Rock, Danzer and his case agents planned their next move. Firmly convinced that David, Michel, and Jack Pardue wanted to have the Harringtons killed, and influenced by the letters from Garrett, which they accepted at face value, the agents decided to force the pace of events. According to their later trial testimony, the agents believed that if the FBI did not take some action, the Pardues would independently arrange for the Harringtons to be killed.

On September 10, 1990, more than two months after Danzer's last conversation with Michel Pardue, Special Agent Dick O'Connell, the lead case agent for the investigation, stood with some FBI colleagues and local police at an extraordinary scene. It had taken a couple of hours to get it right, but all agreed the end result was worth the effort. They had staged the murder of Harrington and his wife.

Bob Harrington, who had been told his life was in danger, had been pleased to help, but his wife was reluctant, so a policewoman took her place. That night a Bureau photographer took two color Polaroids of Harrington lying on a road with silver duct tape across his mouth and blood all over his face. The pictures clearly showed a messy and obviously fatal bullet wound in the back of his head. One of the pictures revealed a woman lying behind him, her wrists bound with duct tape. She too looked dead.

Shortly afterward Danzer called Michel Pardue again. Michel testified later that he was terrified. He had begun to believe he'd heard the last of the scheme and to be approached again was a shocking experience. The tapes show that he was virtually silent as Danzer, in his usual abrasive mood, told him that the murder would take place on September 18 or 19. Michel and his grandfather had better get their alibis arranged.

On September 20, Michel Pardue and Special Agent Gary Danzer were back at the corner table at Shoney's in Fayetteville. For Michel the moment was full of dread. Earlier that day Danzer had called and said he wanted to meet to show Michel some "proof" and arrange to collect his money. For Danzer this was hook time, when, if all went according to plan, the fish would bite down hard on the bait. His body recorder had been tested and was running, and he knew this could be the key moment in the case. But he had to play it carefully.

"You got your alibi set?" he asked.

"Well, I just, uh, yeah."

"How about your grandpa?"

"I just don't like talking in here or anywhere else. I just don't like talking about it. The whole fucking deal makes me pretty nervous, you know," said Michel.

Then Danzer pushed a copy of *People* magazine slowly across the table and asked Michel to open it up. Taped to the center pages were the gruesome photographs of Bob Harrington and his wife lying in a pool of blood.

"I really didn't know what to say," Michel confessed later. "I was trying to look for some evidence from the photographs that maybe this hadn't happened. I asked to look at them again, and I couldn't see anything that would lead me to believe that it hadn't been done."

In fact Danzer's tapes show that he said very little. Danzer pressed home the attack.

"You tell your dad what you saw. If your grandpa wants any evidence past that, he'll have to come look."

In a subdued, choked voice Michel asked him what happened next. Danzer, as ever, had the details. The $4,500 should be sent to him at a post office box in Westville, Oklahoma — over the state line. "You get that money in the mail at the latest Monday. I'll be looking for it Tuesday."

Later that evening, Michel and Jack Pardue sat in Jack's living room and tried to decide what to do. But they knew they had no choice. They either paid up or angered someone they now knew was a professional hit man. There just wasn't any way to avoid it.

The next day they went back to the Varner Unit at Cummins and met David in the visitors' room. In low tones they described the pictures of the Harringtons. David Pardue agreed: "Chuck Ross" would have to be paid. The following morning, after gathering the money together, Jack Pardue drove across the Arkansas border carrying a plainly wrapped package. In it was a copy of the Bible (to give the parcel some weight) and $4,500 in used notes. Even as he mailed it, he felt that something was deeply wrong about the whole setup.

Two days later, he and Michel were arrested. Michel was at the livestock auction grounds, where he worked part-time, when a woman called out his name. He turned to see who it was, and two FBI agents moved in and grabbed his arms. Michel later said in an interview that his first feeling was one of deep humiliation that he had been arrested in front of his colleagues and his boss.

The cases against David, Jack, and Michel Pardue came to trial six months later. The prosecution set out to prove that the three defendants "did use the mail or other facilities of interstate commerce or caused others to use such facilities and to travel in interstate commerce or caused others to so travel to commit murder in Arkansas" — or, in layman's terms, they tried to hire a hit man. The jury heard Special Agent Gary Danzer, Special Agent Dick O'Connell, inmate Gary Garrett, and others, backed up by the tapes and transcripts of the many meetings between Michel and "Chuck Ross," give a convincing account of the Pardue conspiracy. Despite a well-ordered and at times impassioned defense, the jury found the three defendants guilty as charged.

But Michel Pardue's attorney, Jennifer Horan, was convinced beyond any doubt that her client had been set up. It was her first case in a federal court, and she had tried hard to persuade the jury that her client had been deliberately entrapped. She argued that he had had neither the desire nor the motive to see the Harringtons killed, and that without the direct involvement of an experienced, aggressive, and manipulative undercover FBI agent, he would have quietly ignored the wild suggestions of his father. But proving entrapment is always difficult, because such cases rely on fine legal distinctions and arcane technical details that are over the head of the average jury member. In this case, the jury found the entrapment claim unproved and irrelevant.

After the trial Horan went back to her law books and hunted for a last resort. After hours of late-night reading she found one. She could ask Chief Judge Franklin Waters to reject the jury's verdict and acquit Michel Pardue on grounds of "outrageous government misconduct." She didn't have much hope: Waters was a Reagan appointee, a dyed-in-the-wool law-and-order man who counted the local FBI bosses among his closest friends. But she tried anyway.

On May 10, 1991, Waters came to a startling decision. "In almost ten years of doing this job," he wrote in a forty-one-page opinion, "this judge has not been faced with a case as troubling as this one, or one that has caused this court as much concern, worry and conflicting thoughts and emotions. The court has a great deal of concern about whether Michel and his grandfather really planned any of the matters that took place or whether they were instead pulled along into this criminal act by the authorities much as someone is caught in a violent undertow at sea.

"While [this court] recognizes that law enforcement personnel must be free to vigorously and indeed creatively pursue criminals engaged in criminal activity, they must not be allowed to make crime or to make criminals out of otherwise innocent civilians. . . . The court is convinced that FBI agent Gary Danzer and the government's agent Gary Garrett, working together, by deception and improper conduct, implanted the criminal design and intent in the otherwise innocent mind of this young man."

But Judge Waters was not so indulgent toward David Pardue's role in the affair and found there was no evidence to suggest that he was similarly entrapped. The verdicts of guilty against Jack and Michel Pardue were overturned; that against David Pardue was upheld.

Perhaps understandably the FBI and the federal prosecutors were not happy with this decision. They petitioned against Waters's opinion, and a Justice Department specialist was dispatched from Washington to argue the case before the U.S. Court of Appeals for the Eighth Circuit. In January 1993, after considering the prosecution's contention that "judges are not free to impose their personal notions of fairness on law enforcement officers under the guise of due process," the court came down on the side of the government. Michel and Jack Pardue's cases were referred back to Waters for sentencing.

The judge, unshaken from his conviction that the two had been caught up in events beyond their control, was determined to be lenient. Both men were confined to their homes for six months, Jack was fined ten thousand dollars, and Michel was fined fifteen thousand dollars. The government, after considering a further appeal, let the sentence stand.

Waters, who is otherwise a great supporter of the FBI, believes it should learn some lessons from the case. "I think they need to recognize that there are some moral principles involved here," he said later. "It's not sufficient to merely use whatever means are necessary and available to catch criminals. We do have a serious crime problem, but I think we need to recognize that we also have some very treasured personal liberties. I'm afraid that in this case they were trodden on to some extent. The war on crime is not so important that we ought to forget about those principles that we've all revered for so many, many years in this country."

The more the FBI relies on undercover techniques, the more it is going to become involved in cases like that of Michel Pardue and his family — cases in which the line between guilt and innocence becomes blurred by the active involvement of an agent provocateur. The Bureau believes it has enough safeguards in place to prevent any miscarriages of justice, and it can cite numerous instances in which undercover investigations have been rejected at the outset or halted early on because there was insufficient evidence to proceed. But obviously there will always be times when the only person who is capable of making a judgment about the validity of an operation is the undercover agent himself. It is a weighty responsibility, and making the wrong decision can be costly.

Although as a breed they are usually highly motivated, intelligent, and intuitive people, undercover agents are not superhuman. To do what they do calls for more than just a lot of guts and an ability to act. They often have to live out a role that is totally contrary to all their values and beliefs. This can be dangerous not only because their lives might be at risk but also because it can warp their judgments about people. If an agent spends all day every day for months, even years, with people who are hardened criminals, it is almost impossible for him to remain unaffected by it. If he then works on a case where guilt is not clearly defined, he may find it difficult to distinguish between the obvious crook and the border-line case.

Some agents don't think this is up to them anyway. As one agent put it, "When I am undercover, I spend most of my time worrying about keeping my identity covert. I don't know if I am typical, but I think that it's up to my case agent or my supervisor to worry about the big picture. I provide information for them to act on, and they give me stuff which helps fill everything in from my end. But frankly, I don't worry too much about the guys I'm in with. I can maybe get to like them, sure, but if I'm told they are punks then I generally believe they are punks, unless something tells me otherwise. It's just not my problem. I'm there to do a job — in and out as fast as I can to get a conviction."

It can also be difficult for an agent to maintain the distinction between his real self and the persona he has adopted for his work. Bill Butchka, the agent who spent time in jail in Missouri, expressed it this way: "The guys who end up in trouble are the ones who try to be something else. When I was a hit man I was Bill Butchka, when I was an art dealer I was Bill Butchka, when I was a drug dealer I was Bill Butchka. The problem with some of these guys is that because they are pretending to be a drug dealer, say, they think they have to act like one. The risk is that they get wrapped up in it so much they go the other way. It's like integrity, okay? I'll give you an example. I was doing this job a while back — it was a narcotics thing — and I had this six hundred thousand dollars in cash to make a buy. Well, I lost my surveillance and I was sitting there with all this money and I could have just taken off with it. If anyone says it doesn't go through your mind, they're wrong; it does. So I had to come face to face with this thing. I came down on the side of integrity — but it's a thin line."

Of course the practical pressures of working undercover are immense. First and foremost there is the obvious danger that someone, somehow, will identify the agent for what he really is. While such incidents are comparatively rare, most undercover agents have their favorite stories of how their cover has almost been blown.

Then there is the problem of establishing a believable identity. This can be especially critical in Cosa Nostra cases, where family ties are so important. In many long-term LCN cases the Bureau has to devise a way in which the agent's credentials can be established by a third party already known to or trusted by the target. For instance, Special Agent John Doe, who is working his way into a crime family in Las Vegas may tell the mob that he has a history of association with the New York Gambino family. The FBI meanwhile primes one of its Gambino informants to claim a long relationship with John Doe if anyone from Las Vegas asks awkward questions. Once John Doe is securely in place inside the family organization, he can then attest to the bona fides of other agents working undercover in other parts of the country. In his role as a connected guy from out of town, John Doe might even show up in a bar in another agent's territory to show that agent's targets that he has the right sort of friends.

There is also the chance that an agent will have to prove himself to his criminal associates by breaking the law in some way. It is often assumed that the most common hurdle agents have to cross is being asked to use narcotics. This is actually quite rare, because, more often than not, the people who sell drugs (at least the high-level sellers the FBI goes after) are not users themselves and make a point of never getting a habit. When agents are asked to use drugs, they can usually talk their way out of it by pleading bad health or claiming that they are not comfortable doing drugs in the company of strangers. They know that if they do agree, even in order to reinforce their credentials, any testimony they later give in court will be severely tarnished by an admission that they used narcotics.

This fact also applies to other criminal activities. An undercover agent is supposed to be able to avoid entangling himself in any crime, although minor offenses against property that can be put right at a later date are quietly condoned. Sometimes, an agent has to show that he has access to money, stolen property, or narcotics in order to get involved in a criminal enterprise; in those instances, the proof is supplied by the Bureau, which is authorized to use property, cash, or drugs recovered in the course of its investigations.

Of course, much of an undercover agent's life is repetitive. Spending long periods of time with crooks or even terrorists can be wearing — there is no law that says targets have to be interesting people. Weeks spent listening to criminal conversations, even those enlivened by the occasional boast of past scams, can be exhaustingly dull. On some occasions operations have been blown because agents have become so fed up with the delays and the waiting around that they have tried to force the pace. As most veterans will testify, though, nothing makes a target more suspicious than an agent's overeagerness or inquisitiveness.

All the psychological stress caused by working undercover — the isolation, loneliness, boredom, fear of discovery, living a lie, and the enforced absence from family and friends — sometimes puts too much strain on agents. These problems aren't always obvious during the operation — the agent is too busy trying to build a case to have time to reflect on what it may be costing him personally — but when he comes back, his family and colleagues sometimes see a person they thought they knew well becoming moody and introspective, prey to sudden anxieties, and seemingly incapable of readjusting to ordinary life. In the mid-1980s, these symptoms had become so recognizable that the Bureau's Behavioral Science Unit got some specialist medical help to establish a program for monitoring and assessing these agents' mental and physical health before they returned to their everyday lives.

Well before they are allowed to work undercover, potential undercover agents (who volunteer for the work) attend a two- to three-week course at Quantico. It blends legal and psychological training with seminars given by agents who have had firsthand experience of what the rookies might encounter. They are taught how to talk themselves out of difficult situations, how to react to physical threats, and how to deal with the isolation, and they receive more specific instruction on street slang, narcotics recognition, the behavioral traits of criminals, and legal matters. During role-playing exercises at Hogan's Alley, they are also assessed for their resourcefulness, ingenuity, and self-assurance, and poor performers are weeded out.

Despite this kind of training, in the last ten years there have been a number of undercover agents who couldn't take the strain and have had to be pulled off their cases. There have also been instances, though much rarer, when agents have succumbed to the temptations of the job. In plain language, they have turned bad. Most commonly this happens on narcotics investigations, where vast sums of easy money can bedazzle an agent on a modest government salary.

In contrast there are the big successes. Some undercover exploits have become the stuff of legend, even among hardened agents who know how often war stories get blown out of proportion. Of these, perhaps the most remarkable is the story of Special Agent Joseph D. Pistone.

For six years, Pistone posed as a Cosa Nostra associate, jewel thief, and con man to infiltrate the Bonanno organized crime family. He shared the family's darkest secrets and became so much of a fixture that when he was pulled out in 1982 he was only weeks away from being made a wiseguy. It was one of the most audacious sting operations in the agency's history.

Initially, the operation was meant to last only six months and was aimed at high-echelon dealers in stolen property. Pistone was working as "Donnie Brasco," a connected guy from California who had hung around on the fringes of the Cosa Nostra in Miami and elsewhere.

His specialty was fencing stolen jewelry, but like any budding Mafioso he took an interest in any crooked deal. His first contacts were with a low-level Colombo family street crew in Brooklyn, but after a few months he got involved with a more sophisticated Bonanno operation run out of a social club on Madison Street in Manhattan's Little Italy.

There he met and befriended Benjamin "Lefty Guns" Ruggiero, a respected Bonanno soldier, and began to establish his credentials. Before long he was passing on to his FBI handlers details of protection scams, gambling rackets, truck heists, and a variety of other swindles and thefts. He even began to pick up details of the Bonannos' heroin operation, which was run by Sicilians who had been brought in after Carmine Galante, the family godfather, was murdered. This information later helped the Bureau crack the famous Pizza Connection case, in which heroin was peddled through a nationwide network of fast-food outlets.

Gradually it became obvious to Pistone and to his handlers that he had become so well established inside the family that he would be able to provide the agency with unprecedented information for years to come. And so he stayed, becoming so trusted that he was traveling widely on Bonanno family business. He even used his New York connections to set up bogus LCN operations in California, Milwaukee, and Florida. Every now and then he provided backup for other agents by introducing them to Bonanno operations or to those of other Cosa Nostra families. As a result Pistone became involved in and even helped initiate a network of interlinking criminal conspiracies, and he began to uncover the astonishing Cosa Nostra infiltration of legitimate businesses across the United States.

When Pistone was finally pulled out of the family in 1982, six years after he first went into deep undercover, he embarked on a four-year round of court appearances in which he testified against dozens of Mafiosi. The Cosa Nostra put out a $500,000 contract on him and distributed his picture to wiseguys throughout the country, and he and his family had to be guarded twenty-four hours a day. Some of the Mafiosi he had worked with were gunned down on dark nights — a savage reminder of what would happen to anyone else who violated Cosa Nostra security.

Today Pistone is still in danger, although he has officially left the FBI. The contract against him is outstanding, and he knows that any number of young hoods would like to "make their bones" by nailing Donnie Brasco. Neither he nor his family will ever be totally safe from the Mob. The Pistones live under an assumed name in a town where no one knows their true identity. Pistone is suspicious of strangers, and he has to keep reminding his children to be careful of what they say. It is a heavy price to pay for just doing his job.

But Joe Pistone hasn't completely lost touch with his past life. Every once in a while he is called upon to testify in a Mob case, and occasionally he acts as a consultant to the Bureau, passing on his hard-won experience to rookie undercover agents being trained at Quantico.

As he explained in an interview, ""It takes a certain kind of individual to work undercover. You have to be a certain type. The rewards are not as great as the sacrifice. You don't get any extra consideration or pay — in fact, it hinders your promotion. A lot of people have the misconception that you are out spending money, having a good time, but actually it is the opposite, because you are the one who makes the case. You have to be a self-starter. The conversation is all on one level — illegal activities and who is trying to kill who — and it gets very boring. The hours are tough, too.

"You have to know yourself — you have to have a lot of confidence, and you mustn't mind being alone or isolated. You have to have self-respect and be dedicated to what you are doing. A lot of it is mental toughness. There were times when I got pissed off, when I thought that the Bureau wasn't helping very much. You are dealing with people at headquarters who have never been undercover and who don't understand. For example, an undercover agent is given a budget to do the job. When the money runs low, the field office goes to headquarters and asks them to replenish it. Often the Bureau is slow in doing that, because the agent handling it might be on leave or have other cases. So the undercover agent has to worry about the car payment, rent, and telephone bills — things which he shouldn't be concerned about."

Like Bill Butchka, Pistone believes that the secret of being a successful undercover agent lies in not acting out of character or telling too many lies. The more an agent can be himself, the more relaxed he will be.

"The other art of undercover work is being able to talk the right way," he explained. "You have to encourage your associates into an illegal situation that you can carefully control, and all the time avoid the entrapment issue. The situation has to be something that they were already planning to do anyhow. You have to be able to craft your conversation. Most good undercover agents do very little talking — they just promote topics of conversation, without making it look as though they are doing it for some reason."

Pistone admits there is something a little ironic in the fact that the Cosa Nostra put out a contract on him, since the Mob doesn't usually kill law enforcement officers if it can help it, as this brings too much heat down on their heads. But he believes that they never fully accepted who he was. He had been with them so long, had been with them on so many jobs, had become friends with them, and had even eaten with their wives and children — all things that they could not associate with an FBI agent. Three years after dropping his undercover role, when testifying against Nicky Marangello, a Bonanno capo, the Mafioso came up to him and said, "Donnie, how could you do this to us, you are one of us?"

"The difficulty in long-term undercover work is that you have to become friendly with someone and you get to see the good in them," said Pistone. "I didn't just look at these people as thieves. I had to see them as people too, and that made it hard. But ultimately, you can never forget who you are, because if you form a bond with someone, you are not doing your job properly."

Most undercover agents do seem to do their job properly. If the agency's own statistics are anything to go by, the vast majority of FBI undercover operations are successful. Whether any of the resulting convictions could have been obtained by other, more conventional methods is open to question. Nor does anyone know exactly how many innocent people or institutions have been damaged along the way. But given the sophistication of the criminal and terrorist organizations it is now faced with, the agency could not possibly meet its investigative responsibilities without resorting to the technique. UCOs are here to stay. The era when J. Edgar Hoover could afford the luxury of banning undercover work because it might tarnish his organization's rosy image is long gone.

These days, on average, the Bureau conducts between three and four hundred Group I undercover operations every year, and hundreds of Group II investigations are in progress at the same time. That means that somewhere, right at this moment, an FBI special agent is pretending to be someone else, dealing with the enormous pressures of staying ahead of the game, and maybe even risking his life. It is a sobering thought.

CHAPTER 5

FILE MOUNTAIN

O F ALL the fundamental public concerns about the FBI, none has been more deep seated than that regarding the agency's practice of gathering and storing information. Not surprisingly, fears about what the Bureau knew about whom reached their height in the 1970s, when a succession of exposés and revelations showed that the FBI had become a repository for mountains of data with questionable law enforcement value. Gossip about the sex lives of politicians, civil rights campaigners, Hollywood starlets, presidents and their first ladies; notes on the secret and suspect ideologies of the rich and famous; data about the financial embarrassments, alcoholism, and drug dependency of newspaper columnists, diplomats, and members of the Supreme Court — the post-Watergate inquiries showed that the FBI had for many years meticulously collected and filed all this information and on some occasions had used it for its own advantage.

These days such worries have faded. Most people accept that the Bureau is fairly responsible in the performance of its duties, that it gathers and files information for legitimate purposes, and that that data is securely held and protected from abuse. But are these assumptions justified?

Although the Bureau certainly says yes, the issue is not quite as straightforward as it would like people to believe. Even a cursory examination of the modern FBI's information-gathering procedures gives rise to basic questions about privacy which affect millions of people across the United States. Nowhere is this more apparent than in the agency's computer systems, the vast data reservoirs that are the cornerstone of the FBI's investigative achievements and the site of the most tangible legacy of the Hoover era: the legendary FBI files.

There is something quite awesome about the sheer physical presence of the agency's mainframe computer system at FBI headquarters. Occupying the whole of the first floor — an area the size of a football field — it could almost have a life of its own. Row after row of cream-colored containers, stretching away in an impenetrable maze, hum gently in a temperature-controlled environment. To one side is shelf after shelf of discs and tapes, to another is a vast array of batteries, ready in case the emergency generator fails. There are few signs of human activity. A small team of technicians mans a central command console twenty-four hours a day at one end of the room, but unless something goes wrong, they rarely leave their seats.

Deep within the bowels of this immense technological marvel lies a complex of interlinking systems and subsystems that hold countless millions of records — more than an army of FBI agents could ever hope to read. Containing everything from secrets so sensitive that they could topple governments to details of recently issued speeding tickets in Boise, Idaho, the Bureau's computer system is the most remarkable source of information in the world.

There is nothing especially questionable or spooky about the Bureau's reliance on this system. Given its image, the FBI would look pretty ridiculous if it failed to take advantage of modern technology. Indeed, many agents complain bitterly that in some respects it lags twenty years behind other organizations. Oddly, almost all special agents still have to record their memos and reports on cassette tapes, which are then transcribed by a typist. Apparently the FBI maintains this practice in the belief that individual word processors would tie agents to their desks and slow down investigations.

In contrast, though, the mainframe computers at headquarters are about as sophisticated as money can buy. Although endlessly complex, they have two main functions. The first is the National Crime Information Center, or NCIC, as it is more commonly known. This provides a national criminal records database for local, state, and federal agencies, as well as for the Royal Canadian Mounted Police and criminal justice agencies in Puerto Rico and the U.S. Virgin Islands. NCIC is up and running twenty-four hours a day, seven days a week, and it contains almost 20 million records on everything from stolen vehicles, guns, and boats to missing persons, foreign fugitives, and U.S. Secret Service protection. Its Interstate Identification Index subsystem, known as Triple I (III), provides access to criminal history records maintained at the local and state levels. Currently, NCIC information is officially accessed about 100,000 times a day through about 97,000 terminals servicing almost 70,000 police and federal agencies. In all, there are some 500,000 authorized individual users.

The second function is the FBI's own internal network, which is broken down into eleven subsystems. David Nemecek, who is responsible for its smooth operation, is an assistant director, a rank that shows how much importance the FBI attaches to its computer weaponry. He is also a passionate advocate for its effectiveness. Sitting in the hushed, temperature-controlled environment of the main control center, he explained why the computer network was so vital to Bureau operations.

"It's used over two and a half million times a day, and all of the FBI's fifty-six field offices and five hundred auxiliary offices have access to it," he said. "It's an essential part of getting our job done, particularly in combating the technology that the criminals have. The types of cases that the FBI is being called upon to work on and solve these days, whether they are massive bank frauds or involve hundreds of thousands of pieces of data and cases on a national or international scale, make it impossible to review all this data and in many cases to make the linkages to solve the cases without the network. In many cases it's a matter of running computers for hours just to assess the data, just to look for the leads that will help us focus our investigative attention. Before we had this system we had paper — millions of three-by-five index cards, reference files one and two inches thick, hundreds of thousands of files that were stored in various field offices — and no central access, no way to find the data. It used to require hundreds of agents to do the same job the computers do.

"Even in the recent investigation of the bombing of the World Trade Center in New York City," Nemecek continued, "it's probably fair to say that without computer assistance it would have taken many months for us to have been able to identify the particular van that was used and track it back to the people who used it. The computers made it possible for us to really solve that case and begin arresting people within just a week."

Although the FBI system works as an investigative tool that helps agents analyze incoming information, it is also a database that contains details of every FBI investigation from years past. Furthermore, the Bureau has access to a number of other major intelligence and information systems in other agencies. Some, such as the ones in the Department of Justice, are maintained by the FBI and are networked into the FBI system. Others are maintained by organizations such as the Drug Enforcement Administration and the Immigration and Naturalization Service, but the Bureau can gain entry without too much trouble.

It is a rather crude analogy, but logging onto the FBI computer is a little like walking into the lobby of a large office building. In front of you, running into the distance, are a number of corridors. Each corridor will take you to a different lobby or a subsystem packed with files. There you find yet more corridors leading off to yet more subsystems and yet more piles of files. Each subsystem has its own security and operating procedures, but before you can access a subsystem, you have to get into the building — and of course every computer-literate FBI agent will have a key.

The Bureau maintains that all the information contained in the computer system has been gathered for totally legitimate purposes — and in general terms that is likely to be true. But the sheer size, complexity, and power of this interlinking network make it almost impossible to police the data adequately. This raises a number of questions. Can the people who use it truthfully say that every one of the tens of millions of files contained in this system is accurate? Are all these files compiled and held legally and legitimately for the furtherance of justice and in the interests of the country as a whole — every single file? And just what is in these files anyway?

Many people might think first of the hundreds of thousands of crimes that the FBI has had reason to investigate: the cases of murder, rape, arson, narcotics trafficking, public corruption, armed robbery, car theft, bank fraud, espionage, terrorism, racketeering, and the like. Others might think of more famous examples: the Kennedy assassinations, Watergate, the Patty Hearst kidnapping, the Iran-Contra scandal, the Walker spy scandal, the death of Marilyn Monroe. The FBI files contain details on all these and more. Here are records of countless forgotten words of FBI agents about countless forgotten investigations, countless leads pursued and abandoned, countless interviews that have come to naught, countless more that have proved fruitful. Undercover operations are described by the thousands, electronic surveillances by the tens of thousands; tip-offs, witness testimony, cases opened, closed, and pending by the millions.

Of course the files also contain other kinds of information, in less obviously exciting categories: personnel and administrative records, applicant checks, details of contacts with the media, Congress, and the public, letters written, speeches made, money spent, statistics compiled — the recorded history of every dealing in every area. Data is the DNA of the FBI, its very lifeblood, and in one sense the reason for its existence. The wheels of the Bureau's bureaucracy are oiled by facts and figures, notes, memos, reports, abstracts, and conclusions, and like any large and hungry animal, it needs a constant diet to keep going.

Where does all that information come from? It isn't just crime related, that's for sure. In all probability, if you are American, or if you have ever visited the United States, then you or someone you know has contributed to this information mountain in some way. There's a better than average chance that the FBI has some sort of record of your existence.

Many agents dismiss this idea. As one said, "It's the thing I get all the time. People find out I'm a special agent and they say, 'Hey, have you got a file on me?' The first thing I say is 'How the hell would I know?' Then I say, 'Why would we bother? We've got more important things to worry about.' Then if they persist, I say, 'Go ahead and file a FOIA [Freedom of Information Act request], that's your right. But I'll bet you a hundred bucks there's nothing there.'"

But clearly it is comparatively easy to have your name recorded in at least one file. Consider the FBI's central records system, which has five main categories of people kept on file. The first category is for anyone who is involved in any manner with an official FBI investigation, "including but not limited to subjects, suspects, victims, witnesses and close relatives and associates who are relevant." The second category comprises "applicants for and current and former personnel of the FBI and persons related thereto who are considered relevant to an applicant investigation, personnel inquiry or other personnel matters." The third applies to "applicants for and appointees to sensitive positions in the United States Government and persons related thereto who are considered relevant to the investigation."

For obvious reasons most people do not fall into these categories, but the other two spread the net much wider. The fourth classification is for "individuals who are the subject of unsolicited information, who offer unsolicited information, request assistance and make inquiries concerning record material, including general correspondence and contacts with other agencies, businesses, institutions, clubs, the public and the news media." The fifth category is for "individuals associated with administrative operations or services, including pertinent functions, contractors and pertinent persons related thereto."

One of these categories has a catch. According to the provisions of the Freedom of Information Act, anyone who wants to know if he or she has a file at the FBI has to write with a request for details. The fourth category specifically refers to people who ask about record material. Therefore, even if someone doesn't have a file at the FBI, the process of writing to confirm that this is the case will get him or her on file anyway.

Of course most people reading this list would never be tempted to write an inquiry letter, believing that since they have never had any contact with anyone from the FBI, there is little chance that the agency knows of their existence. But this is not necessarily true. By looking into the subject categories that govern the use of the files in this system, and into the indexes the Bureau has designed to make the material more manageable, one can find more clues as to who is included.

The 277 subject categories largely mirror the federal violations over which the FBI has jurisdiction. Predominantly, these are for the kinds of crimes and security matters one would expect the FBI to be investigating. The categories have names such as "C91 Bank Burglary; Bank Larceny; Bank Robbery. Title 18 United States Code, Section 2113"; "C98 Sabotage. Title 18 United States Code, Sections 2151–2156"; and "C200 Foreign Counterintelligence Matters. Attorney General Guidelines. Executive Order 11905." If a name has found its way into any of these categories, there is a fair chance that it is there legitimately. Remember that someone need not have committed a crime to merit inclusion; being interviewed about a crime that he or she may have witnessed is enough.

But the subject list also includes a number of categories for minor violations, as well as categories that seem to have no direct relevance to any serious crime but are included on civil or administrative grounds, such as "C43G Unauthorized use of Johnny Horizon Symbol"; "C63 Miscellaneous — Nonsubversive. Concerns correspondence from the public which does not relate to matters within FBI jurisdiction"; and "C142 Illegal Use of a Railroad Pass."

The management indexes are also revealing. Again they are predominantly concerned with vital criminal and intelligence investigative matters. One index entry is named "Computerized Telephone Number File (CTNF) Intelligence," which contains lists of telephone numbers used by subjects under investigation; another is the "National Security Electronic Surveillance Card File," which contains details of authorized bugs used in foreign counterintelligence cases. But there are also some strange titles, such as "Veterans Administration (VA) Federal Housing Administration (FHA) Matters Index," which contains details about people who have been the subject of investigations concerning VA and FHA matters — incorrect mortgage inquiries, perhaps, or mistakes over disability benefits?

Some of these categories are effectively obsolete, but while the central records system is far and away the biggest FBI filing system, it is not the only one the Bureau uses. For instance, with the Bureau's help, the Department of Justice maintains a system known as the "Congressional and White House Referral Correspondence Log File," which contains details on present and former members of Congress, and on citizens whose correspondence is received directly or indirectly by members of Congress or congressional or White House staff. In other words, anyone who has ever written to his or her congressman can be named in a file accessible to the FBI.

All this is in addition to the NCIC, which as noted, contains a comprehensive record of a vast array of criminal investigations and prosecutions pursued by city, county, state, and federal law enforcement agencies, plus lists of stolen cars, boats, airplanes, guns, missing people, and so forth. The NCIC is one of the most useful tools American police have at their disposal, and it is inconceivable that they could manage without it, but one should bear in mind that this system contains details about millions of minor traffic violations as well as more serious crimes. If anyone has ever had a speeding ticket, the records should be in the NCIC at the FBI's disposal.

Whether or not any of this should be regarded as sinister is open to question. Many people believe that the FBI needs all the help it can get and that as responsible members of society they should not be worried that information about them is lodged somewhere in the Bureau's records. After all, their personal information is just as likely to be recorded at their bank, the IRS, and the Social Security Administration. Others believe that those who have never been investigated or convicted of any crime shouldn't be listed in any law enforcement files, no matter how innocent the reference.

The FBI points out that there are stringent legal safeguards on how the material is used. Many agents also take issue with the very word *file*, which they say conjures up an ominous image of thick dossiers packed full of intriguing information, whereas the reality in most noninvestigative cases is little more than a name, a date of birth, and an address.

The Bureau's ultimate argument, of course, is that it has neither the time, the money, nor the inclination to compile dossiers on even a tiny proportion of the American public. Agents smile wearily when asked about the files and suggest that anyone who is skeptical spend a few days watching them work through a backlog of real cases to see what they have to contend with. One even said, "To be honest, I find the suggestion that I or any of my colleagues might want to waste our time trawling through the private lives of law-abiding citizens deeply offensive. If they have broken the law, that's another matter, but if they haven't, then what is supposed to be in it for me? I believe in the Constitution as much as they do anyway — probably more, as it happens. I go to work to defend it every day. That file stuff is all just so much paranoid garbage."

Cynics, however, note that times and attitudes change, and even though the people who run the Bureau today may be fine, morally upstanding supporters of the Constitution, the people who run it tomorrow may not. Hoover showed that one person was able to use the fruits of a vast information-gathering apparatus for his own purposes. Given the Bureau's increasing technological sophistication, it is chilling to think of how much greater the potential for future abuse might be.

The more the FBI relies on this massive information mountain, the more important it becomes that the records be reliable. Unfortunately, with systems this size it is difficult to ensure that every entry is up to date and accurate — particularly in NCIC, which depends on the input of thousands of people in police agencies across the country. How many times has someone been arrested for a crime and then subsequently released without charge, and how many times has the correct disposition of that case not been recorded on the computer? How many arrest warrants have lapsed without notation on NCIC? How many innocent people have been arrested because they share a hometown and a name with a wanted criminal? Unfortunately, the answer to all these questions is the same: too many.

Terry Dean Rogan's case is typical. An unemployed part-time student in Saginaw, Michigan, Rogan lost his wallet one day. Among the few bills and documents was his driver's license. Like a good citizen, he reported its loss to the police and requested a new one through the proper channels.

A few months later Rogan was spending the evening with his girlfriend when they got into a heated argument. She called the police, who turned up and asked him to leave the house so the situation could cool down a little. It was snowing outside and he was furious with his girlfriend for bringing the law into their domestic problems, so he refused. The police officer, who probably felt he had better things to do than stand around arbitrating a family dispute, called his dispatcher for advice. After the conversation his attitude changed dramatically.

"He started reaching out to grab me," said Rogan, "and he was trying to handcuff me, and then another one came behind me and put a flashlight around my neck, and they pushed me down on the bed and sprayed Mace in my eyes. Then they handcuffed me and carried me out to the car."

On the way to the station, one of the officers turned to Rogan and asked if he had ever been to California. When Rogan said that he had not, the officer told him that there was an outstanding arrest warrant on armed robbery and murder charges for him in that state. Rogan spent the rest of the journey in dumbstruck silence.

At the station he was fingerprinted, photographed, and questioned. Did he have a tattoo on his chest? How tall was he? Had he ever been to Los Angeles? Rogan tried to explain that he had no tattoo and had never been to California. They must have the wrong guy. Perhaps his lost driver's license had fallen into the wrong hands?

Eventually he managed to persuade a detective to check with California, but he spent a further three days in custody before the police were convinced they had the wrong man.

Terry Dean Rogan was an ordinary citizen with ordinary problems, but he had never been in trouble with the law before, and his time in jail was a frightening experience. Nor did it do much for his romantic life. When he got out, his girlfriend was nervous about seeing him, and it took some time before he could convince her that the police had picked up the wrong person.

A few weeks later he was out with his brother-in-law when five police cars screeched to a halt around his car. Suddenly he found himself surrounded by officers who were aiming shotguns and automatic pistols at his head. They made him climb out of the car and spread his arms on the hood while one went away to do a document check. A few minutes later the officer came back looking slightly abashed and told him he was free to go. A few weeks after that, the same thing happened again, although this time he spent five hours in the county jail while his identity was checked out.

Not surprisingly, Rogan was getting angry about these frequent and very unwelcome intrusions by the police into his life. He went to his local police station to complain, and they suggested he see the local FBI. Down at the Saginaw resident agency he explained his problem to Special Agent Peter Engley, who agreed to check his name in the NCIC. After a few minutes he confirmed that a man with the name Terry Dean Rogan was wanted in California, and he agreed that someone was probably using Rogan's lost driver's license. However, Engley also said that until the fugitive was caught, Rogan's name would have to remain on the computer.

Eventually the worried Rogan managed to persuade the local police to give him a letter and a copy of the arrest warrant for the man who had usurped his identity. Shortly afterward, he went looking for work down in Texas. A few miles over the Oklahoma border he was stopped by a Texas Ranger.

"He asked for my ID," said Rogan, "and then he came back with his pistol pointing at me and told me to get out of the car. He says, 'There's a warrant out for you, a life sentence for armed robbery and murder.' I says, 'Oh man, I ain't the guy,' and I took out the paper the police had given me. He looks at it and says, 'OK, but I still got to take you in.' So he took me down to the station and handcuffed me to something and I had to wait four hours until they cleared it all up."

In the meantime, Rogan's friends, neighbors, and employers began to shun him because he always seemed to be in trouble with the law. Sometimes he couldn't face leaving the house since people pointed at him in the street. His parents became very worried about him and even began to wonder if he was telling them the truth.

After several months, the right man was arrested and Terry Dean Rogan's name was taken off the NCIC fugitive list. Not long after that, Rogan successfully sued the authorities for the distress the problem had caused him and received fifty thousand dollars in compensation. But he still may be on file — all his arrests were undoubtedly entered into the computer, and he hasn't yet been able to find out if those records have been expunged.

Such cases are not uncommon. Sheila Jackson Stossier, an Eastern Airlines flight attendant, was arrested coming through customs at New Orleans after a flight from Mexico. She spent three days in jail before she could convince the authorities that the NCIC information that was the basis of her arrest was for a woman with a similar name. Dr. Richard Sklar was arrested and held in prison for two days in California on the basis of a warrant issued against someone who had assumed his identity. Dorothy Sullivan, of Carlsbad, New Mexico, was arrested on suspicion of being a fugitive wanted in a grand theft case, even though her eyes, hair, weight, height, date of birth, and driver's license number were all different from those on the warrant. Suke Omere Emma, a graduate student in Boston, was arrested for stealing a car, even though the car in question had never been stolen. Dale Ray, of Chula Vista, California, was returning from a vacation in England when customs officers at Los Angeles International Airport turned up a warrant for child stealing in San Diego County. He had to go to jail before he could prove it was a case of mistaken identity.

The Bureau, after much criticism, has tried to amend the flaws in the system that lead to such mistakes, and it is in the final stages of testing a new computer called NCIC 2000. Even faster and more sophisticated than the current NCIC, it will be able to transmit photographs and fingerprints directly to NCIC terminals and even to police cars, which should eliminate most of the mistaken identity cases. But this system is still some way from coming on line.

When it does, NCIC 2000 should also address the potential threat from computer hackers, another visible problem. The system is now so vital a part of day-to-day law enforcement activity that any disruption to it would create havoc. With thousands of terminals and hundreds of thousands of users, the potential for malicious damage is enormous. It is not beyond the bounds of possibility that one corrupt or disaffected agent, police officer, or technician with the right expertise could insert a virus into the system and cause chaos. If this sounds implausible, consider that in 1988 hundreds of man-hours and hundreds of thousands of dollars were spent repairing the damage caused when a hacker inserted a virus into computers operated by the Environmental Protection Agency, NASA, the National Oceanic and Atmospheric Administration, and the United States Sentencing Commission. All these systems had high levels of security.

What NCIC 2000 won't be able to guard against, of course, is abuse by authorized users. The FBI is strangely quiet about this problem, although Nemecek said, "We don't believe NCIC has ever been cracked. We have no evidence for it, and we look for that a lot."

He seems as sure about the security of the FBI's internal system as he is about the NCIC. "It has as much security as the highest secrets the government has. We have a variety of protections. Obviously, I'm not going to describe them all, but we have software protection, we have protection that relates to background investigations of our personnel, we have a lot of oversight, a lot of checks and balances. We have audit trails — a team of nine people checks every access request — and we have periodic inquiries of those audit trails. We have a variety of surprise inspections, encryption. The list goes on and on."

Unfortunately, these safeguards do not seem to be working, either for the internal system or the NCIC. There is direct evidence that NCIC is penetrated regularly and indirect evidence that the FBI's own system has been targeted at least once.

The clearest evidence of how the FBI's files have been penetrated comes from a man called Allen Schweitzer. His case shows that despite sophisticated security measures, secret, official, and classified information is regularly bought and sold by people who have no legal right to it. It is an intriguing story, because of what it reveals

about the FBI's determination to guard its own and other government files, and because it provides fascinating insight into the way
the Bureau handles investigations that might be embarrassing to the
agency.

By December 18, 1991, Schweitzer had been working for ten years
as a private detective, and he knew how to handle the unexpected.
The ability to adapt, to think on his feet and to talk his way out of
a corner, was a prerequisite of his chosen career. The trick, or so he
had learned, was to look for the advantage in any situation, no
matter how unfavorable it might seem at first. But at 6:30 in the
morning, with a posse of determined-looking FBI agents standing on
his front steps asking his five-year-old daughter if he was at home,
that might be difficult. It was obvious from the agents' demeanor
that it was not a social call.

Schweitzer got up from his couch to greet the agents as they came
in. There were nine in all, brandishing warrants and credentials but
no guns. If the men were armed, they weren't making it obvious;
indeed the atmosphere was calm, orderly, and very polite. He recognized one or two faces. Four months earlier the same men had
appeared, asking questions for a vague and unspecified "administrative inquiry." Now they had a warrant for his arrest. Ten minutes
later, after a brief discussion with the agents and some quiet words
with his wife, Schweitzer pulled on his coat and slipped into the
back seat of a Bureau car. It was only a short trip downtown to the
U.S. marshal's office, in Sumner, Washington.

A few blocks away on Main Street, a second team of agents was
climbing the stairs to a two-room suite above Sharkey's Bar, a popular Sumner watering hole. A sign outside told them they were at the
corporate headquarters of the Security Group. Few of them spared
it a glance. They knew exactly where they were; Schweitzer's office
had been under surveillance for some time. Within minutes they
were through the door and into the inner office. As one agent began
to leaf through the correspondence and notebooks on Schweitzer's
desk, a second pulled open the top drawer of an adjacent filing
cabinet; a third began unplugging the cables and wires that ran from
the back of a desktop PC to the wall.

A little over an hour later, after his attorney had arranged bail,
Schweitzer arrived at the Main Street office. He met a startling
sight. The room had been stripped. Agents were manhandling his

filing cabinets out the door, his prized computers sat on the floor awaiting collection, and even his telephone system had been dismantled. Outside the building a large truck was being loaded with equipment and documents. By the end of the morning, all that remained of Schweitzer's empire was an old army helmet and a few sticks of furniture. The FBI had shut him down.

By the time he was arrested, Schweitzer had made himself an extraordinary reputation and millions of dollars peddling confidential data to anyone with enough money to buy his services. As one of the United States' top "info-investigators," he had made a joke out of the FBI's claim to have an impenetrable security wall around its most sensitive filing systems. In the process, he showed how frighteningly easy it can be to gain access to both government and commercial secrets and how widespread the private practice of covert information-gathering has become.

Thirty-three years old, with spiky black hair, a mustache, and a broad smile, Al Schweitzer is a long way from Philip Marlowe or Thomas Magnum. Even though he has had a full private investigator's license since 1986, he's done little actual sleuthing in the conventional sense. Not for him the long hours on stakeout, the tailing of suspects, or shadowy meetings in hotel bars. Schweitzer's techniques and tools belong firmly in the late twentieth century. He deploys the telephone, the fax, and the personal computer to get what he needs. Hard-to-get information has always been his specialty, and he is one of the best in the business.

Like many people who operate on the fringes of the clandestine world, Schweitzer began his career conventionally enough, in the army. He left the military in 1980 with no real ambitions or plans and drifted around California for a while, going from job to job. It wasn't until he became an apprentice P.I. working with a police narcotics squad and corporate investigators in Silicon Valley that he found his métier. In the process he learned two vital lessons. One was that confidential data is a valuable and much sought-after commodity, as tradable as any stock or bond. The second was more practical — that there were much easier and more efficient ways to gather this information than by trailing around asking questions all day.

Schweitzer realized that the simplest and potentially most profitable route into the information business lay in developing a network of inside sources: people who worked for private utility or phone companies like AT&T and Bell systems; employees of credit bureaus, banks, local government, hospitals; and most important, law enforcement people. He learned that a little money wisely spent would bring results, that there are always people in any organization who can use a little extra cash. Gradually, after months of work he began to accumulate contacts. Some came easily, others were hard to spot, but the numbers grew. In the process Schweitzer became a keen student of human nature, learning how to pick out the greedy, the vulnerable, and the corrupt. One of his favorite tricks was to haunt the parking lots of target organizations, noting the license numbers of the shabbier cars, and then tracking down the owners to see if they were susceptible to a bribe. A surprising number of them were — and of course, once they were "on the team" it was hard for them to get off.

It wasn't long before Schweitzer was able to set himself up in business. In 1986 he and his wife, Petra, opened their first company, the Information Desk, in the suburbs of Seattle, Washington. It offered a discreet and prompt service to a variety of private clients, from other investigators and quasi-governmental organizations, to newspapers, hotels, airlines, insurance companies, and other major corporations. As Schweitzer's contacts throughout industry, law enforcement, and government grew, so did the amount and variety of information that he was able to deliver. Social Security numbers, unlisted addresses and phone numbers, bank account details, credit backgrounds, medical histories — there was a market for them all. When his sources failed him, Schweitzer would fall back on his acting skills, pretending to be a repairman calling up a phone company for an address, or posing as a payroll clerk seeking information from the out-of-state division of a company. He was able to garner much of what he sought from public sources such as the property register in a local tax assessor's office, voter registration files, and court records.

As his business grew, Schweitzer recruited others to work for him, people with an ability to sound plausible on the phone or a nose for a potential source. Inevitably, after learning many of his secrets, they would leave him and set up businesses of their own in other cities. This never bothered Schweitzer much; there were always enough clients to go around, and they always paid well. He says some of his most lucrative customers were tabloid newspapers such as the *National Enquirer* and magazines such as *Playboy*, whose appetites for the details about the private lives of the great and glamorous were insatiable. Even today Schweitzer boasts proudly of the directory of information about many Hollywood stars which he compiled for his media clients. Want to find out where Madonna will be next weekend? Schweitzer would know how to find out.

As profitable as this business was, any reasonably well connected P.I. could obtain information of this nature. Schweitzer's particular genius lay in his talent for getting inside supposedly secure government data systems like those of the IRS and the Social Security Administration. Most startling was his ability to penetrate law enforcement systems such as the NCIC and the FBI's internal case-filing system, possibly the most sensitive database in the United States.

As Schweitzer described it in a television documentary, the process of doing business was slick, fast, and effective. His company had a brochure with page after page of numbered codes, each one corresponding to a service his company offered. Clients looked through the brochure and decided whether they wanted a driver's license printout, a credit report, some NCIC criminal history data, or one of the other services the company offered. They would then fax a coded order to Schweitzer, who would obtain the information and send it back with a similarly coded invoice.

"If a client wanted NCIC or criminal history information," said Schweitzer, "they would give me the name and date of birth, and sometimes the Social Security number, which is helpful if you have a John Smith or whatever. At the end of the day, typically, I'd have one request, two requests, maybe ten requests for NCIC information, and I would call one of my sources within the law enforcement community, whether it be in the state police, the local police, or in a federal law enforcement agency. I'd give him the subject's information and I would get it back from him the next morning via the fax." He pulled out a piece of paper to demonstrate.

"This is an actual computer printout, not a fax copy. This came right out of the computer. And it provides quite a detailed synopsis of this individual's criminal history; his name, date of birth, physical description, height, weight, color of hair. It's got his FBI number, any aliases that he might use, the fingerprint codes, Social Security number. And then it goes into the detail of his arrest record. For instance, in 1977 he was arrested for drunk driving . . . then it tells the disposition of that — he pleaded guilty. Then there's several more arrests for drunk driving; it gives the dates and what agency arrested him. Then we go to 1978 — he was arrested for grand theft of property, and they declined prosecution on that, then he was arrested for drunk driving again. But it's very detailed. It can be your entire criminal history, whether you were arrested thirty years ago or twenty years ago. Sometimes they are not entirely accurate; they don't always tell you the disposition or the outcome of the arrest. But for the most part the NCIC is the best system there is."

Schweitzer continued, "The NCIC computer system is supposedly policed by the FBI. They are supposed to maintain its integrity. But they are not doing their job. I mean, almost every private eye in the country has access to this in one way, shape, or form, either through a broker like me, or because they have their own law enforcement sources.

"There are three kinds of sources. There's the one that'll do it because he owes you a favor, one that does it because he's your friend and he's helping you out, and then there's the guy who does it for money. All my people did it for the money."

The price for breaking into one of the world's most sophisticated criminal records systems and obtaining this information was surprisingly low. Schweitzer said that the average charges to the customer for each item of information ordered from him ranged from thirty dollars for standard Social Security data to fifty dollars for individual criminal history reports from NCIC. More sensitive information in other systems was harder to obtain and therefore cost more.

According to Schweitzer, it is almost as easy for his sources to get the information as it is for him to ask for it. "In some departments they require you to enter a case number as well as your badge number," he explained, "but that's easily avoidable. I mean, how difficult is it to put somebody else's badge number in, or to go to a substation where you are the only officer on shift? Any officer within that department can walk up to the terminal, type in his request, and receive it in seconds. Unless the FBI is policing each and every one of those terminals on a constant basis and auditing on a continuing basis, there's widespread abuse."

Schweitzer alleges that despite its public statements to the contrary, the FBI not only tacitly accepts that NCIC is compromised, it knows that the system is most frequently abused by its own former agents, who make up 70–80 percent of private investigators — Schweitzer's major clients. Even more astonishing are his claims that current agents have used his services to get information that would take them considerably longer to find through legal channels.

"In a lot of cases, law enforcement would come to me — both directly and indirectly through former agents, who would then get the information from me and pass it back — and ask me for stuff they didn't have access to legally. They'd have to get a subpoena, it would take thirty days, but I could have it in minutes for them — unlisted phone numbers, telephone toll records, that kind of thing."

This claim may help to explain why neither of Schweitzer's two brushes with the law directly concerned possible abuse by law enforcement personnel and the FBI of the NCIC. The first arrest came in 1988, when Schweitzer was trying to get access to the IRS computer system. His marriage was on hold at the time, and a girlfriend introduced him to a possible informant. It was a setup. The contact turned him in and he was indicted. For reasons that aren't too clear (he is careful not to be too specific) he was able to negotiate a deal and avoid going to prison. The only conditions of that deal were that he would avoid any further violations for a year, and for six months he would "provide full and complete cooperation with the IRS and the FBI with respect to any unauthorized disclosure of, and/or access to, taxpayer information or confidential investigative files of those or other federal agencies." In other words, he had to inform on and thereby close down some of his competitors. Of course, the opportunity this gave Schweitzer to manipulate the information market to his advantage was too good to miss.

However, that condition doesn't really explain the apparent leniency with which he was treated. Was it because he had carefully secreted away details of all his contacts and sources in all parts of the government? He won't say, but it is interesting to speculate on the extensive litigation that might have ensued if some of America's most prominent citizens had been informed through a "show trial" that the government had allowed their ostensibly personal files to be freely obtained by Schweitzer and his kind. It could have been an embarrassing revelation on its own, but it would have been doubly damaging if Schweitzer had revealed in court that former FBI agents were among his best customers.

Schweitzer's big mistake in the aftermath of that case was to push his luck. After the six months were up he was short of ready cash. The Information Desk had folded, and his bargaining had cost a small fortune in legal fees. So he started afresh, this time with a company called the Security Group. He began trading profitably almost immediately, and his former clients welcomed him back with open arms.

This time around not even the FBI could ignore what was going on. Schweitzer was getting a little too big for his britches and clearly would have to be reined in. The opportunity came when the Bureau's Newark, New Jersey, office opened an investigation into privacy abuse. In 1991 one of his clients, a former FBI agent who was cooperating with the Justice Department, asked Schweitzer to get some Social Security data. He took the bait. The dawn raid on his offices in Sumner and his trip down to the U.S. marshal's office were the outcome.

When the fruits of the Newark investigation were exposed to public scrutiny in court, the Justice Department called the operation "one of the most important computer fraud cases in history." Seventeen people were indicted and pleaded guilty. Yet despite the hyperbole, only three of them (including Schweitzer and his wife, Petra) received jail sentences. No mention was made in Schweitzer's indictment of any NCIC penetration, and interestingly, none of his clients was ever approached or interviewed even though the Bureau had impounded many of his records and knew who they were. Schweitzer believes that the reason for this can be found in his customer list.

"You have got to remember who they were, as illegal as it may be: corporate America, the major insurance companies, airlines, magazines, the federal government itself. There are a lot of former federal agents involved in this industry, in the buying and selling of confidential information, who are not being prosecuted. The very day that the FBI raided my office, the agents found documents on my desk implicating two of their former colleagues. They haven't even been looked at."

Why is it that despite Schweitzer's frank admission that he was able to penetrate NCIC successfully, and that he made hundreds of thousands of dollars on NCIC requests alone, the FBI seems unwilling to prosecute him for these actions? Is it because the Bureau doesn't take him seriously? Apparently not. After being found guilty in the Newark case, Schweitzer was sentenced to fourteen months in jail. He appealed and managed to get his sentence reduced to four years' probation and five hundred hours of community service. He says that the appeal was successful because he agreed to a request from the Department of Justice and the FBI that he conduct a seminar for them on how to protect the privacy of their records.

The Bureau may simply not want to advertise its failings in public. On July 6, 1992, Schweitzer received a letter from the House Subcommittee on Civil and Constitutional Rights asking him to testify before a hearing "focusing on the sale of criminal history records," due to take place on July 29 in Washington, D.C. The day before he was to catch a plane from Seattle to attend the hearing, a committee official left a message on his answering machine. The official said he was withdrawing Schweitzer's invitation because it was causing the committee too many embarrassing problems with the Department of Justice. As Schweitzer pointed out, "When did the FBI start picking and choosing who testifies in front of the U.S. Congress?"

It might also be that a congressional probe might have had to deal with Schweitzer's claims that he had penetrated not only the NCIC but also the Bureau's internal and highly classified investigative files. As he said, "Once you become a member of the clique everything is accessible in some shape or form. You may not be able to get the actual documents . . . but you can get the information. Obviously, the more sensitive the investigation — if we're talking about intelligence matters, or domestic intelligence — then it's going to be a little bit more difficult, but they too can be had."

If what Schweitzer says is true (and he claims he has had access to the FBI's organized crime intelligence system "and others"), then what is the public to make of the Bureau's claims about the security of its files? If a private corporation can easily buy such information, then what is to stop a Mafia family, a terrorist organization, or a hostile foreign government from using the same route? How much classified government data has fallen into the wrong hands in this way?

Schweitzer remains unrepentant, and claims that his information has helped locate missing people and clear up unsolved crimes. He now believes that he is being made a scapegoat to warn off others in the same business. He doesn't think it will work; the underground information network is too entrenched.

"They're trying to make an example out of somebody. They have to blame someone, so they blame me for the total U.S. privacy crisis," he said. "I'm just one guy. Heck, the first thing that happened after I got indicted is that all the other brokers or people involved in this industry went after my clients. It hasn't changed — the law hasn't changed, the scale of the operations hasn't changed . . . There is no security as long as the old-boy network is effective, meaning that most of the private eyes in this country are former law enforcement from some level: city, state, county, or federal. That's your membership card into this clique, the old-boy network, and as long as that's allowed to exist and people turn a blind eye to it, the information will continue to be shared illegally."

Al Schweitzer doesn't invite much sympathy; after all, he freely confesses to acting illegally. But clearly he is not the only one breaking the law in this way, and that fact is worrying. Even the Government Accounting Office has recognized this as a problem. In a recent review it gave a number of examples. In Arizona, a former police officer persuaded his ex-colleagues to get NCIC data, and he used it to hunt down and murder his girlfriend. An NCIC operator in Pennsylvania conducted background searches for her boyfriend, a drug dealer, who wanted to know if any of his potential clients were undercover officers.

So where does this leave David Nemecek's statements about the security of the FBI's computer systems? Questioned about a case involving a Chicago police officer named William Pederson who was prosecuted for selling criminal history data, Nemecek reluctantly conceded that the system was fallible but also pointed out that the case demonstrated how swift and vigilant the Bureau was in dealing with such abuses. "All I can say is that when it does happen, we take action," he said. "It's rather like saying that if we pass a law against something making it a crime, we have stopped the crime. If there is a person who is willing to violate the law, then you have to deal with that violation, and we responded very quickly in this case. We sent a message to all those who would consider doing it again."

The accuracy and security of the FBI's files are not the only worrying things about them. What about people who have committed no crime and have had no association with any crime or criminals, however innocently, but are in the FBI's files because of their beliefs, their jobs, or their association with organizations or ideologies the FBI considers potentially subversive? From the very earliest days, the agency has made a point of keeping tabs on Communist and left-wing sympathizers, political radicals and dissidents of all persuasions, opponents of the government's foreign policies, even people who just work for organizations that have taken a stand against the government in some way.

The agency's justification, when asked to account for this, has always been the same: since it has a mandate to look after the national security of the United States, the FBI has to investigate anyone who might pose a threat to that security. Such investigations, it says, may be based on an initial suspicion, but they do not make any assumption of guilt or intent, and innocent people have nothing to fear. If there is no case, then the investigations are completed and the files are closed.

The Bureau also points out that investigations based purely on someone's political beliefs, which were such a feature of the Hoover era, are no longer allowed, and subversion as an investigative category no longer officially exists. For agents to open an investigation of this sort there has to be a strong and justifiable suspicion that a crime has taken or is about to take place. When that suspicion involves a radical political group or individual, it usually means suspicion of terrorism.

Obviously, for most of the Bureau's history such safeguards did not exist. Millions of Americans were investigated simply because they chose to exercise their right of free speech by expressing ideas that ran counter to the prevailing political philosophy. They were considered dangerous because their views didn't fall into the narrow political spectrum of the establishment. And though the Bureau insists that it would never conduct any such investigations today, a loophole allows it to do just that.

Even now, if an investigation is opened under the FBI's foreign counterintelligence guidelines, there does not have to be any suspicion of crime. For instance, the FBI can investigate American citizens perfectly legitimately and without any clear suspicion of wrongdoing if they have come into contact with agencies or individuals from a potentially hostile foreign power. This sounds reasonably straightforward until one realizes that in the not too distant past it encompassed people who visited an Aeroflot office to ask for a travel brochure about the USSR, schoolchildren who wrote to pen pals in Poland, human rights campaigners who took part in a postcard campaign protesting the Chinese government's repression of the Tiananmen Square dissidents, and businesspeople who exported goods to the Middle East. The vast majority of these people were then and are now loyal citizens of the United States and would no more turn crook, spy, terrorist, or revolutionary than the agents who investigated them, yet they will have files on the FBI's computer.

There are many contemporary examples of this kind of investigation. The case of Lance Lindblom and the J. Roderick MacArthur Foundation is fairly typical. It shows how, despite all the guidelines and safeguards that are supposed to govern the way the Bureau operates, the most innocent people can still end up with an FBI dossier.

The J. Roderick MacArthur Foundation is based in Niles, Illinois, and was set up in 1976 as a philanthropic institution to provide financial and legal support to human rights and civil liberties groups. Although it deals with many such organizations in the United States, a great deal of its work has been aimed at parts of the world with a record of suppressing free expression and political dissidents: Central and South America, the former Soviet Union and Eastern bloc, and North and South Korea, to name a few. It has more than $26 million at its disposal and in an average year gives more than $2 million of that away to deserving causes.

There is nothing particularly startling about the foundation's work; the United States has any number of similar institutions, staffed by well-meaning people who care enough about free speech and civil liberties to devote their lives to the support of causes that might otherwise languish on the fringes of the political debate. Most of them try to steer clear of public controversy and would run a mile from any suggestion that they are motivated by any overtly political agenda, be it left-wing or right-wing.

In 1988 the J. Roderick MacArthur Foundation and Lance Lindblom, its mild-mannered chief executive, had some dealings with the New York–based Center for Constitutional Rights, which was representing the Committee in Solidarity with the People of El Salvador and other activist groups in lawsuits against the FBI, which had been monitoring their activities. As Lindblom later stated, his foundation was interested in learning about some of the CCR's techniques.

"The Center for Constitutional Rights was doing a routine Freedom of Information Act request on FBI investigations regarding Central America," he said, "and they came up with the fact that there were twelve foundations like ours that had FBI files. We weren't one of them, but we asked, 'Just so we can know how to do these things on a practical level, should we ever need to know, can you show us how to put a FOIA request in?' And so they said, 'Sure, we'll do one for you.' Anyway, they did, and up we came. All that it revealed was that the foundation was cross-referenced to another file. Of course we wanted to know what that other file was. When we asked the FBI about it, they said they couldn't tell us because of national security."

So the foundation, following the advice of its colleagues in New York, tried another tack. It put in a request that listed the names of all the senior people in the organization. This time Lindblom's name hit the bull's-eye, although again it was cross-referenced to other files and again the foundation had no idea what those other files were.

Lindblom did learn that he would be getting some documents from the FOIA request. Not surprisingly, he waited with eager anticipation — after all, it wasn't every day that he found out the Bureau had been investigating him. But like many other people who have gone through the same process, he was to be disappointed. Of the nineteen documents that were sent to him, only a few scrappy sentences remained. The rest had been blacked out, on the grounds that the FBI has a right to protect national security and keep its law enforcement investigations secret.

When the incredulous Lindblom asked what justification the Bureau had to keep *his* documents secret, he received the same response that hundreds of others were given throughout the 1980s — that the FBI had authorization under Executive Order 12333. This directive, issued by President Ronald Reagan in 1981, gave the agency expanded authority to conduct domestic security investigations and to keep them secret. As Lindblom noted, "It's Kafkaesque. They allude to this order as their authorization, but there's no way to check out if it is legitimate because most of the order is classified." The FBI also cited a number of provisions in the Freedom of Information Act itself which allow the government to keep certain material confidential, to protect national defense and foreign policy interests, to shield the names of FBI informants, and to maintain the confidentiality of agency personnel records.

After considering the options, Lindblom decided to sue the FBI to obtain his records. Since his foundation spent much of its time fighting government intrusion against the First Amendment rights of others, he felt obliged to pursue his own case through the courts, and he hoped it would be a test case for challenging the FBI's secret files.

Not surprisingly, civil libertarians across the United States agreed with Lindblom and put their weight behind the suit; dozens of other philanthropic foundations that knew or claimed to know that they too had FBI files offered support. The petition, filed in December 1990 by the American Civil Liberties Union on behalf of the foundation, charged that by keeping files on Lindblom, the FBI had created a "reasonable inference of FBI surveillance" that inhibited Lindblom's ability to conduct the foundation's work for civil liberties and human rights. Furthermore, it said, the agency's investigation and file-keeping "prevents and otherwise chills" others from freely communicating or associating with Lindblom and the foundation, and it asked that the FBI hand over all original documents on Lindblom uncensored and destroy the file copies.

Even though Lindblom has now left the foundation (in 1993 he became a visiting fellow at De Paul University in Chicago), he and the ACLU are still pressing the suit, although the Bureau has filed a countermotion for dismissal and the case may drag on for years. In the meantime he has been searching his past for any possible reason why he or the foundation might have been under scrutiny. The censored documents he does have seem to refer to the period between January and May 1985, but there is not much else to go on. One of the few clear sentences reads "LINDBLOM described as white male, DOB 6/17/48"; another cites a paragraph from a column in the *Chicago Sun-Times* in which Lindblom is quoted as saying he was "very concerned" about the safety of a South Korean political dissident, Kim Dae Jung, who was sent back to South Korea from the United States in 1985.

When Kim returned to Seoul, Lindblom was one of a number of U.S. citizens, including congressmen, diplomats, and journalists, who accompanied him to help protect him from assassination. The group was roughed up by Korean security police when they arrived at the city's airport; Kim was put under house arrest, and the civil libertarians were asked to leave the country. Others who made the trip have subsequently looked into the possibility that they might be on file at the FBI, although because of the lengthy FOIA process no new information has as yet come to light. However, the Bureau maintains close links with the South Korean police and intelligence services (as it does with all the United States' allies around the world), and there are a number of recorded instances of agents being asked by superiors to gather discreet information on "potential terrorists" to pass on to agencies of foreign powers. It seems probable that if and when Lindblom's file is ever released uncensored, it will show that his record has been compiled for such a reason.

Lindblom's case concerns one of the central dilemmas about the FBI and what it does. The Bureau has a mandate to protect the nation against the hostile intelligence efforts of others and to prevent acts of terrorism. To do that, it must collect information, often about innocent people who may not realize that they have been in contact with others who are not so honest or honorable. The Bureau says that it keeps this information secret to protect the innocence and reputation of law-abiding citizens who are caught up in an investigation. It admits that it shares some of this information with other governments, but points out that for the United States to be effective in combating the IRA or the ETA or the Red Army Faction or the pro-Palestinian terrorists, or any other terrorists, it has to be able to work closely with its allies. It is not the FBI's responsibility, it says, to decide who those allies should be.

Agents also point out that it is all very well for people like Lance Lindblom and his foundation to kick up a fuss, but they can't have it both ways. Lindblom is claiming that his and the J. Roderick MacArthur Foundation's reputations are being damaged in the eyes of others by the FBI's interest, but at the same time he is pursuing a course of action that is bringing the existence of the file to the attention of more and more people. Lindblom knows this is problematic. "But there is a moral imperative here," he said. "If we have fought this stuff around the world, we shouldn't let it happen to us here in the United States. This is the kind of thing we were trying to stop with the Stasi in East Germany. It's back to J. Edgar Hoover's secret files again."

Arguments like these have been raging for as long as the FBI has been conducting investigations of political and social action groups and will no doubt continue as long as the Bureau remains in existence. At various times attempts have been made by the ACLU and liberal politicians to get an FBI charter enshrined in law and in so doing provide a stricter legal framework for the Bureau to operate under. Key principles of their proposals have been that the FBI's investigative mandate should be strictly confined to criminal matters and that the agency should not be allowed to collect or hold information on anyone who is not guilty of or suspected of a crime. The FBI, in response, argues that its activities are already heavily regulated by legislation and that a charter would stop it from operating effectively. So far, every attempt to persuade the Bureau otherwise has failed, and the charter proposals have never made it onto a statute book. In the meantime, the filing goes on.

CHAPTER 6

DALLAS — THE FIELD IN ACTION

THE GROUP OF AGENTS lingering in the gloomy half-light of a basement garage looked like somebody's worst nightmare. Clad from head to toe in all-black combat fatigues and clutching weapons that would make Rambo envious, they were painstakingly checking radios and ammunition, belt buckles and bootlaces. One by one they slipped body armor jackets over their heads, hung goggles around their necks, and picked up their bulletproof helmets. Occasionally one of them yawned or cracked a quiet joke. Their faces revealed tension and lack of sleep. It was just after 4:45 in the morning, and the Dallas FBI SWAT unit was about to go operational.

As the team leader, Biff Temple, went over street maps and plans with his section chiefs, the others looked over their guns. Most carried 9mm SIG pistols, although a few hefted pump-action shotguns or Heckler and Koch MP-5 submachine guns. Each weapon had already been cleaned, oiled, and loaded with lavish attention, but the members of the unit had been trained never to take anything for granted. These last-minute preparations were a ritual anyway, giving them a few brief moments to steady their nerves and brace themselves for what was to come. But it was not always easy. Too much hanging around could be counterproductive, giving them too much time to dwell on the risks, too much time to think of injury and death. They wanted to be on their way.

As the hands on the clock moved around to 5:15, the agents climbed into their vehicles. Those on the Gold Team boarded the jet black SWAT van, emblazoned, like their uniforms, with a simple FBI logo. They squeezed past the cases of tear gas and spare flak jackets and sat with their backs to a partition. On it were stamped the ominous words BODY BUNKER. As the door was dragged shut, one man gave a thumbs-up sign to a colleague a few feet away. Agents in the other sections, already sweating under the weight of forty pounds of body armor and equipment, clambered incongruously into ordinary family sedans and station wagons.

The lead car moved toward the steel-shuttered entrance. The driver pressed the "transmit" switch on his mobile radio to activate the gate. Gradually the cars and vans passed up the ramp into the darkness beyond. A few minutes later, the convoy had gone. The shutters clanked gently shut and the garage fell almost silent, the only sound the office air conditioning units working to cope with the brewing Texas heat. It was going to be another hot day.

Two days earlier, Biff Temple had briefed his team in a sparsely furnished first-floor conference room at the Dallas FBI offices. A sandy-haired, muscular man, casually but neatly dressed in a blue-striped polo shirt and chinos, he stood at the front of the room and glanced up from his papers to the twenty or so agents gathered in front of him. In a flat, terse voice he dispensed names, times, and locations. The agents diligently took notes.

The job was a joint operation among the IRS, the Dallas County Sheriff's Office, U.S. Customs, the Drug Enforcement Administration, and the FBI against a suspected drug ring. A large number of arrests were going to be made at five locations. The arrests at three of the locations promised to be difficult, since the suspects had a record of violence. The FBI SWAT (special weapons and tactics) team had responsibility for one of the three; tactical teams from the Dallas police and Customs would handle the other two.

"The address of our location is 5207 Beman," Temple began. "Once we are there, we have two arrest warrants. One for a Rozario Zapata, Hispanic female, approximately forty years old. We have an arrest warrant also for her son, Marco Zapata, Hispanic male. We've got photographs and physical descriptions that we'll pass out now . . . One thing you might want to note about Marco, who is sometimes called Chicky, is that during this investigation he pursued one of the agents working this thing and chased him from the scene and fired a couple of shots at him. So we've got the potential for an A&D [armed and dangerous] subject."

He let the agents absorb this, then added that there might be other people in the house, including a Valentino Jiminez, for whom there were local warrants. Jiminez should be treated with caution. An agent in the audience, a Hispanic man who would negotiate if the operation came to a siege, had an even more crucial point.

"Biff, I forgot to tell you they have an infant daughter too, between a year and two years old."

Temple paused for a moment. A baby at the scene made things infinitely more complicated.

"Okay, in that case, then, if we do come into a barricade situation, that limits some of the tactics, but we are anticipating that the mother will comply with our instructions to vacate the premises."

He looked back at his notes. "All right, the mission. We will move on command from a staging area to the residence. The Gold Team, led by Joe, will take a position in front of the residence with the SWAT van. They'll take up perimeter and protective positions behind the van covering the front portion of the house. The Blue Team, led by Craig, will come into an open field on the south side of the house. This is the only way to get to the rear. You'll come in two to three cars and establish the perimeter and cover the south side, the west, and also the north side of the house. You'll just need to use whatever cover you can to move into position.

"Now, intelligence on the residence is pretty limited. It's in a less than desirable neighborhood, and they have a lot of lookouts in the area. In a minute I'll pass around the diagram that Rex has used, and it'll give you an idea of the layout."

As Temple described the location, the agents picked up the photographs taken by covert surveillance units over the past few days. They had been expertly packaged together with maps and plans by the case agents. The photographs showed a simple white wooden house with a few small outbuildings. It was in a built-up area and was surrounded by a four-foot-high chainlink fence.

Once on site, Temple said, they would secure the area and make a phone call into the house. The suspects would be advised that there was a search warrant and that everyone was to come outside. They would leave the doors open so the Gold Team could enter and secure the building. Those on the perimeter would hold tight and maintain positions of cover. From the moment that agents went inside, there would be no firing into the house. The suspects were

Spanish speakers, and most of the commands would be in their native language. A few of the agents nodded. All of them knew from experience how vital it was for the targets to understand right away what was expected of them. The team's aim was always to control a situation from the word *go*. That way there was less chance of things getting out of hand. Nobody wanted an exchange of gunfire.

The briefing passed on to administrative details. The first rendezvous would be in the Bureau garage at 4:45 A.M., the second one at a highway rest area a mile from the scene. There the team would wait until they had an all-clear from agents at the command post in the IRS building downtown, who would synchronize the operation with those of the other arrest teams across the city. The intention was to hit at first light, just after 6:30. Radios should all be set to Alpha Three, a secure frequency.

Temple raised his voice slightly and looked at each of the agents in turn to emphasize his next point. "Make sure you've got your full body armor. Make sure you do a good weapons check, radio check. Try to work in pairs — that way you can keep good cover, one guy with eyes front, the other guy with his eyes behind, because it is kind of a bad neighborhood. Now, this family has committed several murders already, so they're not above using weapons. We may not anticipate any problems, but let's not take it too lackadaisically. Okay, that's it."

He stood and awaited the inevitable questions. The SWAT team took its duties seriously and wanted to be prepared for any eventuality. Would there be any need for chemical agents or gas masks? Who would bring out the infant? Should the Blue Team search the outbuildings before or after the Gold Team entered the house? Upon such questions the success of the operation, even lives, could hang, and by the time the agents arrived at the scene it would be too late to ask.

Gradually the room relaxed into its normal postbriefing hubbub as agents checked their notes and gossiped for a few moments before getting back to work. But few stayed long. There was always too much to do.

Few of the agents working on the SWAT team, all of whom are volunteers from other squads (chiefly the Violent Crimes Task Force, the Special Operations Group, the Interstate Property Task Force, and the Narcotics Squad), are able to remember how many cases they've had in the past few years. The workload has been too great. The Dallas field office covers most of north Texas and, with its satellite resident agencies, as far away as Austin and Lubbock, is responsible for a tract of land bigger than many European countries.

On its own, Dallas is a big town, but together with the adjacent cities of Fort Worth, Irving, and Arlington it becomes one vast metropolis, known to locals as the Metroplex. To cover this area the FBI has a grand total of 242 agents, 190 of them in Dallas, the rest in the resident agencies.

As in every FBI office around the country, agents are assigned according to the investigative priorities established by the special agent in charge. In Dallas in 1993 that is Oliver "Buck" Revell, a man who has been all the way to the top of the Bureau. At one time he was executive assistant director in charge of investigations, but a combination of headquarters office politics and a desire to get back to the field brought him down to the South.

Although Revell keeps many of his agents in the usual investigative categories — counterintelligence, counterterrorism, organized crime, and public corruption — his main priorities broadly reflect the two most serious problems associated with this part of Texas: white-collar crime and violent crime. Both have their roots in the roller coaster Texas economy of the last few years.

For most of the post–World War II period the Dallas economy was driven by oil and banking, but in the 1980s the real estate boom was added to the mix, and the local economy was kicked into the stratosphere as land values shot up almost overnight. But as the decade came to a close, the savings-and-loan industry collapsed, and Dallas suffered as much as it had benefited earlier. Outwardly it is still an affluent city, still a place where the ostentatious display of wealth is smiled upon, still a place where entrepreneurial skills can receive handsome rewards, but now that wealth is spread much thinner. The recession hit hard in this part of Texas, and many of the promised and real blue-collar jobs that attracted people from other parts of the United States and from Mexico have vanished. The gap between rich and poor has widened, and that has created resentment. Most poor people swallowed their bitterness and are waiting patiently for better times, but some have sought quicker solutions. Crime, especially among the young, has increased dramatically.

Dallas has always been a violent town, just as Texas has always been a violent state. The right to bear arms has always been taken seriously here — it has something to do with a frontier attitude, perhaps. But in recent years things have been getting out of control. Guns are easily available, and the city has a narcotics problem at least as bad as Miami's. The ethnic mix is undoubtedly a factor too. Every day the city's population is swelled by two-thirds as commuters come in from the predominantly white middle-class suburbs to the north and northeast. Every evening it shrinks, leaving the city in the hands of the poorest and most desperate. For the obvious reasons — poor education, poverty, lack of opportunity, and unemployment — that means the black and Hispanic populations of the inner city. They have suffered the most from the economic downturn, and it is from their ranks that the vast majority of offenders comes.

As these problems took root in the 1980s the situation was made worse by the Texas penal system. As violent crime grew, so did the demand on the state's jails. The obvious answer would have been to build more of them, but that would have required money, and therefore higher taxes. Texas politicians lacked the resolve or the power to get the message across to voters, so the flood of violent offenders filled the existing prisons to overflowing. After the state was successfully sued by an ex-inmate for this appalling overcrowding, a federal judge decreed that the system could never run at more than 95 percent capacity. From then on, the system buckled. Violent criminals received the harsh sentences prescribed by law but served very little of them. Even the most persistent offenders were spending as little as twenty-two days inside for every year of their sentence. A convicted killer sent down for twenty years could be free within two; armed robbers with a string of violent crimes behind them could look forward to a few months in jail before they were back on the streets. The whole basis of judicial incarceration — that it should be a deterrent as well as a punishment — was in danger of being undermined.

That was when the FBI came in. Most homicides, larcenies, thefts, and robberies are still the preserve of local and state police. For violent crimes to become the subject of an FBI investigation, they have to cross state lines or violate a federal law. Banks that carry federal deposit insurance have always been under Bureau jurisdiction, just as the transportation of stolen automobiles across state lines has been. But an armed robbery in a local convenience store, no matter how violent, until recently was not. In the 1980s, under William Webster, the Bureau began to pursue narcotics investigations actively. Later, as the threat of the Cold War receded, it was decided that resources that were once deployed to guard the system against the enemy without could in part be redeployed against violent crime. William Sessions, Webster's successor, began a program called Safe Streets and made violent crime a national priority. Cynics argued that the motives behind the Bureau's new-found interest in such investigations had to do with its desire to redefine its role as one of its major functions was becoming less relevant. But in many cities the additional assets of the FBI have done much to relieve the pressure on harassed local law enforcement personnel.

In Dallas at least, one of the main weapons against violent crime is now the task force, a squad made up of city and state police and FBI agents who combine local know-how and street wisdom with the skills, talents, and resources of the federal justice system. These units have been able to function thanks to the imagination of U.S. attorneys who seem to have found new ways to reinterpret long-forgotten federal statutes. For instance, some robberies at convenience stores now qualify for federal investigative attention if the store is part of a nationwide chain with out-of-state national headquarters.

But the cooperation between the FBI and other agencies extends far beyond these everyday violent crime cases. For instance, the White-Collar Crime Task Force, fully occupied with fraud cases stemming from the collapse of the savings and loan industry, draws upon advice from agencies as diverse as the Federal Home Loan Bank Board, the IRS, and the U.S. Treasury. Another example is narcotics investigations: part of the multimillion dollar cocaine traffic from Mexico and Colombia is routed through Dallas, and the FBI's Narcotics Squad works side by side with the DEA, Customs, and the Dallas Police Department on stemming the flow of drugs and drug money into the city. Many of the narcotics traffickers have a history of violence, and frequently the Dallas FBI's SWAT team is called upon to provide tactical support on the most dangerous of the multiagency operations.

On his way to the staging area, Biff Temple mulled over the latest intelligence report. The target location was in a known drug-dealing neighborhood, and gathering information had not been easy. The dealers posted lookouts around the clock, just to keep an eye out for law enforcement. Aware that strangers could be spotted, the Bureau had sent a plane up to reconnoiter the day before. Nobody ever took much notice of circling aircraft. So far there was no sign that anyone knew what was coming, but Temple planned to send a car through the area just before zero hour, to get a last-minute look at what vehicles or people might be there.

Twenty minutes later the SWAT teams established their staging area in a parking lot a mile away from the target location. A reconnaissance team had cautiously driven by the house and seen lights on at the back. It looked as though the suspects were inside. Temple gathered his men for a last briefing. Much of it was repetitious, but no one minded the chance to go over the details again. As he warned them once more to keep their eyes peeled and their backs covered, a bulky figure in a black FBI baseball hat and blue shirt slipped into the ranks of listening agents. Buck Revell, the SAC, had come to watch over his troops, as he always did.

Everyone tried his best to ignore him. This was Biff Temple's operation, and there was a strict procedure to follow. Nonetheless, Revell's presence was comforting. There are SACs who willingly get up at four in the morning for an operation like this and those who would rather be caught dead. Revell was one of the former, and it earned him respect.

At last Temple looked at his watch and gave the word, and the agents got back into their vehicles. The jokes and the banter stopped. As they moved off once more, the early sunlight fell on a small sign someone had stenciled on the spare wheel housing of the SWAT van. BAD COMPANY, it read. ANY TIME, ANY PLACE.

Beman Avenue could have been any street in any of the working-class neighborhoods that ring the city. Scrubby trees lined the road, modest wood-frame houses sat well back in yards that might have been improved by a cleanup. Most had a battered car or two parked out in front; some had porch swings or whitewashed porticos. In short, the neighborhood was nothing special — until the menacing black SWAT van parked opposite the front door of 5207. It provided cover for six agents. Four stood, submachine guns and shotguns aimed directly at the house; the other two, armed with handguns, knelt at the sides, one covering the target, the other facing into the street.

"Abri la puerta!" The words, amplified by a powerful hand-held megaphone, echoed across the road and scared the birds out of a nearby tree. Somewhere in the distance a dog started barking.

The voice belonged to the unit's negotiator. Unlike his black-clad companions, he was highly visible in white pants, baseball hat, and a blue jacket with the FBI logo. This was intentional. No one wanted the cornered suspects to be distracted from anything he was saying. It was his responsibility to convince them to come out, and in accordance with the plan he was speaking Spanish. His first instruction, to open the door, went unanswered. Then something began to happen.

"I saw the window," he muttered. Temple, standing beside him, peered at the front of the house and agreed. There was definitely some movement.

In their hideouts around the house, the other members of the SWAT unit tensed. This was the key moment, when the suspects either gave themselves up or began shooting. The perimeter teams had been holding their position for about fifteen minutes now, longer than originally anticipated. The first plan, to call the suspects on the telephone, had gone awry, because the previous day the local phone company had cut off the line and no one told the FBI. Now they had to use a megaphone, which had the major disadvantage that everybody else in the street could hear it. In houses all around, people came to their windows to see what was going on. It was making the agents a little jittery.

Everyone's attention was suddenly drawn back to the house. The door opened slowly and a figure came out onto the porch. It was Chicky Zapata. Dressed only in boxer shorts and a gaping red bathrobe, he stood for a moment, peering out through a mesh screen gate.

"Manos arriba. A la cabeza." As Zapata put his hands on his head in response, a second figure came through the door. His hands were already held high. Chicky was sent back to get a key for the mesh screen gate. Seconds later he came back, opened it, and emerged onto the steps. His partner remained on the porch.

The negotiator reverted to English. The next phase, in which the suspects had to be made to understand that the FBI was in total control, was vital. He spoke urgently, repeating his instructions every time he detected some hesitation. His words, and his asides to Temple, were patched through the radio network to every agent

From this window in his office at the Department of Justice, J. Edgar Hoover, director of the FBI for forty-eight years, watched seven presidential inaugural parades pass down Pennsylvania Avenue. *Jeremy Hall/Connaught Films*

Hoover's orchestration of public opinion was critical to his hold over the Bureau and the way it was seen by successive generations of Americans. Beginning in the 1930s, with Hollywood as a willing accomplice, Hoover created the G-man myth. *You Can't Get Away With It* was typical of many movies that glamorized the exploits of the FBI. *National Archives*

Hoover (*center*) and Clyde Tolson, his lifelong friend and deputy (*right*), in a typical G-man pose. Agents were required to emulate the director's smart appearance. *National Archives*

Former special agent Jack Shaw was fired from the Bureau after criticizing J. Edgar Hoover in a private letter to his college professor.
Jeremy Hall/Connaught Films

Don Rochon left the FBI after he suffered racial harassment from fellow special agents. More than five hundred other black agents subsequently filed a class action suit against the Bureau for discrimination. *Connaught Films*

On the range at the FBI Academy in Quantico, Virginia, agents are taught to use a wide variety of weapons, from shotguns to automatic pistols and submachine guns.
Jeremy Hall/Connaught Films

A rare surveillance photo of Billy Grasso, whose skill at evading detection gave the FBI years of problems — until he was murdered. *FBI*

Gaetano Milano (*right*) with Frank and Louis Pugliano after Billy Grasso's murder. Agents saw several men give Milano a "kiss of respect," a clear clue that Milano had been responsible for the death. *FBI*

John "Sonny" Castagna after his arrest on racketeering charges. He subsequently made a deal with the Bureau and testified against the Patriarca family. With his son, Jackie Johns, he provided evidence that brought the Connecticut Mob to its knees. *FBI*

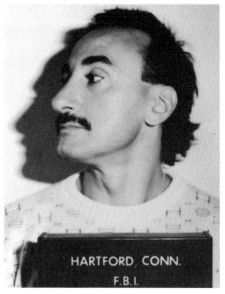

Gaetano Milano, arrested for Billy Grasso's murder, later stood up in court and renounced his membership in the Cosa Nostra. *FBI*

The bogus casino that the Patriarca family established in Manhattan, shortly after it was raided by police and the FBI. That night the Mafiosi were trying to pull off one last sting against unsuspecting gamblers. *FBI*

Raymond Patriarca, Jr., is said to have wept when his soldiers told him he should stand down as boss. *FBI*

Special Agent John Marley in the Fulton Fish Market, the site of Operation Sea Probe. The investigation ended the influence of the Genovese crime family over market business and was a notable triumph for the RICO laws. *Connaught Films*

The Bureau said Michel Pardue was involved in a murder-for-hire scheme, but the trial judge found that he was an innocent victim of an FBI undercover operation. *Connaught Films*

A special agent on surveillance duty. Surveillance photographs are often vital evidence that a crime has taken place and are very difficult for defense lawyers to refute. But such techniques frequently raise concerns about invasion of privacy. *Connaught Films*

Below: Former special agents Paul Brana (*left*) and Guy Berado were among the FBI's first undercover specialists. Hoover frowned on such operations because he thought his men would be tarnished by close contact with criminals. *Connaught Films*

The FBI's vast computer network contains tens of millions of records, from individual criminal histories, or rap sheets, to details of top-secret counter-intelligence investigations. One section, the National Crime Information Center, is used by police forces across America. The network forms one of the largest data reservoirs in the world.
Connaught Films

FBI agents believed that Judge Clarence Gaines was taking bribes, but they were being conned by an informant in what came to be known as Operation Corkscrew. *Connaught Films*

Judge Lillian Burke was also wrongly accused of taking bribes as Operation Corkscrew descended into farce.
Connaught Films

Looking for clues at the FBI lab. The Bureau's forensic specialists have developed techniques now used by police forces around the globe.
Jeremy Hall/Connaught Films

Agents monitoring a wiretap. Despite the Bureau's well-publicized ability to eaves-drop on conversations, the telephone is still the instrument of choice for many criminals, terrorists, and spies. *Jeremy Hall/Connaught Films*

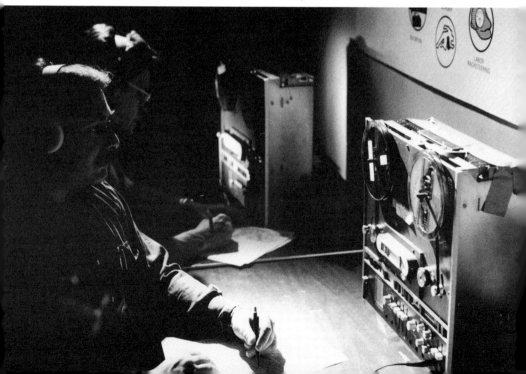

Analyzing fingerprints at FBI headquarters. The identification division handles more than 35,000 law enforcement requests every day. *Connaught Films*

An FBI forensic specialist examines clothing in a homicide case. Forensic evidence is often used to prove innocence as well as guilt. *Jeremy Hall/Connaught Films*

Special Agent Dennis Brady checks his gun before another shift on the streets. Like many agents, he goes to work each day knowing that he might be involved in a violent confrontation. *Connaught Films*

What every agent wears on his belt: his gun, his keys, and his badge. *Diarmuid Jeffreys/Connaught Films*

Special Agent Paul Shannon, of the Dallas FBI Violent Crimes Task Force, on the heels of a fugitive. *Diarmuid Jeffreys/Connaught Films*

Special Agent Biff Temple briefs his SWAT team as dawn breaks over Dallas. The squad's motto is "Bad company. Any time, any place." *Connaught Films*

The SWAT team in action. Agents believe that if they threaten to use overwhelming force, all opponents, no matter how dangerous, will want to surrender. *Connaught Films*

Paul Shannon makes another arrest. *Connaught Films*

Oliver "Buck" Revell, former special agent in charge of the Dallas division and one of the most powerful figures in the FBI, rose to the top echelons of the Bureau before going back to the field. *Connaught Films*

The corridors of power at FBI headquarters, which is known to many agents as the "puzzle palace." *Connaught Films*

Frank Varelli, the informant at the center of the FBI's CISPES investigation, claims the Bureau made him the scapegoat when the operations came under public scrutiny.
Tony Stark/Connaught Films

The monstrous J. Edgar Hoover Building on Pennsylvania Avenue has been the FBI's headquarters since 1974. More than 7,500 of the Bureau's 24,000 employees work behind its fortress-like walls. *Diarmuid Jeffreys*

Top: The devastation at Lockerbie, Scotland, hours after Pan Am Flight 103 was blown up on December 21, 1988. After a huge international investigation, the FBI and British police issued joint warrants for the arrest of the two Libyan terrorists responsible. The Libyan government has yet to hand them over.
The Independent/*David Rose*

Armageddon at Mount Carmel: the Branch Davidian compound going up in flames during the FBI raid on April 19, 1993. Seventy-five people, including David Koresh, died in the fire, although many bodies were later found to have gun-shot wounds. *Associated Press/Wide World*

Opposite: The World Trade Center soon after the explosion on February 26, 1993, which killed six people and caused over $650 million in damage. One week later the FBI began making arrests. *Associated Press/Wide World*

William Steele Sessions at his final press
conference, on Monday, July 19, 1993.
As he spoke, he held his letter
of dismissal from President Clinton.
Associated Press/Wide World

Louis J. Freeh with President Clinton
after his nomination in July 1993 as the
new director of the FBI. After Sessions's
controversial tenure, many feel that
Freeh, a former special agent, is reviving
the Bureau's reputation as the best
law enforcement agency in the world.
Associated Press/Wide World

with an earpiece. For those on the other side of the house, it was the only way of knowing what was happening.

"Chicky. Put your hands up in the air, all the way up. Start walking back towards us. Come back here. Towards me. You, the other one, wait right there. Hold. Keep your hands up, Chicky. HANDS UP! Keep walking. Walk towards me. One more. Backwards. Keep coming. Keep coming."

With his back to the agents, the red-robed figure inched down the path toward the SWAT team. Half a dozen lethal weapons were aimed at his head and torso. The rest of the team kept their guns trained on the house.

Finally, after what seemed like an age, Zapata reached the SWAT van. The negotiator spoke more quietly to him now.

"Stop. Right, get down on your knees. Right now. Okay, get all the way down on your stomach. Put your hands out, all the way out on the street. Palms up. Out to the side, out to the side."

Someone came forward with handcuffs, manacled Zapata, and pulled him up onto his knees. An agent squatted down a few feet away, his finger laced into the trigger guard of his automatic pistol. The negotiator turned his attention back to the man on the porch.

"What's your name? WHAT'S YOUR NAME? Right. Start coming out like he did, backwards, okay? Keep coming. Turn around. You don't need to look this way. Keep your back to us. Start walking back slow."

Once the second man was secured, Temple and the negotiator conferred. Zapata had told them that there were two teenage boys in the house, one fourteen, the other nineteen.

The negotiator picked up his megaphone once again. He spoke slowly and carefully in English, pausing every few words to let their full impact hit home. "Okay. Come on out. Chicky's out here waiting for you. There's nothing to be afraid of. Just come on out. We need to go in there, but we need you to come out first." He tried again. "Just step out through the front door. Chicky is out here waiting for you. Make sure you grab your brother's hand and come out with him also."

At that moment a black sedan turned out of a side street and started up the road toward the SWAT van. About a hundred yards away, the driver suddenly realized what was going on. He stomped on his brakes and reversed hurriedly.

Bob Siller, one of the division's assistant SACs, jumped out of the car he was sharing with Buck Revell and shouted at the knot of agents and police holding the outer perimeter farther down Beman. "Let's have a car block that side of the street. Both ends of the street. Now."

The negotiator finally talked both teenagers into coming out of the house. The eldest grimaced when an agent put the cuffs on him. The younger was a plump kid with a street-tough shaved head and baggy hip-hop clothes, but now he looked lost and terrified. Though left uncuffed, he too was made to lie on the ground.

Now came the most dangerous phase. The team had to go into the house and check to see that it was clear. On previous operations suspects had stayed hidden inside, waiting to shoot anyone who put his head through the door. The negotiator stepped forward with the megaphone and turned up the volume for one last try. It was a dramatic appeal, with all the force of seventy years of law enforcement history behind it: "Come out with your hands up. This is the FBI."

Buck Revell looked on with the insouciance of a man who had seen it all before. He knew that in relying on such techniques the Bureau could be accused of using a sledgehammer to crack a nut. But he believed it was necessary. "We don't want anybody to think they can win," he explained later. "So we seal off the area, maintain a perimeter, and show overwhelming force, prepared to meet any contingency. You have to remember that a lot of these people have automatic weapons, some of them have explosive devices. So what may appear to be excessive force could very quickly turn into minimum necessary force. We always have to be prepared for that ultimate contingency. In this situation, some of the individuals are known to have engaged in homicides, drive-by shootings, gang activities, as well as drug trafficking. So we're dealing with a volatile situation and have to be prepared for it."

The clearance section of the SWAT team approached the house. Even though Zapata and the others had told them that no one else was inside, they were still cautious. One agent crouched behind a bulletproof shield, which he held up to the open door. It was mounted with a flashlight, and he could see the interior through a slit of bulletproof glass. He swung it this way and that, looking for any sign of movement. Six other agents, machine guns at their shoulders, stood to one side. Gingerly they edged inside to start their search for unidentified suspects, booby traps, and contraband weapons. Every door, every passageway was threatening, and they took it slowly.

By now everyone in the area was awake and aware that the FBI was working their neighborhood. People came out to the street and stood behind the perimeter. The young Dallas police officers on duty seemed to share their open fascination with what was going on, but the older ones were nonchalant. They were superfluous and they knew it, but the system demanded that they provide support, so they turned up, parked, and gossiped. There were worse ways to pass a shift than watching the FBI do all the work.

Ten tense minutes later, Biff Temple came out of the house and walked over to report to Buck Revell and Bob Siller. The team had found no one else, but a preliminary search had uncovered an automatic weapon under a bed. The sweep had gone slowly because the team had had to clear an attic. Chicky Zapata's mother had left the house before the agents arrived; they would have to pick her up another time. The nineteen-year-old had not understood any English, and the agents suspected he was an illegal alien. He would be passed along to the Immigration and Naturalization Service. Now the agents could hand the house over to the IRS document team, which would look for any remaining evidence that the suspects had made money from narcotics deals.

As Temple spoke, the suspects were finally allowed to get up from the road and sit on a low wall across the street. Confused and intimidated, they answered questions in dull, listless voices. An agent squatted in front of them, getting details for the arrest sheet. The dog had stopped barking. Suddenly everyone looked very tired.

The headquarters of the FBI's Dallas Regional Division lies in the six-story Landmark Center at 1801 North Lamar, in the heart of the city's oldest neighborhood. To the general public, immediate evidence of a Bureau presence is hard to find. The red brick complex has a number of tenants, both commercial and government, and from the outside it appears to be just another nondescript office building. Even in the main lobby, the only sign of the FBI is on a floor plan next to the elevators. You have to go to the third floor before you can find the Bureau's public entrance. For fairly obvious security reasons, access to the inner labyrinth of offices and corri-

dors is not easy to achieve. Visitors are not exactly forbidden to drop
in without an appointment, but they are discouraged. Most will get
no farther than the reception area, guarded during office hours by
two pleasant but eagle-eyed female employees who sit behind a
glass partition and dispense advice in voices slightly distorted by a
two-way microphone. Their main function seems to be to weed out
those whose reasons for visiting are implausible.

But if a visitor is convincing and patient enough, he or she might
get to meet a duty agent, summoned from behind a locked door at
one side of the reception area. The duty agent will then take the
visitor to a small, sparsely furnished anteroom to explain himself.
Since the Bureau's stated policy is to encourage cooperation and
input from the citizens it serves, the duty agent will usually be
courteous and understanding. It is supposed to be his responsibility
to find out what the visitor wants and to see if the Bureau can help.
Most recognize that a polite approach is the best way to achieve
this. But it is not always easy. Broadly speaking, visitors can be
divided into three categories: the worthwhile, the misguided, and
the seriously unbalanced. If the agent gets it wrong, he knows he
could be tying himself down to a lot of wearisome procedure. A
little caution is in order.

The unbalanced, if not in the majority, are numerous enough. The
Bureau's reputation as the greatest investigative agency in the world
may be a source of pride to its personnel, but it has its disadvan-
tages, and one of those is attracting the kind of people who wish to
inform America that flying saucers have landed at the Texas Sta-
dium. The misguided are normally people who should be elsewhere
— those who want to complain about an aspect of the government's
law enforcement policy, for instance, or those who are simply in the
wrong place and have to be referred to the local police, the DEA,
the ATF, Customs, or some other agency.

The worthwhile, whom the experienced agent can usually spot
within minutes, can have any number of reasons for appearing. The
rarest are people who have information that could contribute to an
ongoing investigation or start a new one. Among the most common
are those who wish to file a civil liberties complaint. Allegations of
police brutality or corruption are fairly frequent, and though no one
in the Dallas FBI (or elsewhere, for that matter) particularly likes
investigating such cases, the agency has responsibility for them and

so takes them seriously. Injuries are noted down and photographed; names, dates, locations, and backgrounds are all scrupulously documented for later scrutiny. That the vast majority of the allegations turn out to be false doesn't seem to matter.

In general, though, a shift as duty agent doesn't hold much excitement. It is on a par with checking applicants for government service — necessary, dull, and to be avoided if at all possible. But just beyond the locked gray door off reception lies a maze of interconnecting corridors that run off in every direction, and that is where the serious work gets done. Go one way and you might come across Buck Revell's office, where the walls are covered with more plaques, awards, photographs, and trophies than can be found in one spot anywhere else in the Bureau; or the offices of the ASACs Tom Rupprath and Bob Siller. Go the other way and you might find your way through to the radio and dispatch room, with huge floodlit maps, computers, and communications equipment. In other rooms you might catch sight of agents and supervisors engaged in a myriad of administrative and investigative tasks: the undercover review committee in session, perhaps, or a meeting between members of the White-Collar Crime Task Force and attorneys from the Federal Home Loan Bank Board. Internal stairways lead to the Special Operations Group (which conducts the bigger surveillance operations) on the fifth floor and to the Violent Crimes Task Force on the first floor.

Security in the first-floor office is as elaborate and sophisticated as it is elsewhere in the building. Every door from a public area is secured with computerized locks, and employees can get in only by keying an entry code on a small black panel. Some doors are also guarded by retina scanners, a relatively new technological marvel that records each employee's "eye signature," so that when they peer into a slit beside the door and punch in the code, the computer recognizes their unique retina pattern and releases the lock. But the retina scanner is awkward to use, and most agents pass it by. Overburdened by work and subject to irregular hours, they save their energy for more important things — like paperwork.

Most agents dislike the incessant administrative chores that go with their job, but recognize their necessity. As Special Agent Paul Shannon of the Violent Crimes Task Force explained, "We've got to do it, there's no way around it. I mean, most of it has a purpose.

When you do your interviews and you talk to people or you take a confession, it has to be documented. When you show photo spreads to people and they say, 'That's him,' and they sign the back of the picture, you have to document that too. It's just part of the job."

But though Shannon accepts that paperwork has to be done, there are times when it gets in the way. At 7:00 A.M. one morning he was hunched in the tiny cubicle that passes for his office, trying to concentrate on a huge stack of money that lay on his desk. He had a busy day ahead, and he had to count the money before he could go out on the streets, but every time he came close to finishing the task, the telephone rang and interrupted him. His temper was close to the breaking point.

The phone rang again, and Shannon picked up the receiver. "Yes," he barked. As he talked, his eyes focused on the small mountain of dollar bills in front of him. He was trying to remember how far he'd got, but it was no use; he would have to go back and start again.

Squeezed in alongside him Special Agent Mark Chapman ignored the noise and counted on. "Forty-seven, forty-eight, forty-nine, fifty." He took his small stack of bills and put it on top of the large pile in the center of the desk, evidence from an arrest Shannon had made the previous week. The two men were counting the money carefully because any minor discrepancies in the amount would be pounced on by a defense attorney. It took two of them because the government is always a little sensitive to any suggestion that its employees could be light-fingered. Each agent was supposed to keep an eye on the other. Both had done this many times before, and the thrill of handling large sums of cash had long since worn off. It was just another chore.

Of the two, only Chapman looked like most people's idea of what an FBI agent should look like. He was tall, slim, and thirtyish, with neat brown hair and a dapper mustache. With his white shirt, gray flannel pants, and quiet patterned tie, he could have walked straight out of Central Casting. Shannon looked more lived-in. His jeans and sweatshirt were neat but anonymous, his sandy hair was less styled, and his eyes were a little warier. He looked a bit like what he once was — an investigative reporter for the *Miami Herald*. Both men had guns on their hips.

As they worked, other agents drifted by on their way to the coffee machine. At this time of the morning there are usually only a few of them here — die-hards who come in early to take advantage of a little quiet time before the day really gets going. The Violent Crimes Task Force is one of the busiest squads in the field office, and most agents spend much of the day away from their desks, testifying in court, answering armed robbery calls, interviewing witnesses, showing photo spreads of likely suspects to anyone who can give them a lead. It doesn't leave much time for the mass of paperwork.

Each agent has a cubicle like Shannon's, a few square feet of space, where phones and filing cabinets compete with more personal clutter: a few photographs, plaques and commendations for courses attended, others for achievement and bravery. Many desks hold personalized mugs (a brave but doomed attempt to make Bureau coffee drinkable), and others have odd collections of FBI baseball caps, each with a different emblem, or mementos from long-ago cases. Nameplates are ubiquitous — most for special agents, a few for Dallas Police Department detectives and Texas state troopers on assignment.

Steve Powell, sitting a few feet away from Shannon and Chapman, was already on his third cup of coffee and his fourth stack of case notes. With a little luck, he hoped he would get through it all before his midmorning appointment at the U.S. attorney's office. He was used to paperwork, having coped with it all his working life. Before he became an agent, he was an FBI clerk and did nothing but push paper. Back in those days, agents still had to wear jackets, white shirts, and ties at all times, no matter what the weather. Although that rule has long since been relaxed, the FBI's love of paper has not diminished one iota, and Powell, like his colleagues, has to scratch together a few hours when he can.

In a smaller office on the other side of the gray hardboard partition, Joe Hersley, the unit supervisor, was similarly engaged. He sat with his feet up on a government-issue chair and worried over future work schedules. Keeping track of which agents were working which cases is a full-time occupation. Every time the phone rang, he snorted with displeasure.

In one corner of the squad room, pinned to a wall, are black-and-white photographs taken by security cameras in the Dallas area. It is hard to make out any faces, as all the figures are hooded or disguised in some way. But the Violent Crimes Task Force has had a lot of practice unmasking these characters, and names and aliases are written under some. The task force has something of a reputation in the FBI. Its proud boast is that on recent trips inspectors from headquarters had waived its annual examination because of its continued successes on the job. Outsiders might not think this much of an accolade, but in the Bureau, where such procedures are more or less carved in stone, it is seen as remarkable.

After twenty minutes of checking and rechecking, Shannon and Chapman were finally ready to bag up the cash and take it down to the basement evidence room. The money had been in their hands since before the weekend, and they were glad to get it into the system. It would not see the light of day again until the case came to court a few weeks later. The evidence room was sacrosanct — not even agents could go beyond the outer office, and the inner storage space was restricted to three evidence clerks. It was piled high with boxes of records, old desktop computers that still had to yield their secrets, guns, narcotics, bloodstained clothing, cigarette butts, furniture, ransom notes — anything, in fact, that could help make a successful prosecution. If one item was lost, damaged, or otherwise interfered with, the cases could be blown and months of careful investigation wasted.

When they got back to the squad room, Chapman wandered off to his cubicle. He was on call, and until he was beeped there was little to do but drink coffee and shoot the breeze with the rest of the response team. Shannon tidied up a few more odds and ends at his desk before he made ready to leave. It was time to hit the streets.

A few days later Shannon climbed out of the car he was sharing with Dennis Brady, his partner. A Continental short-haul jet screamed in low over Bachman Lake to make a noisy landing on nearby Love Field. Although it was just past 7:00 A.M., the heat was intense — in the high nineties and climbing — and neither agent seemed inclined to linger. They hurried inside to the relative cool and quiet of a Dallas Police Department substation. As on most days, they began their "running and gunning" duties with a visit to the DPD to pick up warrants and to check in with the police detectives who would be on the same mission.

Thirty minutes later, after sharing coffee and gossip with the police team, they were back in their car and heading up Preston Lane. Brady explained what was on the agenda.

"We're going after two attempted murder suspects, Nico Riley and Lawrence Mask, both black males about eighteen years old. We have information they might be in a North Dallas apartment building. They got into an altercation with a twenty-year-old black male named Rodney Gray, and at the end of it they weren't satisfied, I guess. They came back, broke into his apartment, pinned him up against the wall and shot him in the chest five or six times, and ran off. According to the report, they had a separate gun battle with some other witnesses in an apartment complex in the southern part of Dallas."

FBI agents like to make their arrests early, when most people are still in bed and off their guard. It is safer that way. But at the first location Brady and Shannon drew a blank, although they did elicit some information. A man walking out of the apartment complex turned out to be the father of Nico Riley's fiancée. He told them that Nico knew he was wanted but was keeping his head down. The family wanted him to turn himself in before he got killed, but for the past few days he had stayed away from them. The father thought that he might be staying at another complex a few miles south.

The agents, by now accompanied by two DPD detectives, drove off to the new address, a place called Copper Creek. It had an elaborate swimming pool and manicured gardens and seemed an unlikely place for a street fugitive to hide out. But after checking with the superintendent and flipping through the rental log, Brady persuaded the nervous maintenance man to get a key and lead them to an apartment at the cheaper end of the complex. On the short walk down the path they drew their guns and fastened their flak jackets. At the last minute Shannon jammed a black FBI baseball cap on top of his spiky hair and stood to one side as Brady hammered on the door. One of the detectives slipped into the bushes at the back of the building in case the fugitive made a break for it. But again they drew a blank. The apartment was empty, and though they checked inside, there were no signs that Riley had been there recently. The agents and detectives walked back to the parking lot to confer.

It was something of an anticlimax. Brady and Shannon normally did this several times a day, preparing themselves mentally and physically for the possibility that the next knock on the door might be followed by a violent confrontation. It seemed both stressful and exhausting, and their adrenaline levels must have fluctuated like the mercury in a thermometer being repeatedly dipped in boiling water. Yet neither appeared to be affected or even frustrated by it.

"It's just the thing about fugitive investigations," explained Shannon. "You can't predict where the guy's going to be. You're liable to come up on him unexpectedly anytime you are out looking for him. Sometimes you don't find him today, maybe you'll find him tomorrow. We have any number of cases working at the same time. I mean, I have two guys who are wanted on robbery warrants that I have a surveillance team on right now. There's just no way to tell how the day's going to go — your beeper goes off and you're going somewhere else. Or somebody who's looking for another guy comes up on the radio and they ask for some assistance and we'll go and help them."

After another two hours of driving around, asking questions, and checking apartments, the agents could find no real trace of the two suspects. They drove back to the DPD substation for a quick lunch. For a few minutes they sat chatting about their families and their plans for the weekend. Then, suddenly, they were on the move again, running out through the sweltering heat to their car. Brady gunned the engine as Shannon took their flak jackets from the trunk and explained what had happened.

"We had a call from an intelligence officer, that's a Dallas police officer in plainclothes, who indicated that he has a murder warrant on an individual and he has the guy put down, either in a house or an apartment, we don't know. That's all the information we have. He said, 'Come on down as quick as you can,' so we are on the way. It's obviously not going to be some planned or staged tactical maneuver. I mean, we are going to have to think fast on our feet. We'll probably hook up with the intelligence officer once we get down there, look at the layout of the place, assess the situation, make some decisions, and do our best to arrest the guy."

In the car, the airwaves erupted with traffic as the radio dispatcher in the downtown FBI office directed others to the scene. Twenty minutes later, Shannon and Brady were outside a single-story house on Checota Drive. Other agents, wearing Bureau jackets and carrying shotguns, had already arrived and were taking up positions to the side and rear of the property. A confusing melee of shouts and instructions followed. Brady and others slipped inside, while Shannon kept a weather eye on an elderly black man on the porch, who had been the first to surrender. He identified himself as the father of the target, and after some questioning he told Shannon that the subject was in a bedroom at the rear of the house. He had decided, the father said a little defiantly, that he wouldn't give himself up. Shannon bellowed this information through to Brady and the others.

The team members inside the house were in something of a quandary. They were crouched at one end of a small hallway that ran the length of the building. Off the passage were three bedrooms, a bathroom, and a number of closets. All the agents knew that, with the forces they had, there was no way to move down that hallway and be secure. A little deception was called for. At first they discussed loudly whether it was time to use tear gas to flush the subject out. This brought two women and an infant to the door of one bedroom, but not the subject himself. They waited a while and then shouted that they were sending the dogs in. A few tense moments later, the suspect gave himself up. The agents and cops breathed a collective sigh of relief. They had neither dogs nor tear gas at hand, and it would have taken at least an hour to call up a fully equipped tactical team.

Outside, the subject, whose name was Michael, was handcuffed and loaded into the back of Brady's car. Small groups of people emerged from the houses nearby to see what all the fuss was about. Standing motionless and quiet a few dozen yards away, they stared at the police cars skewed haphazardly across the street and at the police officers and agents laughing and gossiping as the tension ebbed away. It was as though they were looking upon beings from another planet. At this particular operation, the spectators were almost all black, the law enforcement officers almost all white. This was a poor neighborhood, and those watching knew that in a short while the lawmen would leave, driving back in their fast cars to their downtown offices and their comfortable middle-class homes in the suburbs. The residents would be left out here on the front line. It was easy to understand why resentment showed on some faces.

Thirty minutes later Brady, Shannon, and their prisoner pulled up outside the FBI offices on North Lamar. The agents took him inside to the small "mug room" off the Violent Crimes Task Force suite and handcuffed him to a table. No one said much. Brady and Shannon were polite, but it was a familiar routine, nothing to get excited about. As Shannon went off to make some calls, Brady emptied Michael's pockets and removed his expensive-looking running shoes to search them later. He took his prints carefully and stood him up against an FBI height chart to take photographs. Following instructions, Michael looked first to the front and then to the right. He had a thick gold chain around his neck and several gold rings on his fingers, but his face was creased with stress.

Later Brady and Shannon mused on the day, their chosen careers, and the risks they took every time they got into a car at the start of a shift.

"I don't think about the danger," said Brady, who came from a small town in Idaho and worked as a police officer before joining the FBI. "I think of it as an opportunity to really do something that counts, that matters. Not everybody is willing to do what we do. I'm more than just willing to do it, I enjoy doing it, and I seek out those challenges — I always have. My wife and I have talked a lot about this, and she really believes I wouldn't be happy doing anything else. I do everything I can to defuse the situation, but at some point you're going to have to meet violence with violence. If you can't accept that fact, then you don't only need not be in the FBI, you don't need to be a law enforcement officer at all."

Shannon, the onetime reporter, agreed. He often thought about the contrast between his home life and his work. He was happily married with two great kids, a nice house, and a good car. But from the moment he got to work he was in another world.

"The next thing I might be in the projects chasing some kid down a hallway, where there's trash and water seeping out of the walls and rodents and —"

"Roaches, don't forget roaches," said Brady.

"Yeah." Shannon laughed. "Can't forget the roaches — we find those all the time. Generally speaking, the kind of person we're going after is the kind of person you can and will have violent confrontations with. And as my wife has pointed out to me many times, if they get us instead of us getting them, it's a pretty poor tradeoff. Because there are people in our homes who depend on us and who we're doing the right thing for, and the people we chase are the kind of people who have only left behind a trail of victims." He leaned forward, eager to make a point.

"We have to be prepared when we go to work to have a violent confrontation and possibly to kill somebody. One of the ways we do that — and I know Dennis does this too, which is one of the reasons I like working with him — is that we train. You know — we work out, we take care of ourselves, we get a good night's sleep, we get those pistols out and shoot 'em. That's how we deal with the stress of thinking today might be the day. Training, physical fitness, and through a recognition that you're an FBI agent and you took the oath of office. When you take the oath of office to become an FBI agent, it's not like an idle promise. You take that oath and it changes your life forever, for the rest of your life."

Of course the job does have its frustrations, despite their commitment. As Brady talked, he became more earnest. FBI agents are rarely given the chance to talk to outsiders about their work, and both men wanted people to understand what motivates them.

"Sometimes," said Brady, "I get the feeling that it's going to go on and on, that it's never going to stop. And at that point I feel that maybe it would be better to move on. I've always overcome that feeling, because I feel that I'm doing what I can and maybe I do make a difference, no matter how small. When I was a brand-new agent in the Bureau here in Dallas, one of my first cases was a child kidnapping. A little girl was abducted from behind the apartment complex where she lived. And I worked as hard as I could with the police department. You know, doing whatever I could. We had hoax telephone calls claiming that they had the child and that she was being held for ransom. It was almost laughable, because her family was so poor that there was no way they could afford to pay the ransom. But we went though the entire charade, and just when I was feeling at my lowest, my supervisor came to me and said, 'You know she's dead.' And I said, 'No, I don't know any such thing.' He said, 'You know in these types of cases, with a child of that particular age — she was kidnapped for sexual gratification, and she was used and murdered soon after she was taken. She was probably dead within hours of the time she was abducted.'

"And that was the hardest thing to deal with. I could not accept that no matter how hard I worked, I could never find that child and I could never bring that child back. Eventually she was found — nothing but a skeleton. But that case left a particular mark on me and hit a particular chord with me because my daughter was the same age."

Shannon and Brady derive a great deal of their strength from being part of the wider FBI family. In their book, an agent should be happy to be awakened in the middle of the night with a call to arms. They prize loyalty, tradecraft, and an ability to persevere, never to let up, above everything else. Both are remarkably uncynical. It really is a matter of "us and them," good guys and bad guys, right against wrong. They do not hate criminals so much as despise them. Theirs is a crusade. The people who use violence to achieve their aims are like vermin, to be hunted down and put away.

"I'm not sure anybody can tell you why things are as violent in the streets as they are at the moment," said Shannon. "I know that when we all get together and we talk, we look at our youth, we can look at the way we were raised and the neighborhoods we were raised in and think of the things we did and know that our children are never going to be able to live the way we lived. They're not going to be able to go out, say, on Halloween and trick-or-treat the way we did, because society's changed. And I think that most of us feel like it's changed for the worse."

The belief that the FBI is waging a war of sorts against the forces of evil in society is widespread, not only among agents but among the American people, and not only in Dallas but across the country. These days the idea is more sophisticated than it was in the era of the G-men, but the visible public work of special agents like Brady and Shannon comes so close to what people see on television that it can sometimes be difficult to distinguish between reality and fiction. That line is also hard to define in some of the less public activities of the FBI, such as those undertaken by the Foreign Counterintelligence Unit.

In Dallas, a large part of the FCI Unit's work takes place in an obscure room on the third floor. When fully manned, the wiretap room — or "tech room," as it is sometimes called — is an unnerving sight. Half a dozen agents, each wearing a set of headphones, sit side by side in front of a long row of reel-to-reel voice-activated tape recorders. On the low table before them are their logs, numbered and classified in accordance with the conversations that the agents are monitoring. Every few minutes a set of reels begins to revolve, electronically triggered by someone lifting a telephone receiver in a target house, office, or phone booth. A moment later an agent will lean forward and make a note of the time, date, and nature of the conversation.

To anyone without headphones the room is strangely quiet. Each agent is in his own secluded world, with metallic voices whispering into his ears alone. Occasionally a click and a whir break the silence as a computerized pen register prints out a number that has been dialed; a snap follows as one of the agents leans forward to press the "minimization switch" on his recorder or to adjust the volume.

It is also an oddly familiar scene, one from countless spy movies, reminiscent of le Carré novels and the bad old days of the Cold War. But this is Dallas, Texas, not Berlin or Budapest, Warsaw or Moscow. This is the United States of America, the greatest democracy in the world. Why are all these people engaged in something so obviously intrusive?

Wiretapping has been a standard technique throughout the Bureau's history. Indeed, in the early years, before other kinds of electronic surveillance were developed, it was the agency's single most useful intelligence-gathering tool. Nowadays, of course, it is only one of several ways of monitoring conversations. Body recorders, "spike mikes" hidden in walls, parabolic mikes that can pick up conversations from thousands of yards away, bugs disguised in ashtrays, table legs, light fixtures, pottery, and auto parts, bugs hidden in VDTs, fiber-optic cables, and diodes — the Bureau has them all and uses them frequently. It can also intercept telexes, ciphers, faxes, telegrams, computer modem transmissions, and almost every other form of communication in spoken, written, or electronic form.

Strangely enough, though, despite all this sophisticated technology, wiretapping remains the single most effective and reliable way of surreptitious eavesdropping. Of course, agents no longer crouch at a telephone junction box, wearing a pair of headphones and scrawling on a note pad. For many years wiretapping has involved little more effort than flicking a switch on a tape recorder and picking up a signal that has been kindly diverted by a friendly phone company. But however the conversations are now monitored, the telephone is still the instrument most people use most of the time to communicate. Whether innocent or guilty, crook, spy, or terrorist, everyone makes calls.

Legal authorization for wiretaps has fluctuated over the years, although Hoover was a genius at devising various ways around the minor restrictions that righteous attorneys general and legislators sought to impose on the practice. As far back as 1928, the Bureau of Investigation, as it then was, was benefiting from Supreme Court rulings that left it free to engage in unrestricted tapping of certain investigative targets, such as counterintelligence suspects. In 1940 President Roosevelt overcame the reluctance of Attorney General Robert Jackson (who had tried to bring wiretapping to an end in all investigative categories) and decided that wiretaps could be used against those suspected of "subversive activities" against the United States. This evolved into a general acceptance that espionage and subversive targets were fair game — and of course Hoover took the broadest of views on what could be categorized as subversive.

By and large, criminal investigations were less fertile ground for the Bureau's wiretapping enthusiasts. Though they did take place on a large scale, they weren't officially sanctioned until 1968, when Congress enacted Title III of the Omnibus Crime Control and Safe Streets Act, which established procedures for obtaining judicial warrants, court hearings, time constraints, and the like.

But despite such regulations, there were many loopholes left for the Bureau to exploit. For instance, the Justice Department, the White House, and the FBI continued to take the view that most, if not all, investigations concerning national security matters required only general presidential approval for wiretaps to go ahead. Even in criminal cases, for which judicial approval was supposedly required, the Bureau frequently turned a blind eye to the regulations and instituted covert wiretaps. Since there was little or no oversight, the Bureau was able to operate pretty much as it pleased. One of Hoover's regular practices was to turn off many of the taps just before his annual appearance in front of the House Appropriations Committee, to avoid the problem of having to lie to Congress about the huge number of illicit taps that were in place. Shortly afterward the taps would all be turned back on again.

Like many other features of Hoover's FBI, this unrestrained surveillance came under scrutiny during the post-Watergate inquiries into the failings and failures of the United States' intelligence and judicial communities. Not surprisingly, the considerable public outrage was followed by calls for tougher rules and regulations. The Levi Guidelines of the late seventies (named after the attorney general who drew them up), enhanced by fresh legislation and administrative changes instituted in later years, made the whole process much more straightforward. Today all wiretaps have to be judicially approved; warrants on criminal cases, including domestic terrorism investigations, have to go before a local judge, and warrants on foreign counterintelligence investigations are issued through a presidentially appointed court in Washington. There are various time limitations, but in practice most warrants are issued for thirty or sixty days.

None of this completely removes the possibility of abuse, of course, nor does it address the central dilemma of all wiretaps — namely, that no matter how useful the technique is, electronic surveillance (of all kinds) is undeniably intrusive. The problem was neatly summed up in a report from one of the many congressional investigations into the issue back in the seventies:

> By their very nature . . . electronic surveillance techniques also provide the means by which the Government can collect vast amounts of information, unrelated to any legitimate governmental interest, about large numbers of American citizens. Because electronic surveillance is surreptitious, it allows Government agents to eavesdrop on the conversations of individuals in unguarded moments, when they believe they are speaking in confidence. Once in operation electronic surveillance techniques record not merely conversations about criminal, treasonable or espionage related activities, but all conversations about the full range of human events. Neither the most mundane nor the most personal nor the most political expressions of the subjects are immune from interception. Nor are these techniques sufficiently precise to limit the conversations to those of the intended subject of the surveillance; anyone who speaks in a bugged room and anyone who talks over a tapped telephone is also overheard and recorded.

The procedural panacea dreamed up to deal with this difficulty is called "minimization." According to Dan James, a foreign counterintelligence agent in the Dallas FBI office, "Minimization is a procedure whereby we listen to the phone call, whether outgoing or incoming . . . long enough to determine whether it's going to be a personal call or one of a nature which would indicate whether it's in perpetration of the crime we are investigating. If it's the former, we turn off the phone at that time. We do not listen to the conversation, it's not entered on the log, or nothing more than a personal note goes in the log."

In practice, this means that any agent monitoring a wiretap is supposed to sit with his hand on the pause button, waiting to press it if the callers start discussing shopping or family problems or anything else extraneous to the matter at hand. He is then allowed to dip back in from time to time to see whether the conversation has become more relevant.

But whether minimization is little more than a cosmetic device to reassure anxious liberals about the invasion of privacy is open to question. After all, the fact that the Bureau is legally supposed to abide by such a rule is almost certainly known to many of the criminals and all of the hostile intelligence agents whose telephones are liable to be tapped. It is not beyond the bounds of belief that they would modify their conversations accordingly. Such callers are unlikely to say, "Hi Bob, this is Oleg Vasilyevich. When are we going to get those top secret plans for the stealth bomber? You know, the ones for which I gave you twenty thousand dollars at our meeting in the parking lot of the Hyatt Regency last Tuesday afternoon," or even "José, this is Fernandez. I just wanted to let you know we've got ten kilos of cocaine coming in on Flight 319 from Bogotá tomorrow." Any caller desperate enough to discuss such things over the phone is probably going to speak in code, dressing up his conversation about his narcotics/espionage/bank fraud/murder-for-hire scheme in references to football games, his daughter's boyfriend, or the relative merits of Coors and Budweiser beer.

So how does the listening FBI agent determine when a conversation is relevant and when it is not? Do these people really press the pause button when matters stray away from the strictly relevant, or do they listen to everything just to be sure?

If the agency is to be believed, they press the pause button. Dan James says determinedly that a reasonably well trained agent can distinguish between a potentially criminal conversation and an innocent one. He insists that in his experience, Bureau agents will always opt to be conservative in terms of what they put in the log or retain on the tapes.

It is certainly true that the Bureau has recorded thousands of openly incriminating conversations, in which people speak clearly about their criminal endeavors. Either those with tapped lines are too stupid to realize they are being monitored, or they don't know about minimization, or the FBI has been remarkably successful in keeping a low profile.

"People are wise to minimization, and it's widely publicized," says James. "But surprisingly enough, most people either seem to believe that they're immune to this or don't suspect that we are aware of the allegation that led us to establish the tap to begin with. People are very forthcoming on the telephone."

This is why Dallas, like every other FBI field office in the United

States, has its own tech room. It is not used every day, or even every week, but it is occupied frequently enough, mostly by the squads that run long-term investigations — organized crime, white-collar crime, narcotics, domestic terrorism, and foreign counterintelligence. As a general rule, the more complex a case is, the more useful taps will be.

Dan James, if not a habitual wiretap user, has certainly put in plenty of hours over the years at the boring business of monitoring the taps. For him and the other agents on the foreign counterintelligence squad, wiretapping is a vital weapon, one of the few in a field that is traditionally short of more straightforward methods of investigation. But even though the FCI agents may rely more on the technique than their colleagues who work crime do, they have some advantages. Because their cases are less immediately urgent, they can avoid the graveyard shifts that go with round-the-clock monitoring. Instead they are able to use voice-activated recorders to do their work for them, so they can go in at more reasonable times of the day to replay the tapes and fill in their logs.

Despite the collapse of the Soviet Union, foreign counterintelligence is still regarded as a major FBI priority, and almost a fifth of all agents work on espionage cases. Dallas is no exception. This part of Texas, thick with major defense contractors, has always been a magnet for foreign spies eager to get their hands on U.S. military secrets. But these are strange times for Dan James and his colleagues. The old certainties have been swept away, and the agents have had to make a sometimes painful readjustment to a post–Cold War world. The Russians are still regarded with suspicion — with some justification, as the arrest of Aldrich Ames made clear — but many other former Warsaw Pact countries are now considered to be allies, or at least no longer hostile. In their place looms the second league of bogeymen — the People's Republic of China, North Korea, Vietnam, Cuba, Iraq, Iran, and Libya — and other more surprising targets such as France and Japan, which are believed to be after economic and technological secrets. The constant replenishment of enemies has not gone unchallenged. One of the most frequently heard criticisms of intelligence agencies is that they continually invent new enemies in order to keep the support of their political paymasters. The FBI is as vulnerable as any other agency when funds are limited, and it is just as capable of finding plausible reasons to justify its existence. The problem that Congress and the public face is how to judge whether the new threats are legitimate when the decision-making process that proposes them is wrapped in secrecy.

Dan James maintains that such decisions are not a matter for him and his immediate colleagues in any case. They merely act upon those decisions. "There is a group of countries that the president of the United States, the attorney general, the National Security Council, and the intelligence community back in Washington have deemed as being inimical to the best interests of the United States," James explained. "History tells us that among the visitors from these countries are those who are coming here with a hidden agenda. We know or feel certain that they are engaged in intelligence operations, and we are allowed to open cases on those we think might fill that profile — those assigned to embassies and consulates, what we call the establishment, and those who are coming here to do business."

The FCI squad's office, only a conveniently short walk from the tech room, is indicative of the squad's unchanging agenda, a throwback to an earlier era. For starters, the agents seem older and more conservative than their counterparts in other fields. On their desks and shelves are mementos of the long Cold War. Russian Army hats and epaulettes sit like trophies of an old campaign; stickers on telephones exhort the caller to DENY DENY DENY — COUNTER ALLEGE or warn that that particular instrument "is not secure." Elsewhere, filing cabinets are fitted with combination locks, and worn mock movie posters herald the "Spybusters" who protect the nation's security. Even the furniture seems old and dusty, a somber wooden brown, defiantly distinct from the modern gray plastic and fiberboard found elsewhere in the building. This is a quiet place of murmured conversations and secret industry, overseen by an enigmatic supervisor, Tom Williams. A slightly built, guarded man of indeterminate age, Williams has hooded, unfriendly eyes that gaze out coldly on his small empire. He runs a tight operation, and he has no welcome or patience for questioning visitors from the outside world. "Why?" he will ask. "Why do you want to know these things? They are our secrets." This is very much old Bureau, where Hoover would have felt at ease and where humor seems to be an unaffordable luxury.

But whatever else these agents may be, they are not out on a limb. Buck Revell, the special agent in charge of the Dallas field office, is a counterintelligence enthusiast. Until he took a step down in rank a few years ago, he was the number-three man in Washington, directly responsible for all investigative functions. Throughout his time at the top he was well known as a keen supporter of the FCI squads in the field, and he brought that ardor with him back to Texas. In some offices, foreign counterintelligence is becoming less of a priority — as violent crime and narcotics assume ever more importance. But not here. Although Tom Williams and his team may look like an anachronism, they are rarely short of resources and support.

Unlike other squads in Dallas, they are relatively unconstrained by rules and regulations in their use of wiretaps. They do not need a criminal predicate to monitor a telephone, only a "strong" suspicion that the target may be involved in intelligence gathering. They also, uniquely, have the ability to open a case on American citizens even if there is no evidence to suggest that they may have been involved in a crime — a loose connection with a national security investigation is enough. In other words, agents can eavesdrop on the private conversations of innocent people in the cause of some greater good. Is this not overly intrusive?

"Potentially it is," admitted Dan James. "However, you should stop to consider the fact that the reason we open most of the American citizens as subjects is not because we suspect them of being intelligence operatives or anything, but because we want them to provide us with information directed against the target that we do deem might be an intelligence officer, to use them as an asset. Of course we know there is a fine line between preventing subversion and protecting civil liberties. We simply have to educate ourselves about what is expected of us now — that there are rules and guidelines and they're there for our protection as well as for the citizens', and we can only do what is right and adhere to those. We take that responsibility seriously."

Perhaps. But in some ways the wiretap room is where the old and the new Bureau come together. A handy symbol of much of what was wrong about Hoover's FBI, it is also, inescapably, a tool of the future. Agents investigating white-collar crime, narcotics trafficking, and the rest are using a technique that was first and foremost designed and authorized to help the FBI protect national security. The guidelines and rules under which the criminal investigators now have to operate are probably as strict as they can be, but the foreign counterintelligence agents are less constrained. At a time when many people believe the FBI is looking for potential enemies, this is worrying.

Hoover exaggerated the threat from the U.S. Communist Party and others in order to legitimize his requests for more power and resources. People were deemed subversive and investigations were opened on the flimsiest evidence. The existence of those investigations was then held up as proof that a threat existed. Couldn't the same thing happen with today's FCI squads and their comparatively unrestricted access to wiretapping?

The FBI dismisses such worries and says that, criminal investigations aside, its only concern is national security. It points out that despite the collapse of Communism, there are still numerous foreign powers openly hostile to the United States, and furthermore, that the nation faces an ever-present threat from international terrorism. To meet these threats, the FBI says, its agents must have the right tools, and that wiretapping and other surveillance methods are indispensable. Yet, while all this may be true, with the Cold War well and truly over, it must surely also be time to establish a legal framework that makes a clear distinction between legitimate suspects and innocent citizens.

CHAPTER 7

"WACMUR"

We were prepared for what we'd done, but what we weren't prepared for was some of the hammering we took in the press. It was something we hadn't trained for. I know when the association called and said they would like to present us with an award, we looked at that as our peers in the field who are saying, "Hey, you did a good job." And I think that is what it is all about. When a fellow agent says you did a good job, everything else doesn't matter. So to heck with the press and to heck with some of the other folks.

— A MEMBER OF THE FBI'S HOSTAGE RESCUE TEAM,
ACTIVE AGENTS ASSOCIATION CONVENTION,
CHICAGO, JULY 1993

O N MONDAY, April 19, 1993, seventy-five people, including twenty-five children, died as a raging fire swept through a shabby complex of wooden buildings on the outskirts of Waco, Texas. It was the end of one of the most bizarre and dramatic incidents in modern American history: the fifty-one-day standoff between the Branch Davidian religious cult and the FBI.

The seeds of the disaster were sown on Sunday, February 28. In the early hours of that morning, more than one hundred agents from the Bureau of Alcohol, Tobacco, and Firearms raided the cult's compound in an attempt to serve warrants for federal weapons violations. They were expected. The Branch Davidians were heavily armed, and in the ensuing gun battle four agents were killed, fifteen were injured, and six Branch Davidians died.

David Koresh, the cult's self-styled Messiah, was among the wounded, but he survived, determined to keep the "unbelievers" at bay. For the next seven weeks, under the eyes of the world's media, he and his devotees defied the might of American law enforcement. To his followers he was the chosen one, the last angel of the Apocalypse, the keeper of the Seven Seals. To the FBI, which took over after the ATF agents were killed, he was a grandiose fanatic, a rambling "loony tune" who prophesied calamities while ruthlessly exploiting the naiveté and gullibility of his disciples.

For nearly two months the FBI surrounded the compound, trying negotiations, threats, pleas, and psychological warfare, to little effect. Eventually the FBI decided it had to act. The plan was simple: to knock holes in the walls of the complex, flood the interior with tear gas, and force Koresh and his followers to come out. But something went tragically wrong. Seven hours into the operation, smoke and flames began to darken the skies above, and within minutes the whole compound was ablaze. There were only nine survivors, all of them adults. Koresh was not one of them. Just as he had promised, Armageddon had come to the Branch Davidians.

This tragedy comprehensively illustrates the changing nature of the FBI's role in law enforcement, and the difficulties it sometimes has in adapting its traditional attitudes and methods to new situations. At Waco, the Bureau was faced with something far outside its normal range of experience: an opponent whose motives and aspirations were completely alien to the agents at the scene and to the experts and tacticians elsewhere who plotted strategy. The Bureau deployed its vast armory of techniques against the Branch Davidians, confident that methods that had proved successful in the past would do so again. Allied to this strategy was its publicly expressed belief that Koresh was a con man, murderer, and fanatic who should be treated in much the same way as other violent criminals. When this approach failed, the agency seemed unsure how to proceed. In the end, it opted to follow a tactical solution, believing that that was the only way to bring the protracted siege to an end. But was the FBI right?

One could certainly argue that events would have been different if the FBI had not viewed Koresh in such a stereotypical way, and if agents had not underestimated his defining characteristic: his remarkable ability to inspire absolute loyalty in his followers. However fanciful his claims might have appeared to the FBI, his followers sincerely believed in his religious teachings, his prophecies, and his claims of revelation. Their fundamental devotion overrode normal social conventions and made the Branch Davidians largely impervious to attempts to separate them from their leader. In the face of such profound belief, orthodox siege techniques could only achieve so much. Indeed, as time went by, those techniques seemed to reinforce the solidarity of those inside the compound. If the Bureau had recognized this in time, the seventy-five Branch Davidians might still be alive today.

Like many cults, the Branch Davidians had their beginnings in a larger movement to form a Christian community based on a literal reading of the Bible. That movement, which sprang up in New England in the early nineteenth century, was prompted by the teachings of William Miller, an itinerant carpenter who believed that the Book of Revelation predicted the second coming of Christ in the immediate future. The faithful, who called themselves Seventh-day Adventists, saw various predicted dates for this event come and go, but their church nevertheless continued to grow.

In the early 1930s the church underwent the kind of split that is a feature of many fundamentalist sects. A devotee called Victor Houteff, dissatisfied with the worldly and materialistic direction he thought the church was taking, went off on his own and set up a subsect at Mount Carmel, on the outskirts of Waco, Texas. The community became known as the Branch Davidians.

Like its parent church, the community had good times and bad times. By the 1980s it was barely holding its own, still attracting an occasional convert from the radical fringes of more orthodox Christian groups but in desperate need of fresh blood at the top. The prophet at the time was Lois Roden, an elderly woman who was unable to generate much enthusiasm among her followers. Her son, the erratic and eccentric George Roden, was her logical successor, but he had a rival in one of the more popular members of the sect, a young man named Vernon Howell.

Howell, born in Houston in 1959, had left school in the ninth grade but had developed a remarkable interest in and knowledge of religion. By the time he was thirteen he could recite chunks of the New Testament; by twenty he had been fired for preaching to fellow workers on a construction site. Apart from rock music (he played the guitar), the Bible seemed his only interest. His increasing fervor took him into the Seventh-day Adventist Church in Tyler, Texas, where for almost two years he was one of the loudest and most demonstrative members of the congregation. He even announced his plans to take up a ministry. But in 1982 members of this essentially conservative group decided they had had enough of his enthusiastic and unorthodox interpretations of their theology and they threw him out.

Like Houteff before him, Howell headed down to Waco, where he joined the smaller and more radical Branch Davidian community. There he found his spiritual home, a place where his earnest declamations would be taken seriously. By 1986, when Lois Roden died, he had become one of the community's most popular members, winning over his coreligionists with what seemed to be a divinely inspired knowledge of the Bible. To some of them he began referring to himself as the Lamb of God. He claimed that he had spoken to God, that he alone could ultimately redeem his followers after the Apocalypse, and that he alone could reveal the spiritual mysteries of the Seven Seals. George Roden thought otherwise. Shortly after his mother's death he forced Howell and his followers out of the compound at gunpoint.

A year later, Howell, who had been unsuccessfully trying to set up a rival community, returned with eight armed followers and tried to take over Mount Carmel. Roden was slightly wounded in the affray, and Howell and the others were arraigned on charges of attempted murder. After a bizarre trial involving the appearance of a corpse in court (Roden sought unsuccessfully to demonstrate that he could raise the dead), they were found not guilty, and shortly afterward Roden was confined to a mental home. Howell, who was by now calling himself David Koresh — David after King David, Koresh after Cyrus, the Persian emperor who freed the Babylonian Jews from slavery — took over as leader of the Branch Davidians.

From then on, Koresh's development followed a pattern that cult experts later recognized as typical. He ruthlessly established his leadership and his sole right to interpret the sect's theology. He made several evangelical trips abroad, recruiting particularly among Seventh-day Adventist communities in the United Kingdom and Australia. Both from there and at home he began to attract new devotees, people who followed him back to Mount Carmel and stayed to hear more.

He also became more manipulative. For example, he taught that he was entitled to have sex with female cult members — young girls and other men's wives included — but that all the other men at Mount Carmel had to be celibate. His word was law on matters of money, diet, behavior, and dress. Like other cult leaders before him, he used food as a tool for ensuring obedience: making members go without meals if they disobeyed him, and occasionally, on a whim, changing his followers' diet. Sometimes dinner was stew or chicken; at other times it might be nothing but popcorn. One month the members ate nothing but bananas. He frequently subjected his exhausted followers to marathon Bible study sessions, and even resorted to physical force. Some of those he thought were breaking his rules were beaten with a canoe paddle on which were inscribed the words IT IS WRITTEN; others were thrown into a pool of raw sewage and then not allowed to wash.

As Koresh gained power over the Branch Davidians, he also began to develop a paranoia about authority figures. His teachings about a forthcoming apocalypse became bound up with a growing fascination for guns and a hatred of the law enforcement agencies. Under his orders, the Branch Davidians began assembling a deadly arsenal of heavy-caliber semiautomatic weapons. They established their own gun shop, and through it began to buy large stocks of ammunition and parts for converting rifles to machine guns. Military-style weapons training became mandatory for the cult members, and men, women, and even children were sent over a specially built assault course. Bible classes were often preceded by hours on the firing range. The cult began expanding the compound as Koresh urged his followers to fortify it against the coming apocalypse. Stocks of food and water were brought in, and gas masks were purchased and tested, in preparation for what he claimed would be a final confrontation with the forces of darkness. Frequently Koresh cast the FBI and the ATF in this role, claiming that they would attack and kill everyone in the compound. Armageddon was just over the horizon, he said, and then and only then would he be able to unlock the mystery of the Seven Seals, which would end the world and ensure the Branch Davidians' place in Paradise.

By the time Koresh came to the attention of the authorities, his power over his followers was complete. To many in the outside world he seemed a charming young man with a slightly crazy ob-

session about the Apocalypse. To his disciples, however, he was the
Lamb of God. Like all cult leaders, he appeared to have access to
some inner truth, and this was remarkably attractive to vulnerable
and susceptible people. His followers were prepared to endure humiliation and degradation. The Spartan lifestyle, the sacrifices, the
self-denial — all were worth enduring for the sake of some greater
good. This extreme devotion, coupled with the Branch Davidians'
acquisition of sophisticated modern weaponry and training in its use
made an explosive formula. Mount Carmel was a time bomb.

Into this potentially disastrous situation walked the Bureau of Alcohol, Tobacco, and Firearms, an agency run under the aegis of the
Department of the Treasury but for all intents and purposes independent. Originally established to investigate the smuggling of contraband cigarettes and whiskey, the ATF now concentrates on the
firearms industry, arson, and illegal explosives.

The ATF's interest in the Branch Davidians was sparked by a tip
from a United Parcel Service employee who had made several deliv-
eries of arms and weapon parts to the gun shop in 1992. The subsequent investigation unearthed a major pattern of arms shipments,
many of which were legal. According to a court affidavit, the ATF
believed the cult had obtained grenade launchers, dozens of AK-47
and AR-15 semiautomatic rifles, some heavy-caliber sniper rifles,
dozens of assorted handguns, and hundreds of thousands of rounds
of ammunition — all of them, astonishingly, legitimately acquired
under Texas gun laws, which are about the most liberal in the world.
But other materials were more suspect. Through various informants
and the eyewitness reports of Robert Rodriguez, an undercover agent
who subsequently infiltrated the group, the ATF believed it had
evidence that Koresh and his followers were converting the semiautomatic weapons to machine guns and were manufacturing hand
grenades and other explosive devices. Both of these processes are
illegal.

The ATF began compiling warrants for a search-and-seizure raid.
Why it didn't merely arrest Koresh on one of his frequent forays into
town, or when he was out jogging, is hard to comprehend. Perhaps
someone thought that a high-profile and dramatic operation would
help repair the agency's image, which had become somewhat lack-
luster in recent years. If that was so, it was a tragic error.

ATF agents weren't the only ones interested in the Branch Davidians. The activities of Koresh and his group had come to the attention of the local paper, the *Waco Tribune-Herald*. Its reporters had begun work on a series of exposés and were interviewing former cult members and local people who had come into contact with the Branch Davidians. The first in the series was published on Saturday, February 27, 1993, the day before the ATF raid was to take place. The timing could not have been worse. The day the article came out, an ATF agent tipped off the *Waco Tribune-Herald* and a local TV network about the raid. The word spread to nine other media outlets. By 8:30 the next morning, there were over a dozen TV and newspaper journalists around Mount Carmel.

Inside the compound that Sunday, the Branch Davidians were on edge. The newspaper article had been very critical, and Koresh took it as a sign that the authorities were taking an undue interest in his group. He had also become suspicious of a group of men living in a nearby house, who had told the Davidians that they were students. Since most of them were over forty, nobody believed them. (It turned out that they were part of an ATF surveillance team.) Koresh told his followers to be extra vigilant that day.

One of the Davidians, David Jones, worked as a mailman. He was returning from an errand, driving his official U.S. Mail van, when he saw a car parked a few hundred yards from Mount Carmel. The car belonged to Jim Peeler, a cameraman with KWTX-TV. Jones stopped to ask if he was lost, but then saw the TV station's logo on Peeler's jacket and realized that he wasn't talking to any ordinary passerby. Peeler, for his part, didn't know that the helpful mailman was a Branch Davidian. He warned him to keep clear of the area, as helicopters and agents would shortly be arriving.

Cutting the conversation short, Jones drove off to report to Koresh. The ATF's undercover agent, Robert Rodriguez, was in the compound at the time. Immediately understanding that the raid was compromised, he managed to slip out of the compound and race away to the nearby observation point to warn his superiors. As he left, Koresh began shouting, "Neither the ATF nor the National Guard will ever get me. They got me once, and they will never get me again. They are coming! The time has come!"

His disciples began gathering up their weapons. Douglas Wayne Martin, a Harvard-educated lawyer who practiced in Waco, hung a string of hand grenades around his neck; others moved into positions in the fortified watchtower that Koresh had had built at the center of the compound. One of them carried a .50 caliber armor-piercing rifle that could shoot through a car from a mile away; this same weapon had been used by the U.S. Army to knock out Iraqi light armor in the Gulf War.

By now the ATF knew that it had lost the crucial element of surprise. But in spite of a standing order that the assault should be canceled if secrecy was lost, the field commanders, Philip Chojnacki and Chuck Sarabyn, decided to go ahead. They didn't even bother to modify their strategy.

Shortly after 9:30 A.M., ninety-one armed ATF agents climbed into two sealed cattle trucks in Waco and set off on the fifteen-mile trip to Mount Carmel. Several dozen Branch Davidians crouched behind carefully erected barriers, checked their weapons, and settled down to wait. Shortly before 10:00, three ATF helicopters flew low over the compound and were fired upon, forcing them to withdraw. Almost immediately afterward the assault force arrived and went on the offensive.

Two hours later, ten people were dead. No weapons had been seized, and the Branch Davidians were now firmly entrenched in their compound, ready to defend themselves from the next assault by the forces of evil.

Within a day the abortive raid was headline news around the world. As the debate over what had gone wrong got under way, one question was asked over and over again: What now?

The Federal Bureau of Investigation was supposed to provide the answer. Because four federal agents had been killed in the exchange of gunfire, the Bureau now had jurisdiction over whatever happened next. The debacle had not improved its opinion of the ATF, which many FBI agents privately regarded as a second-rate organization, and though they mourned the deaths of fellow law enforcement officers, the FBI agents were now determined to show the world how such an operation should be run.

But right from the start the Bureau had problems. Because the ATF had effectively botched its own operation, the FBI was at a disadvantage: instead of being in control, it was to some extent at the mercy of the cult, which was on its own ground and could set the pace of events. Since there were so many weapons inside the compound, the FBI could not even overwhelm the Branch Davidians through force of numbers and superior firepower.

A few hours after the assault, the special agent in charge of the San Antonio Division, Jeff Jamar, arrived on the scene. Although the ATF was nominally in command for the next twenty-four hours, Jamar made it clear who was now in charge. Waco fell within his area, and he had all the right links with local law enforcement to be the logical choice as on-site commander. However, this was his first big crisis since he had taken over in San Antonio, and he knew that his every move would be scrutinized by more experienced SACs across the country. Fortunately, Jamar did have a standing contingency plan to work with. Called the Crisis Management Program, it had the principal function of drawing together appropriately qualified personnel from all over the country, and it had been put into effect the moment Jamar was appointed by headquarters.

By the time Jamar arrived at Mount Carmel, an advance party of agents from the Hostage Rescue Team (HRT) had already taken up sniping positions around the perimeter. Others arrived on his heels. Then came personnel from the Special Operations and Research Unit; the Critical Incident Negotiating Team; SWAT units from San Antonio, Dallas, Houston, El Paso, and elsewhere; agents from the local division's Special Operations Group; media relations experts and logistics specialists from headquarters; a behavioral scientist from the Investigative Support Unit; and agents who were experts in dozens of other relevant disciplines. The command chain for the operation, now called WACMUR (short for "Waco Murders"), extended all the way up to the attorney general in Washington. The Strategic Information Operations Center, on the fifth floor of the J. Edgar Hoover Building, would be manned night and day by an emergency team led by Assistant Director Larry Potts, who would in turn report to his superiors, Deputy Director Floyd Clarke and Director William Sessions. Including the hundreds of agents working behind the scenes at field offices across the country and ancillary units from the Texas National Guard, the Texas Rangers, U.S. Customs, the ATF, the U.S. Army, and the McLennan County Sheriff's Office, over two thousand people were directly or indirectly at Jamar's beck and call. On any one day there were between two and three hundred at Waco. It was a heavy responsibility.

One of Jamar's top priorities was to establish rules of engagement. In simple terms, the people at the site were divided into two camps: the tactical squads, led by HRT commander Richard Rogers, assistant SAC of the Washington field office; and the negotiators, coordinated at various times by Gary Noesner, Clinton Van Zandt, and James Botting. In discussions with Larry Potts and Richard Rogers, Jamar decided to follow normal procedure. The tactical squads would not use deadly force except in self-defense or when it was believed that agents or others were at risk of injury or death; the strategy was one of containment, negotiation, and pressure. The Bureau's paramount objective was to convince Koresh and his followers to surrender peacefully without any further loss of life. This policy had been followed with some success in previous hostage crises — because there were children in the compound at Mount Carmel, the operation was considered a hostage situation — and the Bureau had every reason to believe it would be equally successful at Waco.

In the aftermath of the cease-fire, Koresh's first act had been to dial 911 and shout at a bewildered police dispatcher, "You brought a bunch of guys out here and you killed some of my children. We told you we wanted to talk. How come you guys try to be ATF agents? How can you try to be so big all the time?" He also called his relatives and the news networks and claimed that he and the Branch Davidians were the victims of a major conspiracy. CNN interviewed him live on the evening of February 28, and the world got its first real insight into Koresh's mental state. Describing himself as the Lamb of God, he took a meandering journey through the Book of Revelation, focusing on the Seven Seals described therein. This was the way, he said, to Apocalypse. Opening the first seal would reveal a white horse that symbolized evil; the second would reveal a red horse symbolizing war and political strife. The black horse of the third represented famine. The pale horse of the fourth symbolized death. The fifth seal meant suffering, the sixth earthquakes and natural disasters. The seventh seal was to be opened at Armageddon, the second coming of Christ. Only the Lamb could open the seals. "I am the Lamb," he repeated.

A veteran FBI agent watched a replay of this performance on a portable TV as he raced toward Waco in a SWAT vehicle, and he said later, "I looked around at the guys and said, 'Jeez, I've seen some loony tunes in my time, but this guy is a real nut."

After a few hours, Koresh began to make deals. He promised

KRLD-AM, a Dallas radio station, that he would release some of the children if it would broadcast his written statements. That evening, as the first statements were transmitted, two children were released. Two more followed a second broadcast a few hours later. Shortly before midnight Charles Seraphin, the station manager, took a call from the compound. A few minutes later he found himself talking to Koresh. For forty minutes they chatted, the cult leader answering every question with a quotation from the Bible. Then Koresh insisted he wanted to go live.

After checking with the ATF, which was still in the last few hours of its command, Seraphin agreed, though he was terrified that Koresh would commit suicide on the air. At one point Koresh said, "I've been shot. I'm bleeding bad. I'm going home. I'm going back to my father." After a few more minutes he hung up. That was the last the public heard from him for some days. From then on, the FBI was determined to limit his access to the media.

The morning after the siege began, on March 1, FBI negotiators went to work on the long, slow process of trying to talk the Branch Davidians into coming out. Although they would speak to fifty-four different people over the phone in the coming weeks, for the most part they could reach only Koresh, Steve Schneider, his chief lieutenant, and Wayne Martin, the Harvard-educated lawyer. Usually they talked to Schneider, but the talks with Koresh were the longest, since they involved his rambling biblical references. Every word of the 754 conversations — 215 hours' worth — was recorded for later review by the Bureau's panel of experts and psychologists, who examined every nuance, every hesitation or stumble, for possible clues into the characters of those inside the compound.

Meanwhile, two command centers were set up, one in a camper van near the compound's perimeter, which would become the headquarters of the tactical unit, the other at a former air force base some miles away. Bradley armored personnel carriers, on loan from the U.S. Army, were brought in to guard the perimeter, but they were kept at a distance after Koresh warned that he had the ordnance to "blow them forty feet up in the air."

At first the signs were hopeful. During the first five days a thin trickle of Branch Davidians slowly left the compound. Each of these eighteen people, some of whom were children, was immediately whisked away to brief Bureau negotiators. One of them carried a tape that Koresh wanted broadcast on KRLD and on a national Christian radio network. Koresh promised that after it had been transmitted he and the rest of his followers would give themselves up. The taped sermon was fifty-eight minutes long and again contained references to the Book of Revelation. After the tape had been broadcast, religious leaders around the country declared it to be essentially meaningless.

Nonetheless, the FBI was apparently convinced that the cult leader would keep his word and surrender. As the hours slipped by and he made no move, Jamar and his team began to understand that Koresh could not be relied on to do what he said he would do. Some weeks later, a Branch Davidian confided to agents that there had never been any plan to surrender. Instead, he said, four cult members would have brought Koresh out on a stretcher and then they would have blown themselves up with explosives while those in the compound either killed themselves or were killed. But God had told David Koresh to wait. And so the siege settled into a weary stalemate.

By March 6 a routine had emerged. For hours every day FBI agents called the compound; in fact, the phone lines were rerouted to the main command center so that only the FBI could speak to the Davidians. At this stage, the Bureau's strategy was to restrict the activities of those inside and deprive them of a comfortable environment while reassuring them that they would be well treated if they surrendered. On several occasions agents told Koresh and the others that they would not use deadly force against anyone except in self-defense or in defense of another.

Koresh, who said he was irritated by the incessantly ringing telephone, cranked up the volume on his stereo and blasted rock music out at the ranks of agents. "We are ready for war," he told the negotiators. "Your talk is becoming in vain." But at this early stage, at least, he seemed happy to share the chatter. On one day the FBI spoke with the Davidians for over eleven hours, seven and a half of them with Koresh.

Inside the compound, some of the cult members were trying to carry on as usual, preparing food, teaching the children, making minor repairs, and getting what exercise they could. The others, including what was left of Koresh's inner circle of armed guards, which he called the Mighty Men, stood sentry. When Koresh repeated his threat to shoot at the Bradley armored vehicles, the FBI responded by bringing up Abrams tanks (which carried much heavier armor and could survive any firepower the Davidians might use against them). They began clearing fences, scrub, and abandoned vehicles from the outer ring of the fifty-acre compound. Slowly, very slowly, the perimeter began to shrink. On March 8, Koresh ordered a burial service for one of the cult members who had been killed in the February 28 raid, and three Branch Davidians left the complex with the body, drove fifty yards, and buried it in a hastily dug hole. No one attempted to interfere.

On March 10 Koresh broke off negotiations, claiming that he had a splitting headache. He had lost a lot of blood after being wounded in the raid, but he consistently refused all medical help. The following morning Steve Schneider promised negotiators that three Davidians would soon give themselves up. Nothing happened. Later that day Koresh's mother, Bonnie Haldeman, and a defense lawyer from Houston, Dick DeGuerin, arrived to speak with Koresh. They were turned back at a roadblock.

The next day, March 12, two cult members surrendered. One, Kathryn Schroeder, told agents that there were no plans inside the compound for suicide. The Bureau made a video of her emotional reunion with her three-year-old son and sent it into the compound in the hope that it might induce others to reunite with their children on the outside.

Schroeder's report was reassuring. Right from the start of the siege, the FBI experts had been worried that Koresh and the Davidians might commit mass suicide like the nine hundred followers of Jim Jones, who had poisoned themselves in Guyana in the late 1970s. Peter Smerick, an analyst with the Investigative Support Unit, was among those who were most concerned. He had been on the scene since March 3 and had prepared a number of profiles of Koresh for Jamar and his colleagues. In one Smerick noted, "He has significant characteristics associated with psychopaths; that is, he will generally act only in his self-interest, rarely accepts blame for his actions, is manipulative, cunning and has the ability to control the actions of others. He will display rapid flashes of anger if provoked and will act impulsively."

Smerick also warned of the dangers of increasing the tactical pressure. In memos prepared with a fellow profiler, Mark Young, he listed a number of tactical options that could be used to step up the pressure, but he recommended instead that efforts be made to shore up the trust between Koresh and the negotiators. He believed that

FBI commanders were beginning to move toward a tactical solution, and this worried him. On March 8, Smerick and Young stated in a memo, "Koresh realizes that in an environment outside the compound, without his control over the followers, he would lose his status as the Messiah. His orders for a mass suicide would be his effort to maintain the ultimate control over his group in the event of his death."

Others on the negotiating team were equally worried. They believed that Jeff Jamar was not taking their advice sufficiently seriously and that Koresh would lose his mind if pressured too much.

Jamar, who was also being briefed constantly by the tactical squads, was now in charge of one of the biggest siege operations in American history. He was spending most of his days either at the main command center or in the operations room in the camper van near Mount Carmel. Several hundred agents, local police, and state troopers were scattered around the perimeter of the compound, and the area was almost completely sealed off. Just over a mile and a half away a media village had sprung up, and a local farmer, Woodie Lambert, whose land adjoined the compound, was allowing hundreds of sightseers to line up to take a peek at the scene through his high-powered binoculars. The crowd attracted fast-food vendors and souvenir salesmen. For lack of anything else to do, the media interviewed these people and bought T-shirts labeled WACO: WE AIN'T COMING OUT. All in all, the scene was both tense and ludicrous — and there was no end in sight.

March 12 was a red-letter day for Janet Reno: she was sworn in as attorney general in Washington. Her first task was to receive an up-to-date briefing on the progress of the siege, and during this briefing she began to realize the enormity of the problems facing the FBI. After nearly two weeks the Hostage Rescue Team was beginning to feel the strain. For thirteen days trained snipers had been staring at the compound through scopes and night-vision equipment; eyes were getting tired, and tempers a little frayed. The SWAT teams from San Antonio and Dallas were equally exhausted, but because there were more of them and they were not so specialized, they at least had shorter and less frequent shifts. Many of the agents had begun to feel that it was time to do something more dramatic than negotiating.

Every morning FBI and Department of Justice officials held a press briefing, during which they reported what Koresh had been saying but gave away none of their own plans. They stressed that they were in control, but behind the scenes a major debate about possible courses of action was brewing. In Washington, Floyd Clarke, Larry Potts, and Director William Sessions consulted expert after expert about both the peaceful and the violent ways to bring the siege to an end. Sessions, who was already under a cloud for an independent financial scandal, was beginning to attract some unfavorable press about the lack of action. Following advice from the negotiators, however, they decided to continue as they were for the moment. President Clinton was briefed daily by his aides, and George Stephanopoulos, his chief press spokesman, told the media that Clinton had every confidence in the FBI's ability to bring the siege to a peaceful end.

Meanwhile, inside the compound, Koresh's wounds had worsened and he was spending much of his time in his second-floor bedroom. The Bureau already knew where most people in the compound were located. Sophisticated parabolic microphones had been directed at the compound for days, and, according to one source, two teams of agents had slipped in under the guns of the watching Davidians one night and placed wire-thin, sensitive fiber-optic transmitter cables in the walls of three of the compound buildings to broadcast closed-circuit pictures and sound to the command center. According to another source, agents had equipped an airplane with powerful thermal-image equipment borrowed from Britain's elite SAS regiment; by flying over the building, they could see where the cult members were on the inside of the wooden walls. And on the fourteenth day the HRT began to use a battery of 6 million candlepower floodlights to illuminate the compound at night.

Clearly the tactical teams were beginning to make their presence felt. Sometimes they followed the advice of the negotiators, sometimes, as on March 12 when they convinced Jamar to cut off the electricity to the compound, they acted on their own initiative and pushed for more provocative action. Conflict with the negotiating team was inevitable. The negotiators' strategy was to try to gain the Davidians' trust and then create a situation in which the cult members would feel dependent on the FBI. They tried to get the Davidians to rely on them for little luxuries like fresh milk and vegetables, hoping that as a parent opened up a container of milk for her son or daughter, it would dawn on her that this milk had been provided by people David Koresh was describing as tyrants and killers. They also sent a videotape portraying the negotiators as caring, Christian, family men into the compound. But not all their presents were so benign. For instance, acceding to a request for writing materials, they supplied paper and a typewriter for Koresh to work on. Hidden among these gifts, however, were tiny microtransmitters that they hoped would give them clearer intelligence about what was going on inside. A few of these devices worked well for a few days, at least until their batteries ran down, but the Davidians discovered most right away and destroyed them.

In spite of the growing frustration, the strategy was still to negotiate, and new developments continued to give hope to that approach. For instance, on March 15, Special Agent Byron Sage, one of the leading negotiators, and McLennan County sheriff Jack Harwell had a face-to-face meeting with Steve Schneider and Wayne Martin, who met them about sixty yards from the compound. The four men talked for ninety minutes, but although the atmosphere was positive, little was accomplished. The Davidians repeated Koresh's promise to come out eventually, when the time was right, and the negotiators offered them a fair trial and safety from violence.

Some of the negotiators had high hopes for Schneider at that point. Unlike Koresh, he was a college graduate. His wife, Judy, had been appropriated by Koresh shortly after their arrival, and Schneider had been angry when Judy had a child by Koresh. Schneider had become Koresh's lieutenant when Perry Jones, who had previously filled the role, was killed on February 28, and some agents hoped that he could be manipulated into challenging Koresh's leadership. Byron Sage, though, had doubts. He believed that Schneider was not that well respected by the rest of the Davidians and that it would be difficult for him to accept that he had made a mistake in joining the group in the first place.

The negotiators were still spending hours each day on the telephone to Koresh, in conversations that were largely one-sided. Little actual negotiation went on; Koresh usually embarked on rambling religious lectures, to which the weary agents responded with monosyllabic answers. The cult leader was hard to put off his stride, even in the early hours of the morning. A typical discussion, on March 20, began at 12:15 A.M. and lasted until 3:12 A.M. Sometimes the negotiators let Koresh take calls from the Davidians who had already surrendered, most of whom were being held as material witnesses in nearby jails. When the telephone system proved inadequate to the strain of round-the-clock discussions, agents in an armored vehicle delivered an army field telephone to the compound.

Around March 12, Schneider told the FBI that thirty Davidians wanted to surrender. None appeared immediately, but seventy-two hours later eight cult members, mostly elderly men and women, emerged. Koresh had given them a final Bible lesson before they left the compound. Fifty adults and twenty-five children remained inside. Over the next three days several of the FBI's calls into the compound went unanswered.

On March 22 Koresh demanded that he be allowed to preach to his flock once he was in jail, and the FBI sent in a letter signed by Jeff Jamar confirming the terms of the agreement. Schneider thought it was a good sign, but Koresh wadded the letter into a ball and threw it away. That afternoon the negotiators and the tactical teams began to discuss the viability of using tear gas.

On March 24, in the early hours of the morning, the FBI began to blast the compound with a tape recording of Tibetan meditational chants. "We are not going to be jerked around," said Robert Ricks, the SAC from Oklahoma, who had come in to help Jamar. "If they back away from what they promise, we will continue to exert the pressure we feel necessary." A similar step-up in pressure came the next day, when Koresh rejected the offer of a two-hour stint on a Christian television network if he surrendered. "It's not worth the paper it's written on," he said. Negotiators responded by blasting the compound with Nancy Sinatra songs and tapes of rabbits being slaughtered. "Which one is Nancy Sinatra?" a weary SWAT team member was heard to ask his colleagues.

Despite these tactics, on the next two days, March 25 and March 26, two men, both apparently attracted by Koresh's televised prophesies of a post-Armageddon paradise, embarrassed the FBI by slipping past the cordon into the compound. The first, Louis Anthony Alaniz, was an outcast from the Assembly of God Church. Agents failed to spot him until he was knocking on the door of the building. They decided to let him go in. The next day Jesse Amen sneaked through the security barriers. The Bureau tightened up the perimeter, but some of the fifty men in the HRT squad began to complain about the constant pressure they were under.

On March 30, after several requests, the FBI decided to let Koresh's attorney, Dick DeGuerin, into the compound. A lean, boyish ex-prosecutor, known among local defense lawyers as "Clint Eastwood," DeGuerin had a track record of successfully defending apparently hopeless cases and winning the confidence of his clients. He sat on a chair on the porch and talked to cult members through a crack in the door for almost two hours. Eventually, at a subsequent meeting, he was allowed inside. His approach to Koresh's problems, which he explained to the cult members over meals of canned chicken, apple juice, and nuts, was straightforward. The matter would have to be dealt with in the courts, DeGuerin told Koresh, but in his opinion the government didn't have much of a case. A jury could be convinced that Koresh and the Davidians had acted in self-defense. Koresh should consider surrendering now, before matters got out of hand. But Koresh was noncommittal; he would have to consult with God.

DeGuerin later called a press conference and said he was confident that some settlement could be worked out. But away from the cameras, he was more cautious and conceded to agents that the situation might be more complex than he had first thought. After one of his meetings, the Davidians had given him a videotape showing two adults and sixteen children, meant to allay the negotiators' worries about the children's welfare. Agents were disturbed by the pictures, and when Koresh began putting the children on the telephone to ask, "Are you coming to kill me?" they became seriously concerned. They put a temporary halt to their own discussions with Koresh to give DeGuerin more time.

Throughout this period the command team consulted every day with its panel of behavioral and psychological experts, garnered from inside and outside the Bureau. As the days passed they grew increasingly sophisticated in their judgments, but differences of opinion began to emerge. The Behavioral Science Unit at Quantico believed that Koresh was terrified at the thought of prison and had a fear of homosexual rape. Inside the compound he had everything he wanted — wives, food, liquor, attention — but in jail he would be a nobody, an inmate on trial for his life. He was teetering on the edge of insanity, yet still able to think and act in an apparently rational way. The longer the siege went on, the unit felt, the faster his tenuous links with reality would disappear.

Some of the other members of the group (academics and psychiatrists from universities and hospitals across the United States) also expressed fears that the Bureau was playing a dangerous game. Noise and lights at night were part of a tactical strategy aimed at irritating the besieged and keeping them on their guard, so that if an attack ever had to be launched, they would be tired and confused. But the strategy wasn't without its risks. Koresh could be pushed into a violent response, and the possibility of mass suicide was ever present.

And so the discussions went on. There were meetings at the White House, at the command center at FBI headquarters, in the Department of Justice, at the San Antonio field office, amid the massed cabins, camper vans, and SWAT trucks on the perimeter. Some of these concerned logistics — getting resources from A to B, how to handle the press, how to analyze the statements made by Davidians who had already come out. Other meetings were held under rigid security and focused on the last resort — the viability of armed intervention.

With no immediate end in sight, the media village shrank a little. Attention was focusing on Washington. Why didn't the Department of Justice do something? The new attorney general was spending hours every day going over the possibilities. William Sessions, equally under pressure, asked his team to assess the impact of a personal on-the-spot appeal to David Koresh. After all, he reasoned, he came from Texas originally and might be able to explain the legal system in a manner Koresh would understand. But Potts and Clarke dissuaded him from flying down, arguing that he would be in danger, and that experts on the scene were better equipped to cope with the situation. Privately, many within the top echelons of the Bureau thought Sessions was hoping a dramatic personal gesture could help him hold on to his job.

The days passed with few further incidents. On April 4, Jesse Amen, one of the men who had crept into the compound a few days earlier, appeared outside the front door, was embraced by a Davidian, and left. He was immediately taken away to talk to the negotiators, but he made little sense. Several times in the following days Davidians attempted to leave the confines of the buildings and walk around the compound. Each time the FBI drove them back with "flash bangs," tiny explosive charges that gave off bright light, smoke, and noise.

Two days later, DeGuerin and Jack Zimmerman, Steve Schneider's attorney, who had also been allowed to visit his client, left Waco, saying that nothing would change until the cult had celebrated Passover, a fact that Bob Ricks felt might be significant. "Many of his followers who have come out and those around the world have said that David has said this is the last Passover they will celebrate together," he told the press. Later DeGuerin admitted to the *New York Times* that he had been negotiating on Koresh's behalf with publishers for the book and movie rights to the cult leader's story. The Bureau conceded that this might mean Koresh was looking to the future, but few in the FBI still seriously believed he was going to come out voluntarily.

On April 9, the forty-first day of the siege, Steve Schneider brought out a handwritten letter purportedly from God. He left it on the ground some way from the buildings, and it was retrieved by agents in a Bradley fighting vehicle. The message was confusing. It was written in the first person and referred to Koresh as "my friend." "I am your God," it said, "and you will bow under my feet . . . I offer you my wisdom. I offer you my sealed secrets. How dare you turn away my invitations of mercy." The letter warned that the nearby Waco dam might be washed away by an earthquake, and the Texas Rangers put guards on the dam in case anyone attempted to fulfill the prophecy. When the Bureau passed the letter on to psychologists for assessment, they reported that Koresh showed signs of paranoid psychosis. This was confirmed the next day, when Jamar and his colleagues received another letter from God: "This is a warning. Please don't harm my Lamb." The Syracuse University psycholinguist Murray Miron told the FBI, "We are listening to the ramblings of a diseased mind. These are the one-sided delusional tirades made by a paranoiac."

On April 14 Koresh told DeGuerin on the telephone that he would surrender when he had finished writing a manuscript that would explain the Seven Seals. He added in a letter, "As far as our progress is concerned, here is where we stand. I've related two messages from God . . . I'm presently being permitted to document in structured form the decoded message of the Seven Seals. Upon completion of this task I will be freed of my waiting period. I hope to finish this as soon as possible and stand before man and answer any and all questions regarding my activities."

But events were now moving remorselessly to a conclusion. Both inside and outside the compound there was an awareness that the situation couldn't continue as it was indefinitely. On April 18, an HRT sniper, his eyes red with fatigue, noticed a movement in one of the windows. He swung his high-powered scope around and saw that someone had propped up a cardboard sign on the ledge. It read FLAMES AWAIT. He called the information in to the forward command post, but the response was not recorded. By then they were probably busy with other matters.

On April 7, Floyd Clarke and Larry Potts flew secretly into Waco on an unmarked government plane to hear a plan devised by Jeff Jamar and Dick Rogers, the tactical leader, to end the siege. Jamar told the men from Washington that he wanted to send in tanks and pump the buildings in the compound full of tear gas.

Jamar and Rogers believed that a frontal assault was out of the question. They suspected that the entire compound was booby-trapped, and they knew the cult had powerful weapons and night scopes. Sentries guarded the windows around the clock, and whenever agents approached in tanks, members of the sect would hold up children. Jamar and Rogers had explored other ideas — using water cannon, for instance. But they had no armored fire truck at hand to act as a pump, and the water might bring the whole structure down and would certainly destroy any evidence inside. Some of the more fanciful ideas being touted by the press, such as drugging or cutting off the compound's water supply or dropping agents in from helicopters, had been dismissed as unworkable. Any blatant attempt to use force could bring a savage response from the Davidians. But the siege was tying up massive resources, the HRT team had been running shifts for forty days without a break, and the negotiators were running out of ploys. Something had to be done. The agency's reputation was at stake. It was already under fire for the imbroglio involving Sessions, and the lack of a resolution at Waco only added to the public's sense that something was wrong at the heart of the FBI.

Five days later, on April 12, the Bureau chiefs laid the plan out in front of Attorney General Reno. The meeting took place in the greatest secrecy in the "submarine," the lead-lined Strategic Information Operations Center, on the fifth floor of FBI headquarters.

Reno, Sessions, Clarke, Potts, Douglas Gow (the associate deputy director), John Collingwood (the Bureau's media relations director), and a handful of others went through Jamar and Rogers's outline in great detail. As the attorney general flipped through the red leather folder containing the plan, she asked the first of hundreds of questions. She repeated one frequently: "Why now?" After ninety minutes she left, apparently unconvinced. Later that day the team reconvened in Reno's office and went over the same ground. Again the meeting broke up without a decision.

On April 14, Reno widened her circle of advisers to include other FBI officials, members of the army's Delta Force, more lawyers, and Dr. Harry Salem, a Pentagon expert on tear gas. Another marathon question-and-answer session ensued. The first point the attorney general insisted on concerned the likely impact of tear gas on the children in the compound. The Bureau wanted to use a chemical called CS gas (known officially as orthochlorobenzalmalononitrile), which is more debilitating than normal tear gas. Reno listened while Salem told her that the gas would cause eye irritation, crying, coughing, sneezing, and difficulty in breathing, but that it wouldn't permanently harm adults or children and wouldn't start a fire during delivery. It was, Salem assured her, the best nonlethal gas available.

There was also some discussion of whether gas would be the best way to prevent mass suicide. The cult members had gas masks, but the filters would last only a few hours at most, and the plan called for injecting the gas over a much longer period. It would disorient the Davidians and drive them out. The agents also told Reno that they had decided not to use anesthetic gas because of the risk that anyone who inhaled it might not wake up, especially the young children, and that strong men would be the last to be knocked out.

Then Reno returned to the issue that had bothered her earlier. Why now, why not wait? Again the agents had a ready answer. Koresh had prepared well. The Davidians had bought thousands of army surplus emergency rations packs and had stored enough water for a year. They showed no signs of coming out voluntarily; indeed, everyone seemed to be settling into a comfortable routine. Koresh had promised to surrender after Passover, but only he knew when his version of the holiday ended. The passage of time was not going to make the situation any easier; it only increased the likelihood that something would happen to injure the innocent children in the compound, the public at large, or agents at the scene. Sanitation was already a major problem; there were no flush toilets, and cult members, afraid of FBI snipers, had given up burying their waste and now just threw it out the door. The longer the siege went on, the greater the chance of disease.

Then the agents told Reno more about the children. According to one of those present, an agent said that a Davidian who had left the compound earlier had talked of babies being slapped around. "Let me get this clear," said Reno. "Do you really mean beaten?" "Yes," the agent replied. Reno was left with the clear impression that the FBI believed children were being abused at that time. Only later did she find out that the allegation was an old one and was not necessarily still relevant.

Sessions, Potts, and Clarke expressed concern about how long the HRT had been on the scene in a state of constant readiness. Dick Rogers had said that his unit would soon have to be pulled out for retraining if it was going to remain useful. Furthermore, it was the only civil force that had the expertise to secure the extensive area around the compound; the FBI's own SWAT teams, while well trained, did not have the specific experience they needed for this job. Since the idea was not to provoke a major showdown but to increase the pressure gradually, using gas was the last phase in a logical progression. The gas would be inserted gradually, forcing the cult members into the front of the complex of buildings, which had more exits than the others. The more crowded the front buildings became, the more the Davidians would feel the pressure to come out. Gas and negotiate, gas and negotiate: it was a relatively simple strategy.

Then Reno turned to the most difficult question. How would Koresh react? His theology defied any logical interpretation. Those at the meeting discussed whether his obsession with the Seven Seals meant he would commit suicide or encourage others to commit suicide when the end came. Agents pointed out that they had asked Koresh four times whether he planned to kill himself, and each time he had said no. Others in the room argued that there was evidence pointing the other way. One of the children who had come out of Mount Carmel had demonstrated on TV how she had been taught to put a gun in her mouth. Cult members around the world had warned the authorities that Koresh and his followers would never allow themselves to be taken alive.

No one, it seems, discussed the differences of opinion that had arisen time and time again between the negotiators (backed by the Behavioral Science Unit) and the tacticians over how the siege should be conducted. Nor, apparently, did anyone wonder whether the Branch Davidians might become less stubborn if less pressure was applied. Things had gone too far for that.

But Reno fought against the prevailing mood. She probed again to see whether all the alternatives had been explored. Why not put up a fence around Mount Carmel and keep the cult members there? Not possible, the agents replied. There would be an unacceptable risk to construction workers, and the resources needed to provide a guard would be immense. If the perimeter had been breached when the HRT was in control, it would almost certainly be compromised if another agency were in charge. Besides, the FBI could not walk away from a group that had already killed four federal agents. Every day that the Davidians went unpunished was another day that law enforcement was made to look weak and ineffective.

The meeting dragged to an end, but it was followed the next day by another round of discussions and debate. Reno was being forced into a corner, but she shrank from making a hasty decision. On April 15 she asked Associate Attorney General Webster Hubbell to talk personally to Byron Sage in Waco. The phone conversation lasted two hours. The message was clear: the negotiations had reached an impasse. Reno then called for advice from the army's Delta Force. Was the Bureau's plan workable? General Peter Schumacher and Colonel Jerry Boinken told her that it was, but they preferred a much faster solution: gas should be injected simultaneously all around the compound. The Bureau's gradual approach seemed unnecessarily complicated.

Yet more meetings followed. At one point on April 16, Hubbell told colleagues that Reno had said no; a few hours later, however, she was considering the plan again. The Bureau executives were getting impatient, and their mood was not improved when Carl Stern, head of the Justice Department's Office of Public Affairs, commented that going ahead with the plan might be likened by the public to Saddam Hussein's gassing of the Kurds. That night Reno sat in her office in the Department of Justice building and brooded on what she had been told. Was there really no other way? At a final meeting with her staff and the FBI's senior team the next day, she said she had decided to go ahead with their plan. On Sunday, April 18, she called President Clinton and talked for fifteen minutes. "Have you carefully considered it?" he asked. "Do you feel this is the best way to go?" "Yes, sir," she replied. "It's my responsibility, and I think it's the best way to go."

At 4:00 the next morning, Jeff Jamar and his aides gathered in the FBI's forward command post, a mile from the compound. Around them in the darkness a full complement of agents and hundreds of police officers made their final preparations. Dick Rogers was sealed in an Abrams tank on the edge of the compound, and the Bureau had brought in other tanks, M-60s that had been converted to combat engineering vehicles. Attached to the front of two of them were large booms. The plan was to poke these booms through the walls on the far right and left sides of the main compound building and then to pump gas into the upper and lower levels. "Ferret" rounds, small canisters containing gas, would be shot through the windows. The aim was to drive the cult members into the center and then out the front door. The rest of Rogers's team was in the other tanks or in four Bradley armored personnel carriers beyond the perimeter. HRT snipers, their eyes rested after a longer than usual break, were posted in two houses across the road. SWAT units manned the perimeter, and a helicopter hovered nearby ready to catch anyone who might make a run for it. Now everyone was waiting for the wind to die down, so it wouldn't disperse the gas. After a tense hour, the breeze abated.

At 5:55 A.M., Byron Sage picked up the phone and called the compound to say, "There's going to be tear gas injected into the compound. This is not an assault. Do not fire. The idea is to get you out of the compound." The same message was broadcast to the rest of the Davidians over the loudspeaker system. Schneider answered the telephone, and his response was defiant. Shouting, "Everybody grab your masks," he threw the phone out the window.

Five minutes later, Jaime Castillo, a twenty-five-year-old Branch Davidian from El Monte, California, who had been sleeping in the compound chapel, was awakened by a terrible crash. He crept upstairs to the first floor and saw that a massive hole had been punched in the wall. There were piles of rubble everywhere. On the other side of the compound, Koresh had been up all night working on the manuscript that he had told agents would decode the Seven Seals. Surviving Branch Davidians later said that he was wearing an old jogging suit but added a canvas hunting jacket and stuffed its pockets with ammunition.

At 6:02 the gassing began. According to the FBI (although some of the survivors vehemently denied this later), the cult members started shooting at the tanks. The FBI did not return fire, but because agents were under attack they stepped up the rate of the gassing. They were prepared to wait up to forty-eight hours for the cult members to come out — which was about as long as agents expected the filters on the Davidians' gas masks to last. But there were no immediate signs that the cult members were ready to leave. The survivors later said that they read their Bibles through the lenses of their masks. Children in the second-story dormitory wore masks with wet towels stuffed around them to make them fit. Fifty minutes after the gassing began, it was halted to let cult members out. No one emerged. The gassing resumed.

By 8:30 the wind had picked up, gusting to 35 knots. Jamar met with his aides halfway between the command post and the compound. Some agents believed that the doors to the building had jammed shut and people were unable to get out, so a tank was dispatched to knock a hole in the wall by the front door.

At 9:55 cult member Graeme Craddock ran out the front door, grabbed the telephone, and retreated. Five minutes later came the last recorded sighting of David Koresh. He was seen limping up and down the second-floor hallway, adjusting people's gas masks and handing out rounds of ammunition. Thirty minutes later Steve Schneider was seen for the last time, wearing headphones and listening to the radio.

The gassing continued periodically, as the HRT fired tear gas projectiles through windows and walls. At one point the cult members hung a white flag out an upstairs window, but they replaced it moments later with a colored one. This was a sign that they wanted their phone fixed, but that would require an agent to go on foot to the edge of the building complex. Jamar said later that he was unwilling to risk any more lives while the Davidians continued to fire on the armored vehicles.

Janet Reno had been watching the scene on closed-circuit television monitors in the Washington command center since early morning. At 10:00 she left for Baltimore, where she was to give a luncheon speech to judges of the Third Circuit Court. At 11:50 the final round of gassing was completed. Eighteen bottles of gas had been used, more than had been anticipated; the wind howling through the holes in the building had dissipated its effects. The Bureau put out an urgent request to other field offices for more canisters.

At 12:10, an FBI sniper at Sierra One position, some three hundred yards from the compound, reported that a man was kneeling on the ground just inside the front door of the compound. Seconds later, a fire started in that position. Agents who were monitoring the remaining hidden microphones heard more shooting, but this time it seemed to be aimed inside the building. Byron Sage, who had been broadcasting appeals to the Davidians all morning, later said that he grabbed a microphone and shouted, "Don't do this to those people! This is not the way to end it!"

Outside, Jamar saw smoke rising from the front right corner of the building. A circling FBI plane videotaped a huge fire that had started behind the watchtower. Then there seemed to be fires in four places. Bob Ricks stared at the blaze from a vantage point on the edge of the complex and said, "Oh my God. They're killing themselves." Danny Coulson, then a deputy assistant director who had been instrumental in founding the HRT, was watching with others in the FBI's command center in Washington. When the first flames appeared, the room went silent. Coulson began to pray quietly to himself. Down in Waco someone called 911 and asked for the fire department. It was fifteen miles away.

By 12:30 the fire had whipped through the chapel and into the second floor, where the children's dormitory was. The fierce wind made the fire spread quickly in the cheap wooden structures. Occasionally kerosene for the Coleman lamps and stockpiles of ammunition would explode. Some of the cult members struggled to safety. Ruth Riddle jumped through a hole in the wall, with smoke pouring from her clothes. An FBI agent clambered from an armored vehicle and caught her as she tried to get back into the building. Renos Avraam appeared on the roof, his clothes in flames. He fell off, and agents tore his burning clothes from him before rushing him to a Bradley. Six others got out from the rear of the building. But none of the children escaped, and eventually the complex began to collapse in on itself.

To the watching agents and to the world at large, the fire was a nightmare come to life. The only hope the agents had was that

someone might have put the children into an old bus that was
buried underneath the compound at the rear. When the firefighters
arrived, Dick Rogers led sixteen men down into a tunnel and through
a trapdoor, behind which they found the bus. The air was clear and
sweet, free of gas and smoke. There was no one inside.

By 3:00 P.M. the fire was out and agents had begun to sift through
the smoking rubble, looking for survivors. They found one man —
Graeme Craddock, who had been hiding under the edge of a concrete
block. Of the rest, only twisted, smoldering remains were found.

When the attorney general returned to the FBI command center,
she stood watching the scene in silence. Then she turned to look at
her aides and said, "I am responsible." No one among the shocked
group of agents or attorneys contradicted her. This was Washington;
someone would have to be the scapegoat.

Reno's decision to take the flak was a brave act, and a rare one in a
city where covering up your mistakes is deemed a prerequisite for
a successful career. In the days after the disaster she appeared on
countless talk shows and news programs, speaking of the agonizing
decision she had had to make and how she had finally accepted that
the status quo could not be allowed to continue. The media, which
had been sharpening its knives for a major inquest into what had
gone wrong and who was to blame, instead began to applaud Reno's
courage. Political Washington — including the president, who had
been keeping a low profile — joined in the paeans of praise once they
saw which way the wind was blowing.

What criticisms there were, were muted and halfhearted. Reno
had taken the blame and offered her resignation. There didn't seem
to be much point in hounding the FBI after that. Instead the media
focused its attention on the ATF raid, and the ATF in turn blamed
the media for tipping off the Davidians just before the raid. After a
few weeks, the heated investigations began to simmer down as the
American public accepted that no matter what had happened at
Waco, David Koresh was ultimately to blame. An ABC poll showed
that 95 percent of Americans believed he was responsible for the
disaster. Further speculation was put on hold as the media broadly
agreed to give the official inquiry process a chance to come up with
answers.

Somehow the FBI remained untouched. In the first few days after the disaster it was questioned about whether or not it had started the blaze. The Bureau quickly released a fire examiner's report showing that the fires had begun in four separate places. The inferno was obviously started deliberately, an agency spokesman said, as an act of suicide or murder, orchestrated for the Davidians by Koresh and his inner circle. The FBI also pointed out that many of the bodies, including Koresh's, had bullet wounds, which made it probable that the cult members had either shot themselves or had been shot by "third parties unknown." Pressed on why the agency had not anticipated a mass suicide, the spokesman said that they had been told several times by Koresh and others that the Davidians would not commit suicide, and the FBI's own experts had backed this up. With that in mind, they reasoned, the gassing was a legitimate risk that should have been taken.

Somehow, the agency forgot to mention Peter Smerick's memo of March 8, the one in which Smerick said that Koresh's "orders for a mass suicide would be his effort to maintain the ultimate control over his group in the event of his death." Were these prophetic words, or just a good guess? The official Department of Justice report into the affair, released several months later, skated over the issue. Smerick's critical opinions of the pressure tactics used by the Waco team were recorded, but there was no real assessment of whether he had been right in his warning or why it wasn't taken more seriously.

When asked about these issues later on, John Douglas, Smerick's boss at the Investigative Support Unit, did not wish to comment on whether too much pressure had been put on the Davidians. But he did say this: "What is frustrating is when you do give advice and it's not adhered to. This unit was involved in Waco and the Special Operations and Research Unit was involved. They had the negotiators; we were their assistant negotiators. So you do an assessment. Now you have a leader [Jeff Jamar] who's listening to the psychology side in behavioral science and the tactical side. You hope that there's a balance, that the person in charge gets a balance, tactical and behavioral, and then makes his decision. Sometimes when that happens he may shift, go more tactical or more on the negotiating side. It's up to them to make the ultimate decision. Sometimes it's frustrating, whether it's a Waco, Texas, or any type of crime."

Ultimately, of course, it would be grossly unfair for the FBI to take the blame for what happened at Mount Carmel. The disaster would never have happened if not for the hold Koresh had over his followers or the way the ATF botched its raid on the compound. It is also unfair to argue that the FBI's exhausted hostage rescue specialists should have been prepared to sit out the siege for as long as necessary to get all the people out. There is no concrete evidence that Koresh and his followers ever seriously considered giving themselves up, and even if they had, how long should the FBI have been prepared to wait before it happened — six months, nine months, a year? The Davidians had enough food and water for at least another year, and with rationing could probably have extended the period. Should the FBI really have waited that long?

But some criticisms of the way the siege was conducted are valid. It now seems obvious that at various times throughout the standoff there were strong differences of opinion between the tacticians and the negotiators. Privately, some FBI agents concede that a more conciliatory approach might have tempted some of the less devoted Davidians to surrender, and that perhaps fatigue or impatience influenced the Bureau's decision to press for a tactical solution. It is not easy to say, but if more notice had been taken of the warnings that Koresh could incite mass suicide or murder among his followers, then maybe a different and more successful tactical solution could have been worked out.

There are also some valid questions about the attorney general's role in the affair. Was she given the best advice? Did the FBI put her in a position where she could make only one decision? How seriously did the allegations of child abuse influence her decision, and why didn't the FBI correct her assumption that it was ongoing? Janet Reno has said several times that she believes the advice she received was clear and unbiased. She also maintains that she was never pressured to come down in favor of the Bureau's tactical plan. There is no reason to disbelieve her, but it must be remembered that she was sworn into office after the siege was well under way and a strategy had already been decided on. It was an awful crisis for a brand-new attorney general to have to face, and by all accounts she handled herself well. But it takes an unusually strong person to stand up to the real and implied pressure that an organization like the FBI can bring to bear, especially when that person is not used to its ways.

The official inquiry addressed some of these questions but was criticized for glossing over the differences of opinion among various parties involved at the scene. But up to a point its recommendations were sensible ones. If such an extended confrontation arises in the future, the report noted, the FBI should consider rotating the crisis management team and increasing the size of the HRT squad so that fatigue is less of a factor. It should provide for better communications among the different elements of the CMT, and more effective anesthetic gases should be developed. Predictably, though, the inquiry concluded that Koresh was solely responsible, adding that "under the circumstances, the FBI exhibited extraordinary restraint and handled this crisis with great professionalism."

The FBI itself officially considers that there was little else it could have done, although in the aftermath of the Department of Justice report, it expanded its Hostage Rescue Team and began developing a program of siege training for supervisors. Louis J. Freeh, who succeeded William Sessions as director, announced that he and the attorney general would be among a number of senior Bureau executives who would seek advice on crisis management. No blame was attached to any of the agents involved; in fact the Bureau even commended some of the people who took part. On July 16, 1993, barely three months after the tragedy, the Active Agents Association Convention in Chicago gave a special award to the HRT members for their role at the siege. Special mention was rightly made of the bravery of those agents who rescued survivors from the flames and of the courage under fire that others displayed on that awful day. No mention was made of the dead.

This extraordinary story has a dramatic postscript. In February 1994, almost a year after the traumatic events at Waco, eleven Branch Davidians were acquitted by a San Antonio jury of murder and conspiracy to murder the ATF agents who died in the raid of February 28. Seven of the defendants were convicted of lesser crimes. Four were set free. Asked for her comments on the verdicts, Attorney General Janet Reno said that despite the acquittals on the more serious charges, the jury clearly failed to believe the Davidians' claims that they had acted in self-defense. In a quiet aside, she added, "The ghost of Waco will be with me all my life."

CHAPTER 8

THE POLITICAL SPIES

THE AMERICAN PUBLIC'S INTEREST in the FBI is so persistent that barely a day goes by without some mention in the media of its work. For the most part, this coverage concentrates on the FBI's law enforcement operations. The agency's other mission, counterintelligence, traditionally remains clouded in secrecy, ostensibly because the requirements of national security override the public's "right to know." Naturally, the Bureau must be able to frustrate the espionage efforts of hostile powers without worrying that its clandestine operations could be compromised. But there is surprisingly little public debate about the agency's counterintelligence mission, and on the rare occasions when it does fall under the spotlight, usually for espionage cases, the media is quite flattering. The arrest in 1994 of Aldrich Ames, the former head of the CIA's Soviet branch, was a case in point. Although a few critics wondered how such a senior official in the intelligence community could have gotten away with being a double agent for the KGB (and its successor agency, the Russian Security Ministry) for nine years without being suspected, most press accounts focused on the exciting aspects of the story: how the Bureau conducted its surveillance, identified Ames's "dead letter boxes," and finally moved in on him.

Of course, the FBI encourages positive media coverage and does its best to reassure people that its interest in the political opinions of American citizens is confined to cases of foreign espionage. But in reality, the Bureau can open an investigation on any domestic group or individual it considers a threat to national security, regardless of whether the targets are suspected of breaking any law. Investigations like these lie in the murky area between crime, national security, terrorism, and foreign counterintelligence and are difficult to criticize outright because the Bureau often has prima facie evidence of wrongdoing. However, in some instances the Bureau has clearly overstepped the bounds and trespassed into areas that should never be its concern.

The agency's intelligence investigations into groups and individuals opposed to the Central American policies of the Reagan administration constitute perhaps the most disturbing episode in modern FBI history, and show how easily this can happen. In the 1980s, the Bureau embarked on a program to "uncover" the terrorist affiliations of a loose association of religious groups, peace groups, radical political organizations, and well-meaning individuals known as the Committee in Support of the People of El Salvador, or CISPES. Eventually the investigation involved over one hundred distinct political groups that were exercising their constitutional right to dissent from official government policies. By drawing on information provided in part by extreme right-wing pressure groups, the FBI showed yet again that it was unable or unwilling to differentiate between a legitimate criminal investigation and a political vendetta. The whole sorry chapter gave weight to the arguments of those who believe that no matter how effective the FBI is in its criminal and espionage investigations, it cannot always be trusted to abide by the Constitution its agents have sworn to uphold.

The FBI's investigation of CISPES was founded on three factors: the Reagan administration's attitude toward political dissent in the United States, growing turmoil in Central America, and a perceived threat from the Soviet Union's support of "wars of national liberation." Right from the start, as the Reagan transition team prepared to take over from President Carter in late 1980, these three "problems" helped form the thinking of the new national security and foreign policy advisers. Influenced by conservative pressure groups, they believed in an international Communist conspiracy that had the long-term goal of undermining the political, social, and economic stability of the United States. The conspiracy could be seen at work in Central America, where it was embodied in the new Sandinista government of Nicaragua and in the rebel insurgents of the FMLN in El Salvador, and at home, where the Soviet Union was using an old tactic, deploying "active measures" — soft propaganda and disinformation — to influence public opinion.

None of these ideas was particularly new. But unlike previous conspiracy theorists, the deeply conservative Reagan government had the will and the desire to go on the offensive. It was only a short step to involving the United States' two leading intelligence agencies, the CIA and the FBI, in covert countermeasures, both at home and overseas, against the nation's supposedly Communist-inspired opponents. This action was quickly codified under the catchall phrase "the fight against terrorism." Out of it grew a frighteningly unsophisticated formula: Communists were terrorists; Communist sympathizers, including liberal dissenters, were therefore supporting terrorism; silence the sympathizers, and Communist terrorism would be stopped. From the earliest days of the Reagan administration, this formula was vigorously applied.

One of the new president's first acts was to issue Executive Order 12333, which, like others that came after it, was classified and so not subject to congressional approval. Based largely on recommendations made during the election campaign by the conservative Heritage Foundation, it restored to the CIA and the FBI many of the intelligence-gathering powers that had been taken away from them in the years after Watergate. Not only were they once again allowed a wide use of wiretaps, surveillance techniques, informants, and so on; they were also allowed to contract secretly with private intelligence-gathering sources when and where it proved necessary. That these sources would be predominantly conservative in nature was no coincidence.

For the U.S. intelligence community to act effectively, such powers would have to be kept secret. Over a comparatively short period, the executive branch placed new restrictions on the issuance of government records under the Freedom of Information Act. Civil servants above a certain level were forbidden to write or speak about any aspect of their work, and most government employees became liable to random polygraph tests. Secrecy wasn't the only objective; these procedures had the added benefit of allowing the government to control the flow of information to the public, so the administration could manipulate the debate over U.S. foreign policy in its favor.

While these changes were being made in the United States, the administration was putting its policies, both covert and open, into effect in Central America. Massively increased political, financial, and military aid began to flow south. In Nicaragua, American aid funded the rebels known as the Contras, who were battling the left-wing Sandinista government for control. In El Salvador, the situation was equally complicated.

In the last days of the Carter administration, the military dictatorship of General Carlos Romero had been ousted by a junta led by José Napoleón Duarte, a moderate whom the Democratic White House had hoped would return democracy and stability to the country while maintaining its status as a bulwark against Communism in Latin America. But Duarte soon fell out of favor with almost everyone. Conservative Salvadorans regarded him as a U.S. puppet and a closet Communist, and they suspected he was ambitious to press ahead with land reform. They believed that the Reagan administration might pressure Duarte to crack down on their political opponents, but until that happened they continued to sponsor and actively organize the death squads that roamed the country murdering their enemies, members of the FMLN. The Communist guerrillas of the FMLN, though, who had been fighting the army and the military government since the early seventies, were at best only lukewarm about Duarte. When they realized he had neither the will nor the desire to make fundamental political changes or stop the death squads, they renewed their attacks with savage force.

Into this chaotic situation came the Reagan administration with its simplistic view of world affairs. It had to support Duarte with political and military aid, as his junta was the best available option for restraining the creeping tide of Communism. Apart from anything else, El Salvador was a handy base for supporting the Contras. But the administration was anxious to remain on good terms with the conservative elements in El Salvador and help them advance their influence. This policy, Reagan explained to the American public, was in the United States' best interests.

Despite its best efforts, however, the administration did not go unchallenged. News about Central America normally only appeared on exceptionally slow news days, but eventually enough was reported for opposition to the White House's Central American agenda, particularly in El Salvador, to grow. Support for the long campaign of the Salvadoran dissidents was fueled by media accounts of the brutality and violence in that country. Some people established small grass-roots organizations to provide a focus for protests against the United States' military support of Duarte; others, particularly in religious communities, banded together to help the thousands of refugees from the violence in the region. This inevitably brought them into direct conflict with the Reagan administration's conservative immigration polices, but hundreds of churches, synagogues, and convents nonetheless provided sanctuary for people who were, in effect, illegal aliens. By the mid-eighties, thousands of concerned citizens were involved in groups that questioned the morality and the consequences of the administration's policies.

Not surprisingly, the administration and the intelligence community became even more entrenched in their view that many of these groups were fronts for Soviet "active measures." As a result, the intelligence agencies — the FBI foremost among them — increasingly sought to establish that links between the Communists in El Salvador, Nicaragua, and elsewhere and the growing protest movement at home had little to do with authentic political activity and everything to do with Soviet-inspired terrorism. Thus the stage was set for an extraordinary campaign of character assassination, disinformation, infiltration, surveillance, and intimidation against people who were merely expressing their legitimate opposition to government policies.

According to William Sessions's testimony before Congress in 1988, the Bureau first became interested in CISPES in September 1981, when the Department of Justice suspected that the organization had violated the Foreign Agents Registration Act. In fact, however, the investigation was based not on this alleged crime but on suspicion of terrorist activities, and that suspicion in turn was based on documents that were almost certainly not what they purported to be.

These documents were supposedly taken from diaries compiled by Shafik Handal, the leader of the small Salvadoran Communist Party, and his brother, Farid Handal. According to the CIA, which passed them on to the FBI, the papers had been captured by the Salvadoran National Guard in 1980, during raids on guerrilla camps. They revealed a secret Soviet-Cuban plan to arm and train the Salvadoran rebels and implied that a concerted operation to influence liberal public opinion in the United States in support of the rebels had been initiated. Farid's travel diaries were particularly crucial: they detailed a trip he made to the United States to set up a network of solidarity groups to oppose U.S. military aid to the Duarte regime. According to the papers, he had met with officials from the U.S. Peace Council, which the intelligence community regarded as a Soviet front organization. As a consequence of that meeting, or so it was believed, one of the officials, Sandy Pollack, suggested setting up a conference to discuss the situation in El Salvador. The two conferences that were subsequently held in Los Angeles and Washington were attended by a wide variety of left-wing and liberal groups, and from them sprang a fledgling organization known as the Committee in Solidarity with the People of El Salvador.

The conclusion to be drawn from the documents was plain, indeed inescapable, if you were already looking for it. CISPES was a key part of a concerted and far-reaching plan to spread Communism across Central America.

Some months after the Bureau received this material, an article appeared in *The Review of the News*, a newsletter published by the ultraconservative John Birch Society. The article had been written by John Rees, a British-born journalist, who had worked as an FBI informant and was a fervent watchdog of America's liberal left. It quoted verbatim from the still classified Handal diaries and went on to say (without any further documentary evidence) that CISPES had been set up by groups under the control of the Communist Party of the United States and Farid Handal. It added,

> What is incredible is that to date the Justice Department has taken no action against CISPES as an unregistered foreign agent. In El Salvador, the Reagan Administration appears to be trying to encourage unity between Salvadoran moderates and Conservatives to stop armed terrorist aggression by Moscow's proxies. But it will take sustained American support to defeat this threat to the security of our hemisphere. A move against the unregistered foreign agents of the U.S. Committee in Solidarity with the People of El Salvador would show the Communists we mean business.

The article, in tone and content, was typical of Rees, and of the ultraconservative groups he represented. During the early Reagan years, he worked for the Western Goals Foundation, part of a larger organization called the World Anti-Communist League, which included the Moonies, former Nazi sympathizers, death-squad leaders, and officials from right-wing governments around the world. Rees published articles for various WACL organizations, as well as an influential newsletter, *Information Digest,* and by 1980 the FBI was taking him seriously. But that had not always been the case.

Rees's first contact with the Bureau had come in the early 1960s in London. He was working on the *Daily Mirror* newspaper at the time and had become engaged to a secretary in the FBI's British office. Agents there did a background check for his fiancée and discovered that he was already married. Rees subsequently emigrated to the United States, and after becoming involved in a number of questionable activities, he worked as an unofficial undercover agent for the House Un-American Activities Committee, taping political meetings in Chicago. In September 1986 he offered his services (for the second time) as an informant to the FBI but was turned down; as a memo from a senior Bureau official said, "We should not initiate any interview with this unscrupulous, unethical individual concerning his knowledge of the disturbances in Chicago as to do so would be a waste of time."

Undeterred, Rees began publishing *Information Digest,* which was zealously anti-Communist, and mailing it to conservative politicians, including California's governor, Ronald Reagan. Using false names and disguises, he and his third wife infiltrated progressive and left-wing circles in Washington, D.C., and, through their contacts in police departments, passed the information they garnered to the intelligence community. Eventually, for reasons never explained, the FBI began to pay Rees for his services.

By the time President Reagan took office, Rees was firmly established as a reliable conservative source. Along with others on the far right, he and his theories were influential at the highest levels. Although the Bureau couldn't directly solicit political intelligence, it was legally entitled to draw on such material if someone sent it, and Rees's polemics often made their way into the files.

Thus Rees's article and the Handal diaries became critical elements in the FBI's proposal to open an investigation on CISPES on the predicate that it had contravened the Foreign Agents Registration Act. But the diaries were almost certainly false. The Bureau, for reasons that have never been adequately explained, did not try to verify their authenticity at the time, and years later, when it came under pressure to explain its interest in CISPES, its Inspection Division was unable to find information that would directly corroborate the diaries. Nor did the agency ever give a convincing explanation for why it used a wildly speculative article from an ultra-right publication, written by a journalist who was named in its own files as unreliable, as part of the official request to initiate a probe.

Indeed the original CISPES conferences, far from being the carefully coordinated first shot in a Soviet-Cuban conspiracy to spread Communism across Latin America, managed to establish only one thing: that violence in El Salvador, fueled by U.S. military aid, was getting out of control. Although some representatives of the FDR (the Salvadoran Democratic Revolutionary Front, the political wing of the FMLN) were invited to attend as observers, they did not participate directly. Those at the conferences simply debated the long-term goals of the group: the best ways to bring public pressure on the American government to stop supplying the Duarte regime with money, arms, and military advisers. In other words, right from the start it was clear that CISPES was what it said it was: a grassroots, liberal movement that had been established in response to the tragedy of the escalating violence in El Salvador. Even if the Handal documents had been legitimate, they did not reveal any foreign control of CISPES, and it was extremely unlikely that an organization composed of such disparate elements *could* be controlled by Moscow or anyone else.

In truth, the idea that CISPES was part of a Soviet-Cuban master plan sprang out of the preconceived notions of the American intelligence community, which was institutionally incapable of accepting an innocent explanation. Although the initial investigation lasted only three months and concluded with a finding that CISPES had not violated any law, plenty of people in the FBI, the CIA, and the administration could not be shaken from their belief that the organization was supporting terrorism in El Salvador and could import that terrorism to the United States if left unchallenged. The Bureau, responding to Reagan's doctrines, seemed to have made up its mind that CISPES was a serious threat. The first attempt to counter the threat had failed, but for some time the FBI had been quietly preparing the ground for a bigger operation. Fortunately it already had the means at its disposal.

For some years the FBI had been employing a man named Frank Varelli, who had been born in 1950 as Franklin Augustín Martinez Varela to a powerful political and military family in San Salvador.

Varelli had received a degree from Tennessee State University and had become a Baptist minister in 1977. He had even served for two years in the U.S. Army. But more important, he had a lifelong hatred of Communism and had preached both publicly and privately against the Marxist-Leninists' efforts to gain control of his homeland. After his family fled El Salvador in 1980 because of an assassination attempt against his father, who had once been head of the Salvadoran National Police, Varelli had hastened to change his name. Soon thereafter, while in Los Angeles, he received a visit from Special Agent John Esparza.

Esparza told Varelli that the FBI was preparing for a major investigation of possible Salvadoran terrorism in the United States and was particularly concerned that the FMLN might be infiltrating the influx of Salvadoran refugees coming across the border from Mexico. Would he be prepared to help? Varelli said he would. A week later he moved to Dallas, where the investigation was based.

The Bureau was keen to tap into Varelli's family's network of contacts. For some time it had been looking for its own sources of intelligence so it could operate independently of the State Department and the CIA, whose information the FBI distrusted. Some in the Bureau believed that the CIA was not passing on all the data it received. When Varelli told them that plenty of people in Salvadoran intelligence circles felt the same frustration, the FBI agents believed they might have found another way in.

In December 1980, Varelli met Daniel Flanagan of the Dallas FBI, and impressed him with his extensive knowledge of Salvadoran affairs. Flanagan asked him to meet others in the counterterrorism unit with a view to signing up as an FBI analyst. Meeting followed meeting until March 10, 1981, when Varelli agreed to work for the Bureau for one thousand dollars a month. His principal contacts would be special agents Daniel Flanagan and Jim Evans, and Dallas ASAC Park Stearns.

A few weeks later, on April 10, Varelli was sent on his first operation. The mission was to return to El Salvador, contact the right-wing National Guard, find out who the guard's antiterrorist units were looking for, and determine whether any organizations in the United States had contacts with these people.

In San Salvador, Varelli met first with Antonio Villacorta, a counterinsurgency specialist, then with Colonel Eugenio Vides Casanova, the director of the National Guard. He explained the FBI's desire to open up a separate line of communication that would bypass the CIA and allow it to respond directly to the threat of the FMLN. What the agency wanted most was information, especially on the movements and U.S. contacts of suspected Salvadoran terrorists.

Casanova, who had served under Varelli's father when both had been in the Salvadoran army, was not fond of the CIA and was excited by Varelli's arguments that the FBI could give the National Guard another way to influence Washington. So he agreed to Varelli's plan, and suggested that Villacorta serve as the contact between them. For its part the National Guard wanted to know the names of Salvadorans being deported from the United States and their expected date of arrival. It also wanted the names of those living in the States who were opposed to the National Guard. In return Villacorta supplied Varelli with a list of those being sought by the death squads, a list of political opponents, and propaganda materials and documents that he said had been seized from the Communist guerrillas. All in all, Varelli was handed almost 1,500 names of people sought by the Salvadoran authorities.

During the trip, Varelli also met with a group of senior figures on the far right of Salvadoran politics. They too were frustrated at the apparent lack of resolve in the Duarte regime and the Reagan administration, and they wanted more action sooner. They told Varelli they had established their own private intelligence and propaganda networks in the United States, and in effect they put these at the FBI's disposal.

When Varelli arrived back in Dallas three weeks later, he told the FBI that he had recruited fourteen major intelligence sources to help in the fight against Salvadoran terrorism. These ranged from an official in the passport section of the country's immigration department to people in the Ministry of Culture, the health service, the army, the death squads, and the National Guard. Among the dozens of documents Varelli gave his handlers was the text of a speech made by a leading FDR strategist to a conference at a Mexican university, including broad details of how the FMLN was planning to respond to the policies of the Reagan administration. One of the points referred to a plan to set up 180 "groups of solidarity" with the people of El Salvador in the United States.

This was just what the Bureau had been looking for — fresh evidence that the American protest groups might be under the control of Russian-backed Salvadoran terrorists. During subsequent meetings, as Special Agent Flanagan and his colleagues debriefed and congratulated Varelli, they told him that the next stage of the investigation was about to start. In the meantime he was to keep up his contacts with the National Guard.

In later interviews, Varelli claimed that for the next few months he did as he was told: calling Villacorta and others in El Salvador every couple of days to pass on names the FBI had given him of people who had been deported, and of American citizens who were hostile to the administration's policies and were visiting El Salvador. The National Guard responded with more names of suspected FMLN supporters.

Then, in June 1981, Varelli came across an article in a magazine, *Mother Jones*, about the Central American protest movement. It included details of how to contact the growing number of protest groups. When Varelli showed it to his handlers, they told him that they had prepared a new identity for him: that of Gilberto Mendoza, a Salvadoran refugee whose family had been killed by the death squads. He would have a new social security card, a post office box, two driver's licenses, and other papers to authenticate his new character. His task now, they said, would be to infiltrate CISPES.

As Gilberto Mendoza, Varelli was a humble refugee from a war-torn country, a stranger in a new land, grateful to the decent Americans he met through the leads in *Mother Jones* for their enthusiasm and support. The activists he contacted believed his tale; Mendoza was exactly the kind of dispossessed refugee they were trying to help, the embodiment of all the tragedy and unhappiness they were working to prevent. Little did they know that their letters to him went to an FBI-funded box number or that many of their phone calls were routed directly to the foreign counterintelligence squad room in Dallas.

All of these contacts elicited new names, new addresses, new telephone numbers, which Varelli dutifully passed on to Flanagan and his other handlers. It wasn't just a one-way process — Varelli also gave the activists news from home, which came from his contacts at the National Guard and was carefully constructed to reflect the right-wing viewpoint on events in El Salvador. Then he would tell the National Guard about new CISPES chapters, planned events and demonstrations, and individuals they might be interested in.

After a while Varelli felt confident enough as Mendoza to sign up with the Dallas chapter of CISPES. He began to attend meetings and would often make impassioned little speeches on behalf of his battered homeland, which had the desired effect of taking him closer to the leaders of the organization. After every meeting he made lists of the names and addresses of those who had attended and took down the license plate numbers of the cars parked nearby. These too he shared with Flanagan, Evans, and others. He was debriefed at the Dallas FBI office every couple of days, an activity he was happy to undertake. As he later said, "Based on the briefings I received from the FBI about CISPES, I was prepared for the worst. The FBI led me to believe that CISPES was a radical terrorist organization of the type I had encountered in El Salvador. I was instructed to watch for arms, arms shipments, and safe houses for the hiding of terrorists."

By now, though, he wasn't the only one looking. Using the information provided by Varelli, the Handal diaries, Rees's articles, and other information, the agency had formalized the CISPES probe with the Department of Justice. It now involved twelve field offices and was a legitimate criminal investigation.

Before long, however, Justice attorneys took a look at the evidence the Bureau had amassed to support its theories and came to the conclusion that it didn't amount to much. There had been no violation of the Foreign Agents Registration Act. The investigation was suspended, although the agency noted that if a formal connection between CISPES and the FMLN was determined in the future the case would be reopened. In the meantime, Varelli was told by Evans and Flanagan to maintain his links discreetly with both CISPES and the National Guard, as the probe "was not over yet." They were right. It was only the end of the first phase.

While Flanagan, Evans, and the others waited for their superiors in Washington to sanction a bigger, broader investigation, Varelli did as he was told and maintained his contacts. He also kept in touch with the Dallas FBI, which, he later claimed, decided he could spend some time analyzing the information he had already gathered and preparing entries for the new FBI terrorist photo album. This was to be more than just a book: it was to be a careful log, held on computer as well as on paper, of known or suspected terrorists and people suspected of supporting terrorism. The FBI gave Varelli a camera and a brief course in how to use it and sent him off to find possible subjects for inclusion. As his "beat" was Central America, all of his targets had had some involvement in that region. He obtained details about possible targets from books, newspapers, and magazines, and some from the FBI, which gave him the "right" information from other related investigations. Some names came from his contacts in the National Guard and the private monitoring groups set up by Salvadoran right-wingers in the United States, still more from intelligence assessments prepared by right-wing organizations and individuals like the Western Goals Foundation and John Rees. All the material was put on file forms, which Flanagan supplied.

Ultimately, in the three years he worked on the album, Varelli compiled over seven hundred entries. Each entry included a photo and a brief summary of the supposed terrorist connections of the person. The group was a very mixed bag. Some of the people may have been described legitimately as terrorists, many quite obviously could not. As Varelli said later, in testimony to Congress, "The stated purpose . . . was to have a collection of the individuals who were active or interested in Central American politics who might have terrorist tendencies. In reality, the terrorist photograph album frequently contained persons who really just opposed Reagan's Central American policy."

The album, which came to public attention in 1987, is interesting for the light it sheds on the FBI's view of who is an honest political dissident and who is something more dangerous. If Varelli is to be believed (and as he was able to produce the physical evidence during congressional hearings, there is no reason he shouldn't be), he was instructed to prepare entries on such threatening characters as Senators Claiborne Pell and Christopher Dodd and Representatives Michael Barnes and Patricia Schroeder. The entry on former U.S. ambassador Robert White, who had been President Carter's representative in El Salvador, is typical; under a photograph, it reads:

Narrative of activities . . . Fired by the Reagan Administration in February 1981 because of White's open support for the Marxist-Leninist fronts of El Salvador, the FDR-FMLN. Because of his left-wing position, White is hated by the right wing groups of El Salvador and been sentenced to death by the Maximiliano Hernandez Martinez Death Squads. He was very instrumental in the formation of CISPES in the US and works very close to Sandy Pollack (CPUSA). Teletype to all FBI Field Offices.

SECRET. Attention Boston, MA and Washington, D.C. Robert White is actively pushing to stop present administration policy in El Salvador via CISPES, Solidarity World Front, Communist Party of the United States of America. Urgent to all Bureau offices. Prepared for SA Dan Flanagan FBI Dallas TX. Field Office. Terrorism of El Salvador. CISPES-FDR-FMLN investigation. Signature Franco.

Other entries reflect the common mistrust the Salvadoran right-wingers and the Reagan administration had for members of various church and peace groups, particularly radical Roman Catholic organizations. For example, the entry for Sister Peggy Healy, a leading activist in the sanctuary movement, reads:

She is a nun with the Maryknoll Order . . . a community of priests, brothers and sisters and lay people that are supposed to be spreading the gospel all over the world. Instead they are front runners in preaching the Marxist Leninist "Liberation Theology." In El Salvador, as well as Nicaragua, the Maryknoll priests and nuns are guilty of protecting and supporting the communist terrorists of the FDR-FMLN and FSLN . . . Operating under the banner of "human rights violations" they are operating against the US government.

While Varelli was compiling such "facts" and staying in touch with the Salvadoran National Guard and the people he had met through CISPES, the senior figures in the Bureau continued to consider whether to pursue a CISPES investigation on the predicate of suspected international terrorism, based on information provided by Varelli and by the privately funded intelligence groups on the far right.

In mid-March 1983 Varelli and Special Agent Dan Flanagan were called to a high-level, top-secret conference on counterterrorism in Quantico. Their briefing was to help the Bureau's specialists come to grips with the complex structure that was CISPES and to paint a picture of the organization's supposed ties to the FMLN. As Varelli went to work with flow charts and diagrams, his audience, many of whom now knew him by reputation, took copious notes.

He must have convinced this impressive gathering of some of the FBI's most senior figures, because on March 30 an airtel (an internal agency telegram that carries instructions and reports between Washington and the field) went out from headquarters under the signature of Buck Revell, then head of the agency's counterterrorism and criminal divisions. Thirteen months after ending the initial criminal investigation into CISPES, the Bureau was beginning its second investigation, and this time it was more serious.

The first investigation had been conducted under the Domestic Security Guidelines, which control all criminal, domestic security, and domestic terrorism investigations. These guidelines allowed the Bureau to target only those people whom it reasonably suspected were actively involved in criminal activity. The second was to be conducted under the Foreign Counterintelligence (FCI) Guidelines, which control all investigations of suspect activities of foreign origin and allow the agency to target whole groups, even if it suspects only a few members. The Domestic Security Guidelines say that the FBI should consider all circumstances, "including (1) the magnitude of the threatened harm; (2) the likelihood that it will occur; (3) the immediacy of the threat, and (4) the danger to privacy and free expression posed by an investigation." The FCI Guidelines, some of which are classified for national security reasons, seem by contrast to contain none of these provisions. They also fail to include the caution on "speculation" contained in the Domestic Security Guidelines. In other words, having failed to make a case against CISPES using the high standards of the Domestic Security Guidelines, the Bureau opened a second investigation based on the lower FCI criteria.

At the time the agency believed it had good cause to do so. Data from its sources continued to fuel the FBI's conviction that CISPES had terrorist connections. Indeed, Varelli's handlers now took up his assertion that CISPES support for the FMLN extended far beyond money, food, clothing, and medical supplies to include the covert funding of military aid, "forwarded through Mexico for ultimate use by guerrilla forces in El Salvador."

So CISPES came back under the spotlight. Right from the beginning, the new investigation was aimed at the organization itself rather than at the activities of a few suspected members. Agents attended public meetings, listened to public speeches, gathered membership lists and CISPES literature — activities that could not possibly be effective in tracking down secret terrorist links. FMLN guerrillas were not going to stand up in homes, church halls, and community centers across the United States and blurt out their plans for blowing up the White House and overthrowing Duarte's regime by force. Nor were they likely to address small gatherings of housewives, church workers, gay rights advocates, trade unionists,

Salvadoran refugees, or any of the other myriad CISPES-related groups, on how their umbrella organization was buying arms in Mexico to give to guerrillas in mountain hideouts in El Salvador.

Even if these terrorist links existed, which they didn't, there was no reason whatsoever for the Bureau to spy on the First Amendment activities of people who its own internal memos made clear were extremely unlikely to have any knowledge of such associations. And if the Bureau shouldn't have been spying on these people, then it certainly shouldn't have been putting all the data it gathered into its files. But the investigative philosophy seems to have been that the Bureau could uncover terrorists by penetrating CISPES at every level. Maximum surveillance was in order. Some of the instructions from FBI headquarters did warn that purely political activity was not the target of the investigation, but this apparently made little impression on agents in the field.

Indeed, it is clear that the whole CISPES investigation was enthusiastically embraced. For the first few months it was extended only to a few divisions, but in October 1983 headquarters opened it up to almost every field office in the country. From the first week information flooded between offices, into headquarters, and back out to the field. Agents began identifying CISPES members, detailing forthcoming demonstrations, speculating on the possible links between CISPES and other ongoing terrorist investigations, duplicating CISPES documents, and so on and so forth. Dallas, as the office of origin, was at the center of this traffic and kept all its sister offices up to date with known intelligence about chapters in their region. Sometimes the data was passed on to other intelligence organizations.

This mass of secret teletypes, thousands of which — heavily bridged and censored — have since been released under Freedom of Information Act requests, ranges from the pedantic to the detailed, from the speculative to the aggressive. The following excerpts are very typical:

NEW ORLEANS FM TO DALLAS AND FBI HQ (10/10/83) It is imperative at this time to formulate some plan of attack against CISPES and specifically against individuals [deletion] who defiantly display their contempt for the U.S. Government by making speeches and propagandizing their cause while asking for political asylum.

DALLAS TO ALL FIELD OFFICES [date obscured] For those offices just beginning investigation of CISPES, Dallas submits the following which could be useful in determining their activities. 1. [deleted] 2. CISPES often advertises social events such as dances, Bar-B-Ques, Bake Sales etc to raise funds. These events can be attended without difficulty. 3. CISPES closely aligns itself with church groups. In fact most CISPES offices have set up sanctuaries in churches, and have publicly boasted the fact that they can protect illegal Salvadorans without interference of government agencies.

DIRECTOR FBI TO ASSISTANT ATTORNEY GENERAL, CRIMINAL DIVISION, DIRECTOR DEFENSE INTELLIGENCE AGENCY, US SECRET SERVICE, SECRETARY OF STATE (November 1983) The following information was obtained from the assets of several of our field offices. The information pertains to the peace march scheduled for November 12, 1983, in Washington D.C. and other major cities in the United States. The Chicago chapter of CISPES plans to be well represented at the march. According to CISPES literature the Chicago organization has a goal of sending ten buses from CISPES and other groups. The seats on the buses will cost each individual $60 for the round trip. Over sixty organizations have signed on to make the march the largest ever on Central America.

SAC MOBILE TO DIRECTOR FBI (1/4/84) Investigation disclosed that on 11/29/83 a Mobile radio station, WRKG, ran a two hour program featuring one Dr Steve Schaeffer, a Professor of Pharmacology, University of South Alabama Medical School, Mobile, Ala. who spoke on behalf of CISPES. Dr Schaeffer advised that his wife was from El Salvador and that he had resided there for several years. He advised that CISPES was against the United States knowingly supporting the right wing death squads of the El Salvadoran Government, who were allegedly responsible for 30,000 deaths since 1979. A review of the current directory for professors at the University of South Alabama indicates that one Steven W Schaeffer was Assistant Professor of Pharmacology, University of South Alabama Medical School.

SAC ATLANTA TO DIRECTOR FBI (3/4/85) Observation of the Little Five Points Community Center, the evening of February 22, 1985, determined that there were only about a dozen vehicles in the parking lot and that a dance program was scheduled at the facility that evening. On February 23, 1985, the following license plates were observed on vehicles parked at the Little Five Points Community Center . . . [Forty-one numbers follow.]

There are thousands of pages of this kind of thing, secretly detailing the activities and identities of people and groups involved in nothing more threatening to American national security than some mild political protests. Unfortunately, as these excerpts show, the data was being compiled by people who seriously believed in the CISPES conspiracy. The language is quite clear: agents saw reds under every bed.

To be fair, not everyone was caught up in this insanity. A teletype from Denver to headquarters raised the troublesome question of First Amendment rights. "Denver concurs with New Orleans that in spite of attempts by the Bureau to clarify guidelines and goals for this investigation, the field is still not sure of how much seemingly legitimate political activity can be monitored." But few other offices seemed as concerned as this. CISPES was the latest game in town, and almost everyone wanted to play.

Varelli, of course, remained at the center of things, at least for a while. In addition to providing information and research to the increasingly demanding field offices, he continued to spy on the Dallas chapter of CISPES, trying through it to get close to the national leaders of the protest movement by demonstrating his credentials as a Salvadoran refugee. How effective he was is open to question. Varelli claimed that he became an important member of the chapter, but Sister Patricia Ridgley, a prominent member at the time, said that he didn't leave much of a mark except for his unusual habit of making regular contributions to their funds. This struck her as odd, because he was supposed to be a poor immigrant who barely had an income. "He did not have that big a role in the organization," she remembered. "He came to some meetings but he didn't volunteer for any task. I don't recall him as being a key person in that way."

Varelli also made frequent trips to the FBI's Houston office to help with its CISPES investigation. One of his tasks was to arrange a small network of informants inside Taca, the Salvadoran national airline, based in Houston. Varelli claimed that by making judicious appeals and regular small payments to some Duarte supporters in the company, he and the agency were able to get hold of the passenger lists for every flight between the United States and El Salvador. Using information from the Immigration and Naturalization Service, Varelli says, he was able to forward to his contacts in the National Guard lists of people whom the FBI thought the guard should watch when they arrived. What happened to Salvadorans who were targeted in this way is not known, but it is clear from reports by Amnesty International and other such groups that many returning deportees were later killed by the death squads. It is not possible to say with any certainty that these people were mentioned on the lists that Varelli sent to the National Guard.

Varelli spent some time in Washington too. In November 1983 he and Flanagan worked on an investigation of a bomb attack on the U.S. Senate, and he visited the national headquarters of CISPES, just a few blocks away from the J. Edgar Hoover building on Pennsylvania Avenue. He wasn't inside long, but he met a few of the national executives and took a good look around. He left with yet more literature and a clear idea of the office layout, both of which he passed on to Flanagan. Over the next few days they drove by a number of churches, bookstores, and offices that Varelli believed had some kind of connection with CISPES. At some such places, like the Institute for Policy Studies, he was able to get a quick look inside. The data he passed on to Flanagan and also into the FBI files.

Flanagan was back in Washington for another terrorism conference at Quantico in April 1984. Varelli wasn't invited this time, but he prepared a report that brought together all the disparate strands of the CISPES investigation, including the true identities of a number of assets and informants. This went into Flanagan's briefcase along with other top-secret documents. After Flanagan arrived, on a beautiful spring day, he drove down to the Potomac River to take a look at the cherry blossoms — or so he later told investigators. When he got back to his car, his badge, his gun, and the briefcase were gone.

Twenty-four hours later, one of Varelli's contacts in the Dallas FBI office called to tell him that his cover was blown. Flanagan, who had been unable to make the presentation at Quantico, flew back to Dallas and was immediately suspended pending a full investigation. During the subsequent inquest, Varelli found out that Flanagan had been cheating him on his expenses and had withheld a number of payments that were due to him. Flanagan stuck to his story about the briefcase, though, even when he failed a polygraph test. He was told quietly to resign.

By now everything that Varelli had been working on was falling apart. Tom Kelly, then the Dallas SAC, and two other FBI agents went to his North Dallas apartment to question him about Flanagan and were furious to discover that he had Bureau documents in his possession. A few weeks later Varelli had to undergo his own polygraph examination, involving questions about possible connections with foreign agents, perhaps the KGB. The test showed, as far as any polygraph is able to, that he was telling the truth, but he decided he had had enough of the FBI. He felt he had been cheated of money that was rightly owed to him and that his integrity had been questioned. Two months later he resigned in disgust. For the moment, at least, Frank Varelli was out of the loop.

The mystery of Flanagan's briefcase was never resolved, although Varelli later told journalist and author Ross Gelbspan that he believed the documents might have found their way to the National Security Council, which could have passed them on to the private right-wing intelligence organizations that were helping it with its secret and by now illegal dealings with the Nicaraguan Contras. It is impossible to say how accurate this claim might be, but not long after the documents were lost, CISPES activists across the country began to suffer a series of break-ins, fire bombings, and death threats, which went on for the next five years. Among the targets were some of the offices, bookstores, and churches that Varelli had visited in Washington a few months before. Dozens more had been mentioned in reports he had passed on to the Bureau.

After Flanagan's briefcase disappeared, Dallas ceased to be the office of origin for the CISPES probe, and headquarters took over all responsibility for running the investigation. The case continued until June 18, 1986. It closed because the Bureau finally accepted, after twenty-seven months of intensive inquiries, that it could find no evidence of any links between CISPES and international terrorists.

However, by then, the investigation had expanded to take in scores of other groups that had dealt with CISPES in some way, and the agency continued its hunt for the elusive Central American terrorists in fresh pastures. It was prompted, as before, by many people, both private and professional, who were eager to ensure that the agency didn't lose sight of the continued threat from Communism to the region.

For the administration, though, El Salvador was now only one problem among many. It was worried about events in Nicaragua, Honduras, and Guatemala, and about how to respond to the growing political opposition to its Central American policies back home. Farther afield, it had even more pressing concerns — most significantly, the plight of American citizens taken hostage in Beirut. The FBI, as the nation's lead agency for counterterrorism matters, was also interested in the hostages, but on the face of it the separate issues in Central America and the Middle East seemed unrelated. Others thought differently, and they were working on a single extraordinary solution to the administration's problems in both regions. The Bureau, by default if not by design, became inextricably linked to this venture — which exploded into one of the worst political scandals since Watergate.

At first sight, there would appear to be no direct connection between the FBI's CISPES investigation and the Iran-Contra scandal. However, some strong links did exist between Lieutenant Colonel Oliver North and the Bureau, and when the connections are made, they raise three important questions that have to be answered: How much and when did the FBI know about the Iran-Contra scandal? How much did Oliver North know about the Bureau's CISPES investigation? To what extent, if at all, was that investigation influenced by North's desire to know what his opponents had found out about the illegal Contra supply networks?

One clue can be found in the weekly meetings of the Operations Subgroup of the Terrorist Incident Working Group, a top-secret subsection of a highly classified interagency intelligence committee. Oliver North was a member; so too was Buck Revell, the head of the FBI's counterterrorism and counterintelligence programs. The group's mandate was to advise the government on what action it should take in response to terrorist activities against American citizens overseas. In the early and mid-eighties, one of its major preoccupations was how to obtain the release of the American hostages in Lebanon.

The committee had no responsibility or mandate to investigate or consider any possible violations of U.S. law, and Buck Revell later categorically denied that there was any official discussion of the FBI's domestic CISPES or Central American investigations during its meetings. He did admit that some informal discussion could have taken place, however, and there are numerous indications that North did know about the Bureau's Central American investigations and that he tried to influence them on several occasions.

One example involved Philip Mabry, a former CIA operative and private security consultant, who wrote to Attorney General Ed Meese in 1983 to ask how he could help the "freedom fighters" in Nicaragua. Meese passed his name to North, who had just assumed responsibility for the administration's Nicaraguan initiative. With North's tacit support, Mabry set up a group called Americans for Human Rights and Social Justice, whose public aim was to use media lobbying to counter the efforts of Central American protest groups. Its private aim may have been more sinister.

In November 1984 Mabry sent William Webster, the FBI director, a list of names, among them those of the actors Michael Douglas and Charlie Sheen, the musician Jackson Browne, Robert White (the former U.S. ambassador whom Varelli had included in the terrorist photo album), and ten members of the U.S. Congress, including Jim Wright, the majority leader at the time. Mabry wrote that all these people were, "from their statements and actions, pro-marxist rhetoric and their opposition to United States Policy in Central America, a threat to our National Security." He asked that they be investigated. Just over six weeks later he received a letter from Buck Revell assuring him that his "concerns and comments will be carefully reviewed." Mabry later said that Oliver North had given him the names.

Sometime later another list surfaced. Drawn up by Mabry in 1985, it was entitled "The Liberal Pro Nico Groups monitored for North and State" and included CISPES and many other human rights and political action groups. Under a separate heading, "News Media Watch and Discredit," were the notations "Raymond Bonner — ex NY Times Reporter (Marxist?)" and "Sam Donaldson — CBS News (real S.O.B.)." A note at the bottom of the document, just below the names of seven prominent politicians, said, "Keep close watch & discredit, disinfo, on all above. In interests of US Nat Security and C.A. Policy." As one of the people on this list said when told of it, "This is a kind of nice organization for the FBI to be doing business with, don't you think?" Others, however, were more appreciative of Mabry's efforts. Among the known financial backers of his group were the Moonies, staunch members of the World Anti-Communist League.

There are indications that the FBI not only knew something of the National Security Council's interest in keeping the pressure on foreign policy dissenters, but also turned a blind eye to the growing illegalities of the Contra support schemes. From documents released under the Freedom of Information Act it seems clear that the Bureau had conducted at least one Neutrality Act investigation into Contra weapons supply as early as 1984, and over the course of the next year its agents spoke to at least a dozen people who knew of the National Security Council's links to the Contra supply network. Even more startling is an assertion made to a *Boston Globe* reporter by a former CIA official, Allan Bruce Hemmings. He claimed that in October 1985 an FBI agent called the CIA's Iran section to say that an FBI informant in Tehran had reported that an American plane had been carrying weapons into Tabriz. The agent asked if the plane was on a CIA mission. He was told that it wasn't, but that there might be some White House involvement and he should forget the matter.

But the clearest indication that the agency either did know or should have known about the Iran-Contra scandal, well before it broke, can be found in the details of an extraordinary investigation involving an Arab prince, a mysterious missing teletype, a Philadelphia bank, and a freelance National Security Council asset called Richard Miller.

On May 9, 1985, based on information from the U.S. Federal Reserve Board, the FBI opened an investigation into an allegation that a major fraud had been perpetrated on the William Penn Bank in Philadelphia. The probe centered on a $250,000 check drawn via the William Penn Bank from a closed account at the Saudi French Bank in Saudi Arabia by one Mousalreza Ebrahim Zadeh, otherwise known as Prince Ebrahim bin Abdal-Aziz bin Saud al-Masoudy. While the check was being cleared, $240,000 was transferred by wire on Zadeh's behalf.

Zadeh had told the William Penn Bank that he was a banker, commodities dealer, and member of the Saudi royal family. He also claimed that he was involved in selling some Saudi oil, and that he intended to donate millions of dollars from this sale to the Nicaraguan Contras. The money transfers were to be part of this process. Zadeh gave the name of Richard Miller as a reference. Miller, who ran a Washington, D.C., company called International Business Communications, was a contract operative for the National Security Council. Hearing at least some of this, the William Penn Bank came to the conclusion that the scheme was part of some secret CIA operation and that Zadeh was what he claimed to be. Unfortunately for them, the check bounced after Zadeh had received his money.

On June 10 and 11, 1985, Miller had the first of five interviews with agents from the white-collar crime section at the FBI's Washington field office. During those meetings a number of facts emerged. First, he was already known to the FBI; he had been interviewed some weeks before by Special Agent David Beisner, from the counterterrorism unit in the Washington field office. Beisner later told his colleagues that they had discussed suspicions that Nicaraguan security agents had been trying to get information from Miller about his links to the Contras; that he had been able to confirm that Miller ran a legitimate business; that Miller did occasional contract work for the National Security Council and the State Department; and that his contact at the NSC was Lieutenant Colonel Oliver North. He had also found out that Miller had a "top secret" security clearance.

Miller told the white-collar crime agents, who by now must have been wondering what they had wandered into, that he believed Zadeh really was a Saudi prince, that he had large amounts of money in Europe, and that he was vice president of the Arab National Bank. For confirmation of this, he said, the agents should speak to North. After filing a routine request for an interview with headquarters, the agents saw North on July 18, 1985, at his office in the Old Executive Office Building.

The results were sent out that day in another routine teletype from the Washington field office to FBI headquarters, with copies going to Philadelphia, New York, and Sacramento, the other offices involved in the investigation. The FBI later claimed that this teletype had disappeared; it was never received at FBI headquarters, Philadelphia, or Sacramento. A copy did surface in New York two years later.

The teletype said first that North had confirmed that Miller was engaged in confidential contract work for the NSC and the State Department, and added, "Miller's work concerns the funneling of private funds to Nicaraguan freedom fighters who oppose the Sandinista government."

North then told the agents that he had come into contact with Zadeh through a "right-wing ideologue" named Kevin Kattke, who had had frequent contacts with U.S. intelligence. Kattke told North that he represented a member of the Saudi Arabian royal family called Prince Ebrahim bin Abdal-Aziz bin Saud al-Masoudy. The prince, or Zadeh, as he was known, wanted to donate a large sum of money to the Contras. According to the teletype, "North advised Kattke that inasmuch as U.S. public law forbids expenditures of Government funds to aid Nicaraguan insurgents, it was inadvisable for the member of the NSC [North] to meet with the Prince directly. North advised Kattke that Richard Miller would contact Kattke to meet the Prince." The memo added: "Information regarding the Prince's expressed interest in donating to the Nicaraguan Freedom Fighters was discussed by North personally with President Ronald Reagan and National Security Adviser Robert MacFarlane as recently as June 1985."

After noting that Congress would probably reinstate funding for the Contras around July 22, the memo concluded,

> North specifically requests that attempts by the FBI to interview the Prince be held in abeyance until after the week of 7/22/85 due to the critical timing of the Prince's possible, remote but large donation to the Nicaraguan Freedom Fighters. In no way does North want to interfere with a criminal investigation of the Prince, but North feels that contact by the FBI prior to NSC determination of the Prince's intention may reverse any possibility that the Prince will follow through with his expressed intention to donate this money. North was advised that his request would be made known to FBI.

This teletype is vitally important, because it clearly states that Oliver North, a senior government employee, was helping to channel funds to the Contras at a time when it was effectively prohibited under U.S. law. The previous year Congress had passed the Boland Amendment, which prohibited the government from expending any funds during the 1985–1986 fiscal year, including salaries, "which would have the effect of supporting, directly or indirectly, military or paramilitary operations in Nicaragua by any nation, group, organization, movement or individual." The teletype also said that North had discussed this illegal activity with President Reagan and his national security adviser, and that North was asking the FBI to stall its investigation until Congress reversed the Boland Amendment and Zadeh's money was no longer needed.

Yet this bombshell, which gave the FBI a clear indication of at least part of North's illegal schemes a year before the rest of the world found out about them, never got through to FBI headquarters, or to William Webster, to whom it was addressed. Despite the fact that hundreds of teletypes routinely manage to get from the field offices to Washington in perfect safety every day, this one never even made it the three miles from the Washington field office to the J. Edgar Hoover headquarters building — or so the FBI later said. The agency surmised that the teletype must have broken down that day, or that the information hadn't been properly sent.

If that isn't odd enough, it is clear that a few days later the FBI had a second chance to do something about the situation. On July 31, 1985, the Washington field office sent FBI headquarters a teletype, which was received, saying that "North . . . advised WFO that Richard Miller and Prince Ebrahim bin Abdal-Aziz bin Saud al-Masoudy are currently in Europe reportedly arranging transfer of funds from the Prince to Nicaraguan Freedom Fighters as set forth in referenced tel." Still, no one at headquarters thought to ask why North was taking such an active interest.

During the following months the fraud investigation against the prince developed, and eventually he was called before a federal grand jury. Shortly before the hearing, in April 1986, Buck Revell took a call from North, who said that Miller had been issued a subpoena to attend. North was worried that his contractor might be asked questions about his relationship with the government. If he was, he might reveal that he was involved with negotiations to get American hostages released from Lebanon. Those negotiations were about to go into a sensitive phase. Could Revell get the hearing postponed?

Revell later said that at the time he had no knowledge of Oliver North's arms-to-Iran scheme and that he didn't find out until he was briefed with everyone else at a meeting of the Terrorist Incident Working Group later that year. Nor did he know anything of North's involvement in arranging private aid for the Contras. But he did know that North was responsible for coordinating interagency activities with regard to the hostages, so he didn't see North's request as inappropriate. He went ahead and made a few phone calls of his own. A few days later, he told North that the U.S. attorney's office in Philadelphia had no intention of asking Miller about his connection to the hostage negotiations and that therefore a postponement wasn't necessary. Zadeh was subsequently indicted, and in February 1987 he was convicted and sentenced to five years' imprisonment, a $10,000 fine, and $309,000 in restitution.

It does seem strange that Buck Revell, perhaps the most experienced and sophisticated counterintelligence and counterterrorism official at the FBI, if not in the American government, did not work out what was going on. He must have known the background to the Zadeh investigation, and if not a brief review of the case file would have revealed Zadeh's connection with North's pro-Contra operative Richard Miller. Now Revell was being told by North himself that Miller was involved in negotiations about the hostages in Beirut.

Given that North had already confided to the white-collar crime agents a year earlier that he was indirectly engaged in fundraising for the Contras, it seems strange that he didn't reveal more to a man who was several ranks above those agents and who was in charge of the Bureau's counterterrorism activities. A question from Revell would surely have brought the whole Iran-Contra business into the open. It wasn't as though he didn't have the opportunity to ask that question; he saw North almost every week at the Operations Subgroup meeting. Perhaps Revell was hindered by the fact that the crucial Washington field office teletype had never made it to headquarters.

These exchanges were not the only links between the FBI and Oliver North at this time. North had frequent contacts with David Beisner, the FBI agent in the Washington counterintelligence unit, to discuss the possibility that Nicaraguan intelligence officers might be out to expose North's dealings with the Contras. At least one of those meetings led to an intimidating investigation of a former mercenary called Jack Terrell, who had decided to cooperate with congressional investigators into the Iran-Contra affair.

North also frequently talked with Buck Revell, at one point hinting that an investigation into the crash of a C-123 transport aircraft in Nicaragua (which was shot down by a Sandinista missile in October 1986 while carrying ammunition for the Contras from North's supply network) could jeopardize the hostage negotiations. Shortly thereafter the attorney general asked the FBI director to suspend the inquiry.

That was one of North's last attempts to manipulate the FBI. On November 3, 1986, the American press was full of stories that the United States had been selling missiles to Iran, in violation of its own policies, in order to get hostages released in Lebanon. Three weeks later, Attorney General Meese announced to an astonished nation that profits from the arms sales had been sent to the Contras. Oliver North had been fired; his boss, John Poindexter, had resigned. The Reagan administration's covert wars were beginning to come to light.

The question remains, how much of all this came as a surprise to the FBI's top management? How was it that in spite of all the contacts that Revell and others had had with North on a wide variety of subjects, including times when North directly or indirectly told agents of the Contra supply networks, the FBI officials were able to remain ignorant for so long?

Many of these questions were raised at hearings of the Senate Intelligence Committee into the nomination of William Webster as CIA director in 1987. Webster stuck to his claim that he remained in the dark about Iran-Contra until Meese gave his press conference. After some muttering about the missing teletype, the Senate gave him and the FBI the benefit of the doubt. Not much has ever been said about it since. But as one congressional insider remarked five years later, "Ask me why the FBI didn't put two and two together on Iran-Contra, and the only thing I can say is this: that's a very good question."

Meanwhile the FBI's investigations of Central American protest groups had not gone unremarked by the increasing numbers of people who had signed up with CISPES and other organizations to protest Reagan's policies. Nor did any of them notice any appreciable letup in government pressure after June 1985, when the CISPES investigation officially ceased.

The Center for Constitutional Rights, a Manhattan-based group of lawyers interested in public affairs and civil liberties, had begun to notice that something was up as early as 1982. This organization was well placed to pick up complaints from irritated activists. At first these grievances were mild — people returning from El Salvador, Nicaragua, and elsewhere were being grilled by Customs at entry points, others were reporting that their mail was going astray or that they were being visited by FBI agents who wanted to know their views on Central America.

But by the end of 1983 the CCR was hearing more serious stories: of unexplained break-ins in which money and valuables were ignored but documents and membership lists were taken; of the confiscation of papers by U.S. Customs; of telephones that made strange noises and people who tailed activists in the street. More than a few people suffered unexplained IRS audits, a traditional FBI harassment technique (and an old favorite of Hoover's FBI). Some people, particularly those involved in the sanctuary movement, began to ask the FBI for their files under the Freedom of Information Act. When the files weren't forthcoming, they turned to the CCR for help.

The list of offices, homes, and churches that had been broken into continued to grow. The Guatemala News and Information Center in Oakland, California, was burglarized on November 20, 1983; files were rifled but no cash was taken. The Old Cambridge Baptist Church in Massachusetts was broken into on November 11, 1984, the first of several such incidents in which money and valuables were usually not taken. The Amnesty International Offices in Los Angeles was burglarized on June 17, 1985, and a donor list was stolen. The office of the University Baptist Church in Seattle was ransacked on July 17, 1985. The Home for Justice and Peace in Saginaw, Michigan, was broken into in December 1985; no money or valuables were taken. And so on and on. In almost every case money and valuables were not taken, although cash boxes, radios, telephone answering machines, and computer equipment sometimes disappeared. There was usually evidence that files had been rifled, desks opened, and drawers gone through. The break-ins continued until late 1989.

By mid-1985 the CCR had begun to receive FBI documents that gave some indication of what was going on. Staff members noticed that CISPES appeared as a reference in many of the files. Then, one day in May 1986, Ann Buitrago, the center's expert on deciphering Bureau documents, was sent a copy of the *Dallas Morning News* which carried a story about Daniel Flanagan's lost briefcase. The pattern now had some sense behind it. The CCR began to file FOIA requests with every FBI field office in the country. When more documents arrived, the CCR was particularly dismayed to discover that the investigations were being carried out under foreign counterintelligence guidelines, which permitted the agency to use such intrusive investigative techniques as forced physical searches and infiltration and disruption of targets.

With others, the CCR began to lobby Congress to do something. Finally Don Edwards's Subcommittee on Civil and Constitutional Rights began hearings, in February 1987. Frank Varelli, who seemed to be getting nowhere in his attempts to receive his back pay from the FBI, testified, as did Buck Revell. Although his testimony was noncommittal, Revell did concede that CISPES had been under extensive investigation. He insisted that the Bureau had no involvement whatsoever in the break-ins. The agency had conducted a preliminary investigation to see whether there was any pattern to the burglaries and had concluded that there was no evidence of a conspiracy. The break-ins thus remained the responsibility of the local police departments.

Varelli's testimony was electric. He told the committee about his recruitment, his trips to El Salvador, his work on the terrorist photo album, and the way in which he had traded information between the FBI and the Salvadoran National Guard. He also said that he had been told by Flanagan and Jim Evans that they had participated in break-ins at Bethany House, the headquarters of the Dallas CISPES chapter. He went on to claim that they had shown him phone records taken from the office of one of the nuns who ran the group. (The FBI later investigated these allegations and concluded that they were without foundation.)

Although at this stage Varelli kept much information to himself, the CISPES investigation was now out of the bottle. Interestingly, he also told the panel, "Ironically, never once during the three years of my association with CISPES, did I once encounter anything even close to the picture painted by the FBI as to what CISPES was supposed to be. Not once did I find, see, hear or observe any illegal conduct of any nature. The CISPES organization was peaceful, non-violent and devoted to changing the policies of the United States towards Central America by persuasion and education . . . I now realize that the purpose of the FBI's attention directed towards the CISPES was political and not criminal. The aim of the FBI was to break CISPES for its stand against Reagan's policy in Central America."

By the time Williams Sessions, the new director of the FBI, testified before Congress about CISPES a year later, many of the facts about the investigation had been revealed. At the time Sessions was credited for accepting FBI responsibility for the "unfortunate aligning of mistakes in judgment in several levels that cumulatively led to an investigation of which the FBI is not proud." But arguments have continued to rage over his assessment of Frank Varelli's role in the affair.

Sessions sought to blame Varelli for much of what had gone wrong. When the CISPES stories first began to receive national attention, Varelli was being quietly portrayed by a number of people in the FBI as an untrustworthy person who had exaggerated his influence in and knowledge of FBI affairs. Yet when documents about CISPES began to surface, they showed that Varelli had indeed had a major role in the FBI's investigations. Subsequently some of those same people changed their stories. Varelli, they said in private conversations, was a clever and sophisticated Salvadoran disinformation specialist who had duped the FBI into pursuing a vendetta against the enemies of the right-wing Salvadoran regime.

In his statement to Congress, Sessions said, "Absent the information provided by Frank Varelli, there would not have been sufficient predication for an international terrorism investigation of CISPES. The case pivoted on the information Varelli provided, and there were clear deficiencies, both operational and supervisory, in the way Varelli was handled. His background and reliability were never investigated adequately, and during much of the investigation the accuracy of Varelli's information was not adequately verified. By the time it was realized that Varelli's information was unreliable, the investigation had been under way for approximately one year. The investigation would not have developed as it did had Varelli's reliability been properly scrutinized at the outset."

But the documents don't entirely bear this out. It now seems clear that Varelli was only one of several FBI sources that indicated that CISPES might be a potential terrorist organization. Although Sessions claimed that Varelli was found to be unreliable a year after the probe began, documents describe Varelli as "knowledgeable and reliable," of "great benefit to the FBI," and even "intelligent and eager" throughout his five-year association with the Bureau. In fact, a year after he quit, the Houston field office attempted to rehire him.

Then there is the curious matter of his polygraph test in 1984. The examiners at the time found that he was telling the truth about his association with the FBI, his contacts with the National Guard in El Salvador, and the rest. After the results had been reviewed, a memo from headquarters to Dallas said, "This review disclosed that the examination is satisfactory in all respects and review personnel concur with the results of the examination." Yet three years later, a few weeks *after* Varelli had testified before Congress, the FBI altered those results, claiming that a fresh examination of the tape had revealed discrepancies. A fresh memo to Dallas said, "This review disclosed that the responses indicated that the examinee was deceptive." These new findings were shown to congressional investigators in closed session and were hinted at in off-the-record briefings to reporters. Not surprisingly, they did nothing to enhance Varelli's reputation.

This leaves the question of whether there is any truth to the theory that Varelli had a hidden agenda. He was, after all, a Salvadoran by birth, and a very conservative one at that. To this day he believes that there was a Communist conspiracy at work in his country, and he has never abandoned his right-wing political opinions. But his contention that his three years of work uncovered no evidence of terrorist involvement in CISPES, despite the fact that his political opinions would have motivated him to find such evidence, undermines the double-agent theory. By admitting that CISPES was clean, he did his political cause nothing but harm. What possible motivation would he have for coming forward? It certainly wouldn't endear him to the FBI, from which he was still trying to recover unpaid expenses.

Nor was it strictly the case, as Sessions claimed, that the CISPES investigation had been handled by low-level Bureau agents who had left headquarters in the dark. The top managers were well aware of what was going on. Buck Revell initialed scores of reports sent in by the field offices, and he authorized the expansion of the investigation in October 1983. If Sessions was looking for a scapegoat, he could have looked a lot closer to home. But because Varelli took all the blame, no one at FBI headquarters was ever disciplined.

Whatever the reasons for starting the CISPES investigation, twenty-seven months of agents' time and hundreds of thousands of tax dollars were spent on spying — and there is really no other word to use — on the political activities of thousands of citizens who didn't agree with what their government was doing. No matter what the justification was, or where the blame ultimately lies, that fact is inescapable. It also seems clear, although the FBI refuses to admit it, that the one hundred or so break-ins at CISPES-related offices and sanctuary churches were politically motivated. Since the agency would not agree to investigate those burglaries, it is impossible to say who was responsible. Some blame the FBI, and some blame the private intelligence-gathering and lobbying groups that swam like feeder fish around the official intelligence community. Of the two theories, perhaps the latter is more likely, but it seems certain that no one will ever really know.

The fallout from the CISPES investigation has continued right up to the present. William Sessions's acceptance of at least some measure of FBI responsibility before the House and Senate went down very badly in the FBI at the time and did little to endear him to the senior people he inherited from Webster. At the time, Sessions now says, he had heated discussions with John Otto, the former acting director of the FBI, Buck Revell, and others about whether he should make any admission of culpability. Five years later, Sessions privately blamed many of those same people for engineering his departure from the FBI.

He still maintains, though, that his internal review showed that the investigation was based on a legitimate suspicion of terrorism, was not orchestrated by the White House, and went wrong because of the way Varelli was handled. He says that the break-ins were all properly investigated and that there was no justification for a federal investigation. "There was no evidence then, and none now, that the FBI had any involvement in those incidents," he said.

Frank Varelli still lives in Dallas and nurtures his resentment against the FBI. He has pursued his claims for reimbursement of his expenses through the courts and has won some recompense, but nowhere near the amount he was seeking. He continues to believe that the CISPES investigation was politically motivated and that he was set up as the fall guy when things went wrong. His former handler, onetime special agent Daniel Flanagan, was last known to be working for a Texas insurance firm and has refused all requests for interviews.

John Rees, who, when asked recently if he was still a British citizen replied, "You bet," is still publishing *Information Digest* out of an office in Baltimore, Maryland. These days his main obsession seems to be the "international terrorist conspiracy" rather than the evils of Communism. Though well into his seventies, he is as forceful and as difficult to pin down as ever. He describes the idea that he is a "right-wing spymaster" as "absolute bullshit" and claims to investigate the extreme right as vigorously as he investigated Marxist-Leninist groups. People within the American intelligence community continue to subscribe to his publication privately, though not officially. According to Rees, this means that the material it contains is not available under the Freedom of Information Act, which only applies to official government documents. He happily admits his role in getting the CISPES investigation off the ground: "Of course I wrote that article. I wrote several other articles on CISPES and other Marxist revolutionary groups, and some people in the Bureau took the CISPES story seriously. Which I thought they should do then; which I still think they should have."

Buck Revell served as SAC in Dallas until his retirement in late 1994. Although he publicly denies it, many of his contemporaries say that he was bitterly disappointed when he was not made director of the FBI after Webster moved to the CIA. However, he remained one of the most powerful men in the Bureau. He is characteristically sure of his ground about CISPES. Recently he said, "There was clearly some misunderstanding at some levels in the FBI about what the investigation was meant to achieve. Varelli was an unscrupulous individual who misled many people with his claims that the FMLN controlled CISPES. He was also inadequately supervised. But it was a legitimate investigation, and the allegations that it was politically motivated are totally false and without foundation. Look at our track record. Ninety-eight percent of our counterterrorism investigations are successful, and I think that concentrating on this one investigation takes no account of that."

The Senate Select Committee on Intelligence disagreed. In 1989, while concurring with the FBI's claim that Varelli was to blame for much of the CISPES inquiry, it concluded that "the CISPES case was a serious failure in FBI management, resulting in the investigation of domestic political activities that should not have come under governmental scrutiny. It raised issues that go right to the heart of this country's commitment to the protection of constitutional rights. Unjustified investigations of political expression and dissent can have a debilitating effect upon our political system. When people see that this can happen, they become wary of associating with groups that disagree with the government and more wary of what they say or write."

Certainly many, many ordinary American citizens have come under FBI scrutiny while pursuing their constitutionally guaranteed right to free speech. Over the years, the Bureau may have shifted its emphasis — in the 1950s, for instance, it focused on members of the Communist Party; in the 1960s on student activists and groups protesting the Vietnam War; in the 1970s on those who opposed nuclear power — but the underlying basis for all these investigations seems to have been the target's disagreement with government policies. As the CISPES story reveals, the official end of this kind of investigation does not necessarily signal the end of the Bureau's interest in those who were targeted. And as the CISPES story also reveals, such investigations have a way of spreading to include thousands of citizens whose activities could not be considered suspect by any rational criteria.

Although the Bureau makes much of the fact that it investigates left- and right-wing groups with equal vigor, evidence of this is hard to find. The few right-wing groups that have been investigated, like the Ku Klux Klan, have all come under scrutiny because they have been breaking laws, such as those prohibiting racial violence — a different order of things from peaceful political dissent. With this in mind, it is difficult to escape the conclusion that the FBI is unduly influenced by the political views of those on the far right of the political spectrum, and that its interpretation of the line between a citizen's exercise of his or her civil liberties and that citizen's potential as a revolutionary or terrorist is sometimes made solely on political grounds. Whether this will change as the perceived threat from Communism recedes into history is open to question, but already environmental protestors are claiming that they are now being investigated in the same way as the left-wing groups of earlier generations.

All this leaves one question remaining. Why, given that they are by and large intelligent and decent people, do FBI agents go along with investigations like these? Why are agents prepared to photograph, keep under surveillance, and otherwise monitor those whom they know, almost from the word go, are innocent of any crime or terrorist activity?

The answer is very simple. The FBI is a paramilitary organization. Its disciplinary and loyalty codes are so strong that when agents are told by their superiors to carry out an order, they do so, regardless of how ridiculous or ethically questionable it may seem at the time. Obviously, unless there are compelling issues of national security at stake, very few agents will knowingly break the law, but many investigations fall into gray areas where they may be morally debatable but still strictly within the letter of the law. Even in cases like these, a special agent will almost always do as he is told.

It can be argued that this is as it should be. FBI agents are not unthinking automatons, but they do serve in a government agency with rigid codes of conduct. They have taken an oath and they have to respect it. It should not be up to them to decide which investigations they can or cannot carry out. Nor, it must be said, are field agents always aware of the big picture. They can act only on what they are told. In an operation as significant as CISPES, for instance, they could be excused for believing that those who decided to authorize the investigation knew what they were doing, and that all the necessary legal guidelines had been met.

But this doesn't excuse the FBI's senior managers. Even if one accepts the Bureau's incredible suggestion that the whole CISPES investigation was based on the testimony of one Salvadoran refugee, it is impossible to understand how the senior officials allowed this state of affairs, which eventually involved almost every FBI office in the country, to continue for almost three years.

The CISPES scandal shows quite clearly the dangers the FBI faces when, directly or indirectly, it follows an overtly political agenda set by an administration either under fire for some of its policies or convinced that a major conspiracy is out to undermine its effectiveness. Every time this has happened in the FBI's history, the agency has apologized and promised to behave — and so it does, until the next time, when the whole sorry process begins again. Eventually the Bureau will have to learn that its mandate to investigate political dissent must be limited to purely criminal matters and very legitimate concerns of national security. If it doesn't, the time will surely come when Congress will have to prescribe its intelligence responsibilities by statute. As Sister Patricia Ridgley, one of the Dallas nuns investigated by Varelli and his associates, said, "The edge of the law should be a real edge, not a smooth rock that gets kind of pushed here and there. This you can do. This you cannot do."

CHAPTER 9

TERROR

DESPITE ITS TENDENCY to get caught in the wringer over investigations of purely political groups like CISPES, the FBI does run many very effective and legitimate operations to combat terrorism. When there is real evidence of terrorist activity — when there is in fact a real crime to be solved — the Bureau is truly among the best in the world. Its ability to harness vast resources to solve a problem can lead to the resolution of cases that would leave many other law enforcement agencies baffled. And when resources are coupled with those of other world-class agencies, the results can be astonishing.

In simple terms, the FBI has to deal with two forms of terrorism, domestic and international. The former, as its name suggests, encompasses acts of violence planned or carried out by American nationals on U.S. soil. Terrorist groups of the 1960s and 1970s, such as the Symbionese Liberation Army (famous for its kidnapping of Patty Hearst), fell into this category; so do groups as varied as the Animal Liberation Front, the Aryan Nation (a white supremacist group), and the Pedro Albizu Campos Revolutionary Forces of Puerto Rico, which counts as a domestic group because of Puerto Rico's administrative ties to the United States.

Compared with the Provisional IRA in Britain, the Basque group ETA in Spain, and the Red Army Faction in Germany, American terrorists are comparatively unsophisticated. They have attacked much less frequently and have been the cause of many fewer fatalities. In a typical period, between 1986 and 1990, there were only fifty-four confirmed terrorist incidents in the United States, and of those, thirty-six were in Puerto Rico, where a number of revolutionary groups operate. Many of these incidents, with the exception of some in Puerto Rico (which have become progressively nastier), would not even be recognized as terrorism by the people of Northern Ireland. Until 1993, when a huge bomb went off under the twin towers of the World Trade Center, big explosions were rare in the United States. Widespread, random death and destruction for political reasons were horrors that seemed to be reserved for the rest of the world.

There are a number of reasons for this. The first and most obvious is that the continental United States is free of the nationalist problems that bedevil other parts of the world, such as Northern Ireland or the Basque region of Spain, where terrorists claim (whether justly or not) that they are acting on behalf of an oppressed community. The United States also has fewer big issues that drive a whole sector of society into supporting violence. For instance, the problems that gave rise to a spate of Native American direct actions in the late sixties and early seventies (incidents that were wildly exaggerated by Hoover's FBI) were eased over subsequent years when the Indians gained greater political and economic autonomy. Although many of the problems remain today, they are not, it seems, bad enough to push large numbers of people into committing acts of violence against their fellow citizens.

The United States, for all its flaws, is also a society that offers citizens many peaceful and effective ways of expressing discontent. Although some Europeans regard the States as a politically apathetic place, American politicians are vulnerable to pressure and will take up causes that will get them votes. It is also true that in a society where violent crime is rampant, where guns proliferate, and random killings associated with drugs are an everyday occurrence, terrorism is simply not that effective as a way of getting the system to change. This is not to say that the United States is immune to the threat of domestic terrorism or that the future will not bring some extremely violent terrorist group into existence. There will always be those who attempt to influence the political agenda through the use of violence. Issues such as abortion, environmentalism, and animal rights have already prompted some people to advocate a kind of low-grade terror, and there are fears at the highest level of American law enforcement that economic disparities could cause the poor to turn to terrorism in years to come. But for the moment, things could be a lot worse.

The FBI, which since the early eighties has had primary responsibility for investigating and preventing terrorism, is also quite effective in dealing with the problem. When there is a domestic threat, the agency's resources and manpower usually enable it to catch those responsible.

A well-known example is the case of the United Freedom Front, a small group of political radicals who established a pattern of robbing banks and setting off bombs at "capitalist" targets in the early 1980s. Headed by a Vietnam veteran named Ray Levasseur, the UFF became proficient at evading law enforcement authorities by planning carefully, frequently changing its base of operations, and constantly assuming new names and identities. In fact, for some time the Bureau was not even sure that a single group was responsible for the UFF's actions.

The FBI got its first break in the case in 1980, when one of the terrorists was caught with two explosive devices on the back seat of his car. Then, in December 1981, two members of the group shot and killed a New Jersey state trooper who had pulled them over for a traffic violation. Although they escaped, agents used fingerprints from their abandoned car to find one of their hideouts, where agents found documents that identified other UFF members. Armed with these clues, they were able to obtain photographs and dental and medical records, which they publicized all over New England in an effort to establish the remaining terrorists' true identities.

By August 1984 the Bureau had expanded its investigation into a multiagency operation, code-named BOSLUC. When a state trooper on the UFF-BOSLUC task force found some old catalogs addressed to a Jack Horning in Derby, Connecticut, he followed up the lead and discovered that Levasseur's wife, using the name Judy Hymes, had had a minor traffic accident there. The FBI ran the name through its computer and found that "Hymes" was currently holding a driver's license in Ohio. They checked out the address and discovered that it was a mail drop.

From then on, success depended on vigilance and manpower. The Bureau put a twenty-four-hour surveillance team on the mail drop, kept a small force of airplanes on standby, and alerted the Hostage Rescue Team at Quantico. SWAT teams in Pittsburgh and Detroit were made ready, and the director was kept abreast of developments via the command center at FBI headquarters. When "Judy Hymes" finally showed up, the agents kept their distance, monitoring her from a surveillance plane as she drove to a secluded farmhouse many miles away. One group of agents was then able to follow another UFF member to an apartment in Cleveland, while a second group kept an eye on Levasseur and his family.

On the morning of November 4, 1984, Levasseur left the farmhouse with his wife and children, and the Cleveland SAC decided to act. The SWAT team, trailing the terrorists' van, swerved in and captured Levasseur and his wife, while agents in Cleveland crashed through the door of the apartment and took three other UFF members into custody. A few weeks later, the FBI was able to use chemical and laser technology to trace some of the group's weapons to an address in Virginia, and in April 1985 agents captured the last two UFF terrorists.

Like most counterterrorist operations, the UFF investigation required determination, teamwork, perseverance, and technological resources, all of which are arguably the FBI's strong points. Though such domestic probes take up much time, money, and manpower, they are usually successfully concluded before many lives are lost.

But if domestic terrorism is a relatively minor irritant, international terrorism, which the Bureau defines as attacks on American citizens and property by groups or individuals based in another country, is a major headache. The last ten years have seen numerous instances, many of them quite horrific, in which Americans have been victims. To many other nations, groups, and individuals, the United States is the Great Satan. As the world's richest and most powerful country, it is the cause of all their problems, and attacks on Americans are therefore seen as legitimate.

Examples drawn from a few years in the mid- to late-eighties give some idea of the scope of international terrorist activities that the FBI has investigated.

On October 23, 1983, a suicide bomber drove a truckload of dynamite into a barracks building occupied by U.S. Marines in Beirut. Two hundred and forty-one people were killed.

On June 14, 1985, Islamic Jihad hijacked TWA flight 847 and took it to Beirut. After a thirty-one-day standoff, most of the 153 passengers were released unharmed, but a U.S. serviceman named

Robert Stetham was murdered and his body was unceremoniously dumped on the tarmac in full view of the world's media.

On October 7, 1985, four Palestinians hijacked the Italian cruise ship *Achille Lauro*. They surrendered after a few days, but by then a passenger named Leon Klinghoffer had been killed.

In September 1986, four pro-Palestinian gunmen disguised as airport security agents boarded Pan Am flight 73 from Bombay to New York. Two U.S. citizens were killed during the subsequent siege.

On June 28, 1988, Navy Captain William E. Nordeen, the U.S. military attaché in Greece, was assassinated by a car bomb in Athens. A radical left-wing group claimed responsibility.

All this occurred in addition to the numerous kidnappings of American citizens in Lebanon during the period, all of whom were held hostage and some of whom were later killed.

The FBI's responsibility for responding to such incidents is drawn from a number of statutes, the most important being the Comprehensive Crime Control Act of 1984, which established a new section in the U.S. criminal code for hostage taking, and the Omnibus Diplomatic Security and Antiterrorism Act of 1986. The agency has used (and interpreted) these laws in a number of ways. It has always been ready to send its experts overseas to help gather forensic evidence, but after this legislation was passed it began to take a more active part in investigations abroad, helping out local police and even taking direct action on its own. One of the most dramatic examples of this was the extraordinary operation it set up to capture Fawaz Younis.

On June 11, 1985, Younis and others hijacked a Royal Jordanian jet in Beirut and demanded that it be flown to Tunis, where the Arab League was in conference. The plane was denied permission to land and returned to Beirut. There the crew and passengers, who included a number of U.S. citizens, were allowed to leave and the plane was blown up. Younis, a key member of the Amal militia group, then disappeared into the chaos that was Beirut at the time.

However, CIA and FBI terrorism units kept track of his movements. A warrant was issued for his arrest, and agents in the Terrorism Section at FBI headquarters, together with Justice Department attorneys, devised a scheme to capture him. Knowing that Younis, who had once been a wealthy Beirut car dealer, was susceptible to the charms of narcotics and beautiful women, they decided to offer him both. On September 13, 1987, he took the bait. An undercover agent, posing as a friend and sympathizer, lured him onto a yacht off Cyprus for a brief cruise to some Mediterranean hotspots. As he stepped aboard, two very attractive young women, sunbathing in bikinis on the deck, smiled and waved in greeting.

What Younis didn't know was that the yacht was floating in international waters, that the scantily clad women were FBI agents, and that crouched in the companionway beneath his feet were several members of the Bureau's Hostage Rescue Team. Nor did he appreciate that just over the horizon, Buck Revell and a few senior colleagues were sitting in the darkened "war room" of a small warship, the USS *Butte*, monitoring every stage of the operation.

Younis was immediately arrested, somehow breaking his arm in the struggle, and was taken back to the United States on a U.S. Air Force jet. He was convicted in March 1989 at a federal district court in Washington, D.C., of air piracy and hostage taking and was sentenced to thirty years' imprisonment.

The agency doesn't resort to such methods very often; it prefers to rely on extradition treaties and powers of persuasion to bring foreign terrorists back to the United States. Unfortunately, this process doesn't always work out. Sometimes the extradition process itself contains loopholes, but sometimes the U.S. government is accused of having double standards. For instance, until the late eighties, IRA terrorists who surfaced in the United States on arms-buying trips were able to argue successfully that they were political activists and should not be sent back to the United Kingdom for trial. Not surprisingly, other countries seized on this as justification for not handing over terrorist suspects to American law enforcement agencies.

On other occasions, the Bureau's attempts to extradite terrorist suspects have been frustrated by a prior claim by another country. The case of Mohammed Hamadei is a good illustration. In January 1987 Hamadei was arrested in Frankfurt by West German police and charged with carrying explosives. During the subsequent investigation it emerged that he was wanted by the FBI for the 1985 hijacking in which Robert Stetham was murdered. The Department of Justice applied for extradition, and a section from the HRT flew to Frankfurt and began making arrangements to take Hamadei back in an air force plane that had a sealed interrogation module on board. Somewhere over the Atlantic, a Justice Department attorney said, the FBI planned to "ask him some questions." But then two West Germans were kidnapped in Beirut, and the authorities in Bonn decided that it might be a good idea to keep Hamadei in Germany in case they needed to exchange someone for the hostages. Despite heavy American lobbying, Hamadei was convicted in a German court. FBI agents testified at the hearing and he was sentenced to life imprisonment, but many in the agency were unhappy that he hadn't got his just deserts in the United States.

Of course, there are other countries from which there is absolutely no chance of extraditing terrorist suspects, not least because those countries have actively sponsored the terrorism in the first place: Libya, Iran, Iraq, and Syria, to name the most obvious. For instance, the Abu Nidal organization, frequently cited by the FBI as the most effective and dangerous anti-American terrorist force in the world, has received a warm welcome in all these countries at one time or another, and the People's Front for the Liberation of Palestine has been an equally favored guest.

One result of the frustrations of dealing with terrorism in relation to these nations is that the Department of Justice and the FBI have actively considered ways to capture suspects without the knowledge or consent of the hostile governments involved. This process, which became official policy in 1989, allows the Bureau to snatch suspects from their hitherto safe havens overseas. Not surprisingly, it engendered a considerable amount of heated debate over what was allowable under international law. Some legal experts even argued that sending armed agents into action in this way could justifiably be seen by a foreign government as an act of war.

But in response to questions about the policy from a congressional committee in November 1989, Buck Revell said, "Let me give you an example of where we believe it would be justified: a situation where there is no law, where there is no effective government, and where from that territory there were attacks being made against our civil aviation, hostages being held, and there was an inability of the law enforcement agencies of Government to do anything to protect U.S. citizens. Under those circumstances we would be derelict if we did not attempt to execute in a positive fashion the law of the United States."

If this statement sounds like a veiled threat, perhaps that is no accident. At the time the FBI was in the middle of an investigation of one of the most dreadful terrorist attacks of modern times, the bombing of Pan Am 103.

On the evening of December 21, 1988, Pan Am 103 was twenty-five minutes late, not an unusual occurrence at Heathrow, the world's busiest airport. That night, as on many previous nights, there was a backlog of traffic, and the ground control staff had kept the plane at the gate until it eased. Few of the passengers cared very much. Some of them had been traveling all day, flying into London on a connecting flight from Frankfurt. They were tired and hungry and looking forward to dinner and a drink. But in general, as the 747 taxied out from Terminal Three prior to takeoff, the atmosphere on board was jolly. Most of the passengers and crew — 193 out of 259 — were Americans returning home for Christmas. The rest were British or European, with a sprinkling of Canadians, Argentines, and Japanese.

The plane finally took off at 6:25 P.M. and headed out on a normal flight plan for the seven-hour trip to John F. Kennedy Airport in New York — north to Glasgow and Stornoway and then west over the Atlantic. Thirty minutes later it entered Scottish airspace, and the pilot reported in to the air traffic control center in Prestwick, which had responsibility for monitoring its path until it was well out over the sea. The mass of electronics in the nose of the aircraft sent out a signal every ten seconds which appeared as a green diamond-shaped blip on Prestwick's radar screens. Just after 7:00 P.M. the plane reached its prescribed altitude of 31,000 feet and cruising speed of 550 mph. Then, at 7:19, the green blip abruptly disappeared.

For the three thousand residents of Lockerbie, it was a normal Wednesday evening, tinged with anticipation of the forthcoming Christmas holiday. Families were eating supper, mothers were putting reluctant toddlers into bed, people were watching TV or having a quiet drink in the King's Arms, one of the town's few pubs. It was an ordinary sort of place. Ten miles east of Dumfries and fifteen miles north of the Scottish border, it stood astride the A74, a major road running up from England. Nothing much had ever happened there, and the people of Lockerbie liked it that way. But at 7:20 on December 21, 1988, their quiet, peaceful world blew apart.

Stephen McLeister, a truck driver, was driving past the town on the A74 when suddenly the cab of his vehicle lit up. "I couldn't believe it," he said to reporters later. "A huge aircraft came over just a few feet above me and hit the ground a hundred yards away. I jammed on the brakes and came to a halt. There was a terrible bang."

Another eyewitness, John Glasgow, said, "The whole road was ablaze. Two houses were blazing. The road was completely covered with masonry and apparently parts of the plane. There was a lot of smoking debris on fire. It went up in a fireball."

Two hundred and seventy people died that night — all the passengers and crew members of Pan Am 103 were killed, and so were eleven residents of Lockerbie. Dozens more were injured, and hundreds were treated for shock. It was the worst air disaster in British history. It was also, though no one knew it until a few days later, an act of cold-blooded murder.

The FBI was involved in the investigation right from the start. As accident and emergency services sped to the town, the news that an American plane had gone down at Lockerbie was passed to the U.S. embassy in London. The ambassador, Charles Price, immediately decided to visit the site and flew to Scotland, accompanied by a special agent attached to the embassy. Meanwhile, Darell Mills, the FBI's legal attaché, spent the first of many weary hours on the phone to Washington. During the following week, as British army troops and Scottish police began the slow process of combing an 800-square-mile area for clues and parts of the plane, more agents, including FBI forensic specialists, started arriving in London.

After only a couple of days, British examiners found unmistakable signs of an explosion among the debris: a twisted piece of metal panel showed telltale signs of indentation and pitting, present whenever a blast has occurred. The hunt was now on to find the bombers. The investigators' first task was to call on their intelligence counterparts for a list of likely suspects. In the weeks prior to the explosion, several different sources had passed on to U.S. authorities unspecified warnings that an attack on an American plane by Arab terrorists might be imminent. Though these warnings were apparently not taken seriously at the time, they now seemed deadly accurate. Right from the outset, therefore, no one had any doubts that the culprits could be found in the Middle East. The question was, in which country? To find out, the FBI began working with the Scottish police, CIA, MI6, Interpol, and law enforcement and intelligence agencies in Germany, Sweden, Switzerland, Malta, and France.

The first clues came from among the twisted piles of wreckage, painstakingly examined by forensic specialists in Britain and the United States. The British authorities had agreed to share information with the FBI, which meant there was a constant flow of technicians and evidence between the two countries. With tens of thousands of pieces of airplane, clothing, and other materials to process, this transatlantic trade in airplane debris and forensic data went on for months, but eventually forensic teams came across a small metal plaque that had been inside a baggage compartment. The damage it had sustained indicated that the bomb had been in the passenger luggage area, not in the larger cargo hold. This gave investigators a major break, since it saved them from having to track down and interview the owners of the eighteen tons of commercial cargo that had been on board. Now they could concentrate on the passengers' belongings instead.

More important, this metal plaque contained a piece of yellow plastic about the size of a penny. Under a microscope it was revealed to be a section of a computer chip, part of a Toshiba "Bombeat" radio cassette recorder. FBI counterterrorism specialists heard this with interest, since two members of the Popular Front for the Liberation of Palestine–General Command (PFLP-GC) had been arrested in Frankfurt a few weeks earlier with explosive devices hidden in similar Toshiba radios. The information gave credence to intelligence reports suggesting that the Syrian-backed PFLP-GC had been asked by the Iranian government to bomb the plane in revenge for the 290 people who died the previous July when an Iranian airbus was shot down "in error" by a surface-to-air missile from the USS *Vincennes*. This theory, now reinforced by the forensic evidence, gave the FBI and Scottish police their first clear leads, and they focused their attention on the PFLP-GC and its leader, Ahmed Jibril.

But as the investigation continued, fresh clues began to indicate that other groups might be involved. Experts had recovered and examined the remains of a brown Samsonite suitcase. Chemical analysis showed that it had contained Semtex, the odorless and undetectable plastic explosive, beloved of terrorists worldwide. After conducting experiments with similar explosives and a stack of luggage identical to that which had been recovered from Pan Am

103, FBI investigators determined that the bomb had used up to fourteen ounces of plastique and that the case had been stored in a part of the hold reserved for bags from other airlines. This meant that it must have belonged to a passenger in transit, and not one who boarded at Heathrow.

Crucially, the investigators were also able to identify some clothes that had been inside the case when it had gone off. Special Agent Thomas Thurman, one of the FBI's leading forensic investigators, went to work on these and found that a tiny sliver of circuit board was caught in the fibers of a shirt. He identified it as identical to parts of a circuit board that had been seized after a terrorist operation in Senegal. When he subjected the Senegal board to a fresh examination under the microscope, he saw that something had been erased from its surface. Whatever it was, it was now illegible, so Thurman passed it on to others in the lab. Using chemical and laser techniques originally designed to raise scratched-out numbers from stolen weapons, they managed to identify the word *MEBO*.

FBI and CIA analysts then went through the registers of all known electronics manufacturers and learned that MEBO AG was the trademark of a company called Meister et Bollier, based in Zurich. This information was passed on to Scottish police and to the FBI's legal attaché office in Bern, from which agents made discreet inquiries. Through Interpol and the Swiss authorities, they learned that the company had some interesting connections, so the agents made an appointment to see Edwin Bollier, one of the directors. He was concerned about client confidentiality, but finally told them that the company sold components to the Libyan military and had done some contract manufacturing work for the Jamahirya Security Organization (JSO), the main Libyan intelligence agency. In 1985 and 1986, Bollier said, MEBO AG had made and delivered to the JSO twenty "prototype digital electronic timers, Model MST-13, capable of initiating an explosion at a predetermined future time." Agents later found out that Meister and Bollier had also sublet office space to a Libyan front company called ABH.

At the same time, FBI agents and Scottish police officers were searching for the origin of the clothes from the brown Samsonite suitcase. Extensive research, led by Detective Chief Superintendent John Orr of the Strathclyde police, traced scraps of shirts and underclothes to manufacturers in Italy and Malta, and from there to a small boutique called Mary's House in Sliema, on the Maltese island of Valletta. A joint FBI and Scottish police team went to interview the shopkeeper, Tony Gauci, and struck pay dirt. He told them that on the afternoon of December 7, 1988, a heavily built, clean-shaven man had come into the shop and bought a large stock of clothing. To Gauci's surprise he hadn't seemed at all interested in his purchases and had bought various odd items, including a baby's romper suit and a black umbrella. He had paid in cash. Gauci knew this man was a Libyan, he told the astonished investigators, because there were many on the island and their accent was unmistakable.

The investigators couldn't quite believe what they were hearing. Gauci's memory about what had happened ten months earlier seemed unusually specific. Was he telling them the truth?

A few days later the British authorities went through their macabre collection of smashed suitcases, ripped fabrics, and airplane parts. They had the tattered remains of a number of umbrellas, but on closer examination one of the black ones bore clear signs of close blast damage. It had obviously been inside the suitcase with the bomb. The Libyan connections seemed to be coming together.

The FBI lab now made up a facial composite based on the description provided by Gauci. When agents compared this with photographs of known Libyan operatives provided by the CIA, they were able to narrow the list of suspects down to a handful, including a man called Abu Talb — not a Libyan, but a PFLP-GC terrorist, who was known to have visited Malta in the weeks before the bombing. They took this photograph and others back to Mary's House in Malta. Tony Gauci looked at the photographs a while, but eventually he passed over Talb's picture and put his finger on the face of another man: Abdel Basset al-Megrahi, a known JSO agent.

The FBI did further research in the Middle East and came up with some interesting facts about al-Megrahi. At various times in his checkered career with the JSO he had worked with its Airline Security Section, which placed JSO agents in positions with Libyan Arab Airlines. He had also spent some time working in connection with ABH, the Libyan firm that had sublet office space in Zurich from Meister and Bollier. The FBI discovered that in the fall of 1988 al-Megrahi had made a number of flights from Tripoli to Luqa Airport on Malta. On one of these trips, on December 7, he took a room at the Holiday Inn in Sliema, registering under the name Abdel Basset

A Mohmed, a "flight dispacher" *(sic)* for Libyan Arab Airlines. That afternoon he walked three hundred yards to Mary's House and bought some clothing. Two days later he traveled to Zurich.

While they were finding this all out, the Bureau and the Scottish police were also looking into the activities of one Lamen Fhimah, the station manager for Libyan Arab Airlines at Luqa Airport. The Maltese authorities had told them that Fhimah was one of the few people who could put luggage on flights without sending it through the normal security checks first. By now FBI investigators had learned that an Air Malta plane had flown to Frankfurt on the morning of the Lockerbie explosion. Although FBI agents won't be specific about how they managed it (probably because it came from a CIA under-cover agent or informant), they obtained some very important information about Fhimah. First, they found out that he too was a JSO agent and that earlier that year he had received a batch of Semtex, which he had stored in his desk in his office at Luqa Airport. Probably, law enforcement gained entry to his office and took samples, which the FBI lab later found to be positive.

The Bureau also learned that Fhimah kept a diary, which agents mysteriously managed to obtain. It contained a number of interesting entries. For instance, on December 15, 1988, Fhimah wrote, "Abdel Basset is coming from Zurich with Salvu" and "take tags from Air Malta." Elsewhere he noted, "Bring the tags from the Airport." On December 17, Abdel Basset al-Megrahi traveled from Zurich to Luqa Airport and from there to Tripoli. The next day Lamen Fhimah went to Tripoli and met al-Megrahi. Two days later, they both flew back to Malta, al-Megrahi traveling under a false name. They arrived at 5:20 P.M., carrying a brown Samsonite suitcase. Later that evening they spoke on the telephone and met again. The FBI was convinced they had been discussing the final stages of the plot.

According to the Bureau, the next morning, a brown Samsonite suitcase marked with Air Malta tags that said RUSH JFK was some-how put onto KM flight 190 to Frankfurt. The airplane left at 9:50 A.M. Just over thirty minutes later, Abdel Basset al-Megrahi, travel-ing under yet another assumed name, took Libyan Arab Airlines flight 147 to Tripoli. That evening Pan Am 103 blew up.

There were still a number of holes in the evidence, most notably the question of how an unaccompanied piece of baggage eluded the attention of the security staff at two major international airports, at a time when international airlines and airport authorities had been warned of a possible terrorist threat. Nonetheless, the Bureau and the Scottish police believed they had a strong case. In the fall of 1991, it was bolstered by the defection to the United States of a Libyan intelligence official called Abu Maged Jiacha, himself a former assistant station manager at Luqa Airport. In return for a "financial consideration" (thought to be $2 million in cash) and a promise of resettlement in California under the witness protection program, Jiacha agreed to testify against his fellow Libyans. He was quite clear: al-Megrahi and Fhimah had planted the bomb. On November 14, 1991, in simultaneous press conferences on both sides of the Atlantic, Lord Carmyllie, Scotland's leading law official, and U.S. Attorney General William Barr announced that Libya was solely responsible for the bombing and that al-Megrahi and Fhimah had been indicted under Scottish and U.S. law. Arrest warrants were immediately issued via Interpol.

Three years later, international wrangling over the two Libyans was still going on. Colonel Qaddafi's government flatly refused to hand them over, and international sanctions had had no effect. The regime denied its involvement and tried to convince the British and Americans to try the two men in Libya or in a neutral country such as Malta; they even offered to let a British or American judge preside at such a trial. But the British and U.S. authorities held firm. Al-Megrahi and Fhimah would be tried in one of their jurisdictions or Libya would bear the consequences.

Meanwhile, Buck Revell's earlier hint that direct action might be taken in such circumstances hung in the wind. A source in the Bureau has said that the agency has been reviewing its plans for arresting fugitives in hostile countries and it is likely that some members of the Bureau's elite HRT squad have been ready to go ever since the indictments were handed up.

The most common theory about the motive for the bombing is that the Libyans wanted revenge for the U.S. air raid on Tripoli in 1986. But several European intelligence sources still privately maintain that the PFLP-GC was the principal organizer of the attack. They say that Ahmed Jibril, the leader of the organization, was contracted by the Iranian government to carry out the bombing but turned to Libya when his own men were arrested in Frankfurt. According to these people, the FBI and police investigators did not follow

up the PFLP-GC leads because the investigation coincided with the
Gulf War, and the U.S. and British governments did not want to
alienate Iran and Syria and force them into adopting a pro-Iraqi stance.

Others have even stranger theories. Lester Coleman, an American
journalist who once worked for the Drug Enforcement Agency and
the Defense Intelligence Agency, is one of a number of people (including some of Pan Am's private investigators) who claim that a
massive government cover-up was put into effect after the bombing
to hide the fact that the bombers took advantage of a heroin smuggling route used by a group with close links to Syria's President
Assad. According to this theory, the CIA and DEA had allowed the
route, code-named COREA, to remain open because they wanted
Syria's help in getting American hostages released in Lebanon. The
route was allegedly so well protected that the terrorists were able
to slip a Semtex-packed suitcase onto Pan Am 103 without being
detected. The couriers who carried it on board would have believed
they were smuggling heroin in the normal way.

Coleman, who has co-written a book about the affair called *Trail
of the Octopus*, also says that he was working undercover for the
DEA in Beirut when he became aware that the heroin route was
compromised and that terrorists could take advantage of it. He
claims he warned his controllers, but they left the route open. After
the bombing, when the alleged PFLP-GC connection began to leak
out to the press, Coleman says the DEA tried to silence him by
having the FBI arrest him on bogus passport fraud charges. He jumped
bail and is now living in exile in Sweden, where he is resisting all
U.S. attempts to extradite him. He says he is making all this information public now because it is the only way he can ensure that he
stays alive. Perhaps not surprisingly, the FBI, CIA, and DEA all
categorically refute these charges and insist that Coleman is just a
criminal fugitive.

Determining the truth of all these claims and counterclaims is
difficult, not least because the FBI steadfastly refuses to open its files
on the affair on the grounds of national security. It is certainly true
that both the FBI and Scottish police seem to have ignored the
strong advice implicating Iran and Syria, and it is equally true that
the American and British governments had a vested interest in
keeping those countries out of the spotlight at the time of the investigation. However, the evidence against the two Libyan suspects
is strong and convincing. If the men ever come to trial, perhaps

some of these questions will be resolved. If they are convicted as a result of a trial, then the verdict will surely stand as an endorsement of the power of international law enforcement cooperation, and as a clear symbol of the Bureau's determination to respond effectively to terrorist violence.

As the 1980s gave way to the 1990s, two major incidents significantly affected the FBI's counterterrorism operations. The most obvious was the collapse of the Soviet Union. Despite what many intelligence officials would have had the world believe, the USSR hadn't been a major sponsor of terrorism for many years. Like the United States it had its own problems with terrorists and wasn't that anxious to encourage them openly in the rest of the world.

However, during the Cold War, the United States and the Soviet Union frequently engaged in proxy conflicts around the world, from Korea to Vietnam, from Cuba to Afghanistan, from Angola to the Middle East. Perhaps inevitably, whenever one superpower supported a combatant, the other offered military and intelligence aid to its enemies. This created a climate in which other countries were able to rely on the tacit support of one or the other nation while pursuing their own political agendas. This occurred most obviously in the Middle East, where Syria, Iran, Jordan, Libya, the PLO, and even Egypt at times, were able to summon up Soviet military advisers, MIG warplanes, and KGB intelligence support in times of crisis, while the United States pumped billions of dollars of aid and arms into Israel.

But from the moment that Mikhail Gorbachev first dreamed up perestroika, this agenda began to change, and when Gorbachev was finally ousted and his hard-line Communist opponents fell in their turn, it came to an abrupt end. For all his faults, Boris Yeltsin needed billions of dollars of Western capital, and he knew that he wouldn't get it by providing aid and comfort to the United States' enemies. Terrorists and their supporting states, which had flourished in the late Cold War years, realized that playing off the superpowers against each other was no longer an option. Countries like Syria, Libya, and Iran were now out in the cold, and forced to reconsider and scale back their sponsorship of terrorism. The number of significant foreign terrorist attacks on American targets which the FBI had to investigate declined accordingly.

This isn't to say that Middle Eastern terrorism, or indeed any other sort of international terrorism, came to an abrupt halt. On the contrary, Moslem fundamentalist and some radical pro-Palestinian organizations continued to denounce the Great Satan and its allies. So did Peru's Shining Path guerrillas, Filipino Communist insurgents, and many others. Attacks continued; people continued to die. However, the oxygen of tacit superpower support that had indirectly sustained many of these groups was slowly seeping away. By 1994 the Palestinian question, one of the most divisive political issues of modern times and the cause of most of the major terrorist attacks on the United States and its allies, was finally being settled. It is probably fair to say that if the USSR were still in existence, Palestinian policemen would not be patrolling the streets of Jericho as they do today, American hostages would still be held captive in Beirut, and the FBI and other agencies would still be spending considerable time and resources on monitoring the various political shifts in the various Palestinian and pro-Palestinian organizations, trying to assess where the next terrorist attack was coming from.

The other significant event that influenced the FBI's international terrorist agenda came on August 2, 1990, when Saddam Hussein's massive but ragged army invaded Kuwait. The subsequent Gulf War was an extraordinary success for the United States and its allies, and not only in a military sense. Through diplomacy and strong political pressure these nations persuaded the rest of the Arab world, most of which loathed Hussein anyway, and the Soviet Union (which still existed at the time), to stand and watch while they comprehensively destroyed Iraq's army and infrastructure. In the process, they gave a demonstration of military and technological power that scared the daylights out of potential adversaries. While Saddam Hussein was calling loudly on his Arab brethren to launch massive retaliatory terrorist attacks on the United States, Israel, Saudi Arabia, and the United Kingdom, governments that had previously supported such acts were busily pretending to be occupied with more important matters — which perhaps was the real goal of the Gulf War in the first place.

Nonetheless, the Bureau took Saddam Hussein's threats very seriously — indeed, some say too seriously. The agency believed that terrorist actions could come from four quarters: the Iraqi embassy in Washington (which was shut down halfway through the conflict); the Iraqi mission to the United Nations; Middle Eastern groups such as the PFLP-GC and the Abu Nidal organization; and from amateurs and zealots inspired by Hussein's "holy war" against the United States. Consequently, FBI headquarters went to almost a war footing. The security police who normally guard all the entrances to the J. Edgar Hoover building initiated hourly patrols around the outside, and cars that parked suspiciously close to agency buildings were towed away. Field offices around the country arranged to have special agents guard buildings round the clock. The Strategic Information and Operations Center at FBI headquarters became a kind of war room for the counterterrorism section, and its chief, Neil Gallagher, Director William Sessions, and other senior staff members spent long hours there, talking to the White House and the Pentagon on secure telephone lines. In the end, of course, they mostly sat and watched events in Iraq on CNN like everyone else.

One of the agency's earliest actions was to put together a lengthy list of potential terrorist targets, from power plants, oil installations, airfields, U.S. military bases, and government offices to police stations, homes of prominent politicians, and media organizations. This was disseminated, along with constantly updated threat assessments, to all field offices and to 27,000 other law enforcement agencies. The FBI also moved quickly to let suspected terrorists know that they were being closely watched. It maintained obvious surveillance on relevant diplomats and business organizations, and it went out of its way to talk to Arab American citizens who might know or hear of any planned attacks. In fact, as one agent happily said later, "To be honest, we investigated the shit out of them. They couldn't take a pee without us knowing about it."

Not surprisingly, many Arab Americans were outraged at what they saw as the assumption that because their background was Middle Eastern, they must endorse Iraq's invasion of Kuwait. Their ranks included many people whose countries of origin were fighting on the side of the United States. As one West Coast man said bitterly, "It got to the stage that if your name happened to be Muhammad or Abdul or you were a brown-skinned Moslem, the FBI would drop into your office or your place of work and ask you questions about Hezbollah. I wouldn't mind so much, and I know they've got their job to do, but I'm a Kuwaiti, for God's sake, and a Christian one at that."

Whether all this enthusiastic activity was effective or not is open to question, but it is undeniably true that no terrorist incidents associated with the Gulf War took place in the United States. In fact, the Bureau prevented at least two incidents that could have occurred. One involved a former Jordanian citizen, Jamal Waryat, who had become a naturalized American citizen. Waryat telephoned the Iraqi embassy during the war and offered to commit terrorist acts on Iraq's behalf. Unfortunately for him, the embassy had more pressing concerns at the time and they paid him no attention. The FBI, which was tapping every call in and out of the embassy building, took him more seriously and sent an undercover agent posing as an Iraqi intelligence official to interview him. The zealous Waryat told the agent that he had a number of schemes in mind, including bombing the Holland Tunnel in New York. When he said he wanted to kill President Bush, the FBI arrested him for threatening a U.S. official. The other incident involved a biochemist in New Orleans who wanted to make the chemical nerve agent sarin and send it to the White House on behalf of the Iraqis. He never explained quite how he planned to do this. The Iraqis also ignored him, and the Bureau again moved in and arrested him.

Neither of these men had any connection with any known terrorist organization — in fact they were both probably certifiably insane — but the FBI seemed to believe that they were a real threat, and more deadly examples of terrorist activities were occurring overseas at the time. In any case, the agency wasn't too dissatisfied. Some agents later felt that their increased focus on the Arab community paid dividends in the long run by helping them learn about Islamic society. It was from that society that the biggest domestic terrorist attack in recent years emerged: the bombing of the World Trade Center.

At 12:18 P.M. on February 26, 1993, a massive bomb exploded in an underground parking lot beneath the twin towers of the World Trade Center, setting off a chain reaction among electrical circuits above ground. Smoke soon billowed from the buildings where there were fifty thousand people in the 110-story towers, in the attached hotel, and on the ground-floor plaza. Six of them were killed, over a thousand were injured, and thousands more were trapped in the offices or in the stairwells. The entire south end of Manhattan Island came to a grinding halt as fire and rescue teams made their way to the scene. Hundreds of banks, insurance firms, and brokerage houses on

Wall Street were evacuated, as was the New York Stock Exchange. The cost of the damage to property and the disruption of business was estimated at over $650 million.

At first the confusion was so great that no one knew this disaster had been caused by a terrorist bomb. In the hours after the attack, radio and TV reporters speculated that a power transformer might have blown on an underground rail line. But by mid-evening, when some of the normal calm had returned, investigators were able to begin finding out what had really happened. The FBI, notified by the New York Police Department, had opened a command center in its downtown building, and after discussions with the police and the ATF, it decided to send in a bomb squad for a look. Within twenty-four hours the agents were convinced that a bomb had been set: the damage to the basement garage bore all the hallmarks of a manu-factured explosion.

At first no one had a clear idea who might be to blame. There were the usual crank calls and letters claiming responsibility, in-cluding one sent to the *New York Times* four days after the bombing from a group calling itself the Liberation Army Fifth Battalion. But since no one at the FBI had heard of the group, and computer intelligence research revealed no information about it, agents in-itially assumed that it was a hoax like the rest. Meanwhile, a num-ber of other theories were quietly discussed at FBI headquarters. Was it Serbian nationalists, worried that the United States might inter-vene in the Bosnian conflict, or maybe Colombian cocaine traffick-ers, retaliating in response to a recent crackdown by the DEA and U.S. Customs? But the Serbians had no real expertise in such mat-ters, and no hints of any action from the cocaine cartels had been heard. Pablo Escobar, the most infamous cartel leader, went so far as to write to the American ambassador in Colombia. "They can take me off the list," he said, "because if I had done it, I would be saying why and I would be saying what I want." For the same reasons, the FBI was able to rule out the few remaining domestic terrorist groups as suspects.

That brought agents back to the groups from the Middle East. The bomb was very similar to the one that had destroyed the U.S. Marine compound in Beirut in 1983, and it had exploded on the second anniversary of the liberation of Kuwait. But the Libyans, Iranians, Iraqis, and Syrians had all been maintaining a low profile, and the radical Islamic groups they supported had been quiet for months. Intelligence analysts came up with a dozen explanations for why one or all of these groups might be involved, but none was particularly convincing.

By now three hundred agents from the FBI's New York office, dozens more from ATF, and hundreds of New York Police Department personnel were working on the case, which the Bureau code-named TRADEBOM. Two days after the explosion one of the ATF's explosives experts found the first vital clue. Buried in the rubble of the parking lot were the remnants of a medium-sized van. Scorch marks showed that the bomb had been inside the vehicle. What was left of the chassis also bore the remains of a vehicle identification number (VIN), the number stamped onto every car in the United States. These are always useful to investigators, because state vehicle registration files always list them alongside the vehicle's license number.

The investigative team hunted for other parts of the van and soon determined that it had been a yellow Ford Econoline E-350. Armed with this information, the FBI was able to match the VIN against records and come up with a license plate registered to the Ryder Truck Rental Company in Alabama. The company searched through its computer and discovered that on February 23, the vehicle had been rented out of its Jersey City office for a week, to a man named Muhammad Salameh.

Interviewing the Ryder staff, the agents learned that three hours after the bombing, Salameh had come into the Ryder office and requested a refund of a cash deposit. He said that the van had been stolen from a grocery store parking lot the night before. An employee told him that he wouldn't get his money until he had reported the theft to the police and was able to produce a copy of the police report. This information sent agents to the Jersey City police, where a desk sergeant recalled taking Salameh's report on the theft.

None of this was in any way conclusive. Muhammad Salameh, the agents knew, could have been telling the truth about the theft of the van. It certainly seemed unlikely that anyone would plant a bomb and then take a course of action that would positively tie him to the vehicle in which it had exploded. Obviously they needed to find out more about this man. The New York office called up the FBI's computerized terrorism files and found that Salameh had participated in demonstrations the previous year protesting the innocence of El Sayid-Nosair, an Islamic leader accused of murdering Meir Kahane, the founder of the Jewish Defense League. Salameh had also visited Nosair, who was acquitted of murder but convicted of other charges connected to the killing, at Attica prison. Both men had often attended the Al Salam mosque in Jersey City.

This mosque was well known in the Islamic community because of the preaching of Sheik Omar Abdel Rahman, a radical blind cleric. Rahman, an Egyptian exile, was also a long-standing opponent of President Mubarak's government and advocated its violent overthrow. He had stood trial a decade earlier in Egypt for charges related to the assassination of President Anwar Sadat but had been acquitted. The Egyptian authorities had contended since that he was a leader of a movement responsible for a number of terrorist attacks on Western tourists in their country. Quite a few of Sheik Rahman's circle had been under covert investigation by FBI counterterrorism agents for almost two years, since Rabbi Kahane had been killed. Many of those names now began to crop up in the Trade Center bombing case.

The Bureau discovered that Salameh was a twenty-five-year-old Palestinian who had entered the country on a six-month tourist visa in 1988. That visa had long since expired, and it looked as though Salameh was an illegal immigrant. This and his connection to the van gave agents enough information to arrest him and apply for a search warrant. The Ryder rental document included a telephone number for Salameh. The agents traced it to an address on Kensington Avenue in Jersey City. Salameh was not the listed telephone subscriber, but discreet surveillance and questioning of neighbors revealed that he lived there.

As the warrant was being processed, on March 4, Muhammad Salameh strode boldly back into the Ryder office in Jersey City to collect his four-hundred-dollar deposit. Undercover agents were already posted in the office, posing as employees, and they processed his claim. When he left, a Ryder employee positively identified him as the person who had rented the van used in the explosion. Moments later, he was arrested. That afternoon a search team entered his apartment and found tools, wiring, and books on circuitry and electronics. A sniffer dog, trained to detect odors from explosives, had a "hit" on an empty closet.

With Salameh in custody, the Bureau agents began to search for supporting evidence and possible partners in the crime. Soon they were unraveling a complex network of interrelated plots that, though amateurish in nature, seemed to link others to the bomb. Among Salameh's effects was a driver's license, which listed an address in Brooklyn. At one time the apartment there had been occupied by El Sayid-Nosair, but now that he was in Attica prison it had been taken over by his cousin Ibrahim Elgabrowny, a local building contractor. When the FBI went to search the apartment, Elgabrowny — who was also active at Rahman's mosque — resisted and was arrested for obstruction of justice. Inside the apartment, agents found five false Nicaraguan passports in the name of Nosair and his family.

Investigators also discovered that Salameh had rented a storage room in Jersey City. A search of the premises revealed several hundred-pound bags of urea and bottles of nitric acid and sulphuric acid, components in the Trade Center bomb. Another clue was a business card found in Salameh's shirt when he was arrested. It bore the name of Nidal Ayyad, a twenty-five-year-old chemical engineer. Phone records showed that Salameh and Ayyad had spoken several times before the bombing, sometimes when Salameh had been in the storage unit. They had also rented a car together, which resembled the red vehicle that Ryder staff said Salameh had driven when he came to their office in late February. Agents also discovered that they shared a joint bank account.

Ayyad, a naturalized American citizen with Palestinian roots, was arrested by an FBI SWAT team shortly after these facts were discovered. His lawyer loudly protested his innocence, pointing out that he was a responsible man, with a wife and a steady job with a chemical company. The company said it could find no evidence that any of its products had been stolen. But Ayyad, it turned out, was one of the group around Sheik Rahman who had been under surveillance for some time.

While the agents were pleased with their progress in rounding up suspects, they had not fully established a possible motive, although by now there were increasing signs that the attack was the work of Islamic fundamentalists. Then FBI computer specialists examined Ayyad's personal computer, and retrieved from its hard disc a partially deleted letter that was similar to the one received by the *New York Times* four days after the bombing. They now took the original letter, which had been signed by "The Liberation Army Fifth Battalion," more seriously. It read: "This action was done in response to the American political, economical and military support to Israel, the state of terrorism, and to the rest of the dictator countries in the region."

Agents had identified small flows of foreign money into Salameh and Ayyad's bank account, and on the theory that the funds might have come from Iran, they were trying to identify the source. They also took a fresh look at the 1990 assassination of Rabbi Kahane. But the case was getting ever more complicated. Each day there seemed to be a fresh bank account to trace or a new address to check out, and every new development seemed to deepen the mystery. Furthermore, the agents' progress was increasingly hampered by the members of New York's Moslem community, who regarded their investigation with trepidation and anger. Although indictments were being prepared against Salameh and Ayyad, agents were having a hard time with their background interviews.

But whichever route the inquiries took, they always seemed to come back to Sheik Rahman. Further traces on Salameh's and Ayyad's telephone calls revealed that they had spoken several times to a man named Mahmud Abouhalima, an Egyptian-born taxi driver, now a German citizen, who had left the United States the day after the bombing. He now became the third suspect, and agents discovered that he too had links with Sheik Rahman, having been his driver and personal assistant in 1990. Meanwhile, as media speculation about Rahman's possible involvement in the bombing grew, the sheik was facing a deportation order on the grounds that he was an illegal immigrant. His lawyers announced they would appeal. The preacher told the press that he had no links with any terrorist group and that all allegations against him were unfounded.

On March 22, four weeks after the bombing, Abouhalima was captured by Cairo police. FBI agents immediately flew to Egypt to bring him back, and somewhere over the Atlantic he was charged with complicity in the Trade Center conspiracy. Four hours after he arrived in New York, a fourth suspect, Bilal Alkaisi, who had been seen several times at the storage shed with Salameh, walked into the FBI's Newark office and said that he had heard agents were looking for him. He too was charged.

Jim Fox, the SAC in New York, privately told members of the press that the case was looking more and more like the work of ill-trained fundamentalist fanatics. But he told them only part of the story. In September 1992 agents had arrested a Palestinian called Ahmed Mohammed Ajaj as he was returning to the United States from a trip to the Middle East. In his possession were five fake identification kits, including false passports, and bomb-building manuals. Although Ajaj had been in prison at the time of the bombing, agents subsequently interviewed him and discovered that he had been accompanied back to the United States by an Iraqi named Ramzi Ahmad Yousef. Yousef, an explosives expert, had left the country eleven hours after the bombing and was now a fugitive. A further suspect, Abdul Yasin, was also on the Bureau's wanted list. Fox didn't mention these men, but he was quite clear about one thing: the case was being wrapped up and prepared for prosecution.

The Bureau had a few other surprises up its sleeve too, the most important of which was a former Egyptian army officer named Emad Salem. Salem arrived in New York on February 8, 1988, and on August 21, 1991, became a U.S. citizen. A well-built, bearded, balding man, he told associates that he was an Egyptian security agent and that he had been shot three times in the service of Egypt. He also claimed that he was on the podium when Egyptian president Anwar Sadat was assassinated at a military parade in 1981. The Egyptian authorities have refused to confirm or deny this story.

Sometime in 1990 Salem first approached the FBI and the New York Police Department and offered to act as an informant on the Islamic community in New York. Despite meeting with initial resistance, he gradually began to make his mark. Around the time of Rabbi Kahane's assassination he appeared on the fringes of a group close to Sheik Rahman. Among the people he came into contact with was Ibrahim Elgabrowny, who was then on the executive board of the Al Salam mosque. Some sources have said that in 1991 Salem began to pick up hints from Elgabrowny of plans to bomb various buildings in New York. Salem allegedly passed these rumors on to the FBI, though agents insist he had no specific details.

Shortly after the Trade Center bombing, the FBI decided to use Salem to find out what was going on in Sheik Rahman's inner circle. Salem then offered his services to Rahman as an occasional bodyguard, and Rahman accepted. Some of the sheik's confidants were suspicious of this new arrival on the scene, but apparently Rahman trusted him, and he was able to gain the confidence of a number of the preacher's followers.

Salem quickly became aware that one of the most fervent of these followers was a man called Siddig Ibrahim Siddig Ali, a Sudanese national who worked as an occasional translator for the preacher. Either on his own account or because the FBI told him, Salem suspected that the Trade Center bombing was to be only the first of many terrorist actions, and it seemed that Ali was one of the main plotters. The Egyptian worked his way into Ali's confidence until he began to hear information that he knew the FBI would like to have. Then he began to wear a wire.

Between early May and the end of June, Salem recorded 150 hours of conversations with Ali, during which it emerged that Ali regarded himself as an Islamic warrior coordinating the activities of a number of like-minded zealots. He believed the Koran taught that a man could achieve martyrdom by killing an infidel or an enemy of Islam. The World Trade Center bomb, which he boastfully claimed he had helped assemble, was only a start.

In his role as a fanatical and loyal supporter of Sheik Rahman, Salem made himself a key part of the conspirators' plans. After he was introduced to others in the group, he was told that the next target would be the United Nations complex in lower Manhattan. According to the FBI, Ali told Salem that his Sudanese connections would allow him to drive the bomb into a parking lot below ground. Salem was even asked to find a safe house where the terrorists could build and test a bomb timing device. During some of the conversations, Ali would suggest that Sheik Rahman knew all about their activities; at other times he said that the preacher should be kept in ignorance.

After asking the FBI's advice, Salem duly rented a safe house for the conspirators. A few days before the first meeting, FBI technicians installed hidden cameras in the ceiling and walls and put microphones in the light fixtures in every room. Earlier Ali had told Salem that he would conduct surveillance of the target, obtain the right explosives, and find the personnel to plant the bomb. The FBI wanted to confirm this, and it wanted no equipment failures.

Over the next few weeks, Ali and his nine fellow plotters, all devout followers of Sheik Rahman, put their plans into effect. Ali tested the timing device and traveled to Philadelphia to buy explosives. The group continued to hold meetings, and Salem continued to record them. On May 27, he met Siddig Ali, Amir Abdelgani, and Fares Khalfella in the not-so-safe safe house to discuss targets, and Ali suggested that they bomb three places on the same day to make a big impression. A few days earlier Salem had been told that the federal office complex, which included the FBI's headquarters, was on the list; two days later, Ali announced that the Lincoln and Holland tunnels were also targets.

At this stage the Bureau was not sure that it had identified all the conspirators or that it had sufficient evidence to convict them all. Wire-recorded testimony, even with conversations as clear as these, is often regarded with suspicion by courts and juries. Suspects have to condemn themselves from their own mouths, unprompted and in clear and unmistakable terms. Some of these conversations were taking place in Arabic and some in English, and agents were worried that they could be misinterpreted. But on June 23, three days after Ali and Salem drove out to the Connecticut countryside to test the explosive power of their chemical cocktail, the agency decided it could delay no longer.

Salem's wire had told the agents that the terrorists were assembling the bombs in an old warehouse in Queens. At 1:30 A.M. on June 24, a huge FBI SWAT team stormed the building. Five conspirators were inside assembling the explosives. "As we entered the bomb factory, the five subjects were actually mixing the 'witches' brew,'" said SAC Fox to a press conference later. "The smell of fumes from the mixture was almost overpowering." Three others were arrested hours later.

Two months later, Sheik Omar Abdel Rahman was indicted on terrorist conspiracy charges that painted him as the leader of the group that had bombed the World Trade Center, plotted to bomb the United Nations and other targets, and conspired to assassinate Egyptian president Hosni Mubarak. The twenty-count indictment also linked him and several of his followers to the murder of Rabbi Kahane. El Sayid-Nosair, who had been acquitted of state murder charges, was now indicted on a federal charge of "murder in aid of racketeering." Almost a year later, the four conspirators charged with direct responsibility for the World Trade Center attack were convicted and given stiff sentences.

Emad Salem, the FBI quietly acknowledged, had done everything that had been asked of him. He had helped the Bureau round up the entire terrorist group and had provided evidence that would bring a flood of convictions. The whole case had been a triumph from start to finish. But Salem was still an enigma. To what extent had he acted to help capture a violent group before it wreaked havoc on innocent citizens of his adopted land? What were his connections with the Egyptian government, which was desperate to bring down a group it believed was shooting Western visitors and disrupting its multimillion-dollar tourist industry? Like so much about the FBI's counterterrorist work, there are numerous possibilities and no clear answers.

It is doubtful that terrorism will ever be truly defeated in our lifetime. No matter how successful the FBI and its counterparts are in bringing perpetrators of terrorist violence to justice, the conditions that give birth to the phenomenon are unlikely to disappear.

It is true that there are some hopeful signs. The Palestinian question, which has driven so many to seek recourse to violence, is now in the first stages of being resolved. Peace in the Middle East just might be on the horizon. In Europe, terrorist groups from the Red Army Faction in Germany to the Red Brigades in Italy have suffered reverses from which they may never recover. Even the IRA has now declared a ceasefire and begun to negotiate for a peaceful settlement.

But elsewhere the picture is not so rosy. In Peru, India, Greece, Japan, Korea, and elsewhere there continue to be people who believe that the only way to achieve their political or religious ends is through the use of random violence against innocent people and property. And there will always be governments that provide arms and safe havens to these people as part of their foreign policy.

It is also perhaps inevitable that the United States will continue to attract the jealousy and hatred of others. Although many Americans are puzzled by this, there are millions of people around the world who don't like their country, its politics, its values, or the way (in the view of some) it interferes in affairs that are not its concern. Consequently, as long as the United States stands at the top of the league of nations, its citizens are fated to be targets of terrorism.

The FBI, of course, has neither the will, the responsibility, nor the power to address any of the underlying reasons for terrorism. Its role is to catch those responsible for attacks on American citizens and property and bring them to justice. Yet as the primary law enforcement agency in the world's sole remaining superpower, the FBI is increasingly being tempted abroad. Its expertise, advice, and resources are sought by those less well equipped to handle terrorism, and this puts a heavy burden on an organization that already has considerable domestic crime problems to cope with. Questions have to be asked about whether the FBI has the ability and the sophistication to take on the task of combating terrorism at the international level. It has tended in the past to look for simple solutions to complex problems, to see things in black and white; as several cases reveal quite clearly, the agency sometimes jumps to conclusions that are not borne out by the facts. Such an approach could easily lead to disaster in a complex international case involving countries with differing political agendas.

So how should the FBI address its counterterrorism responsibility? Should it always act strictly within the boundaries of U.S. and international law, or should it bend the rules a little to save lives and protect American interests?

In the 1950s, when the United States believed it faced a serious threat from the forces of Communism, a top-secret report on CIA activities was given to President Eisenhower. It was a rationale for the agency's covert operations overseas and can be seen as a blueprint for many of the CIA's actions in later years, from the Bay of Pigs to Afghanistan. The introduction states:

> As long as it remains national policy, another important requirement is an aggressive covert psychological, political and paramilitary organization more effective, more unique and if necessary more ruthless than that employed by the enemy. No one should be permitted to stand in the way of the prompt efficient and secure accomplishment of this mission. It is now clear we are facing an enemy whose avowed objective is world domination at whatever cost. There are no rules in such a game. Hitherto normal standards of conduct do not apply. If the U.S. is to survive, longstanding American concepts of fair play must be reconsidered.

This argument, of course, comes from another era with other problems. But as the Bureau walks onto the international stage, where only a few years ago the CIA acted alone, it will have to be mindful of the danger inherent in thinking like this. There are undoubtedly those within the FBI who believe that terrorism, in conjunction with international organized narco-crime, is the new threat to established society and that strong, even ruthless counter-measures are required. But whether it is dealing with this enemy outside U.S. borders or responding to the enemies within, the FBI will have to ensure that the rule of law, and only the rule of law, forms the parameters within which it operates.

CHAPTER 10

MUTINY AND THE AFTERMATH

O N THE AFTERNOON of Monday, July 19, 1993, William Steele Sessions, director of the FBI, sat in his office on the seventh floor of the J. Edgar Hoover Building in Washington, D.C., and waited for the phone to ring. He knew who would be calling. A few minutes earlier, Assistant Attorney General Philip Heymann had briefed him on what was about to happen. Farther down the corridor, senior FBI officials were trying to work, but it was difficult to concentrate. The rumors had been circulating for hours, and it was obvious that the climax to a long-drawn-out saga was almost upon them.

At 3:50 P.M. the call came through. As Sessions picked up the receiver, his face was a little pale, but his voice remained calm. "Good afternoon, Mr. President," he said.

Clinton was cordial but to the point. Sessions should be commended for his service to the country, but he had decided that Sessions could no longer serve as head of the FBI, and was therefore terminating his appointment as director.

After a couple of minutes, Sessions put the phone down and managed a weak smile for Heymann, who sat across the broad wooden desk. As the lawyer tried to find a few words to soften the news, the phone rang again. It was the White House once more. The dismissal was to take effect immediately, and, the bitterest blow of all, Deputy Director Floyd Clarke was being named as acting director. The details were set out in a letter, which was now being faxed. Hampered by the sling on his right arm, which was broken in a fall a few days earlier, Sessions dug in his pocket for his leather-bound FBI credentials and slid them across the desk to Heymann. Two minutes later Clarke came into the room and received a letter from Heymann informing him of his appointment. He shook hands and left.

A short while later, as Sessions's secretary sobbed behind him, the former director left his office and went down to the ground floor to address a hastily arranged press conference, his FBI bodyguards following on his heels. As he walked through the corridors to the elevator, the power and prestige that had been his for five years seemed to slip away. But there was also relief, release from the burdens and stresses of nine traumatic months. He walked into the press room, lifted his head, and squared his shoulders. After some brief remarks about how he had sought to dedicate his life to public service, he had a few final words. For the first time he let some of the bitterness show.

"Now, so that you will know with clarity the effect of my conversation with President Clinton, I am in the building as a visitor. I am escorted wherever I will be in the building. And I am now a citizen, a private citizen of the United States," he said.

Just after six that evening, after saying goodbye to his aides and collecting his effects from his office, Sessions climbed into his bulletproof Bureau limousine for the last time. That night his words were repeated again and again on television stations across the United States. In homes and offices FBI agents watched and gossiped about who their new boss might be. In headquarters, some just smiled and said nothing.

The rise and fall of William Sessions can be recounted in two ways. Depending on your point of view, it is either a story of petty corruption, bureaucratic incompetence, and high school name-calling, or it is a saga of power, intrigue, and personal rivalry of almost Shakespearean proportions. Either way it offers fascinating insight into the FBI's corporate structure and the complex politics at its byzantine Washington headquarters.

Like most large and complex organizations, the Bureau depends to some extent on senior personnel to define its self-image as well as its public persona. Thanks to J. Edgar Hoover, these perceptions are particularly strongly linked with the FBI's director, who is still in many ways the ultimate G-man. Hoover's successors — first Clarence Kelley, then William Webster — maintained the tradition established by Hoover, portraying the agency to itself and to the world as the very model of hard-nosed efficiency. But William Sessions had a different approach, and the resistance he encountered reflected both the strength of the FBI's traditions and the determination of those in power to uphold them.

The story began in the fall of 1987, when Sessions, a U.S. district court judge in San Antonio, Texas, was approached by the White House. William Webster was leaving the FBI to run the CIA. Would Sessions agree to replace him at the Bureau? When news of the approach leaked out, many Washington insiders seemed surprised. Sessions's only direct experience of Washington had been a two-year stint in the Nixon Justice Department. But to the president's aides, this was a major plus. The Reagan administration was under fire for the Iran-Contra affair and for the messy nomination of Robert Bork to the Supreme Court. It was important for this appointment to be as smooth and as trouble-free as possible. Judge Sessions was a "Mr. Clean," untainted by the system. His middle-class Rotarian charm and his reputation as a keen student of the judicial process made him the ideal candidate.

Sessions, who had been enjoying the comparatively modest fruits of a successful career in the San Antonio legal community, found the lure of the national spotlight irresistible, and accepted. As the administration had hoped, he sailed through the nomination process and took the oath of office on November 2, 1987. He inherited an organization with a $2 billion budget and almost 23,000 employees, 9,500 of them special agents. He also inherited some embarrassing problems.

First, the FBI stood accused of widespread infringement of civil liberties in the CISPES investigation, and Frank Varelli was making public allegations about its motives. Liberal critics were lining up to accuse the agency of reverting to the techniques of the bad old Hoover days. Second, the highly contentious race issue was receiving plenty of public attention. Special Agent Donald Rochon had filed a lawsuit accusing white agents of systematic racial harassment, and hundreds of Hispanic agents had instigated a class-action suit alleging that the Bureau had conspired to keep them in menial and dead-end jobs.

In former days, the Bureau would have dealt with these embarrassments by mounting a major retaliatory attack, launching an unofficial but effective lobbying campaign through its media friends to keep its critics on the defensive. Plenty of FBI officials, including Buck Revell, then the executive assistant director of the Investigative Division, thought this was the wisest course. Revell took a tough approach on the CISPES case, defiantly telling Congress that the Bureau had done nothing wrong.

To the disgust of many in the Bureau's top echelons, however, Judge Sessions was more conciliatory. Not only did he publicly acknowledge Bureau culpability in the CISPES affair, he also settled the Rochon case and established a program to improve hiring and employment prospects for black, Hispanic, and Asian agents. In an organization that has traditionally thrived on macho secrecy and power, and which has a long, if not so honorable, record of standing up to its critics, his actions were bitterly resented. William Concessions, as he was soon being called, had let his men down. Badly.

If Sessions had gone out of his way to make a firm impression on the Bureau from the start, his subordinates might have forgiven these early "lapses," but that wasn't his style. He was a moderate man, who prided himself on his fairness and disliked personal confrontation. Unfortunately, these qualities, which had been enough to get him to the top in Texas, were insufficient preparation for the infighting and intrigue of the political shark-pool that was the capital. As time went by, it became apparent to Sessions's friends, if not to him, that he was in over his head. As one would say later, "He's basically a decent and honest man with a strong sense of what's right and wrong, but he can be very naive about human nature. He finds it hard to believe that he has enemies who are out to destroy him and that makes him very vulnerable. I don't think he was ready for some of the old vipers who run the Bureau."

One of Sessions's most serious problems, it now seems, was the fact that his appointment had come as a considerable disappointment to a small but important cabal of FBI executives who had wanted an insider to get the job. Failing that, they had wanted someone more in the mold of their previous director. William Webster had been a tough, no-nonsense figure of considerable personal power, who rigidly controlled his senior staff. He had been harsh with anyone who tried to usurp his authority and had come down hard on failures and mistakes. Nonetheless, many people in the Bureau had seen him as one of them, working with an agenda agents could understand. He had been interested in the fine detail of complex investigations and had been eager to develop new ways of fighting crime, such as the RICO statutes and undercover techniques. If he wasn't wildly popular, at least agents knew where they were with him.

Sessions was from a more relaxed tradition, alien to the FBI's paramilitary culture. His achievements and interests during his five-year tenure were more administrative. He introduced the concept of "total quality management" to the Bureau, refashioned recruitment procedures, and pushed for and obtained more resources for FBI support systems, such as computers and forensic services. He also went out of his way to meet as many agents as he could, visiting all the field offices and personally handing out commendations and congratulations to agents who had shown particular initiative or courage. These gestures were greatly appreciated by many in the field, who often felt ignored by headquarters. He even notched up a few achievements in the crime area, most notably when he initiated the campaign called "Safe Streets," making violent crime an FBI priority, and when he transferred a few hundred agents from foreign counterintelligence to criminal investigations as the Cold War began to thaw.

But many at headquarters regarded these initiatives as irrelevant. Sessions, they grumbled, was more interested in the ceremonial aspects of the job than in its practical demands. His self-proclaimed interest in administration was all very well, but he seemed to spend more time on the cocktail circuit and making speeches than he did coming to grips with detail. Several people lost patience with what they saw as Sessions's arbitrary and last-minute interference in operational matters, and with his unwillingness or inability to understand the complexities of some of the agency's cases. Perversely, when he did show an interest, they disliked his fastidiousness over legal matters and his preoccupation with the niceties of the rules of investigation. Above all, his hesitancy in making decisions — or at least decisions they agreed with — began to irritate them.

But all of these supposed faults — his vagueness, his posturing, his lack of charisma, even his actions over CISPES and the Rochon case — might have been forgiven in time, had it not been for one thing: his wife. Of all the director's sins, the most unpardonable to Bureau hard-liners was the way in which Bill Sessions relied on his wife, Alice, for support and advice. Right from the start, her determination to guard him from some of the worst snares of the job led her into open conflict with an inner circle of Bureau officials. According to Mrs. Sessions, shortly after her husband took office, John Otto, one of his senior colleagues, told her, "We've never had a wife in the FBI and we don't intend to start now. You should stay in Texas." That, as they soon found out, she wasn't prepared to do.

Milt Alherich, now SAC of the New Haven field office, was in charge of the Bureau's congressional and public affairs unit at the time of Sessions's appointment. One of his duties was to brief the director on his areas of responsibility. But first he had to get past Alice. "I was the first ranking agent to travel to San Antonio to meet then Director Designate Sessions," he explained, "and I could see that there were going to be problems. I didn't want to believe it, but there it was. She was going to be a part of his life, and we had to deal with it."

It quickly became apparent to Alherich, as to others, that Alice Sessions was not only determined to stay by her husband's side during his early days in the FBI, she was going to make sure that she retained her influence. She felt that her husband needed help, support, and management and that she had a legitimate stake in ensuring his success. After all, the two were giving up a lot to come to Washington. The job carried the same pay as Sessions's previous post — about $89,000 a year — but only half the pension. They would have to sell their Texas home and buy another at twice the price in Washington. For the job to work out as they both hoped it would, she would have to be by his side.

Alice also needed allies. She found them in Sarah Munford, the director's new executive assistant, and Ray and LeRoy Jahn, a husband-and-wife team who were to be responsible for the organization of his office. All of them came up with Sessions from San Antonio, and with Alice they formed a close group that he could rely on. The Jahns had worked as assistant U.S. attorneys, and although they found the Bureau frustrating, they managed to gain some respect for their competence in administration. Munford, however, was regarded with increasing hostility and was eventually forced out.

Looking back now, Alherich believes the seeds of Sessions's problems lay in the determination of Alice Sessions and Sarah Munford to throw a protective cordon around the director. Their actions alienated many at FBI headquarters, who saw their influence being diluted by two people beyond their control. "It made things very difficult," Alherich said. "He kept working through these two women, and if he had been able to keep them in check, just a little, then things might have been a bit different. If for a moment he had listened to the advice of those around him then, he'd still be there today."

The inference is that Alice Sessions and Sarah Munford meddled in affairs that were beyond their competence — which helps to explain some of the FBI's extraordinary, tight-lipped fury over otherwise petty matters. Senior figures hated the fact that the director's wife was given her own security pass for headquarters, that she had her own parking space, that she accompanied the director to official events around the country, and that she used official cars to go shopping and to social events around Georgetown. But their deep unhappiness with what many people might merely consider mildly inappropriate behavior shrinks to nothing in comparison with their ire over the issue of the security fence for the couple's home.

When the Sessionses moved into the house in February 1988, the Bureau thought they should replace the existing picket fence with something more secure. The Bureau's security team wanted a substantial six-foot iron fence; Bill and Alice wanted a wooden fence more in keeping with the architecture of the area. The resulting squabble dragged on for a year and a half, generated dozens of memos and meetings, and even led to a two-hour confrontation between the couple and top Bureau officials, including Floyd Clarke, the deputy director, and Weldon Kennedy, the assistant director in charge of administration. Shortly after the meeting started, the director was called from the room to take a phone call. Then, according to Alice Sessions, the others lit into her. She was told that she had become an embarrassment to the Bureau and that she should leave the matter of her husband's security and the fence to the FBI professionals.

When this dispute was reported by the media three years later, there was much speculation as to why the FBI had spent so much attention on something so petty. Even some agents were confused. As one grizzled veteran put it at the time, "For God's sake, you'd have thought they would have all had more important things to worry about than whether or not one style of fence was better than another. What kind of game were they playing?"

Alice Sessions had no doubts about what was going on. For her, the fence issue was just one in a long line of attempts by the Bureau hierarchy to limit her involvement in her husband's affairs. This infuriated her. As far as she was concerned, she was an official wife, entitled to some special treatment but with official responsibilities as well. Her motivation, she later claimed, was not only to support her husband in his job, but also to lend a more human face to the FBI while fulfilling her public duties. She organized employee assistance programs to help Bureau families cope with problems like alcoholism and drug addiction, and, in defense of her habit of accompanying her husband on business trips, she claimed that she was able to meet hundreds of special agents' wives, who were otherwise ignored by the agency. On the face of it, she had a point. It *was* extraordinary that the senior executives of a major branch of the American government's judicial system should have been so concerned about the comings and goings of the wife of its chief executive. But the battles took on a deeper significance in the war between Alice Sessions and the Bureau. They became critical highlights of a report that eventually cost her husband his job.

Sessions may have made himself unpopular inside the Bureau, but that was nothing compared to the enmity he apparently aroused among some at the Justice Department. In recent years, the Reagan and Bush administrations had both focused attention on the criminal justice issue and had backed major budget increases for law enforcement. Consequently, the usually strained relationship between the Justice Department and the FBI had improved. But this closer working alliance didn't seem to benefit Sessions. Shortly after President Bush took over the Oval Office, Attorney General Dick Thornburgh was dropping hints all over Washington that the administration was thinking about appointing a new FBI director. Nothing happened, no doubt because Sessions had by then made some good friends among the Democrats in Congress, which made him hard to remove. Nonetheless, the attorney general reportedly regarded him as an incompetent.

When Thornburgh resigned to run for the Senate, his deputy, William Barr, took over. Barr had close ties with Floyd Clarke, who was regarded by some in the Bureau (perhaps unfairly) as a committed critic of Sessions. Barr too made no secret of his willingness to dump the director when the time was right. When, in the summer of 1992, the department's Office of Professional Responsibility signaled its intention to open a routine investigation into the way Sessions ran the Bureau, Barr's ears pricked up. If what Clarke and others had been telling him was true, this might be the right time.

Again nothing might have happened, but then an incident occurred that brought Bill Sessions and the attorney general into direct conflict and cost the director what little support he had left in the administration. In October 1992, the Central Intelligence Agency and the Justice Department were trading public charges over who had been responsible for allowing Saddam Hussein's regime to receive $4 billion in loans and aid through the Atlanta branch of the Italian-owned Banco Nazionale del Lavoro. The issue was explosive because the money was given to Iraq just prior to Desert Storm. During the trial of Christopher Drugoul, BNL's Atlanta manager, on 347 counts of fraud, allegations were made that both the CIA and Justice had deliberately misled the court about their role in the affair. It was an election year embarrassment the Bush administration could have done without. At the height of the scandal, William Sessions told Barr that the FBI was launching an independent investigation. The attorney general's office vehemently claimed that it ordered the inquiry.

Whoever was responsible, one thing is certain. Three days later, the Justice Department let it be known, even though such investigations are supposed to be secret, that it had asked to see the FBI director's personal files. The routine ethics review had become a preliminary criminal inquiry, and all Washington knew it. It was left to Senator David Boren, the Oklahoma Democrat who chaired the Senate Intelligence Committee, to make the obvious connection. "The timing of the accusations against Judge Sessions makes me wonder if an attempt is being made to pressure him not to conduct an independent investigation," he said. If so, it didn't work. The investigation continued as planned. But by making such suggestions, Sessions's supporters did nothing to improve his standing with the administration.

Until January 1993, it seemed that Sessions would be able to ride out the affair and control his enemies. Although there had been a number of leaks about the investigation, no one from the Bureau had gone on the record to spell out exactly what was at issue. The old discipline of closing ranks in the face of criticism and never doing anything to embarrass the FBI had kept most of the rumblings of discontent out of the headlines. But when the 161-page report from the investigation was finally published, the lid came off. For the first time in the Bureau's history, a number of senior executives publicly accused a serving director of abusing his position for personal gain and private convenience. The knives were out for Bill Sessions.

Either by design or by default, the report was a textbook piece of political assassination. It contained dozens of minor allegations of misconduct. Taken individually, these charges were trivial, but together they portrayed a director who had continually bent the rules. Aside from the issue of the Sessionses' fence, which received detailed attention, the report included accounts of how FBI officials had to make last-minute decisions on the propriety of Alice Sessions's travel, how the legal attaché in Paris was told by Sessions to provide his friends with travel assistance, and how Richard Held, the San Francisco SAC, had to set up receptions and business breakfasts to make Sessions's visits to his daughter seem official. The report also alleged that Sessions failed to pay taxes on his private use of official limousines, that he carried passengers against regulations, and that when he instructed an FBI pilot to land his plane in Fort Smith, Arkansas, for unnecessary refueling, his father turned up with a birthday cake. There was even an accusation (never substantiated) that he had used his position to obtain a favorable mortgage deal from the Riggs Bank.

When the report came out, the press, which had been trawling its FBI contacts for comments ever since it learned that an investigation was under way, had a field day. Sessions seemed doomed. But to everyone's surprise, the director refused to go down without a fight. Up to that point, he had tried to stay out of the affair, but now he went on the attack. He was helped by the fact that Bush had lost the election and William Barr was leaving office.

The report's impact behind the scenes was considerable. Agents who had spent all their working lives in the Bureau had never seen anything like it. As one said at the time, "The only conclusion you can draw is that it says something very important about the way people in the Bureau feel about Sessions. There's a deeper language in all this, there has to be. I know it's difficult for an outsider to accept, but the Bureau isn't like other organizations. We look after our own and we don't tell tales. If they are going after Sessions like this, then he must really have pissed them off." The agent added that though the director had many flaws, he had done much to improve working conditions for agents, and that without him the Bureau would be run by those people who "still think they can act like they did when Hoover was alive."

For the next few weeks, Sessions's future was the number-one topic of conversation at field offices across the country. At one unofficial gathering, the consensus seemed to be that when a new attorney general was confirmed, President Clinton would have to move. One agent thought that Clinton would have a hard time making it look as if he weren't getting rid of Sessions to put one of his political friends in the job. Another agent, who claimed to have disliked Sessions from the day he was appointed (despite never having spoken to him), disagreed, saying that Sessions was "the original empty suit" and that Clinton couldn't keep him on without looking as if he were condoning Sessions's alleged misconduct.

The subtext of this and every other conversation was that such a scandal would hardly have been possible under any of the Bureau's previous directors — or at least if it had been, it would have been kept well under wraps. But though agents are as prone as anyone else to be nostalgic for the good old days, few of them had forgotten that not so long ago they would have risked their careers by even having such a conversation. Talking about superiors in such a way is still seen as a dangerous thing to do in the Bureau, and the open debate about Sessions was a measure both of how much things had changed since Hoover died and of how far Sessions had fallen in their estimation.

While veteran agents described the scandal as a "puzzle palace coup," Sessions stepped up his campaign to clear his name. In hastily arranged press conferences and TV talk show appearances, he denied that he had acted improperly, declared that Barr may have been motivated by animus, and said that he hadn't been given an opportunity to defend himself against the allegations before they were made public. Cleverly, he dropped several hints about a wider conspiracy to scuttle him — always a good tactic in Washington, where hundreds of eager journalists are always on the lookout for government malpractice. He also marshaled support from his friends on Capitol Hill, one of whom — Don Edwards, a former special agent and long-standing critic of the Bureau — called him "the best director we've ever had."

But sniping from within the Bureau continued. Several senior FBI officials privately told reporters that they hoped Sessions would go quietly and bring the embarrassing episode to an end. Buck Revell even went so far as to say publicly, "If he cannot show the new president that he has conducted himself in an ethical and honorable fashion, he should resign for the good of the Bureau and our country."

Gradually the affair drifted into stalemate as the White House struggled to appoint a new attorney general. Then, on February 26, 1993, the World Trade Center was bombed. A week later, the standoff at David Koresh's compound in Waco began. Suddenly the FBI was desperately busy. As the agency went into overdrive, few people at headquarters had time to worry about the director and his problems. For the moment he remained in control, and, in what many saw as a last-ditch attempt to restore his battered authority, he seemed to take a more avid interest than usual in the day-to-day progress of these key investigations. But by now, the atmosphere at headquarters was several degrees below freezing.

In the end, Sessions's tenure at the Bureau and the sorry spectacle of its demise illuminated a number of home truths about the place. Sessions has always maintained that he did nothing "improper, unethical, or in any way questionable" and that "there was an attempt to cripple [him] as director," which he attributes, in part, to resentment over the fact that none of the senior FBI men were appointed director, and to disagreement over his handling of the CISPES and racial discrimination cases. A dignified and thoughtful man, he emphasizes that he was anxious to serve out his term and keep the Bureau free of political pressure, and that Bureau executives had made "scurrilous" attacks in an attempt to get rid of him. But he has refused requests for evidence of a conspiracy against him. His wife has claimed that the Bureau bugged their home, that agents lied to the Office of Professional Responsibility, and that one of the senior executives falsified his résumé to get into the FBI, but again no evidence has been forthcoming.

What seems clear is that many in the Bureau heartily disliked Sessions. Some must have resented having an outsider in charge, especially one who began his term by publicly admitting that the

Bureau had made mistakes. Others may have been frustrated by his management style, which apparently could be both detached and interfering. Still others may have been irritated by his mannerisms — he is sometimes curiously rambling in his conversation, and he has been accused by some of both arrogance and an inability to concentrate. It appears that by the time the investigation into his behavior was made public, he no longer had the support of either his senior subordinates or his junior ones; the ranks of the Bureau had closed, but they seemed to have closed against him rather than to protect him. If someone had to be embarrassed, it was going to be the director, not the agency.

Sessions wasn't a bad director, and he made some brave decisions. Many of the agency's greatest recent operational successes took place under him, and though some dispute his role in them, he at least created a culture in which such successes could happen. Most important of all, he succeeded in keeping the FBI away from the major abuses of constitutionally guaranteed rights that had been a feature of some of his predecessors' terms in office. But he wasn't a good fit with the Bureau's culture. Politically naive, he apparently did not realize how important it was to maintain the FBI's traditional image and present it to the world, and that cost him the trust and respect of colleagues. Eventually, President Clinton had no choice but to fire him. It was time, he said, to "end the turmoil in the Bureau and give the crime fighters the leadership they deserve."

That leader was Louis J. Freeh, who was nominated on Tuesday, July 20, 1993, to be the fifth full director of the FBI. In front of his wife, Marilyn, and four young sons, at a sun-dappled ceremony in the Rose Garden of the White House, Freeh shook President Clinton's hand, and said, "I pledge my total commitment to an FBI whose only beacon is the rule of law, whose sole task is protecting all our people from crime and violence."

His appointment was warmly greeted throughout the Bureau. Freeh was one of their own, or the nearest thing they were likely to get. A forty-three-year-old federal judge from New York, he had spent six years in the FBI and ten years as a federal prosecutor specializing in organized crime cases before moving to the bench. Former colleagues were glowing in their praise. Freeh, they said, had "innate leadership qualities" and combined "the skills of a seasoned investigator with the best instincts of a trial lawyer." Rudolph Giuliani, the former U.S. attorney for New York and Freeh's one-time boss, said, "He is the singularly best-suited person in America to run the FBI. It will be a great morale boost to the Bureau." Senator Alfonse D'Amato said, "He brings instant credibility to the job."

To many people who have faced Freeh in court or dealt with him on cases, he appears as a quiet, sober figure — "a serious kind of guy in a rumpled shirt," as one put it — but close friends say that in private he has a wicked sense of humor. Whatever the case, he has an impressive track record as an agent and a prosecutor and has been described by both friends and enemies as "an investigative genius." Brought up in Brooklyn, Freeh was well aware of the influence of the Cosa Nostra in New York and forged his career by fighting its menace. As an agent, he displayed a talent for organized crime cases that some have called "breathtaking." One of his earliest successes came in an investigation of waterfront corruption which brought down Anthony Scotto, a former official of the longshoremen's union, and resulted in the conviction of more that 125 Mafiosi, labor leaders, and shipping executives. When he left the Bureau to join the U.S. attorney's office in 1981, his interest in LCN investigations continued; it seemed he had the logical mind and the necessary stamina to put together the complicated RICO cases that were beginning to prove effective against the Mob. In 1982 he prosecuted the government's case against Lefty Ruggiero and other Bonnano family members exposed by Joe Pistone, the undercover agent who spent years inside the Mob. From there he went on to work with the FBI on other investigations and began to get a name as a ferocious crusader against the Cosa Nostra.

This reputation was fully justified by his work on one of the biggest LCN investigations the FBI has ever mounted, the Pizza Connection case. In 1979 the Bureau began an investigation focusing on heroin importation and distribution and money laundering by elements of the Sicilian Mafia in connection with the Bonnano family in the United States. The case got its nickname because the Mob used pizza parlors throughout New York, New Jersey, Michigan, Illinois, Pennsylvania, and Wisconsin to facilitate the distribution of $1.6 billion worth of heroin. Working with the DEA, U.S. Customs, and police from Brazil, Canada, Italy, Britain, Germany, Switzerland, Spain, and Turkey, the FBI discovered how a morphine base was transported from Turkey to Sicily, where it was turned into heroin for shipping to the United States. In 1985, fifty-eight heroin traffickers were arrested in the United States and five were indicted in Italy. As well as being the "investigative mastermind" behind the inquiry, Freeh was chief prosecutor at the subsequent seventeen-month trial, which ended with the conviction of seventeen defendants. During the hearing, the body of one defendant was found stuffed into a black garbage bag at the side of a road. Another was critically wounded when he was gunned down in Greenwich Village. But when the case was over, the Cosa Nostra had been dealt a serious blow from which many in the Bureau thought it would never truly recover.

With achievements like this on his record, Freeh was a man whom FBI agents could admire and respect. Of course, no one achieves successes of this order without making enemies, and there were one or two in the Bureau who felt they had more right to the directorship. Freeh's LCN work was all very well, said some, but it was old-fashioned; the focus now was on violent crime, white-collar crime, and Asian, Latin American, and Jamaican organized crime, of which the new appointee had little hands-on experience. Others doubted whether Freeh was qualified to run a large, expensive agency with a difficult political past.

But in his first few months in the job, Freeh endeared himself to those in the field by making all the right moves. He signaled his understanding that they, not headquarters, did the bulk of the Bureau's work by restructuring the top layers of the hierarchy and sending several senior managers back out to the field. Some departments were renamed and reorganized, and startled executives were called in to justify their jobs. The seventh-floor suite of offices, which in Sessions's last days had been a dispirited and unhappy place, began to jump again. One former agent said after a visit that the charged atmosphere reminded him of his days as a rookie, when Attorney General Robert Kennedy was cajoling Hoover's reluctant FBI into taking action on civil rights cases and against the Mafia.

Freeh's first big test as director came in late November 1993, when the Bureau's conduct in the 1992 Weaver case was called into question, and some of the Bureau's top strategists were threatened with criminal prosecution. This case was interesting because it involved some of the senior people who later played a part in the Waco episode.

In August 1992 two agents from the ATF bought two illegal sawed-off shotguns from a white separatist called Randall Weaver in a sting operation. A court summons to answer the charges was sent to Weaver's two-story cabin on Ruby Ridge, near Naples, Idaho. When Weaver failed to reply, he officially became a federal fugitive. On Friday, August 21, the U.S. marshals (who are responsible for serving federal warrants) decided to arrest him. Three officers, armed and wearing camouflage outfits, set off up the mountain to bring him in. Shortly after noon, at a trail crossroad, they bumped into Weaver, his fourteen-year-old son, Sam, and a family friend called Kevin Harris. All three were armed. Who shot first later became a matter of some dispute, but a few minutes after the encounter, Sam Weaver and U.S. Marshal William Degan were dead. Weaver retreated up the mountain path with Harris, while the two remaining officers radioed back to headquarters that one of their number had been killed and they were under fire. The FBI was called in.

That evening, the HRT flew to Idaho and took up positions around the Weaver family's cabin. Sources now say that at the time, agents were told by the marshals that Weaver was an extremist with extensive knowledge of the mountains and a fierce desire to kill as many federal agents as he could — a highly dangerous man.

Dick Rogers, who later led the tactical team at Waco, was in charge of the operation, and after being briefed by the other federal agents at the scene, he decided not to take any risks with Weaver. His agents' lives were on the line, or so he thought. On that basis, he asked Washington if he could change the FBI's rules of engagement, so that his men could shoot Weaver on sight rather than shooting only to save lives.

Rogers later said that he had obtained approval for this rule change from Larry Potts, the assistant director in charge of the criminal division, and that Potts had discussed this with his senior colleagues at FBI headquarters. A serious misunderstanding developed. Apparently Potts disputes this, claiming that he and Rogers had a different understanding of exactly what they were agreeing on. Nonetheless, the rules of engagement were amended.

On the afternoon of Saturday, August 22, although no negotiators had been brought in to talk Weaver and his companions out of the building, eleven HRT snipers moved into firing positions around it. One of the teams was under the command of Lon Horiuchi, a former army officer with a reputation as a crack shot. Just after 6:00 P.M.

Horiuchi saw two men and a young woman leave the cabin. At the same time Dick Rogers flew overhead in the HRT helicopter, carrying out an inspection of the scene.

Special Agent Horiuchi later told investigators that he thought one of the men was about to shoot at the helicopter. He fired one shot, and the bullet struck Randall Weaver in the back of the shoulder — a position that defense lawyers later claimed was proof that Weaver had no intention of firing his rifle. Then Horiuchi saw the three figures run back to the cabin. He aimed his rifle so that the wounded man would run into his next shot. As the three reached the porch, he fired again. The high-velocity round smashed through a panel in the door and into the head of Weaver's wife, Vicki, who had been standing on the other side, cradling a ten-month-old baby in her arms. She died instantly. Kevin Harris was wounded in a ricochet.

Nine days later, Weaver and Harris surrendered to the HRT. Prosecutors in Boise charged them with killing Degan and with a wide-ranging conspiracy to engage in armed confrontation with the government. In July 1993, after the authorities' case had stumbled under a welter of contradictory statements from agents, marshals, and police, Weaver and Harris were acquitted.

During the trial, the FBI was strongly criticized for its tactics by the judge, Edward J. Lodge, who said that it had covered up its misconduct after the affair and that the agency's behavior "served to obstruct the administration of justice." Prosecutors later accused the agency of closing ranks after the killings and dragging its feet in response to urgent requests for trial evidence. When the Bureau's case file was finally dispatched, after a court order, it was sent by fourth-class mail and arrived only after Horiuchi had finished testifying. Lodge was so incensed that he ordered the agent to return to the stand. In a sanction order he wrote later, the judge said that "the actions of the Government, acting through the FBI, evidence a callous disregard for the defendants and the interests of justice."

Shortly afterward, the Department of Justice's Office of Professional Responsibility began an internal review of the affair, warning some of those it questioned that they could face civil or criminal charges, including violations of civil rights laws and obstruction of justice. Among those interviewed were Rogers, Potts, George Terwilliger, the former deputy attorney general, and Henry Hudson, the head of the U.S. Marshals Service. On the day the news of the inquiry leaked to the media, the OPR admitted that it was also seeking to talk to William Sessions, William Barr, and Floyd Clarke. Interestingly, a few hours after the story broke, Clarke announced he was retiring from the FBI. The Bureau said his departure was not linked to the inquiry.

Clarke resigned on November 25, 1993, the same day that Louis Freeh issued a careful statement to the press. He said that the Bureau was committed to upholding the law and discovering the truth of the matter, but that he didn't want to prejudge the OPR's final report. Fair though his comments seemed to be, they also had the flavor of the time-honored Bureau practice of never admitting anything unless forced to. However, the statement went down well in the FBI, as agents favorably compared Freeh's caution to his predecessor's more open approach.

But if Freeh kept a low profile during this episode, he soon made a dramatic public appearance on the other side of the Atlantic. On December 12, the director set off on a two-day visit to Italy. His final stop on the tour was a brief visit to the island of Sicily, the land of the godfathers. The trip had two functions. The first was to make a public gesture of American support for the Italian people's fight against the Mafia. The second was more personal: to lay a wreath at the site of an explosion that had killed one of his oldest friends. In May 1992 Giovanni Falcone, Sicily's leading anti-Mafia magistrate, who had worked closely with Freeh on the Pizza Connection case, was driving along a main road into Palermo with his wife and three bodyguards. As his convoy passed over a drainage tunnel beneath the road, two men watching from a nearby hillside detonated a huge bomb. The explosion left a crater 1,500 yards long; there was nothing left of the cars or their passengers. Two months later another huge explosion killed Falcone's successor, Paulo Borsellino, and his bodyguards.

After visiting the graves of the two men and attending mass in an ornate twelfth-century chapel in the heart of the island's ancient capital, Freeh spoke to the assembled crowd. He said of the Mafia, "You are not men of honor, but cowardly assassins of children, thieves who move in the night and greedy merchants of drugs, terrorists and bullies. We do not fear you, we do not respect you. We challenge you and will hunt you down to bring you to justice.

We will root you out from under every rock, from the dark places where you hide. Your own families and relatives are turning against you and you will inherit the wind. We take up the sword of Judges Falcone and Borsellino and together we will use its weight of justice to smite their killers."

With these words of warning Freeh sought to galvanize the Sicilians to conclude their long struggle against the criminal syndicates that ruled their lives. But the words also made a great impression back home. Freeh was putting his personal stamp on an organization still a little unsure what to expect from its new boss. The fifth director of the Federal Bureau of Investigation was setting out the new ground rules. He had gone into the enemy's territory and thrown down the gauntlet. It was a declaration of war.

Many agents seized on the speech as evidence that they had at last been given the leadership they felt they deserved, and they may be right. Since he made those remarks, Freeh has been maintaining a low public profile, although his occasional forays into the limelight are always effective (his trip to Moscow in August 1994, to open an office to combat the new Russian mafia, made headlines around the world). He also impresses his subordinates with his determination and his capacity for hard work. But it seems that those who wish the Bureau to return to the "good old days" of the Hoover era will be disappointed. Freeh has shown no appetite for mounting politically related investigations, and has demonstrated his willingness to restructure the agency's administration — areas of which have remained intact since Hoover's death. His long-term goal is to make the FBI a force capable of responding to the crime problems of the twenty-first century; whether he can do so will depend on the support he gets from the agency, the administration, and the American public. To earn that support, he will have to show he understands that the FBI must always be the servant of the people, and never their master.

Whatever direction it takes under Freeh and his successors, the Bureau will never be far from the action or free from controversy, and it will no doubt increasingly be judged on how it handles both. For many decades the FBI has occupied a unique position at the heart of social and political life in the United States, and it will obviously continue to do so. While it is envied and admired by other law enforcement agencies around the world, it is feared and hated by the major criminal organizations, the mafias and the drug cartels, with which it daily does battle. Quite simply, it has a fearsome reputation.

But the FBI's true effectiveness is difficult to calculate. This is partly because there are very few standards against which the agency can be judged. It is also because so much of what we think we know about the Bureau is a myth, a self-created chimera that has woven a spell on generations of Americans. The idea of the FBI can get in the way of a clear analysis, and it is the main reason why the Bureau cannot be counted on to assess itself. The agents who work for the FBI fondly believe that it is unmatched in its skills, resourcefulness, determination, efficiency, achievements, and experience. Ask any agent to name a contemporary organization in any field that comes close to these ideals, and he or she will be unable to do so. This admirable esprit de corps, which does so much to tie this vast agency together, is based on the assumption that it is the best law enforcement agency in the world. Nothing can get through that barrier. Agents find it difficult, if not impossible, to accept that they are looking at the Bureau through rose-colored glasses. If they were to understand this, the FBI would probably cease to function.

This unique sense of identity is probably J. Edgar Hoover's greatest legacy. Hoover realized that the American people needed to believe in certainties — that as the nation accommodated itself to the sophisticated communications of the twentieth century and faced new challenges from overseas, it needed rock-solid structures to lean on. The FBI he designed was meant to be one of those pillars, an organization of such probity and strength that it could always be relied on in times of crisis. The G-man, a figure of unbending fidelity who stood for all the traditional values that had made America great, personified this idea.

The tragedy, of course, is that Hoover personally corrupted and abused the unchallengeable power that this image afforded him. In the process, he led the FBI down secret avenues of political intrigue and polluted an ideal that once had great merit. The G-man became a split personality, a two-faced being. One face was that of the avenging angel of justice, holding the Constitution and the other laws of the United States firmly in its grasp. The other was that of a demonic, cynical manipulator of governmental authority and power.

None of this really became clear until the years after Hoover's death, and he continues to be honored as a great man by those who choose to ignore or forget his disservice to the American people. Today the FBI's reputation has been rebuilt. The past is regarded with detachment, because, agents say, they have neither the will nor the means to abuse the Bureau's power again. Most of today's generation of FBI agents are even prouder of their organization than were those who went before them. They have new techniques, new safeguards, new standards. The modern FBI myth is as strong as it ever was in Hoover's time. Are agents right to feel this way? Perhaps, up to a point. The organization is probably not as good as its agents think it is, but it probably is the greatest law enforcement agency in the world. The two thoughts are not mutually exclusive. The Bureau is a remarkable agency, but the reality will never be able to live up to the legend.

Leaving such abstract matters aside, the FBI unquestionably will continue to be the United States most effective weapon in the war on crime. The problems the agency and the country face are desperate ones. The culture of drugs and the easy availability of sophisticated and deadly weaponry, fueled by the kinds of social and economic problems found in any developed country, have created a crisis of frightening proportions. Attempts have been made to address these issues, and there are signs that the United States is waking up to the greatest threat its society has faced this century. But it may be too late. When schoolchildren brandish guns in class and when crack cocaine is openly bought and sold on the edges of playgrounds, when innocent people are slaughtered on commuter trains, and when poverty, racial hatred, and fear can provoke whole communities into open and armed revolt, then no society can be said to be healthy.

The FBI cannot, and should not, seek to find solutions to these problems. These are matters for the American people and their politicians, and fortunately the United States has an enviable range of democratic structures and forums in which to address them. In the meantime, the FBI has a major responsibility for protecting innocent citizens and preventing criminals from repeating their crimes. But is it equipped to do this job?

The answer will depend on how it copes with its many responsibilities, and they never seem to diminish. Almost every year new federal statutes are added to the long list of matters over which the Bureau has jurisdiction. At the same time, the agency is making cutbacks in its staff and budget. Agents in the field clearly are often overworked and under too much stress. Paul Shannon and Dennis Brady in Dallas, for instance, are remarkable men who are totally dedicated to their job, but they are not superhuman. There are only so many hours in the day to catch armed fugitives, bank robbers, takeover artists, and gang members, and at the end of every shift, they leave some criminals on the streets. John Douglas's profiling unit in Quantico consists of ten people, each with a caseload of forty or fifty investigations. They can provide only so much help to the thousands of people who request it. The unit turns down hundreds of investigations every year, and countless people probably die horribly as a consequence.

Then there are the emergencies, which seem to arise so often. Take the savings and loan scandal, for instance. In 1980 the Reagan administration deregulated this sleepy home-lending industry in the belief that it would allow a neglected and uncompetitive financial service sector to grow. Eight years later, economist John Kenneth Galbraith called the result "the greatest financial disaster in American history." More than $500 billion had disappeared into thin air. Cowboy financiers had swindled taxpayers and millions of investors out of federally insured loans — money that could have gone to build homes, schools, hospitals, or even to rejuvenate the economy and address some of the underlying causes for crime. The Bureau had to divert huge amounts of manpower and resources into dealing with this problem. Agents who could have been used on organized crime, narcotics, and violent crime cases had to learn the intricacies of balance sheets, loan agreements, and computer programs. Hundreds of accountants were recruited so that "land flip" deals and Ponzi schemes could be dismantled and analyzed. Although agents were able to obtain a number of well-publicized convictions of some of the leading offenders, many others escaped through a paper maze so complicated that they will probably never be brought to justice.

The S & L disaster is only one part of a major white-collar crime problem that includes health care fraud, computer fraud, boiler room schemes, wire fraud, defense procurement fraud, and check-cashing abuses at Congress. Every year, hundreds of millions of dollars disappear from the U.S. economy in this way, and the damage to the country is incalculable. Elsewhere, the problems are equally immense — gang warfare on the streets of Los Angeles and other American cities, the emergence of new organized crime groups. Even terrorism refuses to go away. As the World Trade Center bombing showed, terrorist incidents cause a massive redeployment of agency resources. Then there are the unexpected events that no amount of planning can prepare for — incidents like the Koresh standoff, which involved thousands of agents and took the Bureau's much-vaunted HRT unit out of action for fifty-one days. What would have happened if a plane had been hijacked at one of the United States' international airports during that time?

The FBI tries to cope with all these competing demands by managing its resources as efficiently as possible while pleading for more and more cash. But more money is not available. There are other equally pressing demands on the American budget: health care, education, defense spending, and so on. And the government doesn't have bottomless pockets.

How, then, can the agency manage its resources so that it is equipped to deal with all eventualities? Part of the solution might lie in the way the FBI is run and which jurisdictions it covers. By addressing both these areas, the agency might be able to find more resources to lessen the demands on its staff. The difficulty is that the FBI would then have to accept changing its historical role and relinquishing some of its power.

It is obvious to any outsider that the FBI is a vast and unwieldy bureaucracy. The spoke-and-wheel structure that Hoover set up to ensure that his authority would be unchallenged still exists today. All power flows to and from headquarters. Although divisional special agents in charge have considerable status, and some responsibility for their own budgets, the constant stream of paperwork to and from the J. Edgar Hoover Building clogs the system, and agents complain frequently that getting a decision out of Washington can take weeks. Almost ten thousand people work at headquarters, and it is impossible not to wonder what they all do. The vast majority, of course, are service personnel, fingerprint clerks, lab technicians, and so forth, but many hundreds more are management types, climbing the career ladder, putting in time at the puzzle palace according to a long Bureau tradition. Some of them work hard, some of them don't. But are they all needed?

Hoover was a great believer in centralization, partly because it helped to impress the White House and Capitol Hill, partly because he sincerely believed that it made the Bureau more efficient. Twenty-two years after his death, however, it is hard to see how this approach can be justified. How the Kafkaesque array of committees and functionaries and managers is supposed to make the FBI operate more effectively is anyone's guess. It is equally astonishing that hundreds of agents are still effectively computer-illiterate. Many of them have no access to even the most basic office equipment. The Bureau spends millions of dollars creating increasingly sophisticated reference and storage systems for its filing and NCIC functions, but agents still have to dictate their reports into a cassette recorder or to a typist because the Bureau refuses to provide them with word processors. It is difficult to think of another sizable organization, governmental or private, that is so good at creating unnecessary work for its staff.

Louis Freeh has already begun tinkering with the infrastructure at headquarters, but he may have trouble making headway against the deeply entrenched interests of those who work in this monument to bureaucratic excess. Some people at headquarters are very comfortable working in a vast and anonymous environment, and they may have powerful friends. They will not be easy to move. Any attempt to make significant changes will be met with resistance on the grounds that change will tear apart the very structure and fabric of a great organization. William Sessions had a go at changing things a little and his enemies branded him a petty cheat and an incompetent.

But kicking life into the dinosaur on Pennsylvania Avenue is only part of what the FBI should do. Perhaps the most important task the agency should take on is a radical re-examination of some of its missions, particularly counterespionage. The FBI seems to have paid little more than lip service to the end of the Cold War. Many agents have been reassigned to criminal cases, but hundreds more have not. In offices across the country, agents now sit and assess the espionage threat from countries like China, North Korea, Iraq, Cuba, Pakistan, and India. Some of this work can be justified on counterterrorist related grounds, but it is hard to understand why the FBI should make the same kind of effort that it did in the years when the United States believed it faced all-out nuclear war with the Soviet Union. After all, the CIA has responsibility for gathering intelligence about these countries. Since few of them have vast spy networks in the United States, the Bureau's continued interest cannot really be explained. Of course, there are some legitimate counterintelligence priorities — stopping former enemies and allies from stealing U.S. industrial and technological secrets, for one — but even this threat is exaggerated.

However, the FBI will fight to its last breath before it relinquishes a fraction of its authority in this area. Since President Roosevelt granted the FBI an intelligence function in the 1940s, the Bureau has clung to it with grim determination. Guarding the nation's security is not merely a source of pride to agents, it is seen as a primary source of the FBI's power, the passport to influence, the cloak behind which the Bureau can hide when it is embarrassed or unwilling to disclose information about less legitimate operations. There are no signs yet that Louis Freeh has either the power base or the desire to rein in the "spooks" and clip their wings.

This is a shame, because as long as the FBI maintains and supports its top-heavy counterintelligence function (in the face of direct evidence that the threats have diminished), it will also retain the ability to initiate operations like the CISPES investigation, which brought disgrace on the agency and reconfirmed many people's opinion that the Bureau is not to be trusted in any kind of politically sensitive area. This ability hasn't been much in evidence for the last five years, but those who have experienced the realities of illegitimate FBI surveillance and harassment know that the agency is perfectly capable of returning to the field whenever it wants. Although the current administration seems less likely than the Reagan White House to begin spying on its political enemies, in five years, or ten years, the political landscape will have changed again. History has shown that the Bureau has not shied away from such activities. Perhaps this is one reason why the Bureau has been so determined to avoid regulation by a legislated charter, which would strictly define the boundaries for its operations, and why it refuses to apply criminal standards of evidence to all cases.

For all these criticisms, the Bureau seems to be in reasonably good shape. If it hasn't yet managed to exorcise the ghost of J. Edgar Hoover, it has at least managed to confine him to a small, dusty closet in a corner. The next step would be to remove his name quietly from the agency's headquarters, which would go some way toward atoning for past misdeeds. In the meantime, the pressing problems remain. Almost every day someone from the FBI is out on the streets of America, attempting to stem the rising tide of crime and violence. The vast majority of FBI agents who do this work are decent, intelligent, honest, and highly motivated men and women. They seem to have high ethical standards, and most try their best to be courteous and fair under difficult circumstances. Many of these agents knowingly put their lives on the line, and sometimes some of them die. If anything, or anybody, can legitimately be said to justify the Bureau's sobriquet of "the greatest law enforcement agency in the world," they can.

NOTES ON SOURCES

This book is principally based on hundreds of interviews, on- and off-camera, conducted by me and by my colleagues who worked on the television documentary series associated with this book (see the Author's Note, p. 343). Most of these interviews and discussions were with FBI agents or former agents, but we also spoke to many academics, lawyers and judges, journalists, politicians, police officers, employees and supporters of civil rights groups, and dozens of other private citizens whose lives had been affected in some way by the Bureau. The data we obtained was supplemented by further research among tens of thousands of FBI documents released under the Freedom of Information Act, and in the published reports and the transcripts of hearings of congressional committees and other government bodies responsible for overseeing FBI functions.

During our research, we visited field offices in Boston, Dallas, New York, Chicago, Richmond, New Orleans, New Haven, San Francisco, Los Angeles, San Antonio, Houston, Miami, and Washington, as well as the J. Edgar Hoover FBI headquarters building in Washington, the FBI Academy at Quantico, Virginia, and many smaller FBI resident agencies across the country. We also spoke on the telephone to agents from eight other field offices. Wherever I have drawn on information provided solely by the Connaught Films production team, I have tried to crosscheck and back-reference that information personally. However, as far as this book goes, the interpretation of the material, the opinions expressed on the basis of it, and of course any flaws are mine alone.

Prologue

The story of Hoover's lying in state is drawn from the recollections of a number of former agents and FBI personnel who attended, from accounts of the funeral found in the *Washington Post* and *New York Times* of May 3, 4, and 5, 1972, and from the archive footage of the funeral, which can be found in the U.S. National Archives, in Washington, D.C.

Congressional eulogies can be found in *Memorial Tributes to J. Edgar Hoover in the Congress of the United States and Various Articles and Editorials Relating to His Life and Work*, 93d Cong., 2d sess., S. Doc. 93-68.

Further details of the involvement of Liddy, Hunt, Barker, et al., are in *J. Edgar Hoover: The Man and the Secrets*, by Curt Gentry (New York: Norton, 1991), and *Nightmare: The Underside of the Nixon Years*, by J. Anthony Lukas (New York: Viking Press, 1976).

1. The Mission, the Myth, and the Men

The FBI mission statement comes from a confidential briefing book the Bureau issues to its executives.

The FBI tour attracts an average of 550,000 people a year. Its ostensible aim is to educate the American public on how the agency operates, but in reality it does little more than reinforce the stereotypical view many people have of the Bureau. Much is made by the tour guides of the Bureau's war on crime since the 1930s, but there is little mention of the FBI's shameful record on political investigations, or of its well-documented abuses of the First Amendment rights of hundreds of thousands of American citizens. I went on the tour four times between 1991 and 1993.

My impressions of the lack of public knowledge about the exact nature of the Bureau's responsibilities was tested in a mini–opinion poll I conducted on the streets of Washington in July 1993. I stopped twenty-two people at random and asked them what they knew about the FBI. Few of those I spoke to were able to give me anything more than the haziest description of what the Bureau did, although everyone knew about Hoover.

The overview of the FBI's responsibilities and functions is drawn from several briefings given to me and my colleagues by Bureau executives at various times between 1991 and 1993. I am particularly indebted in this respect to John Collingwood of the Office of Public Affairs, and to the staff of the Special Productions Unit of the FBI, who arranged meetings and answered our many supplementary questions.

The figure of $2 billion plus for the Bureau's annual budget is borne out by the FBI's *FY 1995 Authorization and Budget Request for the Congress.*

I spent three days on the streets of Los Angeles with Special Agent John Morris and reinterviewed him by phone some months later. He eventually cracked the Wells Fargo case, and many of the people associated with it were later convicted.

The statistics on bank robberies in Los Angeles came from John Hoos, the FBI's media representative in L.A., and were borne out in subsequent conversations with members of the FBI's L.A. bank robbery squad. I am particularly grateful in this respect to the squad's supervisor, Ken Jacobsen. Descriptions of the office are drawn from my own notes made at the time.

The details on gang activities in Los Angeles come from two research interviews with Robert Jones, supervisor of the division's black gangs squad.

The breakdown of the workload of agents in the white-collar crime squad in early 1993 comes from interviews with Los Angeles ASAC Tom Parker and others.

The information on the employee assistance program comes from interviews with Chuck D. McCormick.

2. *Learning to Love the FBI*

The information on FBI training and recruitment procedures comes from various people at the FBI Academy and elsewhere, including Kelly Cibulas, Vernon D. Kohl, Jim Perez, Pat Foran, James Greenleaf, Dave Martinez, and Walter Stowe. Although a hiring freeze was in effect for much of the time I was researching this book, I was fortunate that one of my first visits to the Academy coincided with the training of one of the last rookie classes before the freeze got under way. This, and several subsequent visits, allowed me to supplement my briefings with my own observations.

Information on the structure and responsibilities of the Behavioral Science Unit came from conversations with the staff of the unit, especially John Douglas and John Campbell, and from my own observations.

Although Douglas is the most recognized of the FBI profilers, many agents credit Howard Teten, a former lecturer in applied criminology at the FBI's National Academy, with first seeing the approach's potential.

Donald Rochon described his case to us in several telephone and research interviews and in an on-camera interview for the TV series conducted in 1993.

Kathryn Anne Askin's case is best described in written testimony to the House Subcommittee on Civil and Constitutional Rights, 101st Cong., 2d sess., pp. 432–51.

Different perspectives on how the G-man myth affected the FBI can be gained from *Lawlessness and Reform: The FBI in Transition,* by Tony G. Poveda (Belmont, Calif.: Wadsworth, 1990), and *G-Men: Hoover's F.B.I. in American Popular Culture,* by Richard G. Powers (Carbondale: Southern Illinois University Press, 1983).

Jack Shaw's case was described by him in on- and off-camera interviews in 1993. (There are more contemporary examples of the FBI's determination that its agents should never embarrass the Bureau. In 1992 Special Agent Paul Lindsay published a novel, *Witness to the Truth* [Random House, New York], based on his experiences in Detroit. The book is a thrilling read, but it contains some stinging criticisms of FBI management, and Lindsay got into very hot water with his superiors for writing it without authorization.)

The information from COINTELPRO came from documents obtained under the Freedom of Information Act and from many of the people who fell victim to it, such as Frank Wilkinson, who was spied on by the Bureau for thirty years because of his campaign to abolish the House Un-American Activities Committee. Of the many published accounts of COINTELPRO, perhaps the best is *Spying on America,* by James Kirkpatrick Davis (New York: Praeger, 1992).

William Sullivan's *The Bureau: My Thirty Years in Hoover's FBI* (New York: Norton, 1979) is just one of the many works by Bureau insiders which refers to Hoover's secret files. The most memorable are by Athan G. Theoharis: *Spying on Americans: Political Surveillance from Hoover to the Huston Plan* (Philadelphia: Temple University Press, 1978), and (with John Stuart Cox) *The Boss: J. Edgar Hoover and the Great American Inquisition* (Philadelphia: Temple University Press, 1988). Further information on Hoover's secret files can be gleaned from *Inquiry into the Destruction of Former FBI Director J. Edgar Hoover's Files and FBI Recordkeeping*, House Subcommittee on Government Operations, 94th Cong., 1st sess., December 1, 1975.

That Johnson owed his job to Hoover: *Nixon Memoirs 596.*

Nixon's statement on Hoover's files to John Dean: *White House tapes, February 28, 1973.*

3. RICO and the Wiseguys

John Marley was interviewed on location in 1993.

Information on the size and composition of New York LCN families came from various people of the New York FBI's organized crime squads, especially Brian Taylor and Lyn DeVecchio.

Background information on RICO came from Michael Ryman and Professor Robert Blakey, both of whom were interviewed for the television series.

For the full story of how the FBI brought down the Patriarca family I am indebted to Dave Cotton, Don Brutnell, Bill Hutton III, and Milt Alherich of the FBI's Connecticut division.

Further information came from John "Sonny" Castagna and the Hartford police.

4. Walking in the Shadows

Bill Butchka was interviewed in 1993.

Paul Brana and Guy Berado were interviewed in 1993.

A detailed account of Operation Colcor can be found in *FBI Undercover Operations*, report of the House Subcommittee on Civil and Constitutional Rights, 98th Cong., 2d sess., April 1984.

Information on Operation Corkscrew came from Judges Clarence Gaines, Lillian Burke, and Salvatore Calandra, and from *Oversight Hearings: FBI Undercover Activities, Authorization and HR 3232*, House Subcommittee on Civil and Constitutional Rights, February, March, April, June, and November 1983.

Information on FBI UCOs came from a variety of briefings at headquarters and elsewhere. Special Agent Ed Schubert was particularly helpful.

The FBI's UCO guidelines were drawn up in substantive form by Attorney General Benjamin Civiletti in 1981, and though they have been amended slightly a few times since, they form the basis for all FBI undercover operations today. See *FBI Undercover Operations*, House Subcommittee on Civil and Constitutional Rights, 100th Cong., 1st sess., March 25, 1987.

Details on the Pardue case are from court transcripts and tapes made available to defense lawyers at the time, and from interviews with Michael Pardue and Judge Franklin Waters.

Joe Pistone was interviewed in 1993. His full story is told in *Donnie Brasco: My Undercover Life in the Mafia*, by Joseph D. Pistone and Richard Woodley (New York: NAL-Dutton, 1989).

5. File Mountain

The two most damning post-Watergate inquiries into FBI activities were those of the so-called Church and Pike committees, whose hearings and findings were published as, respectively, *Hearings Before the Select Committee to Study Governmental Operations with Respect to Intelligence Activities*, 94th Cong., 2d sess., 1976, and *Final Report of the Select Committee to Study Governmental Operations with Respect to Intelligence Activities*, 94th Cong., 2d sess., 1976, and *Hearings of the House Select Committee on Intelligence*, 94th Cong., 1st sess., 1975.

David Nemecek was interviewed three times off-camera in 1993 and once on-camera in the same year. Other background information on the FBI's computer systems came from Bill Bayse, John Arbogast, Walter Johanningsmeir, and Tom Walczwkowski, and from personal observations made during visits to the FBI's computer center at headquarters.

Further information about the rules and regulations covering the FBI's computer systems can be gained from the *U.S. Federal Register*, November 26, 1990, vol. 55.

Terry Dean Rogan was interviewed in 1993.

Information on other instances of NCIC failure can be found in "Data Quality of Criminal History Records," U.S. Department of Justice, 1985.

Allen Schweitzer was interviewed on-camera in 1993 and several times later on the phone.

Lance Lindblom was interviewed in 1993 and 1994.

6. Dallas — The Field in Action

All the events described in chapter 6 occurred while my colleagues and I were researching and filming at the FBI's Dallas office in 1993. Therefore, the scenes and information come from our own observations during our seven separate visits, and from the interviews and conversations we had with several dozen agents, from Oliver "Buck" Revell down through the ranks. Revell retired in September 1994 and now runs a private security consultancy firm. His replacement as Dallas SAC is Danny Coulson, a former deputy assistant director at FBI headquarters.

7. *"WACMUR"*

I spoke to many agents who took part in the events in Waco, few of whom — perhaps understandably, given the circumstances — were happy to be identified. The HRT agent who accepted the award at the Active Agents Convention in Chicago in July 1993 cannot be identified for security reasons. Other frequently used sources were the two inquiry reports issued by the Justice Department and the Treasury Department in the late summer of 1993 and the voluminous press coverage at the time, particularly the excellent reports of the *Waco Tribune-Herald*, which covered the story with great distinction from start to finish.

8. *The Political Spies*

The Heritage Foundation report that influenced the Reagan administration's intelligence policies was published in 1980 and is entitled *Mandate for Leadership: Policy Management in a Conservative Administration.*

William Sessions's testimony is contained in *CISPES and FBI Counter-Terrorism Investigations,* hearings before the House Subcommittee on Civil and Constitutional Rights, September 16, 1988.

Detailed reference to the Handal diaries was made by Oliver "Buck" Revell before the Senate Select Committee on Intelligence on February 23, 1988.

John Rees's article appeared in *The Review of the News,* April 8, 1981.

Details on Rees's early career and warnings about his unsuitability as an FBI informant are contained in an internal FBI memo from Alex Rosen to Cartha DeLoach, September 27, 1968, a copy of which is in my possession.

Details of Frank Varelli's involvement with the FBI come from interviews conducted with him in 1993 for this book and the TV series. Further details are from various congressional hearings, most notably *Break-ins at Sanctuary Churches and Organizations Opposed to Administration Policy in Central America,* hearings before the House Subcommittee on Civil and Constitutional Rights, February 20, 1987.

The author and journalist Ross Gelbspan worked closely with Frank Varelli while writing *Break-ins, Death Threats, and the FBI: The Covert War Against the Central America Movement* (Boston: South End Press, 1991), the best and most comprehensive account of the CISPES affair. I am indebted to him for his invaluable and generous help with sources and documents.

Details on the terrorist photograph album are from *Break-ins at Sanctuary Churches and Organizations Opposed to Administration Policy in Central America,* hearings before the House Subcommittee on Civil and Constitutional Rights, February 20, 1987.

Frank Varelli claims that Buck Revell attended the opening reception at the Quantico conference, but he says he cannot remember whether Revell attended the conference itself.

Details on rules governing domestic security investigations are taken from *Domestic Security Guidelines* (Department of Justice), pp. 13–14, sec. 111 (b)(1)(a).

The Bureau reports that show the scale and nature of its investigation of CISPES are among thousands of pages of material released under the Freedom of Information Act, copies of which are in my possession.

Sister Patricia Ridgley's comments are taken from an on-camera interview conducted for the TV series.

In 1987 Buck Revell was asked by Congresswoman Pat Schroeder if the weekly meetings of the Operations Subgroup of the Terrorist Incident Working Group (OSG/TIWG) had ever discussed the opposition to the U.S. government's Central American policies. Revell replied, "That committee meets weekly and I don't know some comments that may have been made at any particular time in an off-the-cuff manner, but I have no recollection of there ever being a focus on any domestic issue that would correspond with your question." See p. 384 of *Break-ins at Sanctuary Churches and Organizations Opposed to Administration Policy in Central America*, hearings before the House Subcommittee on Civil and Constitutional Rights, February 20, 1987.

Copies of Mabry's letter to Webster, Revell's letter to Mabry, and Mabry's 1985 list are in my possession.

In January 1989 Jack Terrell's attorney, John Mattes, won the release of FBI documents that show the FBI had obtained twelve statements from people who knew about the NSC and the Contra supply network.

Allan Bruce Hemming's claims are contained in a profile of former FBI/CIA director William Webster written by Jeff McConnell for the *Boston Globe*: "Coups, Wars and the CIA," May 13, 1990.

Details of the FBI's investigation of the Prince Zadeh fraud, the FBI interview with Oliver North, and the text of the missing teletype are contained in *Nomination of William H. Webster to Be Director of Central Intelligence*, Select Committee on Intelligence, U.S. Senate, April 30, 1987. Buck Revell's account of his discussion with North about the Zadeh affair is contained in the same document.

Details of the FBI's investigation of Jack Terrell are contained in "Memorandum for the President; From John M. Poindexter; Subject: Terrorist Threat: Terrell" (a copy of which is in my possession), and in *Disposable Patriot: Confessions of a Soldier in America's Secret Wars*, by Jack Terrell and Ron Martz (Bethesda, Md.: National Press Books, 1993).

Information on North's discussions with Revell about the C-123 crash are taken from exhibit EM-12, *Unknown Subjects; Possible Neutrality Violation Concerning a C-123 Aircraft Shot Down*. Iran-Contra hearings, 1988.

The list of suspicious break-ins is taken from *Break-ins at Sanctuary Churches and Organizations Opposed to Administration Policy in Central America*, hearings before the House Subcommittee on Civil and Constitutional Rights, February 20, 1987.

The *Dallas Morning News* article on Flanagan's briefcase and Frank Varelli is entitled "The Informant Left Out in the Cold." Written by Christi Harlan, it was published on April 6, 1986.

William Sessions's statement to Congress is contained in *CISPES and FBI Counter-Terrorism Investigations*, hearings before the House Subcommittee on Civil and Constitutional Rights, September 16, 1988.

The two documents showing how the FBI amended its reading of Frank Varelli's polygraph are dated July 19, 1984, and April 24, 1987. Both are from the headquarters file on Frank Varelli.

William Sessions's comments on how his admission of FBI negligence with regard to CISPES may have affected his career were made during my interview with him in December 1993.

I interviewed John Rees over the phone in August 1993.

Buck Revell's comments on Varelli were made during my interview with him in May 1993. He was reinterviewed on-camera in July 1993.

The Senate's conclusion on CISPES is taken from *The FBI and CISPES*, Report of the Select Committee on Intelligence, U.S. Senate, July 14, 1989.

9. Terror

General background information on FBI counterterrorist operations came from a number of special agents, many of whom can't be named for obvious reasons. However, I am particularly grateful for the help of Neil Gallagher, Wayne Gilbert, and Buck Revell in this respect.

The specifics of the United Freedom Front case came from Lenny Cross in Boston, who gave unstintingly of his time and memory.

An account of the international rivalry sparked off by the arrest of Mohammed Hamadei in Frankfurt can be found in *Terrorism: Interagency Conflicts in Combatting International Terrorism*, hearing before the Senate Committee on Governmental Affairs, July 15, 1991.

Details of the Bureau's ability to snatch terrorists from their safe havens overseas, along with Buck Revell's comments on the topic, can be found in *FBI Authority to Seize Suspects Abroad*, House Subcommittee on Civil and Constitutional Rights, November 8, 1989.

The story of Pan Am 103 was pieced together with the help of the above sources and of counterterrorism experts in Scotland and Germany, but a particularly good starting point for anyone who wants to know more is the detailed indictment issued simultaneously on both sides of the Atlantic on November 14, 1991, by the Department of Justice and the Lord Advocate's Office in Scotland.

Lester Coleman's claims are contained in *The Trail of the Octopus* (London: Bloomsbury, 1993).

I was on one of my first visits to FBI headquarters when I was made aware of the Bureau's heightened state of alertness because of the Gulf War. Mine was one of the cars that was almost towed away!

I spoke to a number of Arab Americans about the way they were approached by the FBI during the Gulf War, and most of them, including the one I have quoted in this chapter, were unwilling to be identified. But David Najjab was prepared to be interviewed on-camera for the series. His story was typical. Like the others, he had no knowledge of any terrorist activity, nor did he think he was ever likely to know of any. Not surprisingly, therefore, he felt deeply disturbed by the FBI's approach.

Further details on the way the FBI responded to the two possible terrorist threats it did face during the Gulf War can be found in Neil Gallagher's testimony to the Senate in *Terrorism: Interagency Conflicts in Combatting International Terrorism,* hearing before the Senate Committee on Governmental Affairs, July 15, 1991.

Details of the FBI's investigation of the World Trade Center bombing attack and the subsequent unearthing of a wider terrorist conspiracy were given to me by two agents who will have to remain nameless. They cited as a reason the way in which James Fox, the FBI's assistant director in New York, was disciplined for speaking to the press during the investigation, in contravention, or so it was alleged, of a court order forbidding any law enforcement leaks to the media that might jeopardize the possibility of a fair hearing for the defendants.

10. Mutiny and the Aftermath

The story of the rise and fall of William Sessions comes from a number of people at FBI headquarters, most notably the former director himself, who consented to be interviewed at length about the affair in the fall of 1993. His wife, Alice, was equally forthcoming, through five long telephone conversations, an exchange of faxes, and a Mexican supper in the suburbs of Washington. Rightly or wrongly, she remained totally convinced that her husband was innocent of any wrongdoing and that he and she were the victims of a vendetta at FBI headquarters.

My colleagues and I were conducting the bulk of our research when the Sessions scandal first began to break and so had the opportunity to witness its effect on the field firsthand.

Milt Alherich, now SAC at New Haven, was the head of the Bureau's Department of Congressional and Public Affairs during the early Sessions years. He was one of the few who were willing to go on the record about Sessions, but his criticisms were mild compared with the vituperative comments of other Bureau executives. Sadly, none of them were prepared to let me quote them.

In his book *The FBI* (New York: Pocket Books, 1994), author Ronald Kessler is dismissive of Sessions's claims that the ethics probe into his affairs was launched because of the FBI's investigation of the Justice Department's handling of the BNL affair. His arguments are convincing, and if anyone wants a blow-by-blow account of the Sessions scandal, Kessler's chapter on the affair is one of the best places to start.

By the time Louis J. Freeh was sworn in as director of the Bureau, our carefully nurtured relations with the FBI were beginning to unravel. My colleagues and I had to push our access agreements to the limit in order to obtain the pictures we needed to illustrate the way the FBI operates. This created considerable unease among some at FBI headquarters. We had planned to interview the new director once the rest of our work had been completed. Only then, we felt, could we question him with the benefit of all our accumulated knowledge. However, our requests to see him were held up in the bureaucracy for several weeks, while lists of suggested questions were shuttled back and forth across the Atlantic. The negotiations finally foundered when the Bureau insisted on seeing all of our television film on the FBI before the interview took place. This we refused, on the grounds that it would seriously compromise our editorial independence. We had always agreed to show the Bureau scenes that it feared might jeopardize its operations or the safety of its agents (and indeed had made this plain, in writing, several times), but we had never agreed to a wholesale prebroadcast screening of each episode in its entirety. In the event, we did show the Bureau certain scenes and altered the pictures to obscure the faces of agents who were working undercover, but this, it seems, was insufficient. Despite our lobbying at the highest levels of the Justice Department and elsewhere, Louis Freeh decided against an interview. He was, we were told, unwilling to comment on anything that had taken place in the FBI under his predecessors.

John Collingwood, the head of the FBI's Department of Congressional and Public Affairs, later wrote to explain why three years of "extraordinary cooperation" were coming to an end. Citing our refusal to show the Bureau the films, he said, "Obviously this and other instances where Connaught has sought to go beyond our agreement, as well as questions that indicate a focus other than what was originally described to us, are cause for concern . . . Therefore we will be unable to provide the additional interviews and research you have requested."

The information I subsequently gathered on Louis Freeh was therefore obtained without the FBI's official help. Fortunately, some agents continued to be more forthcoming in private.

AUTHOR'S NOTE

Many people have asked me how I came to be writing a book about the FBI. It all began in May 1990, on a flight from Washington to London. I was returning home after gathering material for a television documentary on the savings and loan crisis, the biggest financial scandal in American history. During the trip I had asked the FBI for background information on various insolvent S & Ls its agents had investigated. The San Francisco white-collar crime squad had been particularly helpful, and as I sat on the plane going over my notes, I began thinking about their organization. One thought led to another, and after about an hour I realized I had sketched an outline for a documentary series on the FBI on the pad in front of me. It seemed perfectly straightforward; all it needed was the agency's cooperation.

Of course, getting that help proved much more difficult than I ever envisaged, as anyone more experienced at dealing with the Bureau would have known in advance. Initially, FBI executives were dismissive, even hostile to the idea. They had been asked to cooperate with several television productions in the past, and they had rejected almost all of them out of hand. But finally, either because of my dogged refusal to take no for an answer or, more likely, because they decided that the publicity would be helpful, they agreed. After eighteen months of phone calls, letters, faxes, and meetings, I received a letter stating that the Bureau was prepared to help. By then I had lined up British and American broadcasters to finance and screen the series. The only thing missing was a publishing deal, for surely the series would generate a mass of material for a book. Two years later, this is the result.

Those years have been something of a roller-coaster ride for everyone involved in this project. First, the agency's idea of access turned out to be different from ours. Every filming request we made took weeks to process and involved a fresh round of negotiations. At times it was obvious that some agents suspected we had a hidden agenda. Others, perhaps more rationally, were worried that our television crew might get in their way while they were doing their jobs, or reveal techniques that would help criminals frustrate their efforts. This was frequently cited as the reason why the Bureau had never allowed cameras behind the scenes before, and one of my hardest tasks was persuading FBI executives that we had no wish to do anything that would make agents' lives any more difficult than they already were.

We were also hindered by the fact that our production schedule coincided with a period of great upheaval within the Bureau. A few weeks before one filming trip, the siege at David Koresh's compound near Waco, Texas, began, and a few days before that the World Trade Center was bombed. Both operations absorbed a lot of FBI time and energy and made it difficult for us to get to the people we needed to see. Even worse, around this time the FBI's director, William Sessions, was publicly accused of ethics violations and petty corruption, a very embarrassing situation for an organization that prides itself on its immaculate public image, and one that made it very sensitive to the presence of journalists and cameras.

We managed to achieve what we did because of the actions of a few people at the FBI and the Department of Justice who came to accept that our intentions were honorable. We finally realized we had broken through some of the barriers when a Bureau executive, watching our film crew in action, said in amazement, "I just don't understand how you guys have managed to do this. The American media has been trying for twenty years to get this stuff."

Over the course of the production, during the research and filming periods especially, my colleagues and I met hundreds of agents at field offices across the United States. Sometimes I supplemented these interviews with further visits of my own. The vast majority were pleased to be given the opportunity to talk (if not always on camera), and several contacted us later. Many agents gave me additional information for this book, and three in particular proved very helpful with facts, figures, names, and dates. Even though very little of this information was particularly sensitive, they have asked specifically to remain anonymous, since the Bureau frowns on any unauthorized contacts with the press and their careers could be jeopardized.

Although there are many similarities between this book and the television series, there are also significant differences. For a start, the book is far more detailed and focuses on some areas of the FBI's work that are not featured in the series, such as training, headquarters politics, and Los Angeles bank robberies. It is also much less historical than the series, particularly in how it deals with J. Edgar Hoover, first because I wanted to look at Hoover in terms of his legacy to today's FBI, and second because I thought it important to concentrate on the present and the future. As it was, I had to choose whether to write a broad overview of the FBI, describing all its operations and responsibilities in encyclopedic terms, or to pick out those elements that could best illustrate how FBI agents work and examine them in more detail. I chose the latter course.

A great many people have given me invaluable help. First, I would like to acknowledge my great debt to the Connaught Films production team and to the many technical specialists who worked with them to make *The Bureau* a documentary series to be proud of. I am enormously grateful to our production manager, Helen Molchanoff, whose near-miraculous administration of a budget that was always too tight and command of the technical and logistical details of our nightmarish schedule were matched only by her patience, calm, and unfailing good humor under pressure. The intelligence, resourcefulness, and determination of our researchers, Lois Lipman and Jeremy Hall, were also fundamental to the success of the project. Both spent months on the road, tracking down interviewees, stories, and documents, and worked absurdly long hours afterward making sure all these things were available to us. I am also grateful to Sally Rodney, our production secretary, who was in at the very start of the project, went away to have a baby, and couldn't resist coming back to help; to Michael Braham, chief executive of Broadcast Communications, who was among the first to see the potential of this project and gave me the time and space to make it happen; and to Susan Lowery, Maria McGrath, Dan Desmond, and Derek Nolan, who were unstinting with assistance and support on many occasions.

On the technical side, special thanks must go to our principle camera teams — cameramen Peter Greenhalgh and Jonathan Harrison, soundman Tim Watts, and camera assistant Jerry Risius — who all did extraordinary work on the series. They were supplemented at various times by Mark Trottenberg, David Barker, Scott Jonas, Dyanna Taylor, Bob Marts, Paul Mailman, Michael Becker, Tom Paul, and Ulli Bennekamp. Thanks also to film editor Steve Barclay, and to assistant editor Julie Lamden, who worked miracles with the rushes; to our composer, Howard Davidson, whose music perfectly complemented the pictures; to Clive Pearson, who "on-line" edited the series; to the ubiquitous Ken Morse, who did the rostrum camerawork; to Bob Jackson, who was responsible for the sound mix; to dubbing editors James Edmonds and Alexandra Sage; to runners Sergei Cherchintsev and Daniel Mumford; to graphic designer Hayden Young; and to archive researchers Joyce Compton and Bonnie Rowan.

Among the many people at Channel 4 who made this project possible, my special thanks must go to John Willis, whose decision to commission the series and whose patience, support, and advice made me understand just why he is so highly respected in the British television industry. At PBS and WETA, David McGowan, John Grant, and Sandy Hebberer took the risk of believing that British journalists could get into places that their own countrymen could not. Above all, I thank Dick Richter at WETA for his professionalism and kindness. During the all too frequent times I called on him for help, he always had a solution at his fingertips.

I owe three more people a particular debt of gratitude, for without them neither book nor series would ever have appeared. The first is my American researcher, John Kelly. His nose for a good source and his talent for tracking down documents, telephone numbers, and interviewees is simply awe-inspiring, and without his expertise and initiative I would have given up long before this book was ever finished. I hope this book lives up to his expectations. The second is Tony Stark, who produced and directed the TV series with great skill, determination, and vision. The four remarkable documentaries he made bear testimony to his talents as a filmmaker and journalist, and, critically, gave me many of the stories that appear in this book. The third is Erica Roberts. As production coordinator on *The Bureau*, as office manager of Connaught Films, and as a colleague and friend, she gave me more help and commonsense advice than I could ever have hoped for.

My agent, Anthony Sheil, was inspiring and a constant source of support and advice. John Sterling, my editor at Houghton Mifflin, was my principal guide to the strange business of writing something longer than an article or a script and was extraordinarily patient with my slow progress. He should take the lion's share of credit for any writing of merit in this book, although perhaps he will have to share it with Liz Duvall who made sense of my tattered manuscript and somehow found a coherent narrative within it. I am deeply indebted to them both. Georgina Morley at Pan Macmillan inherited the book halfway through its development but was supportive from our first meeting. I thank her for her patience and guidance.

Thanks are also due to Nick Claxton, my partner at Connaught Films, who had the unenviable task of keeping the company going while I reworked the manuscript; to Ivan Rendall, who convinced me that writing a book while executive-producing the series was not as insane as it first appeared; and to my parents and my brothers and sisters, for their unquestioning love and support, and for reminding me that there are more important things in life than the FBI.

Obviously, neither this book nor the TV series would ever have seen the light of day without the help and information given to our production team, researchers, and me by past and current agents and staff of the FBI. Some of them feature in the book, some in the series; many just gave background information. Most were glad to talk to us. A few were unwilling, either because they were against everything we stood for or because they did not fully understand what we were trying to do. Yet all these people, whether they realized it or not, helped to paint a picture of today's Bureau. Although there are many I cannot name, and doubtless some I have missed, I would like to thank Carl Adrian, Milt Alherich, Phillip Armand, Grant Ashley, Steve Berry, Anthony Betz, David Bigbee, Robert Blecksmith, Michael Boone, Dennis Brady, Donald Brager, William Branon, Donald G. Brutnell, Richard Buechele, Mark Bullock, Bill Butchka, John Cambell, Swanson Carter, Donna G. Cathey, Mark Chapman, Thomas Christenberry, Kelly Cibulas, Floyd Clarke, John Collingwood, Wayne Comer, Dave Cotton, Herbert Cousins, Curtis Crawford, Leonard Cross, Gary Davis, Lester Davis, Douglas Deedrick, Robert DeMaria, Lindley DeVecchio, Edmund Diem, John Dillon III, John DiStasi, Charles Domroe, James M. Donckels, William Doran, John Douglas, Alan Ducote, William Dyson, David Elder, William Esposito, William G. Eubanks, John Farmer, Vincent G. Fazzio, Patrick Foran, Tom Fuentes, Gary B. Fuhr, Francis Gallagher, Neil Gallagher, Wilber E. Garrett, Wayne Gilbert, Manuel Gonzalez, W. Douglas Gow, James W. Greenleaf, Henry Handy, Joseph Hanley, Richard Held, L. Joseph Hersley, John Hoos, London Max Howard, William Hutton III, Ronald Iden, Kenneth Jacobsen, Jeffrey J. Jamar, Dan James, Robert Jones, Thomas Jones, E. Michael Kahoe, Daniel Kingston, Dave Knowlton, Vernon D. Kohl, Thomas Kubic, Daniel N. Kunsch, Robert G. Long, David Major, John Marley, David Martinez, Roger Martz, Dan McCarron, Charles D. McCormick, Jim Moody, Gary Morley, John Morris, Michael Morris, Rolando Moss, Larry Neaves, David Nemecek, Richard Newth, Daryl O'Donnell, Gene O'Leary, James A. Oppy, John J. O'Rourke, Thomas Parker, Charles J. Parsons, John F. Pavlansky, James Perez, Marjorie Poche, Larry Potts, Steve Powell, Charles S. Prouty, Donald Ramsey, Gerald Richard, Herbert Richardson, Charles E. Riley, Jose P. Rodriquez, Richard Rogers, Michael Ross, Thomas Rupprath, Neil Schiff, Terry Schmidt, Robert A. Scigalski, Paul Shannon, Robert Shaw, Stephen Silvern, Kerry P. Smith, Richard Smith, Walter Stowe, Richard Swenson, Brian Taylor, John Taylor, George "Biff" Temple, Jerry Thornton, Rex Tombe, James Tomlinson, Mark Van Steenburg, Peter Wacks, Lee Waggoner, Nicholas Walsh, Robert Walsh, Patrick Watson, Thomas A. Williams, Vincent Wincelowicz, Edwin I. Worthington, and James Wright.

I should make special mention of Oliver "Buck" Revell, SAC of the Bureau's Dallas office, and former executive assistant director of the FBI. He is featured throughout this book, and indeed comes in for some criticism, but, ironically, few people in the Bureau were as helpful as he was. He is a remarkable man who went out of his way to interpret various guidelines as liberally as he could, and my colleagues and I thank him for all his efforts on our behalf.

Thanks also to Lillian Albertson, the staff of the ACLU, Dick Baker, Matthew Bates, Guy Berado, Chip Berlet, Kim Bishop, Professor Robert Blakey, Paul Brana, Judge Lillian Burke, Judge Salvatore Calandra, John "Sonny" Castagna, Jack Danahy, Cartha DeLoach, Jim Dempsey, William Ellingsworth, Elmer Emrich, James Flynn, Judge Clarence Gaines, Ross Gelbspan, Curt Gentry, Linda Hajek, Robert Hardy, Tom Hayden, John Heagy, Larry Heim, William Higgins, Jennifer Horan, Jesse House, David Jonas, John King, Scott Lane, Lance Lindblom, Paul Marsh, Art Nehrbass, Jack Nelson, Gordon Novel, Michel Pardue, Joseph D. Pistone, John Rees, Don Riddle, Sister Patricia Ridgley, Donald Rochon, William Roemer, Terry Dean Rogan, Jack Ryan, Michael Ryman, Allen Schweitzer, Alice Sessions, William S. Sessions, Jack Shaw, Carl Stern, Wesley Swearingen, Athan Theoharis, Frank Varelli, Vincent Vasisko, Judge Franklin Waters, Neil Welch, and Frank Wilkinson. All of them contributed something to the series or to this book, or helped in some other way.

I cannot conclude without mentioning my children, Laura and Joseph, who become more precious with every passing day. When you grow up and read this book, perhaps they'll understand why Dad was away so much.

And last, but certainly not least, there is my wife, Patsy. I owe her more than thanks. For three long years she bore my frequent absences and my constant preoccupation with the FBI, yet throughout it all, she kept our home and our family together. It is just one of the many reasons why I love her so much.

Diarmuid Jeffreys,
London, June 1994

INDEX